"We are all immigrants to this place."

—Margaret Atwood

"Cultural Bastards ... cultural bastards. Dat is what we is."

—Shani Mootoo

MULTICULTURALISM AND IMMIGRATION IN CANADA

MULTICULTURALISM AND IMMIGRATION IN CANADA:

AN INTRODUCTORY READER

EDITED BY ELSPETH CAMERON

CANADIAN SCHOLARS' PRESS INC.
TORONTO

Multiculturalism and Immigration in Canada: An Introductory Reader
Edited by Elspeth Cameron

First published in 2004 by
Canadian Scholars' Press Inc.
180 Bloor Street West, Suite 801
Toronto, Ontario
M5S 2V6

www.cspi.org

Canadian Scholars' Press gratefully acknowledges financial support for our publishing activities from the Government of Canada through the Book Publishing Industry Development Program (BPIDP).

Library and Archives Canada Cataloguing in Publication

Multiculturalism and immigration in Canada : an introductory reader / edited by Elspeth Cameron.

Includes bibliographical references.
ISBN 1-55130-249-7

1. Multiculturalism--Canada. I. Cameron, Elspeth, 1943-

FC105.M8M84 2004   305.8'00971   C2004-903986-5

Cover design by George Kirkpatrick
Author photo: Eva Tihanyi
Text design and layout by Brad Horning

04 05 06 07 08   5 4 3 2 1

Printed and bound in Canada by AGMV Marquis Imprimeur Inc.

Canadä

For Eva Tihanyi,
who emigrated from Hungary to Canada
in 1962

TABLE OF CONTENTS

EXPERIENCE

Documents and Tables

INTRODUCTION

Canada is one of the best countries in which to live in the world. Since 1975, when the OECD (Organization for Economic Cooperation and Development) began ranking industrialized democracies, Canada has been at or near the top of the 170 or so countries rated. That rating is based on the human development index, which takes into account such powerful indicators as life expectancy, adult literacy, economic prosperity, poverty, and educational levels. As if that were not enough to attract immigrants — especially from those countries rated low on the human development index — Canada's universal health care system alone is a good reason to move here. As well, a 2003 UNICEF study found that foreign-born and first-generation children in Canada were less likely to fall behind in school than similar children in the 22 other industrialized nations surveyed. So much for the commonly held notion that a high proportion of immigrant children will do poorly in Canadian schools.

But perhaps Canada's greatest draw is the now pervasive national ideology of multiculturalism. Why wouldn't immigrants want to move to a country that not only offers a potentially high quality of life, but one that also espouses diversity in its population?

This book offers a series of readings by academics and journalists that explore various theories about multiculturalism in a section called "Theory." These theoretical chapters are supplemented in a section called "Experience," in which the voices of a representative sample of ethnic writers recreate immigrant experiences in Canada in fiction and poetry. We hear, for example, from Adele Wiseman, a Manitoba Jew born in Winnipeg in 1928; Austin Clarke, born in 1932, who moved from Barbados to Canada in 1955; Joy Kogawa, a third-generation Japanese woman born in Vancouver in 1935; Fred Wah, Chinese, born in Saskatchewan in 1939; Maria Campbell, a Métis also born in Saskatchewan in 1940; Clark Blaise, an American born in 1940 to Canadian parents, who moved to Montreal in 1964; Rohinton Mistry, a Parsi from India born in Bombay in 1952, who arrived in Canada in 1975; Neil Bissoondath, an Egyptian born in Trinidad in 1955, who came to Canada in 1971 and lives in Quebec; Eva Tihanyi, reunited with her parents in Canada at age six in 1962 after they fled the 1956 Hungarian Revolution a few months after she was born; Shani Mootoo, born in Ireland in 1958 and raised in Trinidad, who arrived in Canada in1977; and "Fatima," an Iranian mother of two who arrived in Montreal in 1991. Both sections are arranged more or less chronologically to illustrate the ways in which issues around multiculturalism have developed, and to show the shifts in perception that have altered the ways in which we perceive our own ideology.

Canada has only recently — within the last 35 years or so — considered itself a multicultural society. Before that Canada's self-image was quite the contrary. Several of the chapters in this book touch upon the remarkable way in which Canada has somehow transformed itself from a British colony that aspired to reproduce (and improve on) its British antecedents to one that applauds pluralism of race, religion, and culture — a rapid transformation without revolution or civil war.

In fact, Canada began nationhood with a decidedly racist ideology. Canada's Confederation in 1867 occurred only eight years after the publication of Darwin's *On the Origin of Species*, a work whose premises of natural selection and the survival of the fittest were very quickly applied by Herbert Spencer and others to human society. Theories of what was called "social Darwinism" suggested that races — like species of animals — predominated (or were rendered inferior) by the inborn qualities that enabled them to survive in their environments. In Canada, that environment was perceived as "the North." Doctors, journalists, philosophers, politicians, and poets alike speculated widely in the 50 years between Confederation and the First World War that Canada's northern environment was only suited to (and actually enhanced) the white northern races (such as Germans, Scandinavians, and British) and was inimical to the southern races (such as Italians, Greeks, and Poles). As for what we today call "visible minorities," they would have no chance whatsoever of thriving in such a climate. As Carl Berger concludes in his study of the ideas prevalent in Canada during this period, "In the struggle for existence, the northern conditions called forth virtues of self-reliance and strength: only the fittest survived. On the other hand, the 'south' conjured up the image of enervation ... of voluptuous living and consequently of the decay and degeneration of character."[1] One of the more insidious theories of the time referred to the so-called "Teutonic germ" — an inherited ability to handle democratic rule and freedom in white northern peoples dating back to the early tribal communities of Scandinavia. This ideology of Canada as a superior, democratic nation was, in part at least, a way of distinguishing Canada from the United States to the south where Civil War and the slavery that instigated it were held up as a negative model of nationhood. Canada had a long way to go between 1914 and the present to reverse the power of this identification of the North with the superiority of white northern races and its concomitant denigration (and exclusion from immigration) of the so-called southern races, particularly Asians. Several contributors to this collection still see clear traces of racism in Canadian society; some even go so far as to hold the ideology of multiculturalism partly responsible for it. Nonetheless, the very idea of multiculturalism would have been anathema in Canada before the mid-1960s.

The first clear statement of multiculturalism was made by Liberal Prime Minster Pierre Elliott Trudeau in 1971. Canada then became the first country in the world to adopt multiculturalism as an official policy. A Ministry of State for Multiculturalism was created the same year. By 1985, the Multiculturalism Act was formulated, to be made official in 1988 with a budget of almost $20.5 million. That 1987–88 budget was allocated into four areas as follows: citizenship and community participation, institutional change, heritage enhancement, and heritage language education. Initially in 1971, Trudeau clearly called for a multilingual and multicultural society within a two-nation state. That statement — reprinted here in Chapter 35 — seemed and indeed was an oxymoron. As French-Canadians were quick to note, the paradox of a multicultural nation within a bicultural nation made no logical sense.

It is not surprising that Trudeau's recommendations for a multicultural Canada were contained within a firm recognition of a bilingual and bicultural Canada. Ironically it was Liberal Prime Minister Lester B. Pearson's 1963 Royal Commission on Bilingualism and Biculturalism that brought multiculturalism to the fore. That so-called B & B Commission toured Canada with the express purpose of hearing citizens' views on the state of both so-called Charter Group languages and cultures across the country. The impetus for this came in large part from the increasing foment in Quebec to separate from the rest of Canada. The Quiet Revolution — especially the militant FLQ (Front de Libération du Québec) branch—which threatened the English in Quebec had alerted the whole country to the many legitimate grievances that had plagued the French in Canada since Confederation. One of the results of the B & B Commission's investigations had been the Official Languages Act in 1969, which ensured the use of English and French at the federal level. It is profoundly ironic that a Commission set up expressly to negotiate an effective two-nation Canada should result almost immediately in the emergence of a many-nation Canada. For it was the discovery by the B & B Commission (and recorded in Book IV of their report, "The Cultural Contribution of Other Groups") that there were many vocal groups of citizens neither anglophone nor francophone who insisted on reporting their contributions to culture in Canada. Actually, 26 per cent of the population were neither British nor French in ethnic origin. The major group to draw attention to this fact was the Ukrainians in the west led by Paul Yuzyk, author of a book about Ukrainian settlement in Manitoba. And Yuzyk was supported—at least covertly—by Italians, Armenians, Portugese, Greeks, and Jews. Indeed, more or less simultaneously in Montreal, a strong Jewish community had established itself and had found a voice in remarkable writers such as A.M. Klein, Irving Layton, Mordecai Richler, and Leonard Cohen. In this book, the opening chapter of *The Sacrifice* (1953)—one of the earliest Jewish novels of immigration by a Manitoba writer, Adele Wiseman—is included.

Many of the contributions to this book trace the subtle and not-so-subtle confrontations and adjustments that occurred as Canada shifted and lurched toward a multicultural ideology since Trudeau's statement in 1971. Between then and now Canada has changed from a nation based primarily on the cultures of the two Charter Groups and their languages to a nation of many cultures.

Although it was not until Trudeau made his recommendations concerning multiculturalism in 1971 that the ideology of multiculturalism became "official," the general idea was not new. In retrospect, perhaps the main subtext of the long debates in 1964 on the adoption of a Canadian flag (instead of the British Union Jack or the equally British Red Ensign), which resulted in our red-and-white maple leaf flag that is equally representative of all ethnicities, was the unacceptability of a mainstream British (or British/French) ethnicity. Almost simultaneous with the adoption of this new Canadian flag, brilliant sociologist John Porter published *The Vertical Mosaic* in 1965. This book represented 10 years of meticulous and comprehensive research as Porter tried to pin down the precise nature of Canadian society. The title of his book, as well as many of his specific findings, remains with us today. Any investigation into Canadian society could hardly fail to see that Canada owed much to its immigrant population. Natural increase was a much greater factor in the development of French Canada than it was in English Canada. Especially between 1901 and 1914, Canada resembled what Porter described as "a huge demographic railway station."[2] These were the years following the completion of the CPR (employing/exploiting "inferior" Chinese workers admitted for that purpose) in which the Canadian prairies were settled (largely by Ukranian farmers, also admitted for that purpose) under the aegis of Clifford Sifton, minister of the Interior under Liberal Prime Minister Wilfrid Laurier.

Porter documented the large degree to which Canada—especially English Canada—had been formed by immigrants, and he noted strong connections between ethnic groups and social classes. Not surprisingly, he found that new Canadians tended to be stereotyped and stuck in lower economic echelons. He also found that French Canadians and Native peoples tended to be found at the bottom of both social class and economic hierarchies.

Porter's documentation of Canadian society and the image he chose to depict it—the vertical mosaic—paved the way for the multicultural ideology that followed a mere six years after his book. Every Canadian knows the term "mosaic," knows that it applies to Canada as opposed to the (supposedly) more American designator "melting pot." Not many know that just as important is the vertical aspect of the mosaic. As Porter put it,

> in a society that is made up of many cultural groups, there is usually some relationship between a person's membership in these groups and his or her class position and, consequently, the person's chances of reaching positions of power. Because the Canadian people are often referred to as a mosaic composed of different ethnic groups, the title "The Vertical Mosaic," was originally given to the chapter that examines the relationship between ethnicity and social class. As the study proceeded, however, the hierarchical relationship between Canada's many cultural groups became a recurring theme in class and power. For example, it became clear that Canadians of British origin have retained, within the elite structure of the society, the charter group status with which they started out, and that in some institutional settings the French have been admitted as a co-charter group whereas in others they have not.[3]

In other words, the specific ethnicity of immigrants (and the stereotypes or "racial aptitudes" associated with them) trapped them in the lower classes of Canadian society and excluded them from the status and power of the British majority.

Porter's book, which soon became an enduring best-seller in Canada, was an important factor in the onset of a multicultural ideology. Meanwhile, other changes in that turbulent decade of the 1960s contributed to the groundswell that resulted in Trudeau's federal multicultural policy statement. One of the most significant was a shift in immigration policy in 1962 from lists of "preferred" and "non-preferred" countries from which immigrants were (or were not) welcome. Instead of designating desirable countries from which immigrants should come – a hangover from the old ideology of the superiority of northern nations – new policies outlined the type of immigrant (one with the skills needed for positions in Canada) regardless of country of origin that Canada encouraged. This shift in policy, and other policy changes that followed, ushered in an era in which "visible minorities" increasingly constituted a large proportion of new Canadians. In the 1960s and 1970s, most immigrants were from southern Europe. But by the 1980s, more than half were from South Asia, China, Latin America, and the West Indies. By the early 1990s, the percentage had risen to 68 per cent. This profound change in immigration is carefully traced and analyzed in this book.

As some of the writers in this book explain, the onset of multiculturalism was strongly rejected by French Canada. Québécois politicians and intellectuals alike were quick to see that an ideology of pluralism would be virtually suicidal, undermining the already weak position of French Canada vis-à-vis English Canada. The law that forced immigrants to send their children to French-speaking schools and French language law are obvious examples of this anxiety. There was a clear and present danger that the French (who were already situated quite far down on Porter's vertical mosaic) would no longer have clout as one of two Charter Groups, but would soon become one among many ethnic groups marginal to the English mainstream. Quebec's resistance to multiculturalism as both essentially "folkloric" (and therefore derogatory), and a sure path to the ultimate assimilation of French Canada into English Canada, is traced in some chapters of this book. Today many of the goals – economic, political, and educational – articulated during the Quiet Revolution have been at least partially realized in Quebec. Consequently, the climate for multiculturalism has warmed somewhat. A recent poll conducted by the Association for

Canadian Studies in March 2003 found a slight decline in the importance francophones attributed to bilingualism and a slight increase in their endorsement of multiculturalism over the last three years.[4]

Ironically, it was in large part because of French Canada (and the existence of two Charter Groups rather than one) that multiculturalism developed. A unilateral ideology never did exist in Canada. In this country it was as Canadian to be French-speaking, Roman Catholic, and observe Napoleonic law as it was to be English-speaking, Protestant, and observe British civil law. Where there are two solitudes, it is a short step to three as Michael Greenstein theorized in *Third Solitudes*,[5] his study of Jewish-Canadian writing in Montreal in the 1940s and 1950s — or even more. This too was recognized by Paul Yuzyk and the western Ukranians in their formation of the Third Force.

As politicians were busy shaping the nation, Aboriginal peoples in Canada — the nation's real Charter Group — were expected to assimilate into the mainstream. In the same year that French and English became the two official languages, the Trudeau/Chrétien statement on Indian policy called for their complete integration into the wider Canadian society. The First Nations movement for rights and status that gathered momentum in the 1980s — analyzed here by Tony Hall — made it clear that this was not to happen. As Canada's swing toward multiculturalism increased with the Multicultural Acts of 1985/88, the Native rights movement became strong and more visible. In the constitutional debates that followed, various bands insisted on recognition as distinct groups with undeniably special claims. A small sample of the anguish inflicted on First Nations people can be found in Maria Campbell's poem "Jacob." This poem examines — and exemplifies in its language — the results of Christian oppression of native peoples through residential schools and the deliberate obliteration of their cultures.

The collection of theoretical and creative material in this book raises a number of issues — pro and con — that have characterized Canada's shift since 1971 into a full-fledged multicultural society. Quebec was quick to identify an issue that continues to plague us. Is multiculturalism merely a case of the three "Ds": dress, dance, and dinners? Does it, in other words, reduce ethnicities to trivial folklorism or exoticism? Does the "ghettoization" of minorities promote racism on the principle of "divide and rule"? Certainly, with the shift from "preferred" countries of origin to individuals with desirable skills in 1962, issues of racism and discrimination came to the fore because of the increase in "visible minority" immigrants. At the same time there was a growing concern about the impact of immigration on the main urban centres (Montreal, Toronto, and Vancouver), where the majority of visible minority immigrants chose to settle. In order to remedy the split between multicultural cities and non-multicultural rural areas, there has recently been discussion among the provinces and with the federal government about incentives to induce skilled immigrants to settle for their first three to five years in smaller cities or rural areas. Does the very existence of communities within communities fracture the nation beyond recognition? Some immigrants, like Neil Bissoondath, have dismissed multiculturalism as a "zoo of exoticism," convinced that it trivializes ethnicity, ghettoizes minorities, and obstructs their progress as citizens. And in the arts in Canada, the late 1980s have seen bitter disputes about who "owns" voice and story—disputes that especially affect cultures (such as Native peoples and West Indians) that draw heavily on an oral tradition. Anthropologist and lawyer Rosemary Coombe deals comprehensively with the vexed subject of the appropriation of ethnic voices by mainstream writers.

It is indisputable, however, that ethnic voices are now among the most important in Canada. Changes to eliminate systemic discrimination in the publishing industry since the late 1980s have opened the way for writers who might not have seen print a quarter of a century ago. The contributors to this book are only a few of the many who have emerged in the past decade. Of those writers, a number have won major awards in Canada and elsewhere. Rohinton Mistry, for example, was chosen to appear on Oprah's Book Club television show for his novel *A Fine Balance* in addition to winning national and international awards for his work. In his short story "Swimming Lessons," he traces the first year of a young immigrant who must "sink or swim" in the Canadian culture he has chosen. In this story, as in Neil Bissoondath's "On the Eve of Uncertain Tomorrows," which explores the confusion between political and economic refugees (as well as the underground black market in Canadian health cards and social insurance numbers), apartment buildings and rooming houses symbolize the multicultural society where wildly different ethnic groups coexist in uneasy proximity.

What will the future hold for multiculturalism? As Alan Simmons demonstrates in this collection, much depends on the way we imagine that future. In his intriguing analysis, immigration policies have all along been based on an imagined future: first, a white European Canada; then after 1962, a Canada of skilled workers of all colours in a middle power nation; then a Canada that represents and participates in the entire planet, a global village. Early immigrants faced culture shock and racism—"the soft knife of politics," as Parin Dossa in her account of "Fatima's Story" calls it. Adele Wiseman's *The Sacrifice* and Rohinton Mistry's "Swimming Lessons" attest to this. Most bitter in her consideration of these issues is Joy Kogawa, whose writings on the shocking treatment of the Japanese in Canada during the Second World War, including "Road Building by Pick Axe" reproduced here, have awakened the nation to these matters. Fred Wah's ironic treatment of the ethnic group most feared and hated in early Canada—the Chinese—shows how ludicrous prejudice can be and how necessary it is that we discuss these matters. And Eva Tihanyi reminds us that the children of immigrants were among those most affected.

Meanwhile, as barriers continue to break down and familiarity with those whose cultures differ from what is less and less mainstream increases, perhaps intermarriage, increased awareness brought about by those who speak so eloquently of their experiences as immigrants, and other interpersonal connections in public and private life will gradually result in that hoped-for Utopia of Complexity described by Irshad Manji, a young Muslim feminist whose views are sampled here. Perhaps there will be no need to articulate a multiculturalism if such blendings and layerings eventually occur. In 1982, Section 27 of the Charter of Rights and Freedoms stated, "This Charter shall be interpreted in a manner consistent with the preservation and enhancement of the multicultural heritage of Canadians." This somewhat vague (and virtually unenforceable) statement is nonetheless a strong endorsement of our multicultural ideology. In 2002, June 27 was designated Canadian Multiculturalism Day. Certainly, Canada has changed from a primarily anglophone/francophone country that judges and assesses immigrants to one in which immigrants themselves increasingly comprise society and are a vocal part of all decision-making. Perhaps Canada in the future will be polyethnic and the need for multicultural policies will simply disappear.

Meanwhile, many fear that the division and subdivision of culture and language that is occurring in Canada will entirely destroy the nation. But perhaps, on the contrary, some time in the future, the "collective representations" touted by sociologist Emile Durkheim[6] as a necessary adjunct to nationhood will appear. If so, those symbols of nationhood will have to be all-inclusive.

NOTES

1. Carl Berger, "The True North Strong and Free," *Canadian Culture: An Introductory Reader*, edited by Elspeth Cameron (Toronto, 1997), 89.

2. John Porter, *The Vertical Mosaic: An Analysis of Class and Power in Canada* (Toronto, 1965), 33.

3. Porter, "Preface," *The Vertical Mosaic*, xii–xiii.

4. www.acs.aec.ca/Polls/Poll38.pdf

5. Michael Greenstein, *Third Solitudes: Tradition and Discontinuity in Jewish Canadian Literature* (Montreal, 1989).

6. Emile Durkheim, *The Division of Labour in Society*, translated by G. Simpson (Glencoe, 1951).

SECTION ONE

THEORY

THE HISTORICAL BACKGROUND

FROM THE CONTRIBUTIONS OF OTHER ETHNIC GROUPS

"REPORT OF THE ROYAL COMMISSION ON BILINGUALISM AND BICULTURALISM, BOOK IV"

The arrival in Canada of people drawn from a wide variety of ethnic origins can be followed through four distinct phases. The first of these lasted until approximately 1901. In that year the immigration policy of Sir Clifford Sifton, who became Minister of the Interior in 1896 and was determined to see the Canadian West settled, showed its results in the sharply rising census figures. This second phase, which lasted from 1901 until the outbreak of World War I, saw the greatest flow of people into Canada that the country has ever experienced. This influx was halted abruptly by the war, and the level of immigration only began to rise again in the early 1920s. This third phase was in turn halted by the Depression and immigration lapsed until a fourth phase began after World War II and has continued since then. Each of these four phases attracted different types of immigrants to the country. Thus over the years the ethnic background, class, and educational levels of the newcomers have differed widely, as have the geographic areas in which they chose to settle.

The history of these four phases can be traced through the Canadian census records but they give less than the full story. The questions asked in the censuses about ethnic origin have differed over the years and thus the information available is often not comparable for different periods. For the census of 1891 the only classification by origin was between French and all others⌊Other difficulties are that many people have been unable to answer the questions about their ethnic background accurately and at various times people have had reasons to wish to conceal or change their ethnic origin.⌉

Nor are the figures of arriving immigrants very detailed, particularly in the earlier phases. For example, there are not figures available as to the ethnic origin of immigrants other than the three categories of "British," "others," and "from the United States" for the years 1896–1900. An additional problem is that considerable numbers of immigrants either returned home or moved on, often to the United States, so the change in the number of a particular group between two consensuses results not only from natural increase and immigration but also from emigration. There are no official Canadian records of emigration, although broad estimates can be made by examining official United States reports of immigrants who give Canada as their birthplace or as their last place of permanent residence.

A. Immigration before 1901

Although the French and British have been predominant both in their number and in their cultural influence, the population of what is now Canada has always been ethnically diverse. People of many different origins entered British North America during the 18th and 19th centuries as fishermen, farmers, merchants, traders, soldiers, adventurers, slaves, and fugitives. For example, the Jewish community celebrated its national bicentenary in 1959 on the grounds that Aaron Hart, a commissary officer in General Amherst's invading army and the first permanent Jewish settler in Canada, arrived in Montreal in 1759. The Poles can also point to several notable figures of Polish background in Canadian history during the 18th and 19th centuries. These include Frederic Globenski, born in 1790, a judge at Rivière-du-Chêne, Quebec; Sir Casimir Gzowski, born in 1813, a civil engineer and contractor, and builder of the International Bridge at Niagara; and Alexandre Edouard Kierzkowski, born in 1816, a member of the first Parliament after Confederation.

Yet, until 1901, the pace of immigration was slow. By 1871 only 8 per cent of the population was of ethnic origin other than British, French, or native Indian and Eskimo. By 1881 the percentage had risen to nearly 9 and by 1901 to nearly 10. Emigration to the United States was one reason for this slow rate of growth. In his report on British North America in 1839, Lord Durham noted a tendency for immigrants to Canada to move on to the United States and placed the level of emigration at 60 per cent for the decade 1929-39. It has been estimated that more people left the country than entered it in each decade from 1861 to 1901.

Over half the immigrants to Canada of ethnic origin other than British or French before and during the 19th century were German. Small numbers of Germans settled in New France in the late 17th century. Several thousand German Protestants went to Nova Scotia between 1750 and 1753; about 1,500 of them founded the Lunenberg settlement. There were also Germans among the discharged soldiers and immigrants from New England who settled in the Maritimes and what was then the Province of Quebec after 1760, and among the United Empire Loyalists of the 1780s. After 1780 German sectarians—such as Mennonites, Moravians, and Tunkers—entered the British provinces, especially Upper Canada, coming primarily from the United States. Between the 1830s and 1870s immigrants from Germany settled in Upper Canada, many in Waterloo County (particularly the Mennonites), and to a lesser extent in the Maritime Provinces and Lower Canada. Pioneer settlements of German Mennonites who came from eastern Europe were established on the prairies between 1874 and 1878, and were joined by other Germans of different religious groups from Europe and the United States. German settlers also reached British Columbia after 1850. By 1901 residents of German origin were second in number only to the British in Ontario and Manitoba, and were the third largest group in Prince Edward Island, Nova Scotia, New Brunswick, Saskatchewan, and Alberta. They made up the fourth largest category in British Columbia and the fifth largest in Quebec.

The only other origin categories listed in the 1901 census which constituted over one half of 1 per cent of the population were the Dutch and Scandinavians. Like the Germans, many Dutch immigrants entered British North America as discharged soldiers and United Empire Loyalists. It seems probable that some were also Pennsylvania Dutch, who should really be considered part of the German group. In New Brunswick, a Danish settlement was established in the 1870s. In 1875 and 1876, about 1,000 Icelanders set up farming communities on the west shore of Lake Winnipeg, after earlier attempts in Nova Scotia and Ontario had failed. Norwegians, chiefly from the United States, settled near Brown in Manitoba, near Calgary in Alberta, and at several places in British Columbia. Finns also came to Canada in the 1870s settling in the Port Arthur (Thunder Bay) area.

The vast tide of immigration to Canada from central and eastern Europe in the early 1900s was preceded by a settlement of Poles at Wilno in Ontario and by the beginning of Hungarian settlement on the prairies through the activities of Count Esterhazy. He was responsible for several hundred Hungarian families moving to the Canadian West from the United States, and a smaller number directly from Hungary, to settle near Minnedosa in Manitoba and at what was to become Esterhazy and Kaposvar in Saskatchewan. He also persuaded Slovaks, Ukrainians, Germans, and Czechs to come to Canada.

On the west coast, Asians were a significant proportion of the population, although after 1878 they were subject to special restrictions. There were 4,400 Asians in Canada in 1881, mainly Chinese who had entered from California during the gold rush. Between 1881 and 1884, 15,700 more Chinese were brought in from Canton and Hong Kong as contract labourers to work on the Canada Pacific Railway. It has been said that a Chinese person is buried beneath every mile of track of the railway through the mountains of British Columbia. On completion of the railway, the CPR disclaimed all responsibility for the Chinese workers and neither the provincial nor federal governments provided assistance. By 1901 the number of Asians had risen to 23,700 including 4,700 Japanese and some 1,700 East Indians. Most Asians settled in British Columbia, where they made up 11 per cent of the population and, since they were almost all adult males, a much larger proportion of the labour force.

Negroes came to New France and to the provinces of British North America in the 18th century chiefly as slaves. In the 19th century, they formed sizable settlements as freedmen and fugitive slaves in the Maritimes, in southwestern Ontario, and in Victoria. Many returned to the United States in the 1860s, during and after the Civil War. The 1871 census figure of 21,500 for Canada probably represents a drop in the Negro population from an earlier peak. The 1881, 1901, and 1911 censuses record further declines.

B. THE SETTLEMENT OF THE PRAIRIES

The tide of emigration from Europe between 1880 and 1914 has been described as "the mightiest movement of people in modern history." Because of conditions in Europe—the collapse of the social structure, the transformation of agriculture and industry, the precipitous increase in population—millions moved to the United States and Latin America, particularly Argentina and Brazil. Canada received very few of these settlers until the late 1890s, when several factors combined to begin mass immigration to this country. The Yukon gold rush, the completion of the first continental railway and the building of other lines, the closing of the American frontier, new developments in dry land farming, and the Canadian government's first concentrated policy to promote immigration all combined to attract more than three million immigrants to Canada between 1896 and 1914. The number of immigrants arriving in 1913 was over 400,000, the highest it has ever been. Thus Clifford Sifton's immigration policy achieved its major goal, "to settle the empty West with producing farmers." Of those who immigrated in this period, 1,250,000 came from the United Kingdom, and about one million from the United States. Thousands more came directly from continental Europe. Between the censuses of 1901 and 1921 there was an increase of over 800,000 among those whose origin was neither British nor French in the Canadian population, and by 1921 they made up 15 per cent of Canada's population.

Those that were already established in the West increased their numbers greatly during this period. For example, the Germans increased in the three Prairie Provinces from 46,800 in 1901 to 148,000 in 1911, many of the newcomers being sponsored by German Catholic organizations. In 1921, the census listed 242,000 Canadians of German origin in the Prairie Provinces. Those of Scandinavian origin also increased considerably. Norwegian and Danish farmers migrated from the United States as homesteaders and many Swedes came to Canada as railway workers. The census figures give 17,300 persons of Scandinavian origin in the prairies in 1901, and 130,000 in 1921.

The outstanding feature of this period, however, was the influx of immigrants from central and eastern Europe—Ukrainians, Poles, Hungarians, Roumanians, and Russians. National boundaries had been fluid in eastern Europe in the years immediately preceding this period, and the peasants who immigrated were often uncertain as to their exact ethnic designations. Therefore, the census is an unreliable guide to the numbers in any one of these categories. It is particularly unreliable for Ukrainians, since there was no Ukrainian state during this period. An independent Ukrainian state existed between 1917 and 1921. In the late 1940s some Ukrainian immigrants still had difficulty in persuading Canadian immigration officials to accept Ukrainian as an ethnic origin. Between 1901 and 1921, the census recorded an increase in Ukrainians from 5,600 to 96,000 in the three Prairie Provinces, and an increase in Poles from 2,800 to 32,000. Hungarians were not enumerated separately until the 1921 census when their total was 13,200.

The symbolic "first" Ukrainian immigrants to Canada are Wasyl Eleniak and Iwan Pylypiw, who arrived in 1891. The mass movement of Ukrainians began in 1896, under the direction of Joseph Oleskow and in response to Clifford Sifton's urgent invitations. Oleskow, an agriculturalist, was disturbed by the plight of Ukrainian immigrants to Brazil and other South American countries, and therefore studied the possibility of emigration elsewhere. He felt that Canada was extremely promising and the Department of the Interior sponsored a tour of the country for him in 1895. This tour and his contact and correspondence with Canadian officials increased his enthusiasm. On his return to Lvov, he published a brochure promoting immigration to Canada and this had a tremendous influence on the Ukrainian peasants. He also personally organized groups of immigrants. The first group of 107 arrived in Quebec City on May 1, 1896. This initiated a flow of Ukrainian immigrants that continued until the outbreak of war in 1914.

By 1901 the number of settlers of Russian origin in Saskatchewan was exceeded only by those of British, Indian and Eskimo, and German origin. Among the Russians were between 7,000 and 8,000 Doukhobors, who had arrived in 1899 and settled in Saskatchewan before it became a province. A few more Doukhobors arrived in Saskatchewan before the next census in 1911, but many also emigrated to British Columbia during that period. British Columbia had only 27 settlers of Russian origin in 1901 but had 4,400 by 1911 and 7,800 by 1921.

For these thousands of immigrants, the city of Winnipeg was the gateway to the promised land. Most only passed through the city but some stayed. The settlement of the prairies was reflected in Winnipeg's growth between 1881 and 1911 and in its increasing ethnic heterogeneity. In 30 years Winnipeg changed from a town of 8,000 residents to a prairies metropolis of 136,000. The proportion of those of British origin in the population declined from 84 to 59 per cent. By 1921 the population had reached 176,000 and 67 per cent reported British as their ethnic origin. This proportion was probably inflated, however, as a result of strong anti-alien sentiments after World War I and the Winnipeg general strike in 1919. In 1931 the British proportion was 61 per cent, and it has declined at each succeeding census.

Like so many others who came to Canada, the Italians were forced to emigrate by unsettled economic and political conditions at home, and were attracted to Canada by the demand of the railways and other construction enterprises for labourers. The number of Italians in Canada rose from 11,000 in 1901 to 46,000 by 1911 and 67,000 by 1921. The number of Jews also increased from 16,100 in 1901 to 76,200 by 1911 and 126,000 by 1921. Many of these were refugees from eastern Europe. Most immigrants of both groups settled in the towns and cities of Ontario and Quebec, although some Italian labourers worked on western railway construction and some Jews settled in Winnipeg and in pioneer farming communities in Manitoba. By 1921 the Jews in Toronto were second only to the British in number. Although many fewer immigrated to Canada, the Greeks, Syrians, Lebanese, and Armenians resembled the Italians and Jews in their preference for settling in the cities of central Canada.

Clifford Sifton disapproved of the immigration of Asians but on the west coast the Chinese population continued to increase in spite of the imposition of a "head tax" of $100 on entering Canada in 1900, and $500 in 1903. Japanese also began to immigrate in large numbers. In the first ten months of 1907, over 8,000 Japanese arrived. Anti-Asian sentiment and the demand for tighter immigration restrictions increased in British Columbia, finally resulted in racial riots in Vancouver in September 1907, and drew the country's attention to the problem. The outcome was what is known as the "gentlemen's agreement" by which Japan agreed to limit emigration of labourers to Canada unless specifically requested by the Canadian government. The Japanese already in Canada were largely rural settlers, engaging in farming, fishing, logging, boat-building, and mining, and they stayed near the west coast. By 1921, there were 40,000 Chinese in Canada, 24,000 of them in British Columbia, and 16,000 Japanese, 15,000 of them in British Columbia. There were also about 5,000 East Indians, chiefly Sikhs, who came to British Columbia between 1905 and 1908 and found work mainly in railroad construction and in the logging and lumbering industries.

C. IMMIGRATION BETWEEN THE WARS

World War I cut off the movement of people to Canada, and postwar readjustments impeded it for several more years. However, by 1923 another phase of rising immigration was in progress, although the numbers never reached those of the peak years of 1902–13. This phase continued until the Depression caused an abrupt decline in immigration, starting in 1931. The United States developed restrictions on immigration which reduced the total number of immigrants entering the United States each year and particularly the number coming from southern and eastern Europe. Canada therefore replaced its southern neighbor as the favored destination. Canada also restricted immigration to some extent, although a formal quota system was not adopted as it was in the United States. The Canadian government established a list of "preferred" and "non-preferred" countries from which to select immigrants, virtually excluded the Chinese, and severely limited other Asians. However, the proportion of the Canadian population that was not of British, French, or native Indian and Eskimo origin still rose to more than 18 per cent by 1931.

Fewer immigrants went west in this period than in the early 1900s. The wheat lands were filled, the wheat boom was faltering, and the new arrivals were more interested in settling in urban communities than the early immigrants had been. They tended to stay in the industrial and commercial centers of Ontario and Quebec, or to go to the booming mining and pulp and paper towns in the northern part of central Canada. The populations of these centers were also increased by people moving from farms to urban areas. In 1928 a committee of the House of Commons expressed concern that the immigrants who had been intended to provide a labour force for agriculture were instead gravitating to the cities, and often ending up in slum areas. However, no plans to change this situation were implemented.

Between 1920 and 1939 the number of new arrivals giving their ethnic origin as Ukrainian was 67,000. In addition, awakening ethnic self-consciousness during this period now led many earlier immigrants to identify themselves as Ukrainian. As a result, between 1921 and 1941 those claiming Ukrainian ethnic origin rose from eighth to fourth place in the origin categories listed in the Canadian census figures.

The Ukrainian immigrants of this period were often better educated than those who had come to Canada earlier, and many more of them settled in urban centers .... The influence of this trend can be seen in the spread of Ukrainian communities from the prairies, where they had been concentrated before World War I, to other sections of the country. The number in Ontario doubled and in British Columbia tripled between 1931 and 1941. Higher levels of education and technical skills resulting in greater interest in settling in urban centers also characterized the Poles and Hungarians who arrived in Canada during the 1920s. The number of Hungarians in Canada rose sharply during the decade 1921–31.

The census figure for those of Russian origin was 100,000 for 1921, which is unusually high compared with 44,400 in 1911 and 88,100 in 1931. The increases were all in the Prairie Provinces. It is possible that many German-speaking people who had once lived in Tsarist Russia claimed Russian ethnic origin because of antagonisms towards them resulting from World War I. Some Russians did, of course, enter Canada after the Russian Revolution.

Scandinavians continued to come to Canada and to settle in the farming areas of the West. About 20,000 Swedes, 19,500 Norwegians, and 17,000 Danes entered the country between 1923 and 1930. Those of Scandinavian origin increased from 167,000 in 1921 to 228,000 in 1931. In Saskatchewan, Alberta, and British Columbia the population of those of Scandinavian origin increased by 44,000 between 1921 and 1931.

In the 1920s about 6,500 German Mennonites, mostly members of the conservative wing of the group, left Manitoba and Saskatchewan for Mexico. In the same period Mennonite Colonization Associations brought almost 20,000 settlers to Canada. Other immigration organizations brought thousands more Mennonites, as well as members of other religious groups, most of whom settled in the West. As with other immigrants, the Mennonites were now more interested in settling in urban centers than earlier arrivals.

Many immigrants of this period settled in the mining and mill towns of northern Ontario and British Columbia, including large numbers of Finns. They were from the peasant and working class—losers in the class struggle which followed Finland's achievement of independence in 1917. Many went to the Port Arthur area joining earlier Finnish settlers, and they also developed communities in Sault Ste. Marie, Timmons, Sudbury, Toronto, Montreal, and Vancouver.

For the Italians this phase of immigration was of short duration. After 1925 the Fascist government discouraged emigration from Italy, except to North Africa. Canada's economic difficulties and restrictions on immigration reinforced this policy. Immigration and natural increases were not quite sufficient to double the population of Italian origin between 1921 and 1941. Montreal and Toronto continued to be the centers of the Italian population. In 1941, there were 23,800 persons of Italian origin in Montreal, and 14,200 in Toronto.

During this period, 20,200 Jewish immigrants settled in Canada, most of them in urban centres. Regardless of their citizenship, Jews were treated separately by Canadian immigration authorities and were required to meet special conditions. There were also campaigns for tighter restrictions against Asian immigrants, similar to those in force in the United States. From 1923 on, the Canadian government admitted only certain specified classes of Chinese, and the 1908 "gentlemen's agreement" was revised in 1928 to limit the entry of Japanese to 150 a year. Campaigns against the "yellow peril" were so successful that the census of 1931 listed only 85,600 residents of Asian ethnic origin, an increase of fewer than 19,000 in the decade, and the census of 1941 showed a decrease to 74,000. The decrease was especially marked among the Chinese, and reflected the dying out of the original immigrant group, which had had an extremely unbalanced sex ratio severely limiting natural increase, and the lack of replacements through immigration. Negroes also suffered from discriminatory measures after 1923, when it was decided that only citizens of Commonwealth countries with predominantly white populations would be considered British subjects.

During the Depression of the 1930s the government cut off the flow of immigrants into Canada. A total of 1,804,000 new immigrants arrived between 1911 and 1921, and 1,166,000 between 1922 and 1931. Between 1932 and 1941 the figure fell to 140,000 and emigration is estimated to have exceeded immigration by 100,000. Deportation figures, usually small, rose steeply for a few years in the early thirties, when the provision that those who became total public charges were subject to deportation was invoked against some of the unemployed. Between 1931 and 1941 the number of Canadian residents of German ethnic origin fell by almost 9,000, that of Russian origin by almost 4,500, and that of Asian origin by 10,500. The proportion of the population of other ethnic origins held steady in Canada as a whole, and rose by about 3 percentage points in the three Prairie Provinces, but this increase occurred because the population of British origin decreased by 48,000 in Saskatchewan and Manitoba.

The drift to the cities continued during the 1930s. Small concentrations of different cultural groups which already existed in many cities were augmented by people moving away from the drought areas of the West. For example, the Roumanian community in Montreal, which had existed since the turn of the century, grew considerably and a Hungarian community emerged in Toronto.

In the late 1930s some of those arriving in Canada were refugees, but economic recovery was slow and the Canadian government was reluctant to admit even the victims of Nazi Germany. The tendency to give economic considerations priority over humanitarian ones was probably buttressed by the anti-Semitism expressed by small but noisy and even violent minorities in various parts of Canada in the 1930s.

D. AFTER WORLD WAR II

Substantial immigration to Canada resumed soon after the end of World War II, and by 1961 another 2,100,000 immigrants had arrived in Canada.

A wider variety of ethnic origin categories, social classes, and occupations were included in this final phase, which has also continued longer than either of the earlier phases before and after World War I. The ethnic origins most strongly represented among the new arrivals since 1945—other than British—are Italian, German, Dutch, Polish, and Jewish; those of British origin constituted one-third of the total.

During this period, Canada has become increasingly urban and industrial, and the vast majority of these immigrants has settled in towns and cities. A substantial number has gone to Montreal, but Toronto has become the immigrant metropolis of Canada. In 1961, nearly 42 per cent of the residents of Toronto and one-third of the residents of the Toronto metropolitan area were not born in Canada. Twenty-nine per cent of the city's residents and 22 per cent of those in the metropolitan area had immigrated between 1946 and 1961.

This last phase included some 300,000 persons who came to Canada as refugees displaced by political disruptions in their homeland. These disruptions often had a great impact upon persons from all social and economic levels; many of them came from urban centers and were generally well-educated people with professional training, artistic talents, and linguistic skills, along with experience in business, government, the military, or a skilled trade.

Immigration to Canada following the Hungarian Revolution of 1956 is perhaps the most obvious illustration of this development, but Ukrainians, Lithuanians, Estonians, Latvians, Jews, and Poles were also included. Early in World War II, over 2,500 German and Austrian nationals, most of them Jews who had been interned in Great Britain after the outbreak of hostilities, were sent to Canada for internment. About a thousand decided to remain in Canada after their release, and this group included an exceptional number of intellectually and artistically gifted individuals who have since made a notable contribution to Canadian arts, letters, and science. The Jewish refugees who came after the war were mainly from Poland, although there were also small groups among the Hungarian immigrants after 1956 and from Egypt and North Africa after the crises there in the late 1950s. Toronto and Montreal were their usual destinations. Montreal was especially attractive to the French-speaking Jews from the Middle East, as it was for many French-speaking North Africans.

As already noted, most groups of immigrants since 1945 have included relatively large proportions of the educated and the skilled, partly because economic and social development made Canada more attractive to these groups and partly because government policy made admission easier for those with education and skills. Because of their backgrounds and their familiarity with urban life, these immigrants have not tended to establish heavily concentrated settlements in the cities as the earlier, less skilled groups had done. Instead, they quickly spread out into any parts of the cities where they found other Canadians sharing their educational level, occupations, and tastes.

However, most immigrants from the less economically advanced countries such as Italy, Greece, and Portugal still come largely from rural areas, villages, and towns. These groups continued to cluster in specific sections of the cities in which they settled, their residential patterns thus resembling those of earlier peasant groups that settled in Canadian and American cities. Italian immigration has been the heaviest in the postwar period, especially between 1951 and 1960 when over 250,000 Italians entered the country. Immigration from Greece and Portugal had always been light, but in the early 1950s it increased sharply, and has continued since then at a high level. Most immigrants of all these three ethnic origins have settled in cities, especially in Toronto, Montreal, and Vancouver. By the 1960s those of Italian origin were second in number only to those of British origin in Toronto ....

Probably no people in Canada have suffered more because of the war than those of Japanese origin. When Japan entered the war, they were uprooted from the west coast and placed in relocation centres. At the war's end about 4,000 were forced to leave the country under a government "repatriation" scheme. More than half of these were Canadian-born and two-thirds were Canadian citizens. Most of the Japanese who stayed in Canada did not return to British Columbia. Many went to Toronto where, by 1961, there were about 8,000 Japanese in the metropolitan area.

Immigration from Japan did not resume in any volume after the war. Chinese immigration, which had been virtually non-existent since 1923, revived with the removal of some of the government's restrictive measures in 1947. About 25,000 people of Chinese origin entered between 1949 and the end of 1961. Immigration from India, Pakistan, and Ceylon also began to increase in the late 1950s.

The total Negro population of Canada fell from 22,200 in 1941 to 18,000 in 1951, but by 1961 it had increased to 32,100. The decrease during the war and early postwar years may reflect some tendency on the part of Negro youths to emigrate to the United States for their higher education and for employment. Negro immigration began to rise in 1953 and has continued at a high level since then.

British immigration has always been high; in most years the number of immigrants of British origin has been highest or second highest. French immigration was a slow trickle until 1951, when it showed a slight increase. The natural increase of those of French origin has enabled them to maintain their proportion of the population while the British proportion has declined steadily.

Those of other ethnic origins are not equally dispersed across Canada. The Atlantic Provinces and Quebec (except Montreal) have remained largely British or French. Residents of other ethnic origins make up 47 per cent of the population of the Prairie Provinces, 34 per cent of that of British Columbia, and 29 per cent of Ontario. All five of these provinces also have a high proportion of residents born outside Canada. ...

In the 1961 census nearly one-quarter of the population reported their ethnic origin as other than British, French, or Indian and Eskimo. A large proportion of these are in fact Canadian-born. Seventy-seven per cent of those of Ukrainian origin and 73 per cent of those of German, Russian, and Scandinavian origin were born in Canada ....

ENGLISH-CANADIAN OPPOSITION TO NON-BRITISH IMMIGRATION

FROM THE CALGARY HERALD

"THE CHARACTER OF OUR IMMIGRATION," JANUARY 18, 1899

According to the report of C.W. Sutter, immigration agent at Edmonton, the following is a partial schedule of the new settlers who came into Northern Alberta last year. It is interesting as far as it goes (Mr. Sutter admits it is not complete), as showing the mixed quality of the immigration Alberta is getting:

	Ml's	Fml's	T'l
Austria (Germans)	15	9	24
Austria (Ruthenians)	500	575	1375 [1075][1]
British Columbia	7	3	10
Chile, S.America	6	3	9
England	13	7	20
Germany	2	0	2
Switzerland	1	0	1
Scotland	10	5	15
Ireland	5	3	8
Manitoba	16	10	26
Massachusetts	22	10	32
Michigan	71	29	100
Minnesota	38	19	55 [57]
Montana	6	0	6

(continued)

Nebraska	13	6	12 [19]
New Hampshire	13	6	19
Oregon	31	3	8
Dakota	31	14	15 [45]
Illinois	34	19	53
Iowa	5	1	6
Kansas	8	6	13 [14]
Vermont	3	1	4
Wisconsin	53	21	74
Pennsylvania	7	5	12
Quebec	4	6	9 [10]
Nova Scotia	13	6	12 [19]
Ontario	91	33	124
	1239	792	2031
	[992]	[800]	[1792]

1 Numbers in square brackets represent corrected totals.

A suggestive feature of these figures is the insignificant number of English, Irish, and Scotch settlers as compared with the enormous quantity of Galicians.

It would be better for the reputation of this country throughout the world were statistics such as these entirely suppressed. They need a press censor in the interior department just as badly as they need a fool killer. Like a hotel, or other public place, a country is gauged and sized up according to the class of people who frequent it, the same as the company which a young man keeps is made the criterion by which he is judged by others. As against 1,375 dirty, frowsy Galicians, there came to the North West Territories from the Mother country last year 13 Englishmen, 10 Scotchmen, and 15 Irishmen. It looks as if the wrong kind of men entirely were sent forth to talk up the North West in the British Isles. Some incompetent lazy, quasi-politician, who has been thrown out of the saddle, has to be helped to his feet, and he gets pitchforked into a billet with the immigration department with the result that so far as the mother country or Canada is concerned there is no result at all.

What Sifton means by affecting not to know that there is such a place as Great Britain on the map, and ignoring Britishers as desirable immigrants, preferring to minister with the power behind him and the funds at his disposal to the importing of a mass of human ignorance, filth, and immortality is only known to his immediate friends. Silver-tongued Wilf [Wilfred Laurier], Yukon Bill, and other dubious characters. This policy of building a nation on the lines of the Tower of Babel, where the Lord confounded the language so that the people might not understand one another's speech, is hardly applicable to the present century, and deep as was the love evinced by the people for the Liberal Party, at the last general election they certainly did not reckon that the Liberal policy was to be dated from the Eleventh Book of Genesis, the period of the flood. They bargained for a more up-to-date policy.

STEPHEN LEACOCK

RACISM IN EARLY CANADA

FROM ECONOMIC PROSPERITY IN THE BRITISH EMPIRE

[...] We must start, I say, from the fact that the emigrant, or local worker, with whom we are concerned possesses nothing; or, more likely, in the form of a dependent wife and children, possesses, economically less than nothing. We have to start from this. Any scheme of migration dealing with thrifty Scottish farmers who have saved a hundred pounds, or well-to-do Americans from Kansas, or young men whose people will pay a hundred pounds to get rid of them, is quite beside the mark.

The emigrant has nothing, except his capacity to work. If he is disabled and cannot work, his case lies outside of this book. But at present, let us say, he cannot find work; he is one of the 2,000,000 unemployed and the 5,000,000 under-employed of Great Britain.

Citizens of alien countries are not under consideration, do not fit into the scheme. The outer empire needs population and settlement. Part of it, like Canada, can only carry its "overhead" of transportation and capital investment on the condition that a stream of newcomers shall move in. If there were no available British to come, we should very likely have to take in others or drift into liquidation. But it so happens that there are British — millions of them. The others we only need as a second-best choice.

Canada, especially in its northwest provinces, is badly damaged in this respect. As a result of the great foreign immigration before the War, the last census of Canada showed among its inhabitants 459,000 people born in continental Europe, including 57,000 Austrians, 31,000 Galicians, 101,000 Russians, 21,000 Poles, 35,000 Italians, and various others.

From the point of view of the Russians and the Galicians, etc., this meant improvement for the northwest. Not so from others. Learning English and living under the British flag may make a British subject in the legal sense, but not in the real sense, in the light of national history and continuity. A few such people can easily be absorbed — over a large area many thousands can be absorbed. A little dose of them may even, by variation, do good, like a minute dose of poison in a medicine. But if you get enough of them, you get absorbed yourself. What you called the British Empire turns into the Russian and Galician Empire.

I am not saying that we should absolutely shut out and debar the European foreigner, as we should and do shut out the Oriental. But we should in no way facilitate his coming. Not for him the free ocean transit, nor the free coffee of the immigrant shed, nor the free land, nor the found job, nor the guaranteed anything. He is lucky if he is let in "on his own."

IRVING ABELLA
AND HAROLD TROPER

IMMIGRATION AND
CANADIAN ANTI-SEMITISM

FROM NONE IS TOO MANY: CANADA AND
THE JEWS OF EUROPE, 1933–1948

That Jews were not welcome in Canada during the early 1930s is not surprising; neither was anyone else. With one-third of its people out of work, the country was understandably reluctant to accept job-hungry immigrants; in other words, that the economic consequences of the depression throttled immigration cannot be denied. But what should be stressed is that the depression also afforded Canadian government officials a dramatic opportunity to complete a process of restriction begun in the boom years of the 1920s.

Canadian immigration policy had always been as ethnically selective as it was economically self-serving. When economic necessity dictated the admission of non-British and non-American immigrants, it was always in descending order of ethnic preference. Following British and American immigrants, preference was given northern and then central Europeans. At the bottom were Jews, Orientals, and blacks.[1] These "non-preferred immigrants" were acceptable as long as they were out of sight, risking life and limb in the mines and smelters of the west and north, holed up in lumber camps deep in the forest, or farming the more marginal areas of the western wheat frontier. Those who escaped this life for perhaps the even worse one in Canada's urban centres, where they competed for jobs with native- or British-born artisans, were less acceptable. And to Immigration officials, the worst culprits, those most likely to settle in the cities, were

Jews. Jews, according to the director of immigration, were "city people." To almost every request to admit Jewish farmers or agricultural workers, he had the same attitude: it was impossible to keep them on the farm or in the bush; every attempt to do so had failed.[2]

With the inclination on the part of less desirable immigrants to drift into the cities and a gradual decline in the demand for unskilled labourers, the Canadian government had begun, by the mid twenties, to restrict the immigration of those on the bottom rungs of the ethnic preference ladder. When in 1928 the deputy minister of immigration, W.J. Egan, ordered that the admission of eastern European immigrants be cut back by two-thirds, he explained that, although the economy was doing well, these "non-preferred country immigrants had drifted into non-agricultural work almost immediately upon arrival ... and [were] filling positions that might have been filled by immigrants from the Mother Country."[3]

The onset of the depression then gave the government the opportunity to complete drawing the restrictionist ring around Canada. In 1930 an Order-in-Council was introduced, allowing into the country only those with enough capital to establish and maintain themselves on farms. In the following year another Order-in-Council effectively banned all non-agricultural immigrants unless either British or American. To all intents and purposes, Canada had shut itself off from the rest of the world just at the time when it was most needed. And for the remainder of the decade — and indeed beyond it — a determined federal government fought every attempt by the wretched European refugees to break through this protective wall of legislation.

The League of Nations' high commissioner for German refugees, James G. McDonald, repeatedly approached member states, including Canada, to loosen immigration restrictions. In the early spring of 1934 he wrote directly to the Canadian Prime Minister, R.B. Bennett, asking that Canada accept a share of the newly displaced. McDonald followed up his letter with a visit to Ottawa, where he held lengthy discussions with the prime minister and Immigration Branch authorities. Progress seemed to be made, and he was asked by the Canadian government to assemble a number of applications from German refugees detailing their full histories. There was one ominous rider on any deal made: government officials must be persuaded that all those put forward would "not become a factor in the labour market and [would] not become public charges." But as the high commissioner explained in confidence to Canadian Jewish officials, he was also assured some action would "be taken with a view to admitting a small number to Canada."[4]

The commissioner's office prepared the list requested; it was delivered to the prime minister on his visit later that year to the League of Nations headquarters in Geneva. In conversation with the high commissioner at the time, the prime minister was encouraging. Once he was back in Ottawa, however, everything changed. Immigration authorities persuaded Bennett that any breach in immigration restrictions, no matter how small, would only lead to more requests, more concessions; in the end the immigration tap would be turned on again — all this for the sake of a few Jews. Soon after, a contrite prime minister was writing the high commissioner that, although his cabinet's sympathy rested with the work of the refugee committee, the government would offer no help. "We cannot, in fairness to our population," Bennett explained, "authorize the admission into Canada of a number of people who must either remain idle or take the places now filled by Canadians, or for which Canadians are waiting an opportunity."[5] The matter was closed.

After the Liberal party came to power in Canada in 1935, the person entrusted with the task of insuring that restrictions on immigration were upheld was the director of the Immigration Branch of the Department of Mines and Resources, Frederick Charles Blair. Blair's small empire, the Immigration Branch, had been shunted from ministry to ministry as immigration had ground to a virtual halt. The decision finally to place it within the Department of Mines and Resources was likely made as much for administrative convenience as from any functional logic; as immigration receded further into the shadows of government priorities, it mattered little which ministry housed its operations.

Ostensibly, Thomas Crerar, minister of mines and resources, was responsible for immigration; in fact, Blair himself made policy and implemented it. Crerar, now well past his prime as a power on the Liberal party benches, knew little of the workings of the Immigration Branch and cared even less. He relied almost totally on its director for advice.[6] Thus, Blair made almost all decisions about who got into Canada; and nothing that touched his department escaped his personal scrutiny, whether it was authorizing the purchase of stationery or approving a routine application for admission to Canada. And from the point of view of European Jewry this was most unfortunate. Just when they most needed a friend at the gate, they had an enemy; instead of the philo-Semite they required, they had an anti-Semite; instead of a humanitarian, they got a narrow-minded bureaucrat.

Born in Carlisle, Ontario, in 1874, of Scottish parents, Blair joined the Department of Agriculture in 1903 and two years later became an immigration officer. In 1924 he was appointed assistant deputy minister of immigration and in 1936 he became director of the Immigration Branch with full deputy-minister status. He was a religious man, an elder in his church, a dedicated civil servant. Indeed, so devoted was he to his job that, when he officially retired in 1943, four years beyond normal retirement age, he had accumulated about two years of sick leave.[7]

As the man responsible for enforcing Canadian immigration policy, Blair mirrored the increasingly anti-immigration spirit of his times. He believed, said one observer, "that people should be kept out of Canada instead of being let in"; and he was, according to those who knew him, a tough administrator who "stuck to the rules," not so surprising as he had drafted most of them himself. Of course, Blair's ideas were entirely compatible with those of the Canadian government, which kept him in his sensitive position as long as it could. As James Gibson, a Department of External Affairs official, recalled, "He was the single most difficult individual I have had to deal with the whole time I was a public servant. He was a holy terror!"[8] And perhaps this is why he stayed for so long in his job: he was precisely the man the ruling Liberal government wanted: his inflexibility, his fetish for regulations, his wish to control unchallenged all matters of immigration — these traits suited an administration that had no intention of allowing in Jewish refugees but wished to avoid the reproach that might follow from not doing so.

For Blair the term "refugee" was a code word for Jew. Unless "safeguards" were adopted, he warned Thomas Crerar, Canada was in danger of being "flooded with Jewish people," and his task, as he saw it, was to make sure that the safeguards did not fail. Indeed, he was inordinately proud of his success in keeping out Jews. "Pressure on the part of Jewish people to get into Canada," he wrote, "has never been greater than it is now, and I am glad to be able to add, after 35 years experience here, that it was never so well controlled." Blair expressed a strong personal distaste for Jews, especially for "certain of their habits." He saw them as unassimilable, as people apart, as threatening people "who can organize their affairs better than other people" and so accomplish more. He complained bitterly that Jews were "utterly selfish in their attempts to force through a permit for the admission of relatives or friends." "They do not believe that 'No' means more than 'Perhaps'." And Jews, he lamented, "make any kind of promise to get the door open but ... never cease their agitation until they get in the whole lot." Blair saw a conspiracy behind all Jewish attempts to get their co-religionists into the country, "to bring immigration regulations into disrepute and create an atmosphere favorable to those who cannot comply with the law." Self-righteous and justifying, he commiserated with the traffic manager of the Canadian Pacific Railway: "If there is any surer way to close the door in their own face, I do not know of it."[9]

But did Blair see himself as an anti-Semite? No, for he was, in his own view, just being realistic—realistic about Canada's immigration needs and about the unsuitability of the Jew to those needs. To keep Jews out of Canada, he would often argue, did Jews a favor, even if they could not see it. The arrival of Jews would create anti-Semitism in Canada, undermining the security of the existing Canadian Jewish community and little benefiting the new arrival. Those who saw anti-Jewish sentiment in Blair's position did so, Blair claimed, from self-serving motives. "I am sure," he declared, "the treatment received in Canada by Jewish people in no way warrants the charge of anti-Semitism. I suggest that those who hold such a view are putting it forward not on the ground of our past history but probably as an argument in favor of an open door policy, which under present economic conditions is impossible to adopt."[10]

Blair was of course an anti-Semite. His contempt for the Jews was boundless. In a revealing letter to a strong opponent of Jewish immigration, Blair elabourated on the reasons for his prejudice:

> *I suggested recently to three Jewish gentlemen with whom I am well acquainted, that it might be a very good thing if they would call a conference and have a day of humiliation and prayer, which might profitably be extended for a week or more, where they would honestly try to answer the question of why they are so unpopular almost everywhere .... I often think that instead of persecution it would be far better if we more often told them frankly why many of them are unpopular. If they would divest themselves of certain of their habits I am sure they could be just as popular in Canada as our Scandinavians .... Just because Jewish people would not understand the frank kind of statements I have made in this letter to you, I have marked it confidential."*[11]

But, though it was Blair who finally interpreted government regulations and who acted as the de facto judge and jury on individual requests for admission, to blame him alone for Canada's response to Jewish immigration would be both overly simplistic and incorrect; after all, he was, although powerful, only a civil servant whose actions reflected the wishes and values of his superiors. Not to accept refugees was a political decision, not a bureaucratic one. It was Mackenzie King, Liberal prime minister throughout most of the 1920s and again after 1935, and his cabinet ministers who, in the final analysis, were responsible for keeping Jews out of Canada.

The orphan scheme, the needle trades and fur workers schemes, and the first-degree relative program all opened the door, however slightly and however reluctantly, for Jewish refugee immigration to Canada in the postwar years. Compared to the total number of postwar refugees admitted into Canada during this period, the 3,000 Jewish refugees pales in significance. Jews, who made up close to thirty per cent of the European refugee community, represented less than fifteen per cent of the approximately 65,000 refugees admitted into Canada throughout March 1948. Measured against the magnitude of the European problem — in the summer of 1947 it was estimated that approximately 250,000 Jewish survivors of Hitler awaited new homes — the number of Jews who entered Canada in 1948 seems small indeed. On the other hand, compared to prewar and wartime immigration of Jews, this figure represents a monumental growth in Jewish refugee immigration.[12]

Was the cup half full or half empty? It's hard to say. Once again the usefulness of comparisons depends on the argument one wishes to make, but it should be pointed out that Canada's contribution to resettlement of the postwar Jewish refugee community in absolute numbers between 1946 and 1950 was outdone only by Israel's and the United States.[13] Furthermore, it must be noted that the percentage of Jews among displaced persons admitted to Canada was far in excess of the percentage of Jews already in Canada, a prime consideration in American immigration law. In July 1948 David Lewis, national secretary of the CCF, confided his own unease at condemning Canada's role in the postwar Jewish refugee crisis — an unease that grew as much out of what the government was doing and how it was doing it, as from what could be done and was not:

> There is no doubt that there is discrimination. However, there is equally no doubt that the situation in the past year [1947–48] or more has been very much better than it had been for the previous twenty-five years. The fact is that between 15 and 20% of all DP immigrants coming to Canada today are Jewish. In view of the special hardships to which the Jewish DP's were

subject for fifteen years, it certainly is not fair that so small a proportion of all immigrants should be Jews. On the other hand, justice is never complete monarch in the present immoral world. The Department of Immigration is, I think, convinced that if they attempted to increase the proportion considerably, there would be such an outcry and such opposition both in the Cabinet and outside, that even the present 15–20% might be cut off or substantially reduced. Those with prejudice and without the necessary humanity, don't look at the situation in terms in which we do. They are much more likely to demand that the proportion of Jewish immigrants to total immigration should be related to the proportion of Jewish people to the total population in Canada. This would bring the proportion down to less than 2% instead of 15–20%.[14]

For the government, Jewish refugees, and, indeed, refugees in general, remained as a case apart — that is, apart from the normal regeneration of immigration into postwar Canada. Keenleyside, in a 1948 guest lecture at Dalhousie University in Halifax, observed that arrangements made for the admission of displaced persons were "unique in Canadian history and [did] not fit readily into any of the ordinary provisions governing the admission of immigrants." That is not to say refugees did not constitute an important component of postwar immigration. They did. But at the same time the refugee crisis was also understood to be a "temporary" phenomenon of which Canada, if innovative, could take advantage even as it worked for its resolution.[15]

How long need Canada maintain these special programs, these special allowances for refugees? By mid-1948 tens of thousands of displaced persons, including a hard-won contingent of Jews, had been approved for admission. Would it not make more sense, some now argued, to subsume refugees within the general framework of the newly revitalized immigration program, a program of selective encouragement of immigration reminiscent of the turn of the century? Had Canada not done its part for displaced persons?

Norman Robertson, who succeeded Massey as Canadian high commissioner in London, saw no advantage in keeping displaced persons programs alive — not for Canada and not for the displaced persons. As early as January 1947 he cabled Lester Pearson in External Affairs, recommending a simple solution to the refugee problem. Robertson would see all displaced persons, irrespective of national or ethnic origin, granted the "option of legal domicile in Germany" equivalent in all respects with German citizens.

This would give displaced persons a status both different and better than that which they already held. If they held German national status, Canada would be relieved of drifting along an immigration course that, Robertson warned, promised "years of pressure groups, racial, religious and political, all trying to influence and distort [its] immigration policy." Germany caused the crisis, it should be part of its resolution. For those displaced persons who did not wish to establish themselves permanently in Germany, at least they would have a breathing space during which to enter a regular emigration stream out of Germany. For Canada and other overseas countries the plan would offer an "opportunity to develop selective immigration policies adapted to their needs, and absorptive capacities—and relatively unburdened by the special pressures which may well make it impossible for us to work out any coherent and sensible immigration policy at all."[16]

If Keenleyside, who eventually answered Robertson's cable, allowed that these suggestions were "worthy of very serious consideration," he denied Canada was subject to pressure from ethnic or religious interest groups. Replying to the Robertson suggestions almost a year after they were first made, Keenleyside, using Robertson's own words, pointed out to External Affairs that Canada's policy had matured over that year: "As at present defined, directed and administered our policy covering the admission of DP's is *not* unduly subject to 'special pressures' or to 'racial, religious and political' influences designed and applied to distort our programme. Moreover, our policy is scrupulously 'selective' and very carefully 'adapted to [our] needs.'"[17]

For his part Keenleyside would, by late summer 1948, counsel the cabinet to reorganize displaced persons programs, not by changing the status of displaced persons but by closing down programs designed specifically for them.[18] Keenleyside pointed to both a declining Canadian demand for bulk labour of the type still available among displaced persons. He also noted that the acceptance of displaced persons by other countries had eased the immediate crunch (and by the way, picked off the best of the lot remaining). Except where specific industry orders were registered for labourers, Keenleyside recommended closing the immigration office assigned to oversee these admissions. First-degree relatives would, of course, continue to be processed, but in the same way as other immigrants. Rather than normalize the status of displaced persons by granting them German citizenship, Keenleyside would prefer to normalize the process by which they were selected.

With his minister's approval Keenleyside recommended this course to the cabinet in September 1948. Canada, he noted in passing, had nothing of which to be ashamed. In spite of the important contribution of other countries, Canada had still "by far the best record of any overseas countries in its handling of the DP movement." Nor had Canada sacrificed quality in doing good. Keenleyside reassured cabinet members: "Canada has been able, on the whole, to obtain the best of the groups that have gone overseas." Displaced persons should still come to Canada. Indeed, he argued, their number should be increased. However, they should come through the routine and established procedures used by other immigrants.[19]

The cabinet agreed. The Canadian mission was closed. Refugees might come, but only through regular channels. At its meeting in late September 1948 the cabinet authorized the number of displaced persons slated for admission to Canada be increased from 30,000 to 40,000. The additional 10,000 could come from outside existing camps.[20] The immigration door was now wide open, but skewed in favor of recently arrived Baltic refugees outside existing camps. Dismantling the administrative apparatus to process displaced persons who were migrants generally made little difference to Jewish refugees. Emigration out of Europe to Canada was now something Canada encouraged — and the classes that now qualified grew by leaps and bounds. But Jews, for the first time in modern history, were no longer dependent on the good will or self-interest of receiving states like Canada for a place to go. All the while that Canada had held fast in its determination to restrict the entry of Jews, the Jews of Europe stood in abject need. When Canada finally opened its doors to Europe in late 1947, the "Jewish problem" was being resolved elsewhere.

In early 1947 the British government, exhausted and exasperated, dumped its Palestine problem onto the United Nations. For Canada the paramount consideration regarding the Palestine issue was its divisive impact on the North Atlantic alliance. With Britain and the United States at loggerheads over the Palestine question, Canada feared a rupture of Allied solidarity that would leave other pressing problems, including the menacing shadow of Soviet influence, to fester. The Palestine issue, Canada believed, had to be resolved once and for all even if British interests, in this instance, had to be sacrificed for the greater good. In November 1947 Canada broke with Britain at the United Nations and voted for partition of Palestine into two states, one Jewish, one Arab.[21]

It would be wrong to say that the government voted to partition Palestine in order to redirect Jewish displaced persons to their national homeland, easing the pressure on Canada to accept them—thereby making the opening of immigration to Canada more palatable to civil servants, the cabinet, Quebec, and the public in general. This was not the case. Nevertheless, it would also be incorrect to believe that the government was not aware of this potential benefit of their Palestine policy. In February 1947, just as the British were setting Palestine in the United Nations' lap, *Liberty* magazine reported that the Canadian government was still wrestling with the degree to which Canada would be open to displaced persons. Discussion of the issue in Ottawa, the magazine asserted, was "hush-hush" and for a good reason: "No spokesman will link Canada with Palestine but what everyone is going to know soon is that the displaced persons of Europe either come to Canada or go to Palestine. Politically it's a big question. Most politicians are fearful of Quebec, which wants no immigrants not of its faith." Whether this be speculation or not, the Canadian delegation at the United Nations went into the Palestine debate briefed from Ottawa on what a negative majority vote on partition would mean to future discussions of European displaced persons.[22] And Canada voted for partition.

The United Nations' affirmative vote on partition offered, for the first time in almost two thousand years, the all but tangible realization of a Jewish national homeland. To thousands of Jewish refugees this was a dream come true. As Canada selectively lifted the barriers to admission, Jews in large numbers lined up for admission elsewhere—much, one suspects, to Canada's relief.

On May 14, 1948, the state of Israel was proclaimed. That day 1,700 displaced persons entered their new homeland. Mass immigration to Israel, made up in large measure of European displaced persons, began—13,500 per month for the rest of 1948, 20,000 per month in 1949, and 14,000 per month in 1950. Also in the spring of 1948 both pressure on Canada to accept Jewish refugees and Canadian immigration barriers eased. If this was more than judicious planning on Canada's part, it was also less than coincidence. Thus, through the summer of 1948 Canada had approved or admitted more than 180,000 postwar immigrants, including 65,000 displaced persons. Included among the displaced persons were 8,000 Jews—orphans, first-degree relatives, members of the needle trades and fur workers scheme, and a smattering of others.[23] In the same year Canada created a new Immigration Act, under which immigration continued to grow apace. For the next few years the numbers of Jews admitted would be larger than at almost any other time in Canadian history. But total immigration was now so large that the Jewish component remained small, manageable, and, perhaps most importantly, inconspicuous by comparison. In any event, the crisis was over.

NOTES

1. See, for example, *Canada Year Book*, *1939*, 158.
2. PAC, IR, File 644452, Blair to Mrs. I. Grenovsky, December 5, 1938; PAC, MP, Blair to R.A. Bell, February 29, 1938.
3. *Canadian Annual Review, 1928–29*, 153–9.
4. LON, High Commissioner for Refugee Records, Box 5, McDonald to Bennett, March 25, 1934; JIAS (T), File 10A, B. Robinson to A. Brodey, June 11, 1934; ibid., A.J. Paul to Brodey, March 27, 1934.
5. High Commissioner for Refugee Records, Box 5, Bennett to McDonald, November 3, 1934.
6. See Gerald Dirks, *Canada's Refugee Policy: Indifference or Opportunism?* (Montreal, 1977), 44–97; Robert Domanski, "While Six Million Cried: Canada and the Refugee Question, 1938–41," Master's research essay, Institute of Canadian Studies, Carleton University, 1975, 14–16.
7. PAC, Civil Service Historical Personnel Records, File on F.C. Blair; Austin Cross in the *Family Herald and Weekly Star*, June 16, 1943.
8. Civil Service Historical Personnel Records, File on F.C. Blair; Interview with James Gibson.
9. IR, File 54782/5, Blair to Crerar, October 12, 1938; ibid., Blair to F.N. Sclanders, September 13, 1938; ibid., Blair to Crerar, March 28, 1938; IR, File 644452, Blair to H.R.L. Henry, January 30, 1939; IR, File 54782/5, Blair to W. Baird, May 4, 1938.
10. IR, File 209160, Blair to Morris Saxe, January 17, 1934.
11. IR, File 54782/5, Blair to F.N. Sclanders, September 13, 1938.
12. Malcolm J. Proudfoot, *European Refugees: 1939–1952* (Evanston, 1956), 341; Hugh L. Keenleyside, "Canada's Immigration Policy," paper delivered at Dalhousie University, Halifax, November 19, 1948; Herbert H. Lehman Papers, Senate Research Files, Displaced Persons: Australia and Canada.
13. Kurt R. Grossmann, *The Jewish D.P. Problem: Its Origin, Scope and Liquidation* (New York, 1951), 26–9.
14. Jewish Labour Committee Papers, Vol. 16, David Lewis to M. Lewis, July 8, 1948.

15. Keenleyside, "Canada's Immigration Policy."

16. PAC, EA, Box 2113, Robertson to Pearson, January 23, 1947; IR, File 673931, pt. 16.

17. IR, File 673931, pt. 16, Keenleyside to R.C. Riddell, January 13, 1948.

18. DCI, Vol. 121, File 6-1-257, Memorandum of Keenleyside for Minister re: immigration of displaced persons to Canada, August 14, 1948.

19. IR, Orders-in-Council, Memorandum of Keenleyside for Cabinet Committee on Immigration Policy re: immigration of displaced persons to Canada, September 3, 1948.

20. KPC, Cabinet Conclusions, September 28, 1948, vol. 420.

21. For a review of Canadian policy on the Palestine issue, see KPC, Louis St. Laurent to Cabinet, vol. 421.

22. Harold Dingman, "Liberty's Capital Report," *Liberty* (February 12, 1947); IR, File 541782, Pearson to Jolliffe, October 10, 1947; IR, File 673931, Pearson to Jolliffe, October 11, 1947; ibid., Jolliffe to Pearson, October 30, 1947.

23. Proudfoot, *European Refugees*, 357–9; ILGWU, Miscellaneous Correspondence, Toronto Joint Board Record, J.Z. Steinam to Joint Board, December 10, 1958.

JULIE HYLAND

THE GENEVA CONVENTION

FROM "BRITAIN CALLS FOR REVISION OF GENEVA CONVENTION ON ASYLUM"

WORLD SOCIALIST WEB SITE

The Geneva Convention was drawn up in the aftermath of the Second World War and the Nazi Holocaust, which had caused the displacement of more than 40 million people within Europe. The knowledge that the advanced capitalist countries had refused to open their borders to many fleeing fascist persecution led to a broadly held sentiment that never again should refugees be turned away.

These democratic aspirations were incorporated in the Convention, which set out that all asylum seekers—defined as those having a well-founded fear of persecution—were to be guaranteed certain inalienable rights, specifically that of refuge.

But those who framed the Convention were also mindful of broader political considerations. In upholding the right to political asylum, the West sought to strengthen its democratic credentials against the Soviet Union and Eastern bloc countries, and specifically to hold the door open for political dissidents from the Stalinist regimes. As the United Nations Commission for Human Rights (UNCHR) acknowledges, "From the late 1950s US law defined a refugee as a person fleeing communism or a Middle East country, and refugee policy was almost entirely dictated by foreign policy interests."

With the collapse of the Soviet Union and Eastern European states, the major powers felt themselves to have been "liberated" from the democratic restraints imposed in an earlier period. In the realm of foreign policy the US in particular sought to establish its control over strategic regions, resorting to military means, as in the Middle East and the Balkans.

Within the West, international recession, the development of global production and growing international competition saw a restructuring of labour markets through a combination of downsizing, de-skilling and unemployment. Wages fell and indigenous workers increasingly filled jobs previously considered the preserve of migrant labour, thus cutting off another avenue for legal migration.

The numbers of asylum-seekers soared—from under 70,000 in 1983 to over 200,000 in 1989 in Europe alone. The largest increases came from the former Eastern bloc, a process that began with thousands taking the opportunity to flee from the Stalinist regimes and which continued subsequently with tens of thousands more seeking refuge from the consequences of the severe social dislocation and civil and ethnic conflict associated with the restoration of capitalism.

By 1990, significant inroads into the right to asylum were being made. In that year the US adopted the policy of Temporary Protected Status, encroaching on the historic right for permanent residence and possible citizenship after a certain period. In 1996, further legislation established new legal criteria for determining whether those arriving at the US border had a "credible fear" of persecution. This meant that even before their acceptance into the asylum process, each refugee had to prove his or her case before asylum officers. If refused they would be deported.

Alongside this, the US revived its policy of detaining would-be asylum-seekers, which had fallen into disuse during the immediate post-war period. Those accepted into the asylum process were placed in detention. Today the Immigration and Naturalization Service holds an estimated 13,500 detainees, including an unknown number of asylum-seekers—many of whom are held in prisons and denied access to family or legal representation.

In 1993 the European Union (EU) countries signed up to the Maastricht Treaty. Economically this lifted restrictions on cross-border investment, trade and production, but in immigration policy it sought to create a "Fortress Europe." Just months before, the European powers had agreed on the so-called London Resolutions. With applications for asylum in Western Europe peaking at nearly 700,000 in 1992—primarily as a result of the civil war in Bosnia—the EC redefined the right to asylum. Several categories of asylum-seekers were introduced, including one for those that were deemed "manifestly unfounded" from the outset. A "third country rule" was introduced. This meant any refugee who had traveled via a "safe" third country could have his asylum application rejected and could be returned there. Most of these countries were located in Eastern Europe, which thus formed a type of immigrant "buffer" zone along the EU's eastern flank. Having for years decried the Eastern European states for restricting their citizens' rights to travel, the EU bolted the door on the peoples in these countries.

In 1993 Germany, then the recipient of more than 60 percent of all asylum applications in the EU, amended its constitution to remove the unqualified right to asylum. This became the basis for the EU's "Joint Position" declaration in 1996, which introduced a restrictive interpretation of the Geneva Convention, in which only those fleeing persecution by a state were considered admissible for asylum. Adopted by France, Germany, Italy, and Switzerland, it meant that applications from countries like Somalia and Algeria were automatically considered inadmissible.

The 1997 Treaty of Amsterdam committed the EU to developing a common immigration and asylum policy within five years. From this point on, immigration policy was approached as a coordinated pan-European policing campaign aimed at firmly sealing Europe's borders. All regular arrival routes were closed through imposing a series of visa requirements, and heavy fines introduced for any firm or individual found to be carrying so-called "illegals" in lorries, trains, ships, airplanes, and now even private cars.

According to Professor Guy Gordon-Gill, Oxford professor of international refugee law, only 0.3 percent of global refugees ever get anywhere near the EU. Most refugees in Africa, for example, are held in camps in neighbouring countries. With no legitimate means of entering the West, only those applicants able to raise enough money to pay smugglers or desperate enough to attempt other means of entry—such as clinging to the undercarriages of airplanes—stand a chance of making it in. Even then they face being held in reception camps or even prisons for unlimited periods of time, moved from place to place and forced to exist on the most minimal welfare provisions.

Today the concept of asylum is routinely bracketed with that of "illegal immigration," i.e., migration for economic reasons. In the first instance, the attempts of various governments to exclude those seeking relief from often terrible hardship is deeply reactionary. Secondly, the attempt to draw an absolute distinction between economic and political refugees is impossible, given the complex interaction between the two factors. The purpose of identifying asylum-seekers as "illegal immigrants" is to make asylum an issue of criminal policy, with the aim of intimidating and terrorizing would-be applicants.

WILLIAM PETERSON

Canada's Immigration: The Ideological Background

From Planned Migration

French Canada and Immigration Policy

... The most obvious division in the Canadian nation, as well as the one most clearly relevant to the issue of immigration policy, is the subnation of French Canada. The present French population of Canada is descended almost entirely from the approximately 65,000 persons settled there by 1763. The political separation from the homeland effected by the Treaty of Paris became a complete estrangement by the revolution of 1789, with which French Canada had little sympathy. Without immigration, the population increased from this slight base to more than 1,000,000 at the time of Confederation and to more than 4,300,000 today—apart from the French-Canadian emigrants to the United States. "If the population of France had multiplied in the same proportion," Sauvy has enviously noted, "it would today be much larger than that of the entire world."

In the view of Langlois, the author of the principal work on the French-Canadian population, its birth rate was a "demographic defiance of the [British] conqueror,... a declaration that conquest was not the beginning of either subjugation or annihilation." ... Langlois is one of those French Canadians who, as Corbett has remarked, tend "to view immigration cynically as an English-Canadian device for insuring that a majority will never be achieved, no matter how zealously the French Canadians pursue *la revanche des berceaux.*"

While a certain antagonism had existed between Quebec and English Canada ever since the establishment of British rule, French-Canadian nationalism in its present form dates from 1885, the year that Louis Riel was executed. And while in Quebec such a movement of course had a relation to the Catholic Church, it was never merely an extension of it — Riel, a heretic, would not have been the church hierarchy's choice of a national hero. In 1896, when Laurier and his Liberal party were denounced from every pulpit, Quebec gave 49 of its 65 seats to Laurier, the country's first French premier. This popularity was short-lived, however, because the government that Laurier headed instituted the most energetic immigration program Canada had ever had.

The man who spearheaded the French-Canadian attack on this immigration policy was Henri Bourassa, a nationalist member of Parliament. The charges that he and his associates made against the government were principally these:

1. The purpose of immigration was to swamp the French minority in a sea of "drunkards, paupers, loafers, and jailbirds" from England; eccentric Doukhobors; East European Jews; and similar types.
2. The many children of poor French peasants would have liked to emigrate but did not go to Canada because of the complete lack of organized propaganda in France.
3. The railways' policy of granting cheap fares to immigrants was part of a scheme to deny the French access to the West. "It was more expensive for an inhabitant of Rivière-du-Loup to go to Alberta than for a Jew from Galicia or a peasant from the Danube."
4. A fund at least equal to that encouraging immigration from Europe should have been set up to repatriate the French Canadians in New England, who had been attracted by the "vertiginous splendor of American prosperity" but could be recalled by suitable inducements.
5. The grossly inadequate medical examination of immigrants landing in Montreal was made by inexperienced doctors who had been appointed for political reasons. Thus, immigrants swung the population balance against the French in two ways, by their presence in the non-French bloc and by infecting the French with their diseases.

In 1911, when Laurier was defeated in his native province, it was "in large part" because of Quebec's opposition to his immigration policy. During the interwar period, French-Canadian opposition to immigration generally followed Bourassa's arguments. ... An abortive attempt was made to assimilate those Catholic immigrants who arrived into the French-Canadian community; several years before 1914, Abbé P.H.D. Casgrain of Quebec had founded a Catholic Immigration Society, which fell apart during the war. Later, there was apparently little effort to counteract the work of the Protestant proselytizers, who descended on communities of recent Catholic immigrants "like the locusts of Egypt." Emigration from Quebec was discouraged by subsidizing land settlement; between 1930 and 1940, the Quebec and Dominion governments spent more than $40,000,000, or about $1,000 a settler, for the construction of houses and barns and the purchase of livestock and equipment. Even so, almost half abandoned their farms, for they were unable to earn the very modest amount of cash, as little as $200 or $300 a year, that they needed to run them. "A completely satisfactory land settlement policy (for Quebec) has not been found as yet." French Canada is undergoing industrialization, but it would be rash to assume that this implies a rapid transformation of basic sentiments. As distinguished from the rustic areas in the southern Appalachians, for example, rural Quebec is not backward but archaic; that it, its way of life is different not merely because of a lack of opportunity, but principally because it is based on other values. If French Canada were blindly antagonistic to industry, it would be doomed; but in such economists as Esdras Minville and such publicists as Edmond Turcotte, it has articulate spokesmen who welcome the opportunity that industrialization gives it to maintain traditional institutions and attitudes, somewhat adapted to changed conditions but essentially strengthened. Since no more than one-tenth of Quebec's industry is owned and managed by French Canadians, its increased importance has meant that their ethnocentrism has been reinforced by the class antagonism of the mill workers.

Nevertheless, on a verbal level the relations between English and French in Quebec are generally quite good. Everett Hughes has suggested, however, that John Dollard's concept of displaced aggression is appropriate to explain the widespread anti-Semitism. "When French Canadians attack the English, they pull their punches .... Against the Jew, however, attack may proceed without fear either of retaliation or of a bad conscience." If this hypothesis has any validity, it would seem to apply not only to Jews but to any non-English immigrant group. Thus, although the nationalism of French Canadians is in part an expression of a Catholic minority in a predominantly Protestant country, they are notoriously unable to get along well with other Catholics, particularly the sizable Irish group. "Bitter quarrels far exceeding in gravity the point at issue," in Siegfried's opinion, divide the Catholic Church. Attempts have been made to mitigate these differences by appointing French bishops with Irish names, or bishops with French names who speak no French. Appeals to Rome do not generally elicit satisfactory replies; for while French Canada's piety is appreciated, it is associated with a narrowness that hampers the hierarchy's broader ambitions for North America. "The Church refuses to identify itself completely with the small minority who speak the French tongue" — only three per cent of the joint population of Canada and the United States.

During the interwar years, the ultranationalist went beyond Bourassa, to the point almost of demanding separation from the Dominion. Abbé Lionel Groulx, leader of Action Nationale, was one important publicist who has verged on this opinion. "It is clear that at heart he believes in 'Laurentia,' a separate French and Catholic state, rather than in Canada; and ... in 1937, he came so close to advocating it on the radio that he was cut off the air. in Corbett's opinion, there has been an increase in French Canada's nationalism since the war, and thus also in its opposition to immigration. The order-in-council giving natives of France first preference, like those of Commonwealth countries and the United States, was an attempt to allay this opposition, but it was an almost empty gesture — by and large, the French do not emigrate. And "even the admission of Frenchmen has from time to time been viewed sceptically by French-Canadian newspapers, on the ground that European Frenchmen, within a generation or two, tend to identify themselves with the English-Canadian community and seldom or never join the ranks of the *habitants*."

If the French-Canadian opposition to immigration cannot be reduced by admitting a larger proportion of Catholics, or even of Frenchmen, there is also no other way of compromising with it. On the contrary, like extremist views generally, the opposition is likely to grow stronger with each partial success, for this sets a new precedent. This point can be illustrated by a recent article by Dumareau. He divided the eighty years since Confederation into three periods, as follows:

> *1871–1931: Very large immigration and a sizable emigration! of French Canadians. Steady decline in the French-Canadian proportion of the population, from 31.07 to 28.22 per cent.*
>
> *1931–1946: Very light immigration and emigration. Increase in the French proportion from 28.22 to 31.2 per cent, which "would have continued*

*to grow to 32.2 per cent in 1952 except for the sharp change of policy in
1946."*

*1946–1951: Heavy immigration. Decline in French proportion to
approximately 31 per cent.*

That is, since 1871 the proportion of French Canadians in the total
population has remained fairly constant, at 30 per cent plus or minus about
2 per cent; and in the postwar period it has changed only from 31.2 to
"approximately 31" per cent. But for the author, these small differences, the
consequence principally of a larger or smaller number of immigrants, are
of decisive importance, because he compares not the present percentages
but rather their extrapolations: "During the past five years, the effect of
the immigration policy, as well as of the general postwar rise in fertility,
has been to reduce the proportion of the French population in 1951 from
32.2 to 31.0 percent." With the present natural increase and emigration,
moreover, if immigration at the rate of 150,000 annually is continued for
the next ten years, the French sector will be reduced to 30.3 per cent of
the total population without Newfoundland, or 29.6 per cent including
Newfoundland. That is to say, a relatively stable division of the population
among minority groups does not prevent the rise of a competitive spirit; for
nationalists, by arguing in terms of what might have been and what may
be, can interpret a change of 0.2 per cent over five years as disastrous.

Other representatives of French Canada have of course expressed
more moderate views concerning immigration than those cited here,
which are typical of the dominant tendency. French Canada's opposition,
though presently submerged, is a permanent element of the Dominion's
immigration policy.

ENGLISH CANADA AND IMMIGRATION POLICY

The distinction between French-Canada, opposed to immigration, and
English Canada, in favor of it, is often made; but in both elements such
a contrast lacks perspective. Laurier and St. Laurent, supported as
Frenchmen by Quebec nationalists, were also premiers of the Canadian
governments that have initiated two of the most vigorous immigration
programs in modern times. Even French-Canadian nationalists, moreover,
are not necessarily opposed to immigration per se; they would support an
indefinitely large immigration of French peasants who had maintained
more or less intact the values of the *ancien régime*. Similarly, the Empire-

minded English Canadian is really enthusiastic only about the immigration of another disappearing type, English agriculturists. The less virulent prejudices of English Canada are related to the group's more secure status in national life; and they can find expression in a restrictive policy, rather than in opposition to any and all immigration. The difference, thus, in part is one of degree, in part lies in the fact that there are still British emigrants who with sufficient trouble and "expense can be disguised as agriculturists. Originally, when British emigration was directed from Britain, it had two main purposes—to rid the home country of some of its paupers and criminals and to build up the Empire by establishing white settlements in the colonies. Later, when Canadians began to promote immigration from Britain, their purposes were to maintain the high percentage of the supposedly superior British stock and, secondly, to build up a strong Canada within the Empire or, later, Commonwealth. The less than perfect accord between the eugenic, economic, and political aims was hidden, probably often from the participants themselves, by an elaboration of patriotic flourishes; but this was an important reason why so much noble effort came to so little. From the days of Horton and Wakefield, the theories of Empire settlement had little influence on the actual movement of people, which tended to set its own pace and cut its own channels.

In the opinion of J. Bruce Walker, the Canadian immigration official in London before 1914, the persons sent to Canada by the various private or state charitable organizations in England were "for the most part not desirable citizens." Only the unemployed were helped to emigrate, and most of these were from the cities. During the single year 1907, more than 12,000 paupers were sent out by the charitable organizations of London alone. "In my humble judgement," Walker concluded, "the time has now come when the department should devise rigorous and effective measures first to discourage and, secondly, to supervise such charitably aided emigration." Since Canada's principal need before 1914 was for agriculturists, the city-bred Britons required a special effort to adapt to their new lives in rural Canada. There were 180 canvassers in the field to seek out jobs for immigrants. By 1912, the Dominion government had twelve experimental farms and several agricultural colleges where unskilled immigrants could be trained.

There were also various private efforts to establish British settlers on the land in this period. The best known of these was that by two Canadian clergymen, the Reverend I. M. Barr and Archdeacon (later Bishop) G. Exton Lloyd. In 1903, they supervised the settlement of some 2,000 persons from the United Kingdom, most of whom were of urban background and in good circumstances. In spite of the fact that "the Canadian Government spared no pains nor expenses in its efforts to promote the success of the colony," two years later only a quarter of the settlers were still on the land at "Lloydminster," and "deserters," of whom Barr had been one of the first, were still leaving. Another important effort to promote British immigration was that by Montague Leyland Hornby, an officer in the Canadian army. The so-called Hornby Plan, essentially an adaptation of Wakefield's scheme, never got under way: the 1930s were not a propitious time to raise the £60,000,000 needed to finance it. A similar policy was espoused by Professor Stephen Leacock, who believed that Canada could support a population of 250,000,000, provided they were mostly of the "superior" British stock.

These various private schemes, though significant as indices of a trend, were dwarfed by a similar official effort. In 1922, after several years' preparation—involving the work of a special committee of the Colonial Office, several preparatory laws, a meeting of dominion representatives, and a conference of prime ministers—Britain passed the Empire Settlement Act. It authorized the British government to pay up to one-half of the costs of settling "suitable" persons (who were defined by Canada as agriculturists or domestic servants) in the overseas dominions, in accordance with arrangements to be made with either dominion governments or other interested organizations. Either loans or grants could be made to assist with passage costs, initial maintenance, training, or other expenses. Britain was prepared to spend up to £1,500,000 the first year and £3,000,000 in each subsequent year, but during the fifteen years the law was in effect the maximum was never spent. Up to 1931, fewer than 130,000 persons came to Canada under the scheme, or about 40 per cent of the number of unassisted British immigrants during this period. As Carrothers put it, "to speak of this as a redistribution of the white population of the Empire is somewhat flattering." The purpose of the Empire Settlement Act, moreover, had been such a redistribution in a special sense, in line with the concept that Britain was its industrial center and the dominions the agricultural colonies. The failure of the plan was related to the shortage of capital, as various official observers noted at the time, but more fundamentally to the fact that the dominions were themselves becoming industrial nations.

How many Britons placed on the land stayed there? Only estimates can be given, and perhaps the best is that by Reynolds: "While over 146,000 Britishers gave the agricultural West as their intended destination during the decade 1919–29, the actual British-born population of the Prairie provinces increased in the same period by only 3,000." This ratio—3,000 in 146,000, or about two per cent—measures the success of the Empire Settlement Act so far as Canada was concerned, for its purpose was not merely to foster migration but to settle migrants on the land as agriculturists ....

If the preference always given to British immigrants can be justified in terms of Canada's national interest—as distinguished both from the interests of the Empire-Commonwealth as a whole and from mere prejudice—that justification must be their assumed easier acculturation into Canadian society. In most discussions of the matter this is taken for granted, while in others the situation is so defined that the behavior of the British immigrant is the norm of successful assimilation. If the survey that Lloyd Reynolds made among the British-born residents of Montreal can be taken as representative, however, British immigrants to Canada have disadvantages as well as advantages from the point of view of assimilating into Canadian society. The rate of acculturation depends principally on two factors—the degree of difference between the two cultures and the immigrant's attitude concerning his place in the new country. While there are obviously many points of marked similarity between British and Canadian cultures, a Britisher's attitude often makes complete assimilation virtually impossible, for "Canada is but a place of residence; Britain is always 'home.'" Some four-fifths of the subjects of Reynolds' study were successful both by their estimates and that of their neighbors, but a disproportionately large number of the British immigrants, particularly the laborers, were unable to hold their jobs and became dependent on public support. This one study does not invalidate the notion that Britons are more assimilable, but it does emphasize that this assumption, an important basis of dominion policy, has no empirical evidence to support it.

JOHN PORTER

ETHNICITY AND SOCIAL CLASS

FROM THE VERTICAL MOSAIC: AN ANALYSIS OF SOCIAL CLASS AND POWER IN CANADA

FRENCH CANADA AND IMMIGRATION POLICY

[...] Those of European descent are always praised for their contribution to Canada's life. Until 1962 there were still preferred and non-preferred sources of immigrants built into Canadian immigration policy, and although the later attitudes about the relative merits of different cultural groups as immigrants seemed to arise from notions of assimilability rather than supposed racial qualities, there were still groundless assertions, such as the importance of climate (does anyone not feel cold in a Canadian winter?), in official and unofficial pronouncements.[1]

We are here concerned with the formation of social class and the influence that ethnic origin and immigration have on that process. Where such attitudes as the ones reviewed above were expressed in the receiving society, whether they were based on racial theories or on more respectable theories about the ease of assimilation (a not too well-defined concept), it followed that the less preferred immigrants were given "entrance status." They came in on sufferance and were funneled into lower status jobs, and often, if they were agricultural workers or intended to be farmers, they were settled on what was considered to be less desirable land. This method of allocation would seem to have affected the eastern European immigrant who followed those from eastern Canada to settle in the west.[2] Accounts of Ukrainian settlement tell of incredible hardships in the districts that had been passed over by other groups. "Those who did not settle on the land," says Paul Yuzyk in his history of the Ukrainian peasant in Manitoba, took whatever work was available until something better could be secured. Some went to work in mines and factories, and large numbers were hired by construction companies in the towns and cities .... Perhaps the largest proportion went to work on the construction and maintenance of railroads in western Canada."[3] Peter Bryce also pointed out that rough and heavy work was inevitably the main source of money for the poor immigrants from eastern and central Europe, "... just as building the canals of the St. Lawrence and the Grand Trunk Railway supplied work for the thousands of famine-striken Irishmen in the 40s and 50s of the last century in Upper Canada."[4]

The various periods of Canadian economic growth have seen large-scale construction projects as well as the exploitation of natural, particularly mineral, resources. Immigration has been an essential component in the growth of the labour force to undertake these developments, and what seems to have emerged in the process is a kind of scale by which certain European groups are rated more highly than others. As one writer, looking in the 1950s at the various social and cultural factors which appear important in the ranking process, has said of the English, German, and Dutch, "members of these three language groups ... are physically interchangeable .... They have the same standards of personal and household cleanliness. At the higher social levels they dress in identical ways and appreciate the same leisure time pursuits. They profess Christian forms of religion and greatly value military prowess. Understandably such ethnic groups are welcomed in Canada, and they prosper soon after settlement here."[5] There were, however, always the low status jobs, and they were in the main available to European groups ranking low in the preference scale. Canada has never seriously looked beyond Europe. Those from the Orient, having completed the work for which they had been imported, have been excluded since the turn of the century. Without Chinese labour the construction and completion of the C.P.R. would have been indefinitely postponed.[6] Not until 1962 were coloured people from Commonwealth countries looked upon as possible immigrants, except for a small number who were allowed in — without families, or in the appropriate sex ratio to form families — to work as domestic servants, an entrance status previously held by lower class British and eastern European females. Many of these non-British immigrants went into low status occupations because there was a fairly high rate of illiteracy among them, and few of them spoke the charter group languages of English or French. Thus cultural barriers at the time of entry harden into a set of historical relations tending to perpetuate entrance status.

That some ethnic groups have felt, even after their two and sometimes three generation stay in Canada, that they still do not share a status of equality with the charter groups is indicated by some of the briefs submitted to the Senate Committee on Immigration and Labour in 1946.[7] Ukrainian, Polish, Finnish, and Czechoslovak organizations in Canada went to great lengths to indicate both the progress their groups had made since they first arrived and their great contribution to Canadian society. In these briefs are enumerated the number of prosperous farms developed from inhospitable land, the number of enlistments in the armed forces, the number of prizes won for wheat, the number of second generation professionals, and endless quotations from writers praising their contribution to the "Canadian mosaic."[8] One such quotation, from a speech by Professor Watson Thomson, ranks for eloquence with that of Stephen Leacock, except that it expresses the opposite point of view, based on the same kind of stereotype. "British political wisdom, Jewish cosmopolitan, and realism, French lucidity of mind and expression, German emotional depth and capacity for work, Slavonic spontaneity and verve—all these are there in the riches of our Canadian life and each set of qualities can be learned and assimilated by all."[9] Whether any Canadians fit this model of perfection it is difficult to say, but it does represent the often expressed value of the Canadian mosaic.

Speculatively, it might be said that the idea of an ethnic mosaic, as opposed to the idea of the melting pot, impedes the processes of social mobility. This difference in ideas is one of the principal distinguishing features of United States and Canadian society at the level of social psychology as well as that of social structure. The theme in American life of what Geoffrey Gorer has called "Europe and the rejected father"[10] has had no counterpart in Canada although the word "Canadianization" (whatever that might have meant) was used in the earlier immigration periods. In Canada, ethnic segregation and intense ethnic loyalties had their origins in French, Scottish, and Irish separateness from the English. In time they became the pattern for all cultural groups.

S.D. Clark has suggested that the strong attachments to Great Britain on the part of those of British origin, and to their former national cultures on the part of those of European origin, were essential if Canada was to remain separate from the United States.[11] The melting pot with its radical breakdown of national ties and old forms of stratification would have endangered the conservative tradition in Canadian life, a tradition which gives ideological support to the continued high status of the British charter group and continued entrance status of the later arrivals.

An interesting example of the high value placed on ethnic separateness in Canada is the following exchange in the hearings of the 1946 senate committee:

> MR. VICTOR PODOSKI (who had formerly served as Polish Minister in Canada): The Canadian Poles have two loyalties, which I think can be easily reconciled. Canadian Poles have a natural affection for the country of their origin or of the origin of the forefathers; they also have full loyalty and affection for the country of their adoption .... I think the Canadian Poles have a dual loyalty – their loyalty to Poland and their loyalty to Canada, and the two can be merged in a happy combination.
>
> HON. MR. ROEBUCK: If I may interrupt Mr. Podoski? I do not suppose the Polish people in that regard are any different from British immigrants.
>
> HON. MR. CRERAR: And the Scotch.
>
> HON. MR. ROEBUCK: We have the same loyalty to Canada, but we have not forgotten the culture and history of our own particular Motherland, Great Britain. In that respect the Poles are not different from ourselves.[12]

Not until Mr. Diefenbaker's administration was the first Treaty Indian appointed to the Senate, the first of Ukrainian origin to the cabinet, and the first of Italian origin as a parliamentary secretary, each appointment being the occasion for newspaper stories about the absence of such appointments in the past. Segregation in social structure, to which the concept of the mosaic or multiculturalism must ultimately lead, can become an important aspect of social control by the charter group.

In the United States in recent discussions on minority groups there has been a tendency to reject the melting pot theory as both inaccurate and undesirable. Retention of ethnic identity and continued participation in ethnic communities is seen as an important form of adaptation in or adjustment to the mass society of the "lonely crowd." Also, it would seem, that second and third generation members of the non-Anglo-Saxon groups in the United States, after experiencing difficulty in becoming accepted as "true Americans," have returned to their ethnic heritages rather than accept the principle of "anglo-conformity" which is a pre-condition of status equality with the white Anglo-Saxon protestant majority. Within both dominant and minority groups, attitudes and values are often contradictory, with the result that there are conflicting predispositions to both melting pot and pluralistic ideals. Minority groups themselves are not homogeneous, but are differentiated by religion, recent and earlier arrivals, and by class.[13]

A distinction has been made between "behavioral assimilation" and "structural assimilation." The first means the extent to which the minority group has absorbed the cultural patterns of the "host" society and even perhaps had an effect on it. Structural assimilation means the process by which ethnic groups have become distributed in the institutional structure of the receiving society, and in particular have assumed roles in general civic life. As a group of Canadian writers has pointed out, structural assimilation exists when ethnic origin is not a relevant attribute in the allocation of people to positions in the social system or in the distribution of rights.[14] The establishment of fair employment and fair accommodation practices legislation in some Canadian industries and in some provinces is an effort to achieve some degree of structural assimilation.

Structural assimilation, no doubt, leads in time to behavioral assimilation. At least differences in patterns of living between various ethnic groups will be reduced. There are some groups for the view, although writers on the subject are confused on the point, that structural assimilation is incompatible with continued ethnic pluralism, desirable as that may be for its function of adaptation to the mass society, but it is indisputable that some form of group affiliation lying between the extremes of the mass and the individual is a prerequisite for mental health. However, there is no intrinsic reason that these groupings should be on ethnic lines. Where there is strong association between ethnic affiliation and social class, as there almost always has been, a democratic society may require a breaking down of the ethnic impediment to equality, particularly the equality of opportunity.

It is surprising that so little is known about these processes in Canadian society. The relations between the French and the British have no doubt been the most important reason for the ideology of ethnic pluralism. Such an ideology has been congenial to most Canadian minority groups, but as suggested earlier it has also been an important factor in social control. Ethnic groups with their internal hierarchies are themselves stratified. Professor Vallee and others have pointed out the similarity between ethnic associations and professional associations both of which have the task of promoting the interests of their groups. "Both are concerned with establishing the legitimacy of the group; with enhancing and protecting its status and autonomy; with gaining to some extent control over the selection and socialization of its members."[15] The control potential exists in religious segregation. In Canada and the United States ethnicity and religion have reinforced each other in the creation of cultural enclaves. It is clear in the analysis of ethnic affiliation and occupation which follows that we are concerned with structural rather than behavioral assimilation.

ETHNIC AFFILIATION AND OCCUPATIONAL CLASS

Immigration and ethnic affiliation (or membership in a cultural group) have been important factors in the formation of social classes in Canada. In particular, ethnic differences have been important in building up the bottom layer of the stratification system in both agricultural and industrial settings. If non-agricultural occupations are considered alone, there are ethnic differences in the primary and secondary levels of manufacturing and in service occupations. Depending on the immigration period, some groups have assumed a definite entrance status. It is interesting to discover what happened to these various groups over time: whether they move out of their entrance status and show by their subsequent occupational distribution that ethnic origin was not a factor impeding their social mobility. If it was not, they will have achieved an equality of status with the charter group. On the other hand, where cultural groups tend to be occupationally specific, with successive generations taking on the same occupations as earlier generations, we can say that ethnic affiliation is at least a correlative factor in the assignment of occupational roles and thus in social class.

In his extensive study of "racial" origins based on the 1931 census, Professor Hurd referred to "racial aptitudes" or "occupational preferences" of the various ethnic groups: "in the case of the Hebrew preference for commerce, the Japanese for fishing, the Indian for trapping and that of Scandinavian females for household service."[16] But to speak thus is wrong because there is no evidence that genetic factors of "race" are important in occupational aptitude, although perhaps Hurd did not mean to suggest that they were. Moreover, unless choices are open it is wrong to speak of occupational preferences. It is undoubtedly true that when ethnic groups are closely knit their cultural milieu will encourage certain kinds of occupational choice and discourage others. In this way ethnic segregation becomes an important factor in the link between ethnicity and occupation such as for example with the Chinese restaurateur and laundryman, and the Italian plasterer.

It is necessary to remember the changing importance of agriculture in the economy. Some groups have become relatively more urban over time, and others have been predominantly urban from their period of first immigration. In the latter category are the Jews, who were 99 per cent urban in 1951 and 1961, and the Italians, who were 88 per cent urban in 1951 and 96 per cent in 1961. In degree of urbanization in 1951 and 1961 they were followed by the British (66 and 71 per cent) and the Polish (63 and 75 per cent). These four groups were the only ones that were more urban than the total population in both 1951 and 1961. Other groups in descending order of urbanization in 1951 were: French (60 per cent), Russian (52), Ukrainian (50), Scandinavian (47), German (44), and Dutch (41). In the off-farm migration of the 1950's all these groups became increasingly urbanized although they all remained less urban than the general population which was 70 per cent urban in 1961. By the 1961 census the order of urbanization changed slightly to become: French (68 per cent), Ukrainian (65), Russian (65), German (62), Scandinavian (60), and Dutch (53). Thus by 1961 all ethnic groups except indigenous Indians or Eskimos were more than half urban. Between 1941 and 1961 the urbanization of the Ukrainian and Russian groups was particularly striking.[17] Whether or not all groups fare equally in this cityward migration it would be difficult to say. If the movement from farms to cities can be viewed as a process of downward social mobility, or at least a movement of unskilled labour, then groups which were predominantly in agriculture before the cityward movement began will be at a disadvantage compared to those groups predominantly urban throughout.

In the professional and financial occupations (4.8 per cent of the labour force) Jewish, Scottish, English, and Irish were all over-represented. Jewish and Scottish were tied (7 per cent each), followed by the English (6.4 per cent) and the Irish (5.8 per cent). All other origins were under-represented in the following order of decreasing proportions: French (4.0), Dutch (3.7),

German (2.6), Scandinavian (1.9), Italian (1.5), Eastern European (0.9), Asian (0.5), "Other Central European" (0.5), native Indian (0.3).

For the low level, primary and unskilled occupations (17.7 per cent of the labour force) the proportions were reversed. Jews were the most under-represented group (3.2 per cent), followed by German (12.4), Dutch (12.5), Irish (12.8), Scottish (12.9), and English (13.3). All other groups were over-represented: Scandinavian (19.1), French (21.0), Asian (27.9), Eastern European (30.1), Italian (43.8), "Other Central European" (53.5), and native Indian (63.0). In the clerical occupations (3.8 per cent of the male labour force in 1931) which can be taken as intermediate between the high and low levels being considered, the three British origins and Jews were over-represented and all the other origins were under-represented. Unfortunately most of the other census occupational classifications such as "manufacturing" and "commercial" are too broad to be taken as occupational class levels.

There are three female occupations worth noting because they tend to reinforce the occupational class differences for males of the various origins. For females, the professional (17.7 per cent of the female labour force), clerical (17.6 per cent), and personal service occupations (33 per cent) together made up 68 per cent of the female labour force. With the exception of Jews all ethnic groups had more females in personal service than in clerical or professional occupations. The three British origins were under-represented in personal service occupations: English 29.2 per cent, Scottish 29.3 per cent, and Irish 27.1 per cent, compared to 33 per cent for the entire labour force. Also under-represented were Jews (7.4 per cent) and Italians (24.4 per cent). (Italian females were more in manufacturing occupations, particularly textiles.) French (34.5 per cent), native Indian (36.4), Dutch (39.3), German (46.6), Chinese (49.8), Scandinavian (51.4), Japanese (59.7), Eastern European (65.9), and "Other Central European" (73.4) were all over-represented in these personal service occupations. In the clerical occupations Jewish (31 per cent), Irish (23.8), English (23.5), and Scottish (23) were over-represented compared to 17.6 per cent of the total female labour force; and Dutch (14.4), German (12.1), Scandinavian (10.8), Italian (10.4), French (8.6), Chinese (7.5), Eastern European (3.4), "Other Central European" (2.8), Japanese (2.1), and native Indian (0.9) were all under-represented. In the female professional occupations the Scottish, Irish, and French were over-represented. This is the only high occupational category for males or females in which the French were over-represented, no doubt because of the teaching and nursing positions held by nuns. In this category of female professionals, the English and Dutch ranked close together. Both were slightly under-represented.

There are some aspects of this vertical mosaic which are important. One is that, except for the French, the rough rank order has persisted over time. Germans, Scandinavians, and Dutch are the nearest to the British in their occupational levels, in part because more of them than of other European groups have remained in agriculture, and agricultural occupations have been omitted from the preceding analysis. Italians, Polish, Ukrainians, and groups from southeast Europe are still at the lower end of the occupational spectrum. The French could be placed somewhere between these last and the groups from northern Europe. The fact that all ethnic groups have some representation at the higher professional level [...] is some evidence of improvement. It should be remembered, however, that professionals, such as doctors and lawyers, from a particular ethnic group often provide services mainly within their own group. Or to reverse the process, we can say that those of a particular ethnic group as clients seek out one of their own group members. Thus some of the structural assimilation apparent from the 1951 distribution of minority groups in the professional class may have taken place within ethnic enclaves. There would of course be a difference between those professionals with clients, and those who worked for large organizations. Within the total occupational system the vertical mosaic can be summed up as follows: "... the proportion of British in each class generally increases from the lowest to the highest class whereas the reverse is true for the French. The Jewish group follows a pattern similar to that of the British whereas all other origins follow the French pattern."[18]

This relationship between ethnic affiliation and social class varies with the distribution of the various groups across the country. In 1951, about four-tenths of all those of European origin lived in the prairie provinces and one-third in Ontario, but only one-tenth lived in Quebec and the Atlantic provinces combined. Two-thirds of the Ukrainians and six-tenths of the Scandinavians lived on the prairies. Manitoba, Saskatchewan, and Alberta, with about one-fifth of the Canadian population, had more than two-fifths of those of European origin in Canada. Alberta and British Columbia, with about one-seventh of the population, had almost half of those of Asian origin.[19]

Because of this uneven distribution through the society, the perceived class differences will vary, particularly in the large cities. More than one-half of the Italians who lived in Canada in 1951 lived in Ontario urban areas.[20] Their relative status would be perceived differently in Toronto, say, than in some other city where their numbers were proportionately fewer. Also, the low occupational level of the French in the Ottawa-Hull metropolitan area is not a part of the class system experienced by people in British Columbia.

Current immigration tends to fit the existing stratification system. During 1959 and 1960 the largest single group of immigrants were Italians who exceeded British immigrants by about 8,000 over the two-year period.[21] Between 1953 and 1960 British immigration made up 50 per cent of all professional immigration while the Italian contribution to this class was 1.2 per cent.[22]

NOTES

1. See the discussion in David C. Corbett, *Canada's Immigration Policy* (Toronto, 1957). In 1962 Canadian immigration policy was changed to permit immigration from anywhere provided the immigrants had skills that Canada needed. After the 1961 census the *Ottawa Journal* was led to observe in its editorial of August 18, 1962, that the old stock was still strong.

2. "In the case of the Ukrainians the tendency toward segregation was facilitated by Canadian government officials who steered them gently out along the northern fringe of settlement in the Prairie Provinces. Here were some of the least attractive and also the most available settlement areas at the time their mass migration took place." C.A. Dawson and Eva R. Younge, *Pioneering in the Prairie Provinces* (Toronto, 1940), 36.

3. Paul Yuzyk, *The Ukrainian Peasant in Manitoba* (Toronto, 1953), 53.

4. Bryce, *The Value of the Continental Immigrant*.

5. Harold Potter, "The Ethnic Structure of the Canadian Community," Information and Comment (Canadian Jewish Congress), June 1956, 9.

6. This was the opinion of the 1885 Royal Commission on Chinese Immigration. For an important discussion of oriental exclusion see M. Timlin, "Canada's Immigration Policy, 1896–1910," *C.J.E.P.S.*, XXVI, no. 4 (November 1960).

7. "We see before our eyes the picture of the original immigrants, poor and illiterate, but hardy and determined, trekking his [*sic*] way to the homestead

many miles away from the nearest homestead, fencing, plowing, brushing, seeding, reaping, meanwhile building a hut to live in, marrying, raising and educating a family, participating in the social, cultural and political life of the community, his children winning scholastic and civic honors, rising from poverty to comfort, saving his earnings, acquiring new holdings, and finally ending a long and useful life by succumbing only to the grim reaper who takes us all in his stride.

"And these are the immigrants that our Regulations classify as 'NON-PREFERRED.' They are the people who mix freely with our own native-born but are categorized as something inferior. Inferior in what? In fighting qualities, in capacity to learn, in adaptability, in thrift, in perseverance [sic], in honesty, in initiative, in assimilability, in intelligence or in loyalty?" (Brief of Ukrainian Canadian Committee to Canada, Senate Committee on Immigration and Labour, *Proceedings*, May 29, 1946 (Ottawa, 1946), Appendix.)

For a picture of Hungarian immigration to Canada and the success that some have had in moving out of entrance status see John Kosa, *Land of Choice: The Hungarians in Canada* (Toronto, 1957). Kosa also gives a good account of how an extended kinship system in the European group makes for ethnic segregation.

8. The term apparently was first used by Victoria Hayward, an American writer, when she viewed the variety of church architecture in the communities of the Canadian west. See John Murray Gibbon, *Canadian Mosaic* (Toronto, 1938), ix.

9. Committee on Immigration and Labour, *Proceedings*.

10. Geoffrey Gorer, *The Americans* (London, 1948). Gorer likens to patricide the rejection of their former homelands by immigrant groups from Europe.

11. S.D. Clark, "The Canadian Community," in G.W. Brown, ed., *Canada* (Berkeley, 1950), 307.

12. Committee of Immigration and Labour, *Proceedings*, June 25, 1946, 106.

13. See, for example, Milton M. Gordon, "Social Structure and Goals in Group Relations," in M. Berger et al., eds., *Freedom and Control in Modern Society* (New York, 1954); also by the same author, "Assimilation in America: Theory and Reality," in *Daedalus* (Spring 1961). This issue of *Daedalus* is a special one devoted to ethnic groups in American Life.

14. Frank G. Vallee, Mildred Schwartz and Frank Darknell, "Ethnic Assimilation and Differentiation in Canada," *C.J.E.P.S.*, XXIII, no. 4 (November 1957).

15. *Ibid.*, 542.

16. W. Burton Hurd, *Racial Origins and Nativity of the Canadian People*, census monograph no. 4 (Ottawa, 1937).

17. *Census of Canada, 1951*, vol. X, 145-46, and *Census of Canada, 1961*, vol. 1.2–5, Table 36.

18. *Ibid,* 524.

19. *Census of Canada, 1951,* vol. X, chap. XIII.

20. *Ibid.,*vol. II, Table 30.

21. Canada, Dept. of Citizenship and Immigration, *Quarterly Immigration Bulletin* (December 1960).

22. Canada, Dept. of Labour, *The Migration of Professional Workers* (Ottawa, 1962).

FREDA HAWKINS

IMMIGRATION POLICY IN THE LATE 1960s

FROM VENTURE
"THE CANADIAN EXPERIENCE"

Well over three million immigrants have come to Canada since 1945. Roughly a million have moved on to the United States or returned whence they came. They settle in the prosperous provinces and major industrial centres of Canada, which is also where their relatives are.

The pull of the province of Ontario is stronger than any other. In 1969, Ontario attracted 53.6 per cent of the total movement, Quebec 17.5 per cent, British Columbia 13.5 per cent, and Alberta 6.9 per cent. The prairie provinces as a whole received 12.4 per cent of the 1969 movement and the Atlantic provinces 2.3 per cent. Toronto is Canada's major immigration centre, receiving an annual inflow in recent years of at least 40,000 immigrants, more now than any other city in North America.

Since 1945, 28 per cent of all Canada's immigrants have come from Great Britain, 14 per cent from Italy, 12 per cent from Germany and Austria, 9 per cent from the United States, and 5 per cent from the Netherlands. Countries which have contributed a significant, but much smaller number of immigrants include Poland, France, Greece, Portugal, Hungary, China, and the West Indies. But this traditional pattern is changing. Immigration from Europe has been declining. Immigration from the United States and from Asia and the Caribbean is increasing steadily. The percentage of European immigrants, including the British, has fallen from 87 per cent in 1966 to 54 per cent in 1969. The ten major source countries in 1969 were Great Britain (31,977), the United States (22,785), West Indies/Antilles (13,093), Italy (10,383), China, including mainland China, Hong Kong, and

Taiwan (8,272), Portugal (7,182), Greece (6,937), Germany (5,880), France (5,549), and India (5,395). Out of a total movement to Canada of 161,531 immigrants in 1969, 23 per cent came from Asia and the Caribbean.

Immigration has made a less striking contribution to population growth in Canada than it has in Australia, for example, but a very substantial contribution to the size and quality of the labour force and to the stock of highly trained manpower. It has represented an immense saving thus far in national outlay in education and professional and vocation training and can be seen today as a very dynamic element in Canadian postwar development. Immigrants have made a remarkable contribution to the vitality and variety of economic, cultural, and social life in Canada, particularly in the cities, where most have settled. The basic statute in Canadian immigration is the 1952 Immigration Act, an illiberal piece of legislation now greatly modified by subsequent regulations and minor amendments. The first phase in Canada's postwar immigration policy was in fact laid down in a statement by Prime Minister Mackenzie King in 1947. Essentially, only immigrants from Europe and the United States and their relatives were to be admitted. In the early fifties, small quotas were added from India, Pakistan, and Ceylon and a small number of domestic workers were admitted annually from the West Indies. But this approach came under increasing criticism in Canada among those concerned with immigration. By the mid-fifties, immigrants were being actively recruited in the Middle East and in new immigration regulations introduced in 1962, racial discrimination was removed altogether, except in the matter of sponsoring relatives. Fearing a mass movement of relatives from Asia, similar to the one experienced from southern Europe in the fifties, the Department of Citizenship and Immigration inserted a special clause in the 1962 immigration regulations, restricting the range of relatives which could be sponsored by Asian immigrants. This did not apply to the West Indies or to the Middle East and was removed in 1967.

The 1967 immigration regulations were a breakthrough in Canadian immigration policy and management. They established without reservations a policy which is universal, non-discriminatory, selective, and particularly directed to meeting Canada's manpower needs. For the first time, the principles governing the selection of immigrants were spelled out in detail, and a nine point assessment system (with a major emphasis on education and training and occupation demand in Canada) was introduced enabling immigration officers to use the same criteria for admission anywhere in the world. This system has worked remarkably well so far. It has given much more guidance to immigration officers and greatly reduced the use of administrative discretion. It is intelligible to everyone—immigration officials, immigrants, and the whole immigration constituency. This selection system obviously encourages the movement of professional and skilled manpower to Canada and discourages the movement of unskilled workers, except as bona fide relatives. This is a worldwide trend, however, and it must be remembered that Canada has admitted some 900,000 relatives and near relatives in the postwar period [....]

IMMIGRATION MANAGEMENT

Canadian immigration has been managed by a very small group of politicians and officials at the federal level. Under the British North America Act, immigration is a concurrent responsibility of the federal government and the provinces. In the face of massive disinterest on the part of all provinces except Ontario and, very recently Quebec and (to a lesser extent) Manitoba, the federal government has assumed almost exclusive responsibility for this area of public policy. Since the airlift organized by George Drew, then prime minister of Ontario, which brought (from Rainbow Corner in Shaftesbury Avenue) some 10,000 British immigrants to Canada immediately after the war, Ontario has pursued an active immigration programme. This has consisted of a steady and most profitable recruitment of skilled personnel for the province throughout the postwar period, mainly from Britain but also from Germany, Italy, and elsewhere. Quebec, in a dramatic reversal of earlier hostile attitudes, has come energetically onto the Canadian immigration scene with her own department of immigration, an overseas recruitment programme which is just underway and imaginative integration programmes.

Canadian immigration has therefore been a largely bureaucratic exercise, and the bureaucracy has felt a proprietary interest in it and has developed it with some dedication, according to the resources which were available. It was the responsibility first of a Department of Citizenship and Immigration created in 1950 and later of a new Department of Manpower and Immigration, which took over in 1966. Parliament has been involved in a minimal way, although some members of parliament have been energetic defenders of the individual rights of immigrants. All political parties have given nominal support to immigration. But no single party has promoted it with energy and conviction.

Canadians have rarely evinced a real enthusiasm for immigration. But they have been very tolerant to immigrants in the postwar period and Canada has provided a remarkable freedom for creative and energetic immigrants from all quarters and a good life for many others without particular skills or talents. There is an evident feeling among Canadians, more obvious in recent years, that immigrants are hard workers and contribute to economic development and cultural diversity. Some of the striking improvements in the quality of life in large Canadian cities in the last few years is attributed to them. Canadian politicians at the federal and provisional levels, on the other hand have found immigration a touchy, difficult subject and have been reluctant, until very recently, to spend money on immigrants once they had arrived in Canada, apart from immediate welfare and medical assistance and language training. They have given much less thought than their Australian counterparts to the provision of good service for immigrants and to the development of public participation in the immigration process and public understanding of it. Immigrants have, however, benefited very greatly from the energetic development in the last four years of national manpower training, mobility, and other programmes in Canada, and from the creation of a new national employment service, consisting of some 360 Canada manpower centres. The federal government and the provinces of Ontario and Quebec are beginning to move more energetically now into the field of citizenship and immigrant adjustment to give more leadership in this area and provide more money for it.

At the community level, apart from language training, immigrants help immigrants. The boards and staffs of the existing immigration agencies are largely manned by first generation immigrants The immigration lobby, consisting mainly of voluntary agencies and ethnic organizations, is weak but persistent. Two years ago, after years of pressure, the federal government established consultative machinery, at least partly on the Australian model, but in the combined field of manpower and immigration, in the form of a Canada manpower and immigration council and four advisory boards, one of which is concerned with the adjustment of immigrants. The council and boards have now been in action for a year. (For many years Australia has had some effective consultative machinery in immigration consisting of an immigration planning council, immigration advisory council, and immigration publicity council.) Despite the *laissez-faire* approach which has characterized the management of immigration in Canada for most of the postwar period, the two million immigrants who have stayed have settled in without too much difficulty. The 40,000 new immigrants who arrive annually at Toronto's international airport and Union Station, manage somehow to find a place to live and work and most of them become absorbed into the life of this vigorous expanding city.

A considerable expertise in the problems of mutual adjustment between immigrants and host society has been developed in recent years in Canada among voluntary agencies and ethnic organizations. The Canadian community has also become aware of the problems of discrimination in relation to disadvantaged groups and most provinces have some legislation on this subject. The Ontario Human Rights Commission, for example, has done a good job in recent years.

There are problems also. There is a good deal of ethnic isolation. There are a great many immigrants who know nothing about Canadian history or politics. There are ghettos, although with constant movement in and out. The children of immigrants frequently have special educational difficulties and are exposed to serious cultural conflicts. It takes a long time, as it does everywhere, for immigrants to penetrate the political and social structure in Canada. There are in fact the whole range of adjustment problems which characterize all immigration movements, and in which no receiving country and probably no group of immigrants can claim a unique experience. But in Canada at present these problems do not cause, either among Canadians or among immigrants, undue anxiety.

RACE AND IMMIGRATION

Will the presence of many more coloured immigrants in Canada change this relatively comfortable scene? At present, the term "race relations" is not in use in a domestic sense. The public is probably unaware that as much as 23 per cent of the total annual movement now consists of immigrants from Asia and the Caribbean and that these groups are likely to grow to sizeable communities in Canada, concentrated in the major industrial cities. Will the new immigrants who are mainly in the skilled and professional categories share the strong economic motivation and middle-class objectives of their predecessors? Will militant groups bring the race issue to public attention? Will the Canadian impulse to do things differently from the United States exercise a beneficent influence? Is it possible to proceed as if nothing had changed?

British experience would surely indicate that the present phase in Canada, in which there is a lack of concern about these issues and perhaps complacency towards them, will pass and that Canadians will have to come to grips fairly soon with the realities of adjustment, discrimination, and perhaps conflict in relation to much larger numbers of coloured immigrants. In the author's view so far, this is not at all certain. Canada has absorbed two million mainly, but not exclusively, white immigrants without exercising very much effort. In many parts of Canada, immigration is a very familiar phenomenon. The really demanding political and economic problems in Canada now are only marginally related to immigration. The sense of potential in Canadian life today, the sense of space, the vast dimensions of development may act as a strong unifying factor. There may therefore be a case for strengthening existing institutions and community resources in Canada on behalf of all Canadian immigrants, but proceeding in the belief that nothing has in fact changed and that, while other problems may arise in immigration, race relations will not become, and should not be identified as, a serious and worrying issue at least in the near future. The matter, however, is open to debate.

HOWARD PALMER

SOCIAL ADJUSTMENT OF IMMIGRANTS TO CANADA: 1940–1975

FROM IMMIGRATION AND THE RISE OF MULTICULTURALISM "SOCIAL ADJUSTMENT"

Differences of opinion in Canada over the success of immigrant adjustment often spring from different interpretations of the word "adjustment." In Canada, as in the United States, three theories of assimilation have dominated discussion of immigrant adjustment: first, "Anglo-conformity" (and its French-Canadian counterpart, "Franco-conformity") demanded the renunciation of the immigrants' ancestral cultures and traditions in favor of the behavior and values of the Anglo-Saxon group; second, the "melting pot," envisaged a biological merging of settled communities with new immigrant groups and a blending of their cultures into a new Canadian type; and third, "cultural pluralism" (also referred to in Canada as the "mosaic" or "multiculturalism") postulated the preservation of some aspects of immigrant culture and communal life within the context of Canadian citizenship and political and economic integration into Canadian society.

Anglo-conformity was the predominant ideology of assimilation in English Canada before 1940. Proponents of this theory held that it was the obligation of new arrivals to conform to the institutions of Canadian society, which they believed were already fixed. If the immigrants could not conform, they should be excluded. Even most of those who defended the need for immigrants from central and eastern Europe believed in Anglo-conformity. They saw their task as that of convincing anti-immigrant spokesmen that the immigrants could in fact be assimilated. Although Anglo-conformity had many supporters before World War I, it achieved its greatest success during the war, as native-born Canadians made insistent demands for "unhyphenated Canadianism" and absolute loyalty. Provincial governments, schools, voluntary associations, and churches joined in an effort to Canadianize the immigrants. In 1928 R.B. Bennett, then Conservative leader of the opposition, laid down the assumptions of Anglo-conformity in a speech to the House of Commons.

As Bennett's speech shows, the preference in English Canada for British immigrants was related to Anglo-conformist views. English Canadians welcomed British immigrants as an aid in the preservation of "British civilization," into which non-British immigrants would have to be assimilated. The preference for British immigrants, however, did not mean that Canadians were willing to tolerate their expressions of superiority, as selections from a pre-World War I pamphlet for prospective British immigrants indicate.

The second main theory of assimilation, the melting pot concept, was an import. It had been advocated in the United States by a number of intellectuals and politicians, including Ralph Waldo Emerson, Frederick Jackson Turner, Theodore Roosevelt, and Woodrow Wilson. The concept achieved wide popularity in the United States since it harmonized with and articulated deeply held egalitarian values. It also captured the elements of diversity and fluidity which have long characterized American life.

The melting pot idea never achieved the popularity in Canada that it did in the United States, but it had some advocates. Although the concept was not acceptable to French Canadians who wanted to maintain their own culture, some western Canadians found it congenial, and generally ignored French-Canadian feelings about their unique status. The popular Presbyterian minister and writer, "Ralph Connor" (Charles Gordon), succinctly expressed the melting pot ideology in the preface to his novel *The Foreigner* (1909), although the novel itself tends to be a glorification of Anglo-conformity. J.S. Woodsworth, a Methodist minister in charge of All People's Mission in Winnipeg, established to improve the social conditions of immigrants, attacked the assumptions of Anglo-conformity, and advocated something approaching the melting pot in an article for *University Magazine* in 1917. Woodsworth described the work of various voluntary associations — churches, social service clubs, and mission hospitals, for example — in promoting assimilation in order to overcome the cultural and social isolation which separated immigrants from native Canadians. In this sense, the melting pot idea was not so much an attempt to impose cultural uniformity as it was a humanitarian effort to achieve inter-group communication and understanding. Woodsworth later left the Methodist church, but his concern for the plight of the immigrant continued throughout his career as a Labour member of parliament and as a leader of the socialist C.C.F.

Assimilationist pressures by advocates of Anglo-conformity and the melting pot had their effect on ethnic groups. Pressures for conformity, along with the hierarchical ordering of ethnic groups in the socio-economic system, often had serious personal consequences for non Anglo-Saxons. The second generation, tied to the new world by the school system, were more exposed to Canadian society and its assimilationist pressures than their parents were, and they craved acceptance by that society. The conflict of values and expectations which often resulted between the tradition-minded immigrants and the assimilation-prone second generation is reflected not only in many court records, but in some of Canada's best creative literature.

John Marlyn's novel *Under the Ribs of Death*, set in Winnipeg prior to the depression, describes the attempts of a second generation Hungarian-Canadian to overcome the stigma of his ethnic background and the isolation of an immigrant ghetto, in order to be accepted into Anglo-Saxon society. The struggle for material survival is very real to the Hunyadi family, and Sandor learns early that immigrant status is a stigma. He is deeply humiliated by the degradation his father suffers in his work as a janitor and attributes it to his father's pride in his Hungarian past and his notions of brotherhood and the value of learning. Sandor's sense of shame at his parents' apparent handicaps and failure in the struggle for economic survival is the powerful motive behind his vow to be as much like "the English" as possible. In attempting to achieve his goal, Sandor believes he must obliterate any traces of the Old World which his father represents.

As this novel indicates, the second generation often found themselves caught between two social worlds. Economic ambition and the desire for complete assimilation were one response to this dilemma, and political protest was another possible reaction. A study of 236 non-Anglo-Saxons in Ontario who changed their names describes varying responses to the situation of marginality that resulted from assimilationist pressures and the vertical mosaic.

It has been argued that, despite unofficial pressures towards assimilation, the federal government has consistently pursued a policy of cultural pluralism. It is true that the federal government encouraged Mennonites and Icelanders to settle in blocs in Manitoba during the 1870s and gave them concessions (including local autonomy for both groups and military exemptions for the Mennonites) in order to entice them to settle in Canada rather than in the United States. Around the turn of the century, the federal government also encouraged the immigration to western Canada of other groups like the Mormons, Doukhobors, Hutterites, and German and Scandinavian-Americans, who often settled in blocs. But encouragement of the immigration of these groups did not stem from any firm conviction about the desirability of cultural diversity (although politicians sometimes gave lip service to pluralism). Bloc settlements, by providing social and economic stability, were merely a way of getting immigrants to settle in the west and remain there. Prior to World War II, the federal government did not generally promote any ideology of assimilation; its main concern was the economic potential of immigration. Schools, the primary agent of assimilation, were under provincial jurisdiction. There was no explicit federal policy concerning ethnic group, although it was generally assumed that immigrants would eventually be assimilated into English- or French-Canadian society. Immigrants who were regarded as inassimilable were excluded.

For a variety of intellectual, social, and demographic reasons, the ideology of cultural pluralism has been increasingly accepted in the post-World War II period. The decline of racism and the growing influence of theories about cultural relativism opened the way for the emergence of pluralist ideas. With the arrival of many intellectuals among the political refugees from eastern Europe and an increasing number of upwardly mobile second and third generation non-Anglo-Saxons, some of whom felt that they were not being fully accepted into Canadian society, pressures increased at both federal and provincial levels for greater recognition of Canada's ethnic diversity. This could be achieved, for example, through the appointment of senators of a particular ethnic origin, the introduction of ethnic languages as courses (and sometimes as languages of instruction), and ethnic content in the school curriculum.

These demands for greater government recognition of other ethnic groups increased during the 1960s in response to the French-Canadian assertion of equal rights and the Pearson government's measures to assess and ensure the status of the French language and culture. In 1963 the Royal Commission on Bilingualism and Biculturalism was appointed to "inquire into and report upon the existing state of bilingualism and biculturalism in Canada and to recommend what steps should be taken to develop the Canadian Confederation on the basis of an equal partnership between the two founding races, taking into account the contribution made by the other ethnic groups to the cultural enrichment of Canada." Many non-British, non-French groups, but particularly Ukrainians, opposed the view that Canada was bicultural. By 1961, with 26 percent of the Canadian population of other than British or French ethnic origin, with over two hundred newspapers published in languages other than French and English, with fairly well defined Italian, Jewish, Slavic, and Chinese neighbourhoods in large Canadian cities, and with visible rural concentrations of Ukrainians, Doukhobors, Hutterities, and Mennonites, how was it possible for a royal commission to speak of Canada as a *bi*cultural country?

The feeling that biculturalism designated all other ethnic groups as second-class citizens explains the resistance some of these groups expressed to the policies and programs which were introduced to secure the status of the French language in Canada. The place of the so-called other ethnic groups in a bicultural society became a vexing question for federal political politicians, who had originally hoped that steps to ensure French-Canadian rights would go a long way towards improving inter-ethnic relations in Canada. The partial resolution of this dilemma was the assertion by Prime Minister Trudeau that, in fact, Canada is a *multicultural country and that steps should be taken by the federal government to give public recognition to Canada's ethnic diversity* and to give symbolic support through grants for some of the activities of ethnic groups. The leaders of opposition political parties expressed basic agreement with the policy, and four provinces with large numbers of non-Anglo-Saxons — Ontario, Manitoba, Saskatchewan, and Alberta — initiated their own multicultural policies.

The increased acceptance of pluralism in the postwar era has enabled many first, second, and third generation non-Anglo-Saxons to participate fully in Canadian life, and at the same time maintain ties with their cultural heritage. Walter Tarnopolsky, a leading Ukrainian-Canadian academic, expresses support for the federal government's multicultural policy, attempts to draw out some of the implications of the policy for Ukrainians, and assesses the current prospects for survival of Ukrainian identity in Canada.

The increasing acceptance of pluralism by majority groups which these government policies indicate suggests that generational conflict and attempts by the Canadian-born to deny their ethnic origin need not be inevitable. Indeed, the article by a third generation Japanese-Canadian suggests that generational conflict can also be caused by the third generation's disgust with the second for having forsaken their cultural roots in order to be accepted as Canadians. The selection also suggests that growing support for pluralism within some ethnic minorities may be partly due to what has been called "the phenomenon of the third generation":

what the second generation tries to forget the third generation tries to recapture.

Since French Canadians' concern for their rights and cultural survival has been an important factor in stirring other ethnic groups to demand greater recognition, it is ironic that most of the criticism of the various multicultural policies has come from French-Canadian intellectuals. Claude Ryan, the influential editor of *Le Devoir*, reacted negatively to the federal multicultural policy, seeing it both as a distortion of the realities of Canadian life and as a threat to French-Canadian nationalism, since French-Canadian claims to special status depend on a bicultural concept. Ryan and Premier Robert Bourassa both expressed the view that it was contradictory to have a policy of official bilingualism along with *multi*culturalism.

Increased immigration to Quebec in the post-World War II period has raised serious questions for French-Canadian nationalists, already deeply concerned about the status of their culture. The majority have now turned to "Franco-conformity," or the belief that non-British immigrants should be assimilated into French-Canadian society, as the solution to the question of the status of the other ethnic groups in Quebec. [...] J.D. Gagnon, a spokesman for the Parti Québécois, outlines the main causes of the French-Canadian nationalist concern — the declining birth rate of French Canadians coupled with the integration of the majority of immigrants in Montreal into the English-speaking community. This Franco-conformist sentiment focused on the St. Leonard school question in 1968 when a Montreal school board made French the only language of instruction in its schools, much to the consternation of Italian parents. In May 1974, the Liberal government of Premier Robert Bourassa introduced language legislation intended to compel non-English-speaking immigrants to send their children to French-speaking schools. Although many ethnic groups have expressed opposition to the language legislation (Bill 22) of the Bourassa government, it is too soon to tell how they will respond to them. Certainly it is possible that the flow of immigrants to Montreal will decline and that those living there will move to other parts of Canada.

Jeremy Boissevain, in his study for the Royal Commission of Bilingualism and Biculturalism, argues that in choosing English as a language of education, Italians in Montreal are not necessarily opting for the culture represented by that language. While they regard English as a tool for socio-economic success, they have more social ties with French Canadians than with English Canadians. The Montreal Italian newspaper, *La Comunita*, makes a plea for understanding between French Canadians and Italians in an editorial reply to the suggestion of nationalist Pierre Bourgault that immigrants be excluded from the province because of their alleged integration into English-Canadian society.

Although the leaders of the major Canadian political parties have accepted the desirability of Canada's ethnic diversity, the Canadian public does not give unanimous support to pluralism. The debate over ethnicity continues. Questions raised about multiculturalism are not based solely on ethnic intolerance or on fears that it will undermine biculturalism. Does the encouragement of pluralism only serve to perpetuate the vertical mosaic, in which class lines coincide with ethnic lines, or does it help to tear down class barriers by promoting acceptance of the legitimacy of cultural differences? Are the goals of government policy — cultural pluralism and equality of opportunity — mutually compatible? Does the encouragement of ethnic group solidarity threaten the freedom of individuals in these groups, or can ethnic groups provide a liberating rather than a restricting context for identity? Does the encouragement of cultural diversity serve to perpetuate old world hatreds, or will the recognition of the contributions of Canada's ethnic groups heighten their feeling that they belong in Canada and thus strengthen Canadian unity? Is government talk of multiculturalism just a way to get the ethnic vote, or is positive action necessary to preserve cultural pluralism when cultural diversity throughout the world is being eroded by the impact of industrial technology, mass communication, and urbanization?

When they have tried to conceptualize Canada's experience with ethnicity, many people have argued that in both ideology and reality, Canada is a mosaic rather than a melting pot. Some scholars argue that ethnic diversity has greater legitimacy in Canada than in the United States for two main reasons: first, Canada's development of a concrete norm of Canadianism, and second, Canada's greater number of immigrants in proportion to the total population has aided the perpetuation of various ethnic cultures. This does not mean, however, that there have not been assimilationist pressures in Canada [...] , and one can certainly question whether Canadians have been notably more tolerant toward minority groups than Americans. Racist immigration policies, anti-Oriental sentiment, anti-Catholic, and anti-radical nativism have all had long careers in Canada. The Canadian treatment of Germans during both world wars, and of the Japanese during World War II differed little from that in the United States .... Despite the fact that the image of the mosaic versus the melting pot oversimplifies the experience of Canada and the United

States at both the level of ideology and reality, there is still validity in the comparison.

Appendix

Table 9.1: Ethnic Origin of the Canadian Population (percentages), 1871–1971[1]

	1871	1881	1901	1911	1921	1931	1941	1951	1961	1971
Total[2]	100.00	100.00	100.00	100.00	100.00	100.00	100.00	100.00	100.00	100.00
British	60.55	58.93	57.04	55.49	55.41	51.86	49.68	47.89	43.85	44.62
French	31.07	30.03	30.71	28.61	27.91	28.22	30.27	30.83	30.38	28.65
Dutch	0.85	0.70	0.63	0.78	1.34	1.44	1.85	1.89	2.36	1.97
German	5.82	5.88	5.78	5.60	3.35	4.56	4.04	4.43	5.75	6.11
Italian	0.03	0.04	0.20	0.64	0.76	0.95	0.98	1.09	2.47	3.39
Jewish	*	0.02	0.30	1.06	1.44	1.51	1.48	1.30	0.95	1.38
Polish			0.12	0.47	0.61	1.40	1.45	1.57	1.77	1.47
Russian	0.02	0.03	0.37	0.61	1.14	0.85	0.73	0.65	0.65	0.30
Scandinavian	0.05	0.12	0.58	1.56	1.90	2.20	2.12	2.02	2.12	1.78
Ukrainian	0.10	1.05	1.21	2.17	2.66	2.82	2.59	2.69		
Other European	0.11	0.13	0.44	1.35	2.44	2.51	2.45	2.47	3.90	3.71
Asiatic	*	0.10	0.44	0.60	0.75	0.81	0.64	0.52	0.67	1.32
Indian and Eskimo	0.66	2.51	2.38	1.46	1.29	1.24	1.09	1.18	1.21	1.45
Others and not stated	0.84	1.51	0.91	0.72	0.45	0.28	0.56	1.34	1.33	0.96

Source: Censuses of Canada, and Table A–4, *Report of the Royal Commission on Bilingualism and Biculturalism*, Book IV, p. 248.

Table 9.2: Ethnic Origin of the Canadian Population, 1871–1971[1]

	1871	1881	1901	1911	1921	1931	1941	1951	1961	1971
Total[2]	3,485,761	4,324,810	5,371,315	7,206,643	8,787,949	10,376,786	11,506,655	14,009,429	18,238,247	21,568,310
British	2,110,502	2,548,514	3,063,195	3,999,081	4,868,738	5,381,071	5,715,904	6,709,685	7,996,669	9,624,115
French	1,082,940	1,298,929	1,649,371	2,061,719	2,452,743	2,927,990	3,483,038	4,319,167	5,540,346	6,180,120
Dutch	29,662	30,412	33,845	55,961	117,505	148,962	212,863	264,267	429,679	425,945
German	202,991	254,319	310,501	403,417	294,635	473,544	464,682	619,995	1,049,599	1,317,200
Italian	1,035	1,849	10,834	45,963	66,769	98,173	112,625	152,245	450,351	730,820
Jewish	125	667	16,131	76,199	126,196	156,726	170,241	181,670	173,344	296,945
Polish			6,285	33,652	53,403	145,503	167,485	219,845	323,517	316,430
Russian	607	1,227	19,825	44,376	100,064	88,148	83,708	91,279	119,168	64,175
Scandinavian	1,623	5,223	31,042	112,682	167,359	228,049	244,603	283,024	386,534	384,795
Ukrainian			5,682	75,432	106,721	225,113	305,929	395,043	473,337	580,660
Other European	3,830	5,760	23,811	97,101	214,451	261,034	281,790	346,354	711,320	800,300
Asiatic	4	4,383	23,731	43,213	65,914	84,548	74,064	72,827	121,753	285,540
Indian and Eskimo	23,037	108,547	127,941	105,611	113,724	128,890	125,521	165,607	220,121	312,760
Other and not stated	29,405	64,980	49,121	52,236	39,727	29,035	64,202	188,421	242,509	206,090

1. Data for 1871 and 1881 are incomplete, particularly in the treatment of small numbers of those from central Europe. 1891 is omitted because of insufficient data.
2. For 1871 includes the population of the four original provinces of Canada only: Nova Scotia, New Brunswick, Quebec, and Ontario. Newfoundland is excluded until 1951.
* Percentage lower than 0.01.
Source: Censuses of Canada and Table A-3, *Report of the Royal Commission on Bilingualism and Biculturalism*, Book IV p. 247.

EVELYN KALLEN

MULTICULTURALISM: IDEOLOGY, POLICY AND REALITY

INTRODUCTION

In the current Canadian context, the concept "multiculturalism" is widely used in at least three senses: (1) to refer to the "social reality" of ethnic diversity; (2) to refer to the federal government policy, designed to create national unity in ethnic diversity; and (3) to refer to the ideology of cultural pluralism (the Canadian mosaic) underlying the federal policy.

Canada's national ideology of cultural pluralism represents a fairly recent outgrowth of the historical ideal of "cultural dualism" – the original myth legitimating the constitutional separation – and guarantees underlying English Protestant hegemony outside Quebec and French Catholic hegemony with the province of Quebec.

Concomitant with the settlement throughout Canada of the massive, early twentieth century waves of non-English and non-French immigrants from virtually all parts of Europe, the myth of cultural dualism began to lose public popularity, and, by the third and fourth decades of this century, the mosaic myth was increasingly lauded in the speeches of politicians and other dignitaries (Burnet, 1981: p. 29). However, while the myth of the mosaic flourished in the *rhetoric* of public life, public *policy* in Canada continued to be governed by the concept of Anglo-conformity.

The assumption of the dominant English ethnic collectivity was that immigrants would assimilate to the British institutional and cultural model, which included the English language and the Protestant religion. It was not until the early decades following World War II, with heightened concern about human rights and the resurgence of ethnicity throughout much of the globe, that the mosaic rhetoric took on serious multicultural policy implications (*ibid.*).

I will examine the concept of multiculturalism in Canada at three levels: as a societal ideal, as a federal government policy, and as an ethno-political social movement.

THE IDEOLOGY OF MULTICULTURALISM

Isajiw (1981) has recently examined multiculturalism as a set of social values. He has argued that multiculturalism, as a value, can provide a basis for a new kind of universalism which legitimizes the incorporation of ethnic diversity in the general structure of society. Historically, he points out, universal values of modern societies were predicated on the shift from ascribed to achieved criteria for evaluation, and, concomitantly, on complete detachment from particularistic ethnic ties. Integration of individuals into the state collectivity was conditional on total disengagement from ethnicity and fragmentation of ethnic identity.

Today, however, this kind of universalism is losing relevance and validity. For one thing, Isajiw argues, people are questioning the legitimacy of the universalistic ideal of inclusion in the face of continuing ethnic exclusion. Thus, ethnic discrimination has rendered the old universalism invalid in the minds of many Canadians. Also, people are questioning the value of assimilation to post-modern, technological culture, which offers little in response to expressive identity needs. Finally, Isjiw points out that the collective needs of members of ethnic collectivities have changed over the generations. People are coming to the realization that their own personal dignity is bound up with the collective dignity of their ethnic community. Recognition of one thus necessitates recognition of the other.

Given these considerations, what is the meaning of multiculturalism as a set of universal social values? Isajiw suggests that it is threefold: 1) it gives positive recognition to the collective identity of all ethnic communities; 2) it can legitimize multiple identities; and 3) it can become institutionalized as a political value.

In short, Isajiw's argument suggests that multiculturalism provides a set of social values which recognizes both the expressive identity needs and the instrumental power needs of members of diverse ethnic collectivities, and, at the same time, can provide the basis for a new kind of universalism which legitimizes the inclusion of different ethnic units in the general structure of society.

THE MODEL OF MULTICULTURALISM: UNDERLYING ASSUMPTIONS

As a model for reality, the mosaic ideology is predicated on a national goal of one nation/many peoples/many cultures. The mosaic ideal is rooted in the assumption that members of all ethnocultural collectivities are both able and willing to maintain their ethnocultural distinctiveness. This assumption implies that all ethnic collectivities are characterized by high levels of ethnocentrism, but that they also are willing to adopt a "laissez-faire" (live and let live) stance towards ethnocultural collectivities whose values and lifeways differ markedly from their own. Following from this, the mosaic model assumes that levels of prejudice and discrimination between ethnic collectivities are low enough to allow mutual tolerance. Thirdly, the mosaic model assumes a rough equivalence in the distribution of power among the various ethnic collectivities, so that no one population can assume dominance and control over others. Finally, this model assumes that members of the different ethnic collectivities in society will mutually agree to limit and control the extent, spheres, and nature of interaction between them. Thus, processes of acculturation and assimilation will be (mutually) restricted by the interacting ethnic units.

Given these assumptions, inter-ethnic relations within the mosaic society would take the form of ethnic segmentation (Breton, 1978). Each ethnic collectivity would be institutionally complete, and ethnocultural distinctiveness (cultural pluralism) would be maintained through separate ethnic institutions (structural pluralism). As an outcome of cultural and structural pluralism, every citizen's identity would become hyphenated, i.e., ethnic-national, with equal weights on both sides of the hyphen. With regard to human rights, the society would recognize both the individual human rights of all its ethnic collectivities. Given the basic assumption of equality of opportunity built into the notion of a (North American type) meritocracy, the social position attained by individual citizens within a mosaic (as within a melting pot) society would be a function of their demonstrated individual talents, capabilities, and skills, on the one hand, and of the way in which these attributes are culturally valued, on the other. Ethnicity would not provide a criterion for differential personal evaluation or for positional attainment in public life. Ethnicity would, however, provide the recognized basis for collective rights, in that all ethnic collectivities within the society would be guaranteed the freedom to collectively express their religious, linguistic, and cultural distinctiveness.

The most important variable in the operationalization of this model is the relative weights assigned to "unity" and "diversity." The importance of ethnic diversity is reflected in the sphere (or spheres) in which collective (ethnocultural group) rights might be guaranteed. Should the mosaic take the form of pluralism in the public sector, then ethnocultural rights could be guaranteed through political representation, economic (occupational) control in specified area(s), recognition of linguistic rights, and (in its most extreme form) territorial (regional/local) autonomy. The latter form of pluralism provides the basis for *nationhood* based on the geographical separation of ethnic collectivities sharing language, culture, and territory. If viable for all ethnic groups, this kind of pluralism could lead to multinationhood—a multinational society within a common political (federal) administrative framework. In the latter kind of society, the national group rights of all ethnic collectivities would be recognized.

Within the Canadian context, the myth of the mosaic was not (initially) conceptualized in "nationhood" terms for populations other than the charter groups (English and French). Rather, as applied to (later) immigrant ethnic collectivities, the mosaic model relegated cultural and structural pluralism to the private sphere of life. Within the public sector, individual citizens would be accorded equal societal opportunities without reference to ethnic classification. But, with regard to collective (ethnocultural group) rights, the public sector was envisaged as an Anglo or Franco cultural monolith, thus attainment of social positions within the sphere of secondary institutions would be predicated on required acculturation to prevailing Anglo or Franco norms and practices.

MULTICULTURALISM WITHIN A BILINGUAL FRAMEWORK: THE CANADIAN MOSAIC AS GOVERNMENT POLICY

The impetus for Canada's multicultural policy lay in the negative response of immigrant ethnic minorities to the model of bilingualism and biculturalism which underscored the efforts and reports of the "Bi and Bi" Commission in the 1960s. Reacting against the idea of a policy which would relegate non-English and non-French Canadians to the status of second-class citizens, spokesmen for the (alleged) "Third Force" of immigrant ethnic collectivities demanded equal treatment. Spearheaded by Ukrainians, the demands of the other ethnic groups gave rise, in 1969, to Book IV of the *Report of the Royal Commission on Bilingualism and*

Biculturalism: "The Cultural Contribution of the Other Ethnic Groups." This document contains sixteen recommendations for the implementation of an official government policy of multilingualism and multiculturalism designed as a model of integration for immigrant ethnic collectivities.

Prime Minister Lester B. Pearson emphasized the fact that under the newly introduced policy the preservation of ethnic identity is a voluntary matter, both for the individual and for the group. The funding of multicultural programmes would therefore be directed *only* towards those ethnic groups whose members *express a desire* to maintain their ethno-cultural heritage and who can demonstrate a *need for support* in their efforts to maintain their ethnic distinctiveness. Similarly, Mr. Trudeau recognized the right of each individual to be *free to choose* whether or not to maintain his or her distinctive ethnic identity.

Unlike the ideal model of cultural pluralism, which assumes that every individual and group desires to maintain a distinctive ethnic identity and heritage, the Canadian policy of multiculturalism, as espoused by Prime Minister Trudeau, gives recognition to the fact that some people will, inevitably, find greater human affinities outside their ethnic group than within it. Thus, while the policy legitimates the right of each immigrant ethnocultural community to maintain its distinctiveness, it also gives recognition to the right of individuals to *choose* whether or not to value maintenance of ties and loyalties to their particular ethnic group and it supports the right of individuals to participate fully in Canadian society, independent of their (actual or assumed) ethnic classification. The *voluntary* nature of maintenance of ethnic ties, loyalties, and identities under the multicultural policy protects the *individual* rights of members to freely dissent or dissociate themselves from the collective values of their ethnic origin group.

The federal government's policy statement on multiculturalism (*House of Commons Debates*, October 8, 1971) sets forth four objectives:

1. The Government of Canada will support all of Canada's cultures and will seek to assist, resources permitting, the development of those cultural groups which have demonstrated a desire and effort to continue to develop a capacity to grow and contribute to Canada, as well as a clear need for assistance.

2. The Government will assist members of all cultural groups to overcome cultural barriers to full participation in Canadian society.

3. The Government will promote creative encounters and interchange among all Canadian cultural groups in the interest of national unity.

4. The Government will continue to assist immigrants to acquire at least one of Canada's official languages in order to become full participants in Canadian society.

While each of these objectives has received some public and academic support, few scholars who have voiced their views appear to be willing to support the total package. Moreover, opinion is clearly divided on the relative value of the different objectives.

The first policy objective seeks to encourage ethnocultural diversity through support of those ethnic groups which have demonstrated a desire to develop as distinctive cultural entities. Scholars who support this objective (for example, Burnet, 1975, 1976, 1978) tend to view ethnic collectivities in expressive, rather than instrumental terms. They conceptualize the primary function of ethnic communities as one of providing people with havens of security, places where they can escape from the alienating workaday world of post-technological society. Ethnicity provides a sense of group belongingness and rootedness, i.e., a focus for ethnic identity and cultural continuity.

One line of argument put forward by scholars who oppose this policy objective (notably, the late John Porter, 1975, 1979) is that encouragement of ethnic diversity and cultural distinctiveness fosters (implicitly, if not explicitly) ethnic separation, enclavement, and retention of traditional values. Ethnic particularism, in turn, perpetuates the vertical (ethnic) mosaic by creating barriers to upward mobility in post-industrial society, which is predicated on universalistic norms. In this view, government encouragement of ethnic diversity legitimates the proliferation of particularistic value differences among Canadians and thus impedes the development of national unity. Further, some critics have argued, the (original)[1] exclusive focus of the policy of multiculturalism on the other ethnic groups, i.e., immigrants, contributes to the ethnic divisiveness rather than national unity among Canadians. Specifically, Canadian scholars have argued that the artificial separation of the three categories of Canadian ethnic collectivities (immigrants, charter population, and indigenes) for political purposes — endorsed and reinforced by the multicultural policy — represents the age-old Colonial technique of divide and rule utilized by majority ethnic elites to guarantee and perpetuate their ascendancy (Kallen, 1978; Peter, 1979).

A second line of argument against the first policy objective (i.e., maintenance of ethno-cultural distinctiveness) is that there are *no* relevant cultural differences among Canada's immigrant populations other than minor differences in tastes (e.g., food preferences) which neither warrant nor require a multicultural policy in order to be maintained (Brotz, 1980). Members of all of Canada's ethnic collectivities, Brotz argues, aspire to the same "bourgeois-democratic" ways of life, with the exception of the (already transitional) way of life of those indigenes in reservations who continue to be engaged in a pre-industrial hunting and gathering economy (*ibid.*, p. 43). From this view, the multicultural policy "corrupts" the liberal-democratic principle for which Canada stands "by projecting the ideal of Canada as some kind of ethnic zoo where the function of the zoo keeper is to collect as may varieties as possible and exhibit them once a year in some carnival where one can go from booth to booth sampling pizzas, wonton soup and kosher pastramies" (*ibid.*, p. 44).[2]

The expressive emphasis of the first multicultural policy objective, particularly as implemented in programmes featuring "ethnic exotica" has come under sharp criticism by Canadian academics and other scholars (Wilson, 1978; Bullivant, 1981; Peter, *op. cit.*). Bullivant (*ibid.*) argues that this exclusive focus on the *expressive* (roots/belongingness) function of ethnicity deflects attention away from the *instrumental* (corporate group interests) side of ethnic collectivities as politically and/or economically-oriented survival blueprints or designs for living intimately connected with an ethnic group's life chances. Peter (*ibid.*) goes even further than Bullivant in his criticisms of both the first and fourth multicultural policy objectives. He argues that the "we" (Canadian society)/"they" (ethnic collectivities) syndrome, which assumes that Canadian society somehow exists *independently of* (and prior to) the ongoing interaction between the ethnic collectivities which comprise it, relegates the role of minority ethnic groups to that of contributors of quaint customs/upholders of primordial identities, while at the same time it denies them a political and economic reality in Canada. Peter contends that the Multicultural/Bilingual Policy is a policy of appeasement and containment of the conflicting demands made by the other ethnic groups (immigrants), on the one hand, and by Quebecers, on the other. Multiculturalism, says Peter, was originally intended to buy off the compliance of a potential Third Force of immigrants, while bilingualism was intended to appease a revitalized Quebec and to contain its claims to political power (*ibid.*, p. 7). As a whole (according to Peter), the policy served as a technique of domination which legitimated the entrenched powers of the ruling Anglo elite when its super-ordinate, national position was threatened by Quebec's claim to political power, on the one hand, and by the growing numerical and economic strength and increasing cultural vitality of immigrant ethnic collectivities, on the other hand.

With regard to the second and third objectives of the multicultural policy statement, Canadian scholars appear to be far more unified in their positive support. The second policy objective of multiculturalism seeks to overcome cultural barriers to full participation in Canadian society; the third seeks to promote creative encounters and interchange among all of Canada's ethnic groups. Both of these objectives appear to be designed to reduce racial/ethnic discrimination, to protect the fundamental human rights of members of immigrant ethnic collectivities, and to foster Canadian unity.

Canadian scholars generally evince strong support for these two policy objectives. They also point out that the policy *rhetoric* does not correspond with programmes of implementation at the level of social *reality*. Indeed, the weakest and most neglected part of multicultural programmes implemented under the policy has been in this area (Hughes & Kallen, 1974; Kelner & Kallen, 1974; Kallen, *op. cit.*; Burnet, *op. cit.*).

Probably the most contentious aspect of the multicultural policy is reflected in its fourth objective, i.e., linguistic assimilation of immigrants into one of Canada's two official language communities (English and French). The bilingual framework of the policy accords official recognition only to the linguistic rights of the founding peoples, while the linguistic rights of immigrant ethnic minorities are neither recognized nor guaranteed. From the viewpoint of the Third Force, multiculturalism, in the sense of maintenance of viable ethnocultural communities, is meaningless without multilingualism (Yusyk, 1964). Scholars who favor this perspective—the position adopted in the recommendations of Book Four of the Report of the Commission on Bilingualism and Biculturalism—contend that, where numbers warrant, regional guarantees for the protection and recognition of *non*-official as well as official priority languages should be afforded. In direct opposition to this view is the position put forward by the staunch Francophone supporters of bilingualism and biculturalism (Bourassa, 1971; Rocher, 1976). Proponents of this view argue that the constitutional protection of the special status of the French in Quebec places them in a unique position in Canada as one of the two founding *nations*. By virtue of this special status, they argue that in public life their language and culture should be expressed and recognized throughout Canada equally with that of the English. Both arguments—for multilingualism/multiculturalism and for bilingualism/biculturalism—are predicated on the assumption that "living" cultures and "living" languages are inextricably linked. As models for reality, however, the former position more closely approximates an egalitarian mosaic ideal for a multi-ethnic society, while the latter enshrines the dominant status of the (alleged) charter groups.

SUMMARY: MULTICULTURALISM/BILINGUALISM ... THE CANADIAN MOSAIC AS GOVERNMENT POLICY

The multicultural (policy) version of the mosaic (myth) assumes a clear division between *public* and *private* sectors. Within public institutions, and in the interests of national unity, members of ethnic minorities are expected to acculturate linguistically to one of Canada's official languages, English or French. Further, the rhetoric underlying the policy of multiculturalism supports, the idea that in order to achieve upward social mobility (and "earned rights"), especially in the federal government service, Canadians should become bilingual, i.e., they should become Anglo-Franco-speaking Canadians in public life. At the same time, the multicultural policy supports the somewhat contradictory (old) democratic notion of individual equality of opportunity regardless of ethnic (or other ascriptive) classification in the public sector.

It is solely in the *private* sphere of life that the multicultural policy affords minority-ethnic Canadians any kind of social legitimation with respect to collective (ethnocultural/group) rights. In their private lives, ethnic-Canadians are free to sing their ethnic songs, dance their ethnic dances, eat their ethnic food, and (otherwise) engage in ethnic exotic—provided that none of these activities contravenes prevailing Canadian laws. The multicultural policy does not, however, guarantee all of Canada's ethnic *minorities* support for structural pluralism—for educational, religious, language, and/or other ethnic institutions through which a *living* ethnic-Canadian culture could be constantly revitalized and thus remain viable over the generations. Thus the collective *minority rights* of members of non-English and non-French ethnic collectivities are neither protected nor guaranteed. Finally, the multicultural policy with its individual "identities" focus is not designed to meet the instrumental needs of Canada's ethnic minorities. It does not support the kinds of mobilization of corporate ethnic groups interests necessary for the equalization of access by immigrant ethnic minorities to political, economic, and social power in Canadian society. In effect, by stressing the particularistic, expressive (identity) functions of immigrant ethnocultures, the multicultural policy shortchanges the goal of national unity; and by ignoring the instrumental (corporate group interest) functions of ethnic collectivities the multicultural policy shortchanges the goal of ethnic equality.

What seems to be implied by the current multicultural version of the ethnic mosaic is that Canadians are ranked into three classes. The first-class citizens are those whose collective (linguistic) rights are officially recognized and guaranteed in public life and whose cultural norms remain entrenched within public (federal and/or provincial) institutions, i.e., Canada's "founding peoples," the English and French Canadian "charter groups."

The second-class citizens are those whose collective rights are reduced to symbolic diacritica of a past ethnic heritage, legitimated in the private sphere of life only, i.e., Canada's other (immigrant) ethnic groups.

The third-class citizens are Canada's original peoples (i.e., Indians and Inuit), whose *aboriginal* and treaty rights—ignored under the multicultural policy—derive from the historical fact that they occupied and used much of the land in the country we call Canada long before either of the so-called charter groups arrived.

Intentionally or not, the multicultural policy preserves the *reality of the Canadian ethnic hierarchy*, the "vertical mosaic" of ethnic inequality, which the late John Porter (1965) discovered some fifteen years ago. Unlike the mosaic rhetoric, the reality of the Canadian vertical mosaic is a reality rooted in long-term racial/ethnic discrimination and denial of human rights. Questions involving the collective rights of non-Anglo and non-Franco Canadians—whether raised by immigrants or indigenes—have accordingly, become questions of *minority* rights.

THE MULTICULTURAL MOVEMENT: MOSAIC AS SOCIAL REALITY

As an ethno-political movement, the multicultural movement may be conceptualized as a movement for social reform spearheaded by immigrant ethnic minorities in a collective effort to achieve the goal of an egalitarian Canadian mosaic.

As indicated earlier, the multicultural movement arose from the discontent of non-English and non-French immigrant ethnic minorities with their alleged status as second-class citizens under the terms of reference of the Royal Commission on Bilingualism and Biculturalism. At this time, discontent with the biculturalism goal focused on the notion of the two founding races—a term of reference which confuses race and culture—used by the Royal Commission to refer to the English and French charter groups in Canada. This notion, it was argued, relegated all other peoples and cultures to minority status within Canada. In a similar vein, objections were raised against the goal of bilingualism as interpreted by the Commission to mean the languages of the English and French, and as later enshrined in the Official Languages Act (1969).

The earliest and the most powerful spokesman for the multicultural movement was Senator Paul Yuzyk, who, in his maiden speech in the Canadian Senate on May 3, 1964, put forward the idea of a Third Force—a coalition of all non-English and non-French ethnic collectivities in Canada. Yuzyk clearly articulated the *instrumental* goal of the movement when he argued that the Third Force (then) represented almost one third of the Canadian population, and as a united organizational force they could hold the balance of power between the English and French. The *expressive* goal of the multicultural movement soon became evident in demands for a Canadian (mosaic) nation based on a policy of multiculturalism and multilingualism. Spearheaded largely by Ukrainian spokesmen such as Yuzyk, the movement was (at least covertly) supported even in its early stages by representatives of other long-resident immigrant ethnic collectivities, such as Jews, and later by a variety of newer immigrant populations including Italians, Armenians, Portuguese, Greeks, and others.

The majority response to the conflicting demands of the Third Force, on the one hand, and of the French-Canadian nationalists who supported a model of English/French bilingualism and biculturalism, on the other hand, was represented in the compromise policy of multiculturalism within a bilingual framework. Minority ethnic protest against the terms of the policy, since its inception, has indicated clearly that it has not satisfied the demands of either of the constituencies (French or "other" immigrants) whose claims it sought to address. Just as proponents of bilingualism and biculturalism argue that the latter necessitates the former, proponents of the multicultural movement continue to argue that language and culture are indivisible; therefore multiculturalism is meaningless without multilingualism. While the early proponents of the multicultural movement focused on fundamental human rights, especially the right of equal access of all ethnic groups to political, economic and social power, spokesmen for a variety of ethnic organizations over the years have increasingly come to make demands based on collective minority (cultural, religious, and linguistic) rights.

MULTICULTURALISM AND COLLECTIVE MINORITY RIGHTS

Our shared conception of Canada as a multicultural society, it is argued, clearly implies some equitable form of recognition of the collective rights of all of Canada's ethnocultural collectivities. Yet, our original Canadian constitution (the B.N.A. Act) contained only two references to collective (religious and linguistic) rights, namely S.93, dealing with separate (Protestant and Catholic) denominational schools and S.133, concerning the use of English and French in certain federal and Quebec institutions. Under both our original constitution and our 1960 Bill of Rights, the collective (linguistic, religious, and cultural) minority rights of non-Protestant and non-Catholic, non-English and non-French ethnic collectivities have been neither recognized nor protected. In short, only the collective rights of Canada's two founding peoples (charter groups) have been constitutionally secured. Further, the Official Languages Act (1969) provides legal recognition and protection only for the linguistic rights of the English and French ethnic groups, at the federal level.

But what about the linguistic rights of Canada's non-English and non-French peoples? Proponents of the multicultural movement argue that the principle of equality for all Canadian ethnic communities entails the extension of the principle of linguistic rights to include guarantees for the protection of *non*-official minority languages, where numbers warrant.

Douglas (1979) notes that it is only appropriate to speak of language rights where the ethnic collectivity concerned has the requisite population numbers to ensure the maintenance of the effective use of the language. Where numbers warrant, Douglas contends, the effective protection of linguistic rights requires more than a language provision under a non-discriminatory human rights clause. What are also implied are positive measures by the state to ensure the recognition of the rights of linguistic minorities before the courts and with respect to the state apparatus. These rights, Douglas contends, include:

1.   The right to understand and be understood by the state;
2.   The right to use one's language before the courts;
3.   The right to be educated in one's own mother tongue.

While the above-mentioned measures for the recognition and protection of *non*-official minority languages would clearly meet some of the demands of ethnic leaders and proponents of multilingualism and multiculturalism in Canada, they have been rejected outright by Prime Minister Trudeau, first, under the current federal policy of multiculturalism, and second, in the Charter of Rights and Freedoms contained in the *Constitution Act, 1982*. In the current Charter, the sections dealing with languages rights (under Official Languages of Canada, S.16-22 and Minority Language Educational Rights, S.23) are designed to constitutionally enshrine the provisions of the Official Languages Act at the federal level.

MULTICULTURALISM, MINORITY RIGHTS, AND EDUCATION

Spokespersons for the multicultural movement have long criticized the federal multicultural policy for its avoidance of the educational implications of the multicultural ideal through the political strategy of shifting the burden of responsibility to the provinces. Because public education is a provincial matter, the federal policy has conveniently sidestepped this critical issue.

In response to early protest against the focus of multicultural programmes on folk art and museum culture, as opposed to living languages and ethnocultures, multicultural programmes were expanded so as to offer limited support to private, supplementary, minority ethnic schools. But proponents of the multicultural movement continued to argue that failure to provide support for maintenance of language and culture in public institutions — in primary and secondary schools, and in community colleges and universities as well as in public broadcasting and other media — perpetuates the minority status of the other ethnic groups (Burnet, 1981, p. 31). From the viewpoint of the multicultural movement, the present policy continues to violate the collective minority rights of non-English and non-French ethnic collectivities.

Like the question of minority linguistic rights, the question of minority religious rights has become inextricably interwoven with the education issue. Increasingly, spokespersons for the multicultural movement have taken the view that the constitutional recognition of the right of parents to determine the education of their children should apply equally regardless of religious persuasion. Further, it has been argued that in a truly multicultural society the freedom of religion provision under the (1960) Bill of Rights (and now, under the new Charter as well) should be interpreted so as to require the extension of the provisions of S.93 of the B.N.A. Act to include *all* minority religious denominational schools. In practical (economic) terms, proponents of this view have argued that government funds for denominational schools should be extended to include non-Protestant and non-Catholic religious minorities *or* that parents/religious communities who voluntarily choose to support separate denominational schools should be exempt from taxation for public education (see, for example, Glickman, 1976). However, as in the case of linguistic rights, the collective religious rights of Canada's non-English and non-French ethnic collectivities are neither recognized nor protected under our current constitutional arrangements.

MULTICULTURALISM AND RACIAL DISCRIMINATION

Another position put forward under the rubric of the multicultural movement focuses on the second multicultural policy objective, i.e., that of combating racial discrimination. Spokespersons for visible minorities such as Chinese, West Indians, and South Asians have argued that early programmes of implementation under the multicultural policy did not place nearly enough emphasis on eradicating racism in Canada.

In response to this position, in 1975, the (then) Minister of Multiculturalism, the Honorable John Munro, declared a shift in programme emphasis from language and culture to group understanding. The subsequent change in focus of multicultural programmes towards combating prejudice and discrimination sparked a number of important researches in the area, notably the national survey of ethnic attitudes carried out by Berry *et al.* (1977) and a study of racism in Toronto (Henry, 1977), among others. While these academic studies provided important documentation on the nature and extent of racial/ethnic prejudice and discrimination in various parts of Canada, they were not designed primarily to alleviate the negative social and personal consequences of these phenomena for those Canadians found to be most disadvantaged by them, i.e., for visible minorities. It was the various spokespersons for visible minorities who took up the cause of racial discrimination and, under the rubric of multiculturalism, began to press for greater protection (particularly through fairer practices of law enforcement) for their fundamental human rights. For these minorities, the fight against racial discrimination takes precedence over the fight against cultural discrimination so earnestly pursued by the proponents of multilingualism and multiculturalism under the same multiculturalism rubric.

Most recently, in response to the political implications of state funding of ethnic organizations in Canada, criticism of the policy of multiculturalism has come to focus on the syndrome of "state policy as state control" (Kallen, 1981; Anderson and Frideres, 1981). At the level of social reality, it is argued, government funding of minority ethnic organizations legitimated under the multicultural policy represents a major technique of dominant managements of minority ethnic demands. For state funding bodies are controlling agencies: the dominant fund-giving agency sets the terms (conditions) under which funds are allotted, selects the recipients, and oversees and regulates the process through which the funds are distributed and expended. Government funding of minority ethnic organizations thus allows (indeed facilitates) government (and, indirectly, dominant) intervention in minority affairs. Through this subtle (and sometimes not-so-subtle) process the ethnic minority is kept in a dependent position, and minority ethnic protest is contained and diffused. Further, insofar as ethnic minorities must complete against each other for the same scarce resource (multicultural programme grants), ethnic divisions gain in strength and salience.

[margin note: Majority still has overall control]

The implications of ethnic group competition and factionalism for the future of the multicultural movement are manifold. For the tension between the competing and ofttimes conflicting interests of internal lines of division has impeded the instrumental thrust of the multicultural movement as a multi-ethnic coalition in Canada. Nevertheless, at present, the multicultural movement continues to flourish, despite its many vociferous critics. Over and above the competing and conflicting demands of its internal factions, the movement provides a recognized, legitimate forum for minority ethnic protest. Further, as Isajiw (1980) has pointed out, the multicultural *policy* has given ethnic collectivities a legal basis for making claims on public policy and public funds. Thus the policy, despite its (alleged) limitations, provides an important legitimating mechanism for minority claims based on ethnic group demands for recognition of their collective dignity and collective rights.

The evidence presented in the foregoing discussion indicates that the concept of multiculturalism is inherently problematic at all levels of analysis, i.e., as a set of universal social values (ideology), as federal policy, and as an ethnopolitical movement (social reality).

At the level of values, the assumptions of the mosaic ideology pose at least three sets of problems with regard to its potential for implementation. First, as an egalitarian ideology, the mosaic assumes relative symmetry of political, economic, and social power among the constituent ethnic units in the society. What this assumption implies is that the mosaic ideology is inappropriate where there are vast disparities in power between ethnic collectivities. Before the mosaic model could be implemented in an ethnically stratified society like Canada, for example, a major redistribution of power between ethnic units would have to occur. Secondly, the mosaic ideology assumes that all ethnic units in the society are equally desirous and capable of developing and maintaining distinctive ethnocultures. This aspect of the ideology does not take into account the possibility that ethnic units may differ in the degree to which their members desire to maintain ethnic distinctiveness and in the degree to which they have the demographic, economic, and institutional resources which would enable them to do so. While no society can legislate or otherwise ensure any population's desire to remain culturally distinctive, measures can be taken to facilitate this end, if so desired. The scholarly literature on ethnic relations provides persuasive evidence to support the view that maintenance of ethnocultural distinctiveness is best ensured through the development of institutionally complete ethnic enclaves. The latter objective thus would best be served by the geographical distribution of the population into ethnically discrete units, together with the development of relatively autonomous and self-sufficient ethnic communities. In the Canadian context, this would involve not only a major policy and programme of population redistribution but also a major reallocation of societal resources towards ethnic community development. Thirdly, the mosaic ideology assumes that, through tolerant inter-ethnic relations involving the full and equal participation in public life of members of all ethnic communities, a common, national culture and identity would be created. Further, the common national consciousness so created (it is assumed) would be equal in strength to the particular ethnic consciousness of each of the country's citizens. This third set of mosaic assumptions is even more problematic than the first two, on several counts. First, it fails to indicate the specific nature of the common, national culture which emerges in the society. Whose cultural norms, legal and ethical standards, institutional forms, and language(s) would govern the conduct of public life? Except in its most radical (multinationhood) interpretation, what the mosaic ideology *really* assumes in public life is an (empirically, highly improbable) melting pot. A second set of inherent problems arises from the internal contradiction between the objectives of ethnocultural distinctiveness, on the one hand, and full and equal participation in public life, on the other. Here, the long-accumulated evidence from the study of ethnic relations clearly demonstrates that maintenance of ethnic distinctiveness requires geo-ethnic segregation and restriction on participation in public life, while the development of national consciousness and commitment requires extensive ethnic interaction through full and equal participation in public life.

Clearly, as an ideology of ethnic integration, the mosaic model poses formidable problems of implementation in the current Canadian context. The next question, then, concerns the extent to which the adaptations to the mosaic model built into the federal government's multicultural policy have improved its applicability to the reality of Canada's multicultural society.

The initial statement of Canada's federal multicultural policy by Prime Minister Trudeau (*House of Commons Debates*, October 8, 1971) suggest that some of the (above-mentioned) problems inherent in the mosaic ideology were recognized, and that an attempt was made to deal with them in a way deemed appropriate to the Canadian context. Firstly, with regard to the variable nature of the desire of ethnic units to maintain distinctive ethnocultures, the policy statement deviated from the mosaic ideology by making it clear that this was a *voluntary* matter, both for the individual and for the ethnic collectivity. Secondly, with regard to the contradiction between the objectives of maintenance of ethnic distinctiveness, on the one hand, and full and equal participation in Canadian society, on the other, the policy statement adopted a compromise position which posited a clear division between public and private life sectors and which relegated maintenance of distinctive *minority* ethnocultures entirely to the private sphere. Further, the policy guaranteed equal opportunities for all citizens, regardless of ethnic classification, in public life. Thirdly, with regard to the necessity for culturally specific norms, institutions, and language(s) in public life, the policy statement again deviated from the mosaic model: it explicitly offered bilingualism (English and French) and implicitly assumed (parallel) biculturalism. The latter aspects of the multicultural policy are inherently problematic as they clearly negate the equalitarian ethnos of the mosaic ideology. What is probably most problematic, however, is that the multicultural policy says nothing and does nothing (to paraphrase

Bullivant) about existing racial/ethnic inequality in Canada. Thus the long-term effects of structural racism, such as the "welfare colonialism" of Canada's indigenous peoples, and the virtual absence of representation among Canadian elites of visible minorities is nowhere addressed in the multicultural policy statement.

The inherent problems and contradictions of the mosaic ideology as societal ideal and as government policy are clearly expressed at the level of societal reality. Here, the built-in problem of reconciling the principles of equality of societal opportunity and freedom of (distinctive) ethnocultural expression is variously articulated in the ofttimes conflicting demands of different ethnic collectivities. Spokespersons for long-oppressed and racially discriminated against minorities such as Canada's indigenous peoples and visible immigrants point out that the unduly expressive (roots and belongingness) emphasis of the present multicultural policy fails to take account of their more immediate, instrumental needs. In the case of Canada's indigenous peoples (initially excluded, under the policy rubric), spokespersons argue that their special status as Canada's original peoples is negated by the policy. Thus they have rejected multiculturalism out of hand and have chosen instead to lobby for constitutional recognition of their treaty and aboriginal rights.

Proponents of multilingualism and multiculturalism are adamantly opposed to the bilingual framework within which the multicultural policy is couched and they continue to argue, on the assumption that language and culture are indivisible, that the policy perpetuates the minority status of non-English and non-French ethnic collectivities in Canada. A conflicting view, based on a similar line of argument, is put forward by French supporters of bilingualism and biculturalism, notably Guy Rocher and Claude Ryan. They contend that the multicultural context renders bilingualism culturally meaningless, jeopardizes the equal charter groups status of the French, with the English, as "partners in Confederation" and undermines the foundation for national unity which the Royal Commission on Bilingualism and Biculturalism was designed to re-create. A more radical position, rooted in the same kinds of criticisms, is that put forward by Québécois and other supporters of sovereignty-association who argue that Quebecers will never gain equality and national self-determination within Canadian federalism.

To staunch supporters of the liberal democratic view, on the one hand, and the neo-Marxist perspective, on the other, the emphasis on cultural diversity at the very core of the concept of multiculturalism is anathema. Proponents from both of these camps oppose nurturance of ethno-cultural distinctiveness because they view ethnic value differences as well as differential ethnic ties and loyalties as inherently divisive social forces.

From the liberal democratic perspective (Porter *et al., op. cit.*), perpetuation of distinctive ethnocultures is opposed on the grounds that it impedes the development of a strong national consciousness. From the neo-Marxist view (for example, as articulated by Case, 1977), it is similarly opposed because it allegedly prevents the development of class-consciousness.

According to Burnet (*op. cit.*, 1981, p. 31) possibly the largest category of critics consists of those who oppose the multicultural *policy* on the grounds that it constitutes a *political* program, with clearly designed political means and ends, rather than a serious attempt to implement the mosaic ideology. Among the strongest of these critics is the sociologist Karl Peter (1978, 1979), who argues that the multicultural policy is a policy of appeasement and containment, i.e., a political strategy designed to appease the expressive cultural concerns of the other ethnic groups through multicultural programs and to appease the linguistic concerns of the French Canadians through official bilingualism. At the same time, Peter contends, the conflicting instrumental demands for ethnic equality in *political* and *economic* as well as in cultural terms, put forward by each of these constituencies, are contained. However, Peter predicts, containment cannot work, in the long term. For, he contends, we are already witnessing the organization of collective Francophone interests across class lines in Quebec, and the trend of these activities is clearly towards national self-determination. The emergence of the independent Francophone Quebec collectivity, argues Peter, will be the inevitable result. As for the rest of Canada's ethnic collectivities, Peter argues that

> *true multiculturalism [can be achieved through the] mobilization of intellectual resources and political powers on the part of all ethnic groups put into the service of revitalizing and reconstructing a Canada for the 21st century – a Canada that is built by all for the benefit of all. (1979, p. 20)*

At the time of writing, the prospects for "true multiculturalism" in Peter's terms are a long way from realization. Indeed, in the thralls of the present constitutional debate, we are witnessing just the opposite, i.e., a disturbing trend towards ethnic and regional fragmentation. Demands for national self-determination put forward by organizations and coalitions representing the interests of Canada's indigenous peoples; the unflagging efforts of the supporters of the Québécois sovereignty-association to increase public support for their cause; and the threats of cessation by the Western provinces are in the forefront of an already inflamed public consciousness, stirred out of complacency by the snowballing effects of separatist claims and demands. At present, however, the likelihood that Canada's fragile mosaic will be multiply fractured seems no closer to reality than the likelihood that a true (egalitarian) Canadian mosaic will be realized in the foreseeable future.

NOTES

*   This essay is an abridged and revised version of "The Semantics of Multiculturalism," a paper presented for the Consciousness and Inquiry Conference, jointly sponsored by the Canadian Ethnology Society, the National Museum of Man, SSHRC of Canada and the University of Western Ontario, at Spencer Hall, London, Ontario. March 29–April 1, 1981.

1.   In response to continuing pressure exerted by proponents of the social scientific concept of ethnicity—as equally applicable to all peoples—multicultural programmes have been expanded to include all Canadian ethnic collectivities under the funding rubric.

2.   At the level of social reality, the reference in the quote is to events and programmes like Toronto's annual "Caravan," which encourage ethnic voyeurism through the display of ethnic exotica rather than encouraging any real understanding of different and *ever changing* cultural lifeways.

REFERENCES

Anderson, A.B., and J.S. Frideres. 1981. *Ethnicity in Canada: Theoretical Perspectives*. Toronto: Buttersworth.

Berry, J.W., R. Kahn, and D.M. Taylor. 1977. *Multiculturalism and Ethnic Attitudes in Canada*. Ottawa: Minister of Supply and Services Canada.

Bourassa, R. 1971. "Objections to Multiculturalism." Letter to Prime Minister Trudeau in *Le Devoir*, November 17, 1971.

Breton, Raymond. 1978. "Institutional Completeness of Ethnic Communities and the Personal Relations of Immigrants," *American Journal of Sociology* 70, 103–25.

Brotz, H. 1980. "Multiculturalism in Canada: A Muddle." *Canadian Public Policy* VI, no. 1 (Winter), 41–6.

Bullivant, B.M. 1981. "Multiculturalism—Pluralist Orthodoxy or Ethnic Hegemony." *Canadian Ethnic Studies* XIII, no. 2, 1–22.

Burnet, J. 1975. "Multiculturalism, Immigration and Racism." *Canadian Ethnic Studies* 7, 35–9.

———. 1976. "Ethnicity: Canadian Experience and Policy." *Sociological Focus* 9, no. 2 (April), 199–207.

———. 1978. "The Policy of Multiculturalism within a Bilingual Framework: A Stocktaking." *Canadian Ethnic Studies* X, no. 2, 107–13.

———. 1981. "The Social and Historical Context of Ethnic Relations." In *A Canadian Social Psychology of Ethnic Relations*, edited by R.C. Gardner and R. Kalin, 17–35. Agincourt: Methuen.

Canadian Bill of Rights. 1960. An Act passed by the Parliament of Canada and assented to August 10, 1960.

Case, F.I. 1977. *Racism and National Consciousness*. Toronto: Plowshare Press.

Constitution Act, 1981. Proposed resolution respecting the constitution of Canada, put forward by the Special Joint Committee on the Constitution.

Douglas, R.A.S. 1979. Cited in J. Leavy, "Working Paper for a Conference on Minority Rights," 11–14, presented at York University, Downsview, October, 1979.

Glickman, Y. 1976. "Organization Indicators and Social Correlates of Collective Jewish Identity." Ph.D. dissertation, Dept. of Sociology, University of Toronto.

Henry, F. 1977. *The Dynamics of Racism in Toronto: A Preliminary Report*. Downsview: York University.

House of Commons Debates. 1971. Statement of Prime Minister Trudeau, October 8.

Hughes, D.R., and E. Kallen. 1974. *The Anatomy of Racism: Canadian Dimensions*. Montreal: Harvest House.

Isajiw, W.W. 1980. Report of a Conference on Minority Rights, York University, February 29. Sponsored by the Canadian Human Rights Foundation.

———. 1981. "Social Evolution and the Values of Multiculturalism." Paper presented at the Ninth Biennial Conference of the Canadian Ethnic Studies Association, Edmonton, Alberta, October 14–17.

Kallen, E. 1978. "An Evaluation of the Visiting Professors and Visiting Lecturers Programme (Canadian Ethnic Studies)." Report submitted to the Multicultural Directorate, Dept. of Secretary of State, Ottawa, August, 1978.

_____. 1981. "Academics, Politics, and Ethnics." *Canadian Ethnic Studies* XIII, no. 2, 112–23.

_____. 1981. "The Semantics of Multiculturalism." Paper presented at the "Consciousness and Inquiry" Conference, jointly sponsored by the National Museum of Man, the Canadian Ethnology Society, the SSHRC of Canada, and the University of Western Ontario, London, Ontario, March 29–April 1.

Kelner, M., and E. Kallen. 1974. "The Multicultural Policy: Canada's Response to Ethnic Diversity." *Journal of Comparative Sociology* no. 22, 21–4.

Peter, K. 1978. "Multicultural Politics, Money and the Conduct of Canadian Ethnic Studies." *Canadian Ethnic Studies Association Bulletin* 5, 2–3.

_____. 1979. "The Myth of Multiculturalism and Other Political Fables." Paper presented at the Canadian Ethnic Studies Conference, Vancouver, B.C., October 11–13.

Porter, J. 1965. *The Vertical Mosaic.* Toronto: University of Toronto Press.

_____. 1975. "Ethnic Pluralism in Canadian Perspective." In *Ethnicity: Theory and Experience*, edited by N. Glazer and D. Moynihan, 267–304. Cambridge: Harvard University Press.

_____. 1979. "Melting Pot or Mosaic: Revolution or Reversion?" In *The Measure of Canadian Society*, 139–62. Toronto: Gage.

Rocher, G. 1976. "Multiculturalism: The Doubts of a Francophone." In *Report of the Second Canadian Conference on Multiculturalism*, 47–53. Ottawa: Canadian Consultative Council on Multiculturalism, 1976.

Royal Commission on Bilingualism and Biculturalism. 1970. Report: Book Four, *The Cultural Contributions of the Other Ethnic Groups*. Ottawa: Queen's Printer.

Wilson, J. 1978. "Come, Let Us Reason Together." In *Black Presence in Multi-Ethnic Canada*, edited by V. D'Oyley. Toronto: O.I.S.E.

Yusyk, P. 1964. Senatorial Address, May 3, 1964.

TONY HALL

ABORIGINAL PEOPLE AND THE MEECH LAKE ACCORD: CRITICAL PERSPECTIVES

FROM THE MEECH LAKE PRIMER "WHAT ARE WE? CHOPPED LIVER?"

The scope of the first ministers' unanimous accords formulated at Meech Lake and the Langevin Block, and the short duration of the negotiations, shocked many Aboriginal people. The "blow" was especially "tremendous" for the Native leaders that were closest to the previous negotiations.[1] They felt they had been duped—that the March meeting had been an "orchestrated failure" to clear the way for the culmination of the bigger deal at Meech Lake. In the *Bulletin* of the Assembly of First Nations, George Erasmus was reported as having said that the Prime Minister and Premiers "cooked up" the basis of their accord the previous November, and that they "never intended to come to an agreement on Aboriginal rights." Chief Erasmus' comments appear in a story under the title "Constitutional Accord Makes for Disaster."[2]

After four years of being repeatedly lectured by White officials that nothing new could be put into the constitution until exhaustive negotiations clarified all the implications of the added language, Native people learned that the first ministers were unwilling to apply these same standards to themselves in their own private dealings. Hundreds of lines of dense constitutional language of the most significant kind were suddenly unveiled and presented as a seamless web of compromise that could not be changed.

The federal government immediately began advertising the accord as a constitutional fait accompli. A flyer was circulated throughout the country in the mailing of baby bonus cheques, for instance, informing Canadians that "[t]he Accord completes the process of constitutional renewal that began in 1981 .... The 1987 Constitutional Accord concludes our evolution to nationhood in a way that respects the traditions of our country and its people."[3] This kind of pronouncement was hardly calculated to instill confidence in Native people that the new constitution would ever become a vehicle through which they might realize their unfulfilled hopes of attaining a measure of justice and security for their posterity.

Hence, while the first ministers' abandonment without resolution of formal negotiations on Aboriginal matters seemed like a setback for Aboriginal aspirations, news of the Meech Lake accord left Native leaders feeling far more seriously isolated from the process of constitutional renewal. The accord, it seemed perfectly clear, would have the effect of closing off permanently so many possibilities for future movement towards constructive reform. "We could not believe that [the first ministers] were doing that to us," testified George Erasmus.[4]

But remarks made by Premier Don Getty in Ottawa on July 1st, the day before the first ministers reassembled at the Langevin Block to work their Meech Lake document into a legal text, could only confirm Native peoples' worst suspicions about what the accord held in store for them. Alberta's premier as much as proclaimed that with Meech Lake his provincial government was slamming the door on the possibility of making any future constitutional compromises in the area of Aboriginal rights. *The Edmonton Sun* reported his comments as follows:

> Getty said the recent First Ministers' meeting on aboriginal rights is a perfect example of the constitutional unfairness that could drive Alberta to consider separation.
>
> The premier said if Alberta had been forced to accept entrenchment of native rights in the Constitution, separatism would have been seriously considered.
>
> "We would have gone home and talked about maybe having to pull out of the bloody country. I have never thought you go about changing Canada by having 50 per cent of the people dominate the other 50 per cent," the Alberta premier said here last night ....
>
> Getty said an example of why Alberta insists that change take place occurred at the March 26 meeting on whether to guarantee native rights in the Constitution.
>
> At the meeting, Mulroney and the premiers backing constitutionally guaranteed native rights tried to use the current [amending] formula to "bludgeon" Alberta, B.C. and Newfoundland into supporting them, Getty said.

The bid failed, but Getty was adamant last night he fears a recurrence
unless the changes proposed by the Meech Lake pact are signed, sealed and
delivered at today's meeting.[5]

It is clear from Premier Getty's perspective the rights and interests of
Albertans generally are diametrically opposed to the rights and interests
of Aboriginal people. He has no doubt about who must prevail. Similarly,
he leaves little doubt that his interest in signing the Meech Lake documents
had more to do with his desire to contain recognition of Aboriginal claims
than to affirm the distinct character of Quebec society.

The provisions at the heart of the Meech Lake accord that define
Quebec as a distinct society, and that would empower the government of
Quebec to preserve and promote the distinct identity of that province, drew
sharply negative response from a number of Native commentators.[6] It was
galling for them to see such ready willingness among the first ministers to
afford Quebecers the same kind of recognition that had been withheld from
Native groups. "How can the distinctness of Quebec people be explicitly
recognized following the continual denial of aboriginal rights?" asked
Haida leader Miles Richardson.[7]

To make Quebec the one and only society in Canada that could be
defined in the constitution as "distinct" seemed like a distortion of history
and a misrepresentation of present realities. Aboriginal people, some of
whom still speak Aboriginal languages that are often uniquely distinct to
this country, felt themselves once again brushed aside by Euro-Canadian
politicians whose respect for cultural pluralism seemed to begin and end
with acknowledgement of their own major linguistic division. The fact
that the accord would entrench the French and English languages as the
exclusive expression of "the fundamental characteristic of Canada" added
weight to Aboriginal peoples' contention that the Meech Lake accord
symbolically confirmed their exclusion from the key theatres of Canadian
public life. The exclusion was one that might eventually find strong
reflection in the course of Canadian jurisprudence and in the institutional
design of Canadian self-government.

The "distinct society" provision would seem even more inequitable if it
proved that the language and the legal thinking behind the innovation were
actually derived from previous unrealized efforts to define more precisely
the relationship between Native people and the institutions of Canadian
federalism. There is evidence, however, to suggest that this indeed may be
the case. In the British parliamentary debates on the Canada Bill in 1982,
for instance, Sir George Braine explained:

The Native people of Canada are ethnically and culturally distinct peoples who deserve a separate status within Canada .... A greater degree of self-government will achieve for them the most important objective, which is the continuation in future generations of their distinct identity.[8]

In his questioning of George Erasmus in the Joint Committee of the Senate and House of Commons on the 1987 Constitutional Accord, Liberal MP Keith Penner expressed his belief that the idea for the "distinct society" provision originated in the key recommendation of the parliamentary report on Indian Self-Government tabled in 1983.[9] Penner, who was Chairperson of the Committee that produced the report, described the intensity of the debate leading to the decision to advocate that "Indian First Nation governments would form a distinct order of government in Canada."[10] The key phrase in the accord about the Quebec government's powers to "preserve and promote" the province's distinct identity could well have been borrowed directly from section 21(i) of the Cree-Naskapi (of Quebec) Act, legislation of the Parliament of Canada passed in 1984 to implement some features of the James Bay and Northern Quebec Agreement. The germane sections empower Cree and Naskapi Indian band governments "to promote and preserve the culture, values and traditions of the Crees or Naskapis." These powers were granted in recognition that "each band's people are distinct and the culture, values and traditions which make them distinct are of concern to them in their daily functions and activities."[11]

Regardless of whether or not the "distinct society" concept originates in the politics of Aboriginal affairs, the judges that would ultimately be called upon to interpret the new legal language would probably be compelled to study the constitutional use of the word "distinct" as it has historically been used by Crown officials in relationship to North American Indians. The case, Mohegan Indians v. Connecticut colony (1749), for instance, might be consulted. The Privy Councillors who rendered judgment ruled that the Mohegans together constituted a distinct jurisdiction from the colony.

The Indians, though living amongst the king's subjects in these countries, are a separate and distinct people from them, they are treated with as such, they have a polity of their own, they make peace or war with any nation of Indians when they think fit, without control from the English.

It is apparent the Crown looks upon them not as subjects but as a distinct people, for they are mentioned as such throughout Queen Anne's and his present majesty's commission by which we now sit.[12]

As Native leaders were quick to point out, the problem of constitutionally designating a particular constituency as a distinct society, or of specifying a definition of the fundamental characteristic of Canada, is that those peoples not directly covered by the legal provisions are implicitly relegated to the periphery of Canadian statecraft.

At the Langevin Block meeting the first ministers added a provision titled section 16 to the Meech Lake accord. It stipulated that nothing in the "fundamental characteristic of Canada" section affected those parts of the constitution specifically mentioning Aboriginal people or multiculturalism. Rumor has it that Premier Howard Pawley of Manitoba demanded this protection for Aboriginal people while Premier David Peterson, pressured especially by the large Italian-Canadian community in Toronto, sought to defend multiculturalism. A more cynical view would be that section 16 was added as a means to avert any court challenge to the Meech Lake accord on the grounds that it transgressed the spirit and intent of section 35.1, an amendment to the Constitution Act, 1982.

The addition of section 16 aroused ire in several quarters. It worried women's groups whose leaders logically asked why the provisions on gender equality in the Charter of Rights and Freedoms had not also been exempted from the "distinct society" section of the accord. Some feminists saw in the first ministers' actions a constitutional change that would place women at the bottom of "a hierarchy of rights." And Aboriginal groups saw little in section 16 to ease their anxieties. The first ministers once again seemed to be acting on behalf of Native people without including them in the process. Moreover, by grouping the provisions on Aboriginal rights together with the provisions on multiculturalism, the first ministers seemed to be throwing Native people into the same constitutional pot as ethnic minorities. Native people justifiably reject most government efforts to deal with them through the ideological and administrative channels of multiculturalism, a vehicle most readily directed at the cultural requirements of newer Canadians whose first language is neither French nor English.[13]

Section 16 can be criticized further because of the deeper assumptions its inclusion seems to reflect.[14] By describing Native people as separate and apart from the effects of the "fundamental characteristic" section of the accord, there is the symbolic suggestion that Aboriginal groups are not to be included in the dynamic core of Canada. The provision, therefore, gives new articulation to old attitudes informed by a view that Aboriginal cultures are largely inadaptable; they are seen as static, even primitive clumps of humanity that are curious anachronisms in the modern world. Unfortunately, there is really nothing in the Meech Lake accord to give any assurance that its authors have rid themselves of such damaging assumptions long engendered, among other causes, by the way Canadian history has been taught.[15]

While Section 16 speaks of isolating Aboriginal peoples from the effects of that part of the accord defining Canada's fundamental characteristic, there is nothing to exclude Native groups from the many other provisions of the Meech Lake documents. The accord's section on national shared-cost programmes, for instance, has important implications for Indians living within provincial boundaries. If a provincial government was to opt out of such a programme with compensation, as the accord would entitle it to do under certain conditions, what would be the impact on Indian bands in the province? Could these Native people continue to participate in the national programme or would they be tied to the decision of the provincial legislature? The Meech Lake accord is mute on the question, an issue that clearly would be of crucial significance for the future of Aboriginal governments.

Moreover, the spending formula outlined in the accord would entrench a structure without any room for developing Aboriginal governments to make their influence felt, however modestly, in this important field of national decision making. The same could be said of virtually all aspects of the accord. In the area of immigration, in the sections dealing with the appointment of Senators and Supreme Court judges and in the provisions for reform of the key federal institutions of national self-government, Meech Lake is constructed as if Aboriginal nationalities exist outside the democratic structures of Canada. Furthermore, in virtually every facet of its design, Meech Lake would set in motion a transfer of powers from the federal government to the provincial governments.[16]

If the unfolding of Aboriginal politics during the 1980s demonstrates any consistent lesson, it is the following: Aboriginal peoples who currently lack explicit recognition of their own inherent powers of collective self-government must continue to rely heavily on a strong and assertive federal authority to defend and assert Aboriginal claims against the counterclaims of provincial jurisdiction. The Meech Lake accord reflects a failure on the part of Prime Minister Mulroney to live up to this responsibility just as Prime Minister Trudeau yielded similarly in the negotiations of November

5, 1981. What must now be understood about Meech Lake, moreover, is that it would seriously incapacitate the federal government from ever again effectively fulfilling the Crown's old obligations to be vindicator and protector of the Aboriginal interest in Canada.

Meech Lake's yielding of federal prerogatives is nowhere so readily apparent as in the provision that would require unanimous consent of provincial legislatures to reform the rules governing democratic representation in the House of Commons and the Senate. The symbolism of this provision is that the federal government is created out of the deeper constitutional roots of provincial governments, each of which retains a veto power over how Canada's Parliament is structured. It is almost certain that this veto power would be employed by one or more provincial legislatures if ever there was a move towards modest reform of the House of Commons or the Senate to create a few entrenched places for the entry of elected officials primarily accountable to Aboriginal constituencies in various regions of the country. Without such an innovation, how is there ever to be a responsible integration of Aboriginal governments with the larger democratic institutions of Canadian self-government?

The fate that the Meech Lake accord would deal the residents of the Northwest Territories and the Yukon demonstrates a similar example of the results that flow from abandonment of the federal prerogative.[17] Control over the constitutional future of these federal territories was simply traded away to the premiers of B.C., Alberta, and Saskatchewan largely so that their governments could gain a new political lever to regulate the northward development of provincial hinterlands into the arctic. This factor probably also figured in the bargaining strategy of Premier Bourassa of Quebec whose political career has largely been built on advancing the cause of northern development.[18]

The other side of the new provincial veto powers regulating if, when, and how the federal territories became provinces is that territorial citizens are correspondingly blocked from having any formal vote in this same process. Of all the accord's transgressions, this feature is the most overt example of how the deal would place the greatest burden of "Canadian unity" on the most effectively disenfranchised elements of the citizenry. Native people, who still constitute a large percentage of the electorate in the federal territories, face double jeopardy from the accord, especially now that the government of Quebec seems to have joined the side of the assassins of Louis Riel.

AFTER MEECH LAKE

The closing off of formal constitutional talks with Aboriginal delegates followed by the affrontive Meech Lake accord added weight to an already-heavy burden of frustration and alienation that too often comes by virtue of being a Native person in Canada. While the articulation of the new constitution had been seen as an ominous development in some Native circles, a significant portion of Aboriginal people had gotten behind their more optimistic spokespeople. They chose to hold to the hope that more equitable arrangements could be reached for their people through political efforts to elaborate Canada's fundamental laws; they had counted their vote on the side of confidence in the goodwill of Canadians as the nation embarked on its first exercise of full self-government finally cut free from the old imperial structures of the Mother Country. But now that hope and that optimism too, however fragile, were undermined by the stark suggestion that for Aboriginal people Canada's new constitution had merged into the familiar old stream of broken promises. During the late 1980s tempers flared and tension mounted at a number of flashpoints of confrontation.

A catalyst for the re-emergence of more strident forms of Aboriginal activism, reminiscent of the rawer kinds of protests that took place in the early 1970s, was the Olympic torch run sponsored by Petro-Canada. During the autumn of 1987 and the winter of 1988 small groups of Native people and their supporters across Canada met the procession of runners carrying the Olympic torch to the 1988 Calgary Winter Games.[19] While the demonstrations were in the first instance to show solidarity with the Lubicon Crees' efforts to gain an Indian reserve for themselves in northern Alberta, the range of expressed grievances quickly widened. As the run proceeded the protesters replaced Petro-Canada's slogan of "Share the Flame" with "Share the Shame."

While the Lubicon struggle became something of a rallying point for the broader movement to affirm the human rights of Aboriginal people in Canada, the long, unnaturally hot summer of 1988 saw Aboriginal groups in many localities giving physical expression to their grievances. At Kahnawake, Quebec, RCMP officers and arms-bearing Mohawks only barely held back from violent confrontation over clashing interpretations of tax laws governing the sale of American cigarettes on the reserve.[20] At Goose Bay in Labrador, Innu Indians held protest demonstrations on the runway of the jet fighter base there, asserting their unceded Aboriginal interest in lands made less fruitful because of the destructive effects on wildlife of low-level jet training. In Northern Ontario, members of the Teme-Augama Anishinabai Band set up a blockade to stop the building of a logging road through the heart of their ancestral lands.[21] Their action marked a new phase of their fifteen-year-old court action to gain recognition as a distinct Indian band that has never signed a treaty covering its traditional hunting territories.[22]

Gary Potts, the erudite Chief of the Teme-Augama Anishinabai, announced the blockade from the steps of the Ontario Legislature during the last day of the Toronto Economic Summit. Among the speakers sharing the podium with Chief Potts were Aboriginal leaders engaged in most of the major hot spots of tension involving Aboriginal assertion of rights to land and jurisdiction. Haida leader Miles Richardson spoke of his people's struggle to protect with environmentalists the virgin forests of the South Moresby region in British Columbia. Also presented were Lubicon Chief Bernard Ominayak, Kahnawake Chief Joe Norton, Inuit leader John Amagoalik, and George Erasmus, National Chief of the AFN. The intent of bringing together these individuals was clearly to reveal the unifying patterns that make national issues of the various local struggles, to demonstrate Aboriginal willingness to stand together in more strident forms of activism, and to assert the various arguments in a context where the implications for Canada's international reputation became evident. As George Erasmus asserted from the steps of Queen's Park, Indians for a long time

> *thought that reason was going to work. That kind of politics doesn't work in Canada. We must change our actions. We can't change theirs until we change ours ....* [23] *We are a people with tremendous patience but that patience is stretched so thin we must try other kinds of activities.* [24]

These demonstrations of Aboriginal political will were made against a background of a truly appalling human tragedy that sets Native people at the extreme end of virtually every index of social and economic dislocation in Canada. While the last two decades have seen the entry of a small core of Native people into the middle class, the largest number of Indians, Inuit, and Métis still lack any grasp of the levers that regulate the engines of economic productivity in Canada. In many northern communities in particular there has been little success, if not outright backward movement, in mitigating the ravages of alcohol abuse, drug abuse, and family violence.

Statistics on the suicides of Native youths and on the incarceration of Native people—four to seven times the national average—reveal absolutely unconscionable levels of inequity.

Against this background where police, courts, jails, and social workers have become major regulators of the relationship between many Native people and the Canadian state, a series of episodes in the late 1980s suddenly placed a public spotlight on the tremendous suffering wrought by bias in the criminal justice system.[25] The inquiry into the wrongful conviction for murder of Nova Scotian Micmac Donald Marshall, the exposé on the woefully ill-managed investigation that shielded the murderer of Helen Betty Osborne for almost two decades, the killing by a policeman's bullet of J.J. Harper in the streets of Winnipeg[26], and the alleged abuse and neglect by Hull police of accident victim Minnie Sutherland[27] each made haunting statements about the kind of mistreatment too often afforded Native people by officers of the law in Canada.

Given the proven propensity of some of Canada's first ministers to deal with Aboriginal groups as constitutional misfits ill adapted for either their own self-government or for direct participation in the broader exercise of Canadian self-government, it is fair to ask if the problems of law enforcement in the streets are connected to the difficulties in law making at the highest level. What signals are the law makers sending the law enforcers about the need to respect the individual and collective human rights of Native people in Canada? Smokey Bruyere, President of the Native Council of Canada, had little doubt about the answer in the autumn of 1988. He charged that the Meech Lake accord has "revived the worst prejudices of colonialism." He continued:

> *Native people are furious and frustrated. And as the years go by, native people will decide there is no hope or worth to the constitutional reform process. They will decide on more direct action.*[28]

Bruyere's remarks reflect the anxiety shared by many Native people that the best part of their precious political energies over the previous decade had been expended in rather fruitless dialogue with predominantly unhearing government officials. The experience had forced on Aboriginal observers recognition of the fundamental absence of will on the part of the country's political leadership to confront seriously the underlying structural problems in the federal system that so consistently seem to hold Native groups at the edges of the major forums of Canadian political, economic, and social life. Perhaps the most macabre symbol of the renewed thrust to marginalize the Native agenda for change was Meech Lake's replacement of Aboriginal issues with the subject of fish as one of two priorities for future ministers' conferences. The fact that the leaders of the federal Liberal and NDP parties would not make their support for Meech Lake conditional even on amendment of this particularly offensive element of the agreement revealed to Native people once again how easily their interests can be traded off by national politicians intent on courting the support of larger, more cohesive, and more influential constituencies.

The most disturbing commentary on the possible consequences that might flow from the failures in negotiation was delivered by George Erasmus in Edmonton at the 1988 annual meeting of the AFN. As was widely reported in the press[29], he addressed the assembled chiefs as follows:

> *Canada, we have something to say to you — we have a warning for you. We want to let you know that you're playing with fire. We may be the last generation of leaders that is prepared to sit down and peacefully negotiate our concerns with you. Canada, if you do not deal with this generation of leaders, then we cannot promise that you are going to like the kind of violent political action that we can just about guarantee the next generation is going to bring to you.*

Were Chief Erasmus' words too strong? Did he not overstate the extent of the absence of progress in negotiations? After all, had not the 1980s seen the emergence of Aboriginal issues to unprecedented heights of visibility in national politics? Does not this fact alone vindicate the process even if there has been very little concretely to show for all the high-profile talks between Aboriginal leaders and the first ministers?

These questions, of course, defy the possibility of categoric response. A possible index of the relative status of Aboriginal issues in national politics, however, was the televised leaders' debates leading up to the federal election of November 1988. A reporter from Global TV drew the leaders into a discussion of Aboriginal affairs during the last three minutes of a six-hour event composed of three debating hours in French and three in English. Like the legal text of the Meech Lake accord itself, the televised debate reveals a political view of Aboriginal affairs as a kind of afterthought to be briefly considered once the more pressing concerns of the day are addressed. In spite of how integrally Aboriginal affairs impinged into the relatively new forum of constitutional politics during the 1980s, then, it is striking how marginal Aboriginal matters remained in the more familiar theatres of national decision making.

A related argument that could be advanced in defense of the process is the fact that the first ministers' meeting on Aboriginal affairs did succeed in introducing the concept of Aboriginal self-government, a novel idea to many at the beginning of the 1980s[30], into the general currency of political exchange in Canada. Even if the concept was not explicitly introduced into the constitution, Canadians were made more familiar with the notion that Native peoples should have a larger say in determining their own collective futures within Canada. Of course a complicating factor is the vast range of political options that the term "Aboriginal self-government" can be employed to describe.

On the one hand the phrase can describe the transformation of Indian reserves into municipal-like structures whose citizens assume delegated responsibilities from the higher authority of the federal Parliament or provincial legislatures. The agreement concluded in 1988 covering the Sechelt band in British Columbia is of this type. At the other end of the spectrum is the idea of Aboriginal self-government as a distinct or third order of government in Canada. The Sechelt models sees Aboriginal self-government as a right created by Parliament—as a "contingent right"—while the latter is founded on an understanding that treats Aboriginal self-determination as an inherent right rooted in the continuity of Aboriginal peoplehood from a time predating the existence of Canada.

Not surprisingly, government officials in Canada tend overwhelmingly to see the future of Aboriginal self-government more along the lines of the Sechelt model, while most Aboriginal leaders feel the responsibility to hold to the position that they represent peoples who retain the inherent right of self-determination—a right that must never be bargained away. Between 1983 and 1987 a process of first ministers' meetings developed that began to clarify the tensions between these different conceptions. The ground was being prepared for a political compromise that would establish a workable basis for Aboriginal self-determination within the framework of Canadian federalism. In March of 1987, however, Prime Minister Mulroney unilaterally terminated that unfulfilled process with no provisions to continue the negotiations at some later date, or within an alternative political context.

While the termination held the possibility for continuing the process in uncertain abeyance, the terms of the Meech Lake accord seemed drastically to reduce the range of latitude within which future compromise could take place on the crucial issue of Aboriginal self-government. Basically, the accord advanced a vision of a Canadian state without the structural capacity to accommodate the inclusion of a distinct order of Aboriginal government. Instead, the accord was based on an idea of Canada as a pact between the two major linguistic groups and between ten regionally defined distinct societies. Within this rigid framework, with each province gaining veto power over the structural reform of federal institutions, what room would be available for the future expression of the Aboriginal creativity in political, economic, and cultural terms?

The Meech Lake accord allowed Native people little prospect that their Aboriginal governments would ever attain recognition as part of the fundamental characteristic of Canada. Instead a hidden agenda of Meech Lake seemed to be that Aboriginal governments must always be held to the status of a junior order of government with powers derived from the higher authority of federal-provincial structures. For Native people seeking to break free of the legacy of colonialism, what real progress was there to behold in such a prospect?

Of course all these arguments could be turned on their heads if the Meech Lake accord was significantly to advance contemplation among thoughtful Canadians of the parallel requirements that should fall on governments to promote the distinct identity of Aboriginal groups and of the French-speaking minority in the northern portion of North America. It should be no more acceptable to abandon the former to a kind of laissez-faire than it would be to dismiss the historic responsibility to advance the vitality of the French fact in Canada. And yet by leaving Aboriginal governments as shadowy entities in Canadian constitutional law, and by disavowing any constitutional duty to preserve let alone to promote distinct Aboriginal societies, the authors of the Meech Lake accord leave Native groups stranded in inarticulated twilight zones of institutionalized marginalization. A particular difficulty imposed on Native people by these circumstances is the virtual impossibility of establishing a stable constitutional basis for the development of a distinct national system of Aboriginal education. Especially pressing is the need for a strong network of schools to reverse the tragically rapid process of Aboriginal language loss[31], to promote instead a national plan for Aboriginal language renewal.[32]

The failure of Canadian politicians to find workable constitutional adaptations to deal with these problems, and the more general failure in the collective imagination to comprehend Aboriginal self-government as a strengthening feature of a renewed pluralistic federalism, only advance the diffusion of Aboriginal affairs into international forums. Rather than setting a high standard for the world in the treatment of indigenous societies, Canada is instead developing a reputation for human rights violations in this emerging field of international law. If the assessment of Meech Lake's flaws clarifies this current failure in Canada's federal system, then the formulation of the accord may have served a constructive purpose after all.

The importance of finding precisely correct constitutional language to illuminate the ideals that should inform relationships between individuals, groups, and governments in Canada was given enlightened articulation in 1888 by Edward Blake before the Privy Council of the House of Lords in England. In the famous Indian Title Case that saw the governments of Ontario and Canada clash over conflicting interpretations of the rights of Aboriginal people[33], Blake introduced his assessment of the constitutional meaning of the crucial section 91(24) of the British North America Act. Of the document's contents he explained:

> *One sentence, one phrase, even one word, deals with a whole code or system of law or politics, disposes of national or sovereign attributes, makes and unmakes political communities, touches the ancient liberties and the private and public rights of millions of free men, and sets new limits to them all.*[34]

Blake's words serve as a sobering testimonial to the high responsibilities that fall on the shoulders of all parties with a role in transforming the fruits of constitutional deliberations in the 1980s into effective and fair constitutional language.

NOTES

1. The quoted words are from the testimony of George Erasmus. See the Senate of Canada, *Debates*, November 18, 1987.
2. *Assembly of First Nations Bulletin* 4, 7 (May/June 1987), 1.
3. See *The Sudbury Star*, July 27, 1987, 1; August 7, 1984, 4.
4. Senate of Canada, *Debates*, November 18, 1987, 2200.
5. *The Edmonton Sun*, June 2, 1987.

6. See evidence of Zebedee Nungak, *Minutes of Proceedings and Evidence of the Special Joint Committee of the Senate and House of Commons on the 1987 Constitutional Accord*, no. 3, August 5, 1987, 28: evidence of George Erasmus in ibid., no. 9, August 19, 1987; evidence of Ernie Daniels, Interim President of Prairie Treaty Nations Alliance, in Senate of Canada, *Debates*, December 16, 1987, 2458.

7. Richardson quoted in Ellie Kirzner, "Native Self-Rule Omens," *Now Magazine*, August 13–26, 1987, 9.

8. *Hansard*, February 23, 1982, 779–81.

9. Evidence of George Erasmus in *Special Joint Committee*, no. 3, August 19, 1987.

10. Canada, House of Commons, *Indian Self-Government in Canada: Report of the Special Committee*, 1983, 44.

11. Cree-Naskapi (of Quebec) Act, *Statutes of Canada*, vol. 1, Chapter 18, 1984. See also Cree-Naskapi Commission, *1986 Report of the Cree-Naskapi Commission* (Ottawa, 1987), 7.

12. J.H. Smith, *Appeals to the Privy Council from the American Plantations* (New York, 1950), 426, cited in James Youngblood Henderson, "The Doctrine of Aboriginal Rights in Western Legal Tradition," in *Quest for Justice*, 199.

13. See Douglas Sanders, "Article 27 and the Aboriginal Peoples of Canada," in *Canadian Human Rights Foundation, Multiculturalism and the Charter: A Legal Perspective* (Toronto, 1987), 155–66.

14. Much of the following is essentially the author's personal commentary on the Meech Lake accord. See Hall, *Special Joint Committee*, no. 14, August 27, 1987, 57–73, Appendix 1–17; Senate of Canada, *Proceedings of the Senate Submission Group on the Meech Lake Constitutional Accord*, no. 5, March 18, 1988, 50–60; Legislative Assembly of Ontario, *Hansard Official Report of Debates, Select Committee on Constitutional Reform, 1987 Constitutional Accord*, no. C-24, April 13, 1988, C-1243–1251; *The Toronto Star*, June 19, 1987, A21; Hall, "Who Speaks for Canada? The Meech Lake-Free Trade Connection," *Humanist Canada 21*, no. 1 (Summer 1988), 3–6.

15. See J.W. St. G. Walker, "The Indian in Canadian Historical Writing," *Canadian Historical Association, Historical Papers* (1971), 21–47; Walker, "The Indian in Canadian Historical Writing, 1972–1982," in *As Long as the Sun Shines*, 340–57; Sylvie Vincent and Bernard Arcand, *L'image de l'Amérindien dans les manuels scolaires du Québec* (Quebec, 1979).

16. Don Johnson, ed., *With a Bang, Not a Whimper, Pierre Trudeau Speaks Out* (Toronto, 1988).

17. See Senate of Canada, *Report of the Task Force on the Meech Lake Constitutional Accord and on the Yukon and the Northwest Territories* (Ottawa, 1988).

18. See Robert Bourassa, *Power from the North* (Scarborough, 1985).

19. See, for instance, *The Toronto Star*, December 20, 1987, A14.

20. See *The Globe and Mail*, August 2, 1988, A7.

21. *The Globe and Mail*, October 20, 1988, A7.

22. See James Cullingham, "Home and Native Lands," *Saturday Night* 98, no. 4 (April 1983), 7–11.

23. *The Globe and Mail*, June 22, 1988, A1.

24. *The Toronto Star*, June 22, 1988.

25. See "Special Report: A Canadian Tragedy," *Maclean's*, July 14, 1986.

26. *The Globe and Mail*, August 2, 1988, A7.

27. *The Ottawa Sun*, January 18, 1989, 2.

28. *The Globe and Mail*, September 26, 1988, A5.

29. See *The Toronto Star*, June 2, 1988; *The Ottawa Citizen*, June 4, 1988, A3.

30. See Senator Lowell Murray's account of the failure of the first ministers' conferences on Aboriginal affairs compared to the "success" of Meech Lake in *Choices* (Montreal, February 1988) (no pagination).

31. See Michael K. Foster, *Indigenous Languages in Canada* (Ottawa, 1982).

32. See Tony Hall, *The N'ungosuk Project: A Study in Aboriginal Language Renewal* (West Bay, 1987).

33. Joseph Schull, *Edward Blake*, Vol. 2, *Leader in Exile, 1881–1912* (Toronto, 1976), 103–11.

34. *The Ontario Lands Case: Arguments of Mr. Blake, Q.C., before the Privy Council* (Toronto, 1888), 6.

IRSHAD MANJI

THE PING-PONG ETHNIC POLITICS OF CONTEMPORARY QUEBEC

FROM RISKING UTOPIA: ON THE EDGE OF A NEW DEMOCRACY

[...] Witness, for example, the Montreal-area public schools that, in 1994, kicked out two Muslim students [Afra and Mariam Jalibi] for observing hijab, expulsions backed to no small degree by nationalist organizations, newspaper editorialists, and teachers' unions. (One of the schools implemented a strict dress code after the Muslim student enrolled. Both schools are run by Catholic boards. Subsequently, the Montreal Catholic School Commission ignored the Quebec Human Rights Commission, which ruled any hijab ban to be illegal.) Witness, as well, the Muslim School of Montreal, which required all female teachers, including non-Muslims, to don hijab in the name of reinforcing Islamic values. (The school principal insisted that each of the female teachers knew this to be a condition of employment. None, he said, voiced opposition. No matter, retorted Fatima Houda-Pepin, a Liberal member of Quebec's National Assembly. She argued that the condition itself constituted an "assault" on Canada's Charter of Rights and Freedoms. Houda-Pepin spoke not just as a politician but also as a practicing Muslim.) Above all, recall the words of former Quebec premier Jacques Parizeau. On referendum night in October 1995, when he directed blame at the "ethnic vote" for helping to defeat his separatist forces, Parizeau was targeting people like the Jalabis—who, it turns out, are not ready federalists.

Over the past two years, in fact, Afra's sympathies have heightened for Quebec's attempt to preserve its language. The reason? Living in Ottawa, where she is now completing a Master's degree in journalism, has opened her eyes to the Anglo tilt of Canada's capital city. Still, both Jalabis handle the corrosive beast of nationalism with asbestos gloves. Born in Syria, raised partly in Germany, and recently emigrated from Saudi Arabia, they shuttle between Canada and the Middle East — a practice that their mother has long encouraged to avoid romanticizing cultures.

How vexing, then, that to many Québécois, Afra and Mariam would be symbols of a hated multiculturalism. Hated not only because this policy emanates from enemy territory, Ottawa, and was legislated by a supposed turn-coat, Pierre Trudeau, but because it clashes with the provincial policy of interculturalism. "You have a patchwork or mosaic in multiculturalism," opined Madelaine Lussier, a senior Quebec official, in 1994. "But with multiculturalism, you have a common state." Quixotically presented to newcomers as a "moral contract," the paramountcy of the French language and the sovereignty of the National Assembly are not up for negotiation. Interculturalism, by Lussier's own analogy, parrots the melting pot ardor of the United States.

NEIL BISSOONDATH

THE TOLERANT SOCIETY VERSUS THE ACCEPTING SOCIETY

FROM SELLING ILLUSIONS: THE CULT OF MULTICULTURALISM IN CANADA

GLIMPSES BENEATH THE SURFACE

The results of the polls came as a shock to many.

The first, commissioned by the Canadian Council of Christians and Jews and conducted by Decima Research, was reported by *The Globe and Mail* in this way on December 14, 1993:

> *Canadians Want Mosaic to Melt,*
> *Survey Finds*
>
> *Respondents believe immigrants*
> *should adopt Canada's values*

> *Most Canadians believe the multicultural mosaic isn't working and should be replaced by a cultural melting pot, says a survey released today.*
>
> *About 72 percent of respondents believe that the long-standing image of Canada as a nation of communities, each ethnic and racial group preserving its identity with the help of government policy, must give way to the U.S. style of cultural absorption.*
>
> *The survey ... found Canadians are "increasingly intolerant" of demands made by ethnic groups, and are frustrated by "the lack of conformity" in Canadian society.*

"Canadians report a preference for 'homogenization' of the society through adoption by immigrants of Canada's values and way of life," the survey says.[1]

The *Montreal Gazette*, reporting on the same poll, on the same day, chose to highlight not the actual results of the poll but an interpretation of them:

Canadians Harbor "Latently Racist"
Attitudes: Poll

Most reject idea of cultural diversity, saying ethnics should try to fit in.[2]

However, each paper reported one important statistic in a different way. Fifty-four percent of Canadians, said the *Globe*, "believe the current immigration policy 'provides for a good balance of people,'" while the *Gazette*/Southam News report claimed instead that 54 percent "believe current immigration policy allows 'too many people of different races and cultures.'" (The *Globe* puts this figure at 41 percent.) Both figures are high, and should have been surprising to no one with even the most rudimentary sense of the shifting undercurrents in Canadian society.

The second poll, conducted for the federal government by Ekos Research Associates Inc., received front-page treatment in the *Globe* on March 10, 1994. "Four in ten Canadians," it discovered, "believe there are too many members of visible minorities [in Canada], singling out Arabs, blacks and Asians for discrimination."[3] Toronto, a city with an immigrant population of 38 percent, turned out to be the intolerance capital of Canada, with a stunning 67 percent saying there were too many immigrants, up 21 percent from the results of a poll conducted just two years before.[4] Even so, it was pointed out that "nearly three-quarters of those surveyed agreed that a mix of cultures makes Canada a more attractive place to live."

We are a country addicted to lengthy and laborious study. There is hardly a subject we have not polled or Royal-Commissioned to death. We respond avidly to the most intimate of questions. We believe in boards of inquiry, months of testimony, stacks of research papers, final reports too thick and multi-volumed to be read by any but the most avid — not to mention public-opinion surveys confusing even to seasoned reporters.

The effort itself seems to exhaust us: the knowledge, gained at great intellectual effort and financial expense, sits on shelves, glowing like some long-forgotten radioactive waste material. Or perhaps the endless studies simply satisfy the need we have to create the right appearance: we acknowledge the problem, whatever it may be, and then proceed to study it and study it and study it … all to little or no effect.

At the very least, one thinks, we should by now have acquired a little self-knowledge. But self-knowledge does not come from study alone. It comes from a knowledge of history, from self-examination, and from open and vigorous debate, a candid exchange of opposing points of view. Too often in this country we gravitate towards the superficial, and so polls that claim to take our measure can still surprise and dismay us. We are suspicious of debate, anxious about the truths it might reveal. We prefer regulation, the imposition of legal barriers, in our pursuit of peace, order, and good government. We prefer, then, a loaded silence.

And few silences are as loaded in this country as the one encasing the cult that has grown up around our policy of multiculturalism.

In reaction to the Decima poll, Sheila Finestone, secretary of state for multiculturalism, is quoted in the *Gazette*/Southam News report as affirming that "the Liberals have no plans to retreat from a multicultural policy. Instead, she promised to give education in multicultural issues a higher profile." Ms. Finestone then went on to attribute some blame to the faltering economy (which encourages a search for scapegoats) and to racial notions encouraged by Preston Manning and the Reform Party. Like so many others, Ms. Finestone had no hesitation in equating opposition to multicultural policy with racist sentiment.

A month later, when MPs from the Bloc Québécois and the Reform Party criticized federal multicultural funding for encouraging ethnic ghettos through grants to ethnic communities, they were accused, first, of wishing to import the U.S. "melting pot" approach to Canada and, second, of xenophobia.[5] Attempts by the Reform Party to put multiculturalism on the public agenda are routinely rejected with accusations of racism.

It is probably essential that I declare here my complete independence of all political parties. When it comes to the Reform Party in particular — the only official, national party that has dared criticize multiculturalism policy in public — my attitude is at best suspicious. Reform strikes me as a party that suffers from an astounding lack of social generosity and counts among its membership too many who are either racially minded or, to coin a phrase, knowledge-challenged.

But the countering of criticism with accusation is a tactic not unfamiliar to me. My own attempts to contribute to public discourse have been met with nervous silence, a certain vilification, and, finally, the explicit demand at one conference that I *Shut up!*, since criticism of multicultural policy, I was told, served only "to encourage racists like the Reform Party." The cumulative effect of such an attitude is to put what is essentially government public policy out of bounds; it is to afford it an exclusivity extended not even to the country's security apparatus, which is itself subject to constant scrutiny.

Anyone critical of multicultural policy, then, is immediately branded a racist. And if one happens to be, as I am, a "person of colour," one is then graced with words such as "sell-out," "traitor," and "Uncle Tom" from "ethnic" defenders with a stake in the system and from mainstream defenders who expect a little more gratitude. Many are they in this country who fear a serious examination of multiculturalism, its policies, and its consequences. Many are they who will resort to a chorus of vilification to protect their sacred turf.

This reaction, I suspect, has more than a little to do with the psychology of the True Believer, who sees Canada's present multiculturalism policy — generous and laudable, prompted by an inclusive vision of humanity — as the only one possible. But no policy can be written in stone; no policy is immune to evolution. When its defenders come to view a policy as without alternative; when they come to view honest criticism as mere attack; when they come to view critics as enemies, they also indulge in a logic that has led, elsewhere, to unfortunate consequences.

An example — and by this I suggest an intellectual parallel — is the old Soviet attitude towards dissent. If Communism was the perfect political system, the logic ran, then critics of it were, by definition, mentally unstable, for only the insane would criticize perfection. It was therefore incumbent on the state to vilify such people and confine them to mental institutions. Just as the Soviet state responded to criticism by branding its critics mentally ill, so the Canadian multicultural apparatus responds to criticism by branding its critics racist.

It is an easy and, from an ideological point of view, logical way of dismissing uncomfortable truths. And this is what lends to multiculturalism aspects of the cult: the rules are established, you question them at your peril.

A free and healthy society must be wary of all orthodoxies, whether those of the oppressor or the oppressed, of the exploiter or the exploited, of the mainstream or the marginalized. Orthodoxy is itself a form of tyranny, with ideology — political, social, racial, financial — as its angry deity. Multiculturalism has, over the years, acquired aspects of a holy cow for many, a cash cow for some. Both are dangerous creatures. Standing on consecrated ground, they resent being disturbed and, when challenged, are inclined to bite. But a society that wishes to remain healthy and to grow must, from time to time, stare the holy cows down; it must probe and question them, and decide on their merits and usefulness. To fail to do so is to atrophy.

There are many ways of approaching a laudable end. It is incumbent on those who seek it — the end, in this case, being a truly pluralistic society — to define their vision with words weightier than vacuous expressions of goodwill. It is also vital that they not settle into the kind of self-righteous complacency that summarily rejects criticism, for to do so not only calls their vision into disrepute but also proves inimical to the fabric of the society that vision seeks to serve.

Multiculturalism is an emotional subject. It reaches into our past and our present, into the core of ourselves. It engages all that has shaped us. It touches us where we are the most vulnerable and the most self-protective.

For this reason, this book does not claim to be an objective examination of multiculturalism. A subject so personal, one that cuts so close to the bone, defies objectivity. It is, then, a personal attempt to grapple with a policy which, from my earliest days in this country, has presented itself as a social cornerstone; it is an attempt to look at where we are and how we got here.

The question of the financial costs of multiculturalism does not preoccupy me. The federal government dispenses less than $30 million per year to the department, not an insignificant sum but one that does not particularly stand out among government expenditures. Former prime minister Mulroney, after all, spent more than that on a presidential-style aircraft.

Multiculturalism interests me rather as an official government policy and, more particularly, as a government-sanctioned mentality: as a way of looking at life and at the world; for the ways in which it shapes our sense of self and our place in human society. I am interested in the effects of multiculturalism, then, on our individual and collective selves.

Nor, let me add, does this book claim to be prescriptive. I am neither a literary doctor, a sociologist, nor a politician. I do not pretend to have all, or any, answers, although I do offer some suggestions in the same spirit that I offer criticism: as a way of contributing to the necessary discussion on the shaping of an increasingly unhappy and divided land.

ENDINGS

Nobody knows what you integrate to any more. Before the First World War,
you had the sense that here you had an Anglo-Saxon Protestant matrix and
an imperial British culture — and everybody knew what hymn we were all
singing. Now the question is, who's defining the context of integration at
all, and what kind of Canada are you integrating yourself to?

Michael Ignatieff in conversation
December 1, 1993

ETHNICITY

Divisiveness is a dangerous playmate, and few playgrounds offer greater
scope for divisiveness than that of ethnicity. The walls are high, ready-
made, as solid as obsession. Guard towers can be built, redoubts that allow
defense and a distant view into the land of the other. Like all walls, they
can be either accepted as integral to life or breached — dismantled brick by
brick — as restrictive to it. How to view those walls, how or even if to deal
with them, is a decision each individual must make.

For society at large, though, ethnicity and its walls must be barriers
to nothing. No opportunity must be denied, no recognition withheld, no
advancement refused. Neither, however, must ethnicity be claimed as
grounds for opportunity, recognition, or advancement. Tempting though it
may be, a multicultural society can ill afford the use of past discrimination
as justification for future recrimination. It is essential, in such a society, that
discrimination be permissible only on the basis of knowledge and ability.
To do otherwise — to discriminate, for instance, against white males as
a class because of transgressions by other white males in the past — is to
employ the simplistic eye-for-an-eye, tooth-for-a-tooth philosophy implicit
in arguments supportive of capital punishment. There is an element of
class vengeance to it, an element of self-righteousness, that offers victims
or their descendants the opportunity to strike back. It is like arguing that
the victims of torture must be allowed to torture their torturers. Redress
is important, but the nature of that redress is even more so, for it sets the
tone for the future. Yesterday cannot be changed, but tomorrow is yet to be
shaped, and ways must be found to avoid creating resentments today that
might lead to upheavals tomorrow. As Nelson Mandela has made clear,
a peaceful and prosperous future for a multi-racial South Africa cannot
be secured through punitive action for the wrongs of the past; it can be
attained only through the full recognition of human dignity implicit in the
acceptance of equality.

Economic and social imbalance cannot be redressed overnight. Only revolution can effect so radical a change, and if there is a lesson to be learned from the history of the twentieth century it is that revolutionary change is illusory: it merely changes oppressors and the nature of oppression. True and lasting change, then, cannot be imposed; it must come slowly, growing with experience, from within.

The comment was once made that racism is as Canadian as maple syrup. History provides us with ample proof of that. But perspective requires the notation that racism is also as American as apple pie, as French as croissants, as Indian as curry, as Jamaican as Akee, as Russian as vodka .... It's an item on every nation's menu. Racism, an aspect of human virulence, is exclusive to no race, no country, no culture, no civilization. This is not to excuse it. Murder and rape, too, are international, multicultural, innate to the darker side of the human experience. But an orderly and civil society requires that the inevitable rage evoked not blind us to the larger context.

The word "racism" is a discomforting one: it is so easily vulnerable to manipulation. We can, if we so wish, apply it to any incident involving people of different colour: had June Callwood directed her infamous two words at a white woman, it would have been virtually impossible to slander her with the charge of racism. Therein lies the danger. During the heat of altercation, we seize, as terms of abuse, on whatever is most obvious about the other person—or what we may perceive as being a point of emotional (or, as in Ms. Callwood's case, political) vulnerability. A woman, because of her sex, can easily become an intimate part of her anatomy colloquially described (as, indeed, can men). A large person might be dubbed a stupid ox, a small person a shrimp or a pip-squeak. And so a black person might be dubbed a "nigger," a white a "honky," an Asian a "paki," a Chinese a "chink," an Italian a "wop," a Jew a "kike," a French-Canadian a "frog."

There is nothing pleasant about these terms: they are demeaning; they constitute an assault on every decent sensibility. Even so, I once met someone who, with a stunning naivety, used them as simple descriptives and not as terms of abuse. She was horrified to learn the truth. While this may have been an extreme case, the point is that the use of such patently abusive words might not always indicate racial or cultural distaste. It may indicate ignorance, stupidity, insensitivity—but we can be thankful that pure racial hatred, of the Nazi or Ku Klux Klan type, remains, in this society, a rare commodity. There is, thanks to our history of civility, something unCanadian about it. For most people, I would suspect, the blatant racists among us are a source of embarrassment.

Ignorance, not the willful kind but that which comes from lack of experience and uninformed assumption, is often indicated by the defensive phrase, "I'm not racist but ... " I think of a mover, a friendly man, who once said to me, "I'm not racist, but the Chinese are the worst drivers on the road." He was convinced that this was so because the shape of their eyes, as far as he could surmise, denied them peripheral vision.

There is something similar in the vision of the man who rejected apartment buildings with East Indian tenants because of their rumored love for gift-wrapped cockroaches — as there is in the pitifully angry voices of Canadian Legion members as they reject the imposition on them of a rule that would lessen their control of the last space within their influence. Few of these people would think of themselves as racist, and the charge would undoubtedly be wounding to most, if not all of them, and yet their comments, often so innocently delivered, would open them up to the accusation.

True racism is based, more often than not, on the willful ignorance and an acceptance of and comfort with stereotype. We like to think, in this country, that our multicultural mosaic will help nudge us into a greater openness. But multiculturalism as we know it indulges in stereotype, depends on it for a dash of colour and the flash of dance [....]

THE TOLERANT SOCIETY

In a radio interview, the novelist Robertson Davies once spoke of the difference between two words that are often — and erroneously — used interchangeably: acceptance and tolerance.

Acceptance, he pointed out, requires true understanding, recognition over time that the obvious difference — the accent, the skin colour, the crossed eyes, the large nose — are mere decoration on the person beneath. It is a meeting of peoples that delves under the surface to a knowledge of the full humanity of the other.

Tolerance, on the other hand, is far more fragile, for it requires not knowledge but willful ignorance, a purposeful turning away from the accent, the skin colour, the crossed eyes, the large nose. It is a shrug of indifference that entails more than a hint of condescension.

The pose of tolerance is seductive, for it requires no effort; it is benign in that it allows others to get on with their lives free of interference — and also free of a helping hand. The problem, of course, is that tolerance — based as it is on ignorance—can, with changing circumstances, give way to a perception of threat. And such a perception is all that is required to cause a defensive reaction to kick in—or to lash out. Already in this country, we are seeing the emergence of reaction from those who feel themselves and their past, their beliefs, and their contribution to the country, to be under assault. People who are "put up with" in the good times assume aspects of usurpers in the bad. Notions of purity—both cultural and racial—come to the forefront as the sense of self diminishes under the assault of unemployment, homelessness, a growing sense of helplessness.

This tolerance can very quickly metamorphose into virulent defensiveness, rejecting the different, alienating the new. Understanding, in contrast, requires effort, a far more difficult proposition, but may lead to acceptance and, for the newcomers, a sense of belonging. Multiculturalism, with its emphasis on the easy and the superficial, fosters the former while ignoring the latter.

Canada has long prided itself on being a tolerant society, but tolerance is clearly insufficient in the building of a cohesive society. A far greater goal to strive for would be an *accepting* society. Multiculturalism seems to offer at best provisional acceptance, and it is with some difficulty that one insists on being a full—and not just an associate—member of society. Just as the newcomer must decide how best to accommodate himself or herself to the society, so the society must in turn decide how it will accommodate itself to the newcomer. Multiculturalism has served neither interest; it has heightened our differences rather than distinguishing them; it has preached tolerance rather than encouraging acceptance; and it is leading us into a divisiveness so entrenched that we face a future of multiple solitudes with no central notion to bind us.

Quebec

It is its cosmopolitan nature that will ensure Montreal's future, I do not mean by that exotic restaurants, trendy boutiques or cafés; I mean a population that has come from all over the world, that accepts French as a natural fact, English as a convenient means of communication, and that will create a diversified culture grafted on a French-speaking tree.

Jacques Godbout
The Globe and Mail
November 6, 1989

French Canada entered my consciousness in my second year at university through a course in Québécois literature. While the English-Canadian literature I had encountered seemed on the whole to be concerned with gentle days growing up on the Prairies, French-Canadian writing was striking in its intensity. Engaged, passionate, combative, informed by an anger both visceral and intellectual, it seemed designed to unsettle and incite rather than reassure. The honest brutality of the opening scene of Roch Carrier's *La Guerre, Yes Sir!*, in which Joseph axes off his own hand in order to avoid conscription into a war he sees as not his own, marked itself forever in my imagination, and the starkness of the scene tempered my surprise at the election, in 1976, of René Lévesque and the Parti-Québécois.

So it *was* a surprise, during the year I spent in Quebec City (1985–86), to discover that far from being alienated by my speaking English, people were attracted to it. I learned that the language laws that incited so much anger in the rest of the country were intended as a social measure, not a personal one. Service in stores and restaurants and provincial government offices was offered in French and in English—which was at times irritating to someone who wished to practice his French. But more than this, the people of Quebec City were refreshingly friendly, candid in their curiosity. They were not unnerved by difference.

At dinner in a restaurant one evening with an English-speaking companion, a man at the next table interrupted our conversation to say how pleasing it was to hear English again. He was francophone, had moved from Montreal to Quebec City, and found that he missed the sounds of the language. It was, in its implications, a complex statement, for it spoke in subtle ways of the unacknowledged: of a true meeting of peoples; of shared history, shared visions, shared attitudes. It said that, because of overlapping influences and despite the differences between languages, provinces and regions, we have acquired an uneasy similarity. Though sometimes, blinded by the immediacy of political concerns, we are as a people fundamentally blended: our interest in each other cannot easily be extinguished. The right arm may not resemble the left arm, but they belong together on the same body, serving its interests and their own. Each would be poorer without the other.

In Quebec City, one was simply included, accepted, seduced into feeling at home. The Plains of Abraham, historically poignant, assuredly federal, a gathering place for quiet pleasures, remains one of my favorite places in the country. Its open spaces and panoramic views of the St.

Lawrence, its reminders of the past that has shaped us in such fundamental ways, speak on many levels, not all of them definable, to one's sense of belonging.

But Quebec City is one thing. Montreal quite another. More populous, more ethnically diverse, living directly with the challenge of other languages, its tensions — not only linguistic but social and economic, like those of any big city — are at times palpable. The city appears to have accommodated itself less successfully than Toronto or Vancouver to its growing ethnic diversity, almost as if unwilling to accept the changes that would necessarily require it to surrender elements of its personality. While Vancouver and Toronto have proved able to reshape themselves, while they have eased into a remaking of the public face, Montreal, for so long the center of Quebec's struggle to preserve its French character, holds greedily to its sense of self, to the *joie de vivre* that sometimes feels forced, manufactured. Probably because of the anxieties with which they live, Montrealers tend to be less open, more defensive, more self-protective than the people of Quebec City. They take themselves and their reputation very seriously — rather, it must be said, like Torontonians.

The point, simply put, is this: just as English Canada is no monolith of views, interests, and attitudes, so Quebec is no monolith of views, interests, and attitudes. And like English Canada and Quebec, no ethnic group, or "cultural community" as they are referred to in Quebec, is a monolith of views, interests, and attitudes. To pretend otherwise is to indulge in the simplification of stereotype.

In Canada, the old colonial mentality — and I use the term descriptively — has been relegated, kicking and blustering, to the margins, but the attitude of dependence — the comforts of being a follower beholden to forces and traditions larger and older than our own — retains a certain appeal. In twenty-five years, we have moved from Pierre Trudeau, the free-thinker who wanted to sell his countrymen a vision, to Brian Mulroney, the free-trader who simply wanted to sell his countrymen; from an idea of ourselves as a fresh and exciting country that could set its own pace to another idea of ourselves that is simply a retreat to the comforts of yesteryear; from Pierre Trudeau pirouetting behind the Queen to Brian Mulroney catering to the continentalism of Ronald Reagan and George Bush; from deference to one set of betters, to a flirtation with independence, to deference to another set of betters.

It is a picture of social and political drift, of a desire to control our own destiny and a fear of doing so. There is something distasteful, we seem to think, in attempting to be all we can be. We end up, then, like a ship buffeted by winds that gust and probe their way through our disordered staterooms, the passengers lost and wandering, directionless, jealously seizing whatever they can grab while, on the bridge, would-be captains argue endlessly about the direction of Paradise.

One stateroom, though, has managed to batten down and order itself. Some of its passengers go so far as to eye a lifeboat as a means of salvation from the drifting ship.

Here, then, lies one of the essential differences between English-speaking Canada and the province of Quebec.

Beginning in the sixties and accelerating through the seventies, Canada was hurtling through social change. In English-speaking Canada, the old colonial center was being swept away by waves of "non-traditional" immigrants, the old center relegated to the margins, the new Canada redefining itself into a "cultural mosaic." At the same time, change of quite a different order was taking place in Quebec. The old church-ridden, agricultural society was remaking itself, modernizing itself, throwing off restraints both internal and external. While English Canada soon found itself adrift, with no sense of its center, Quebec redefined its own center, strengthened it, sought to make it unassailable. A host of economic measures ensured an economic future for a people long denied widespread prosperity, and a series of laws designed to protect the language and culture were put into place.

Simply put, then, while English Canada saw its defining Britishness dismantled, Quebec saw its defining Frenchness strengthened.

For a newcomer, the difference was striking.

In English Canada, the prevailing attitude seemed to be "Come as you are — Do as you please." The society had few expectations beyond adherence to the basic rule of law.

Quebec, however, was more demanding. The prevailing attitude was "Come as you are, but be prepared to engage with a French-speaking society." This meant that advancement would depend on your ability to work in French; it meant that your children would attend French schools; it meant that if you opened a convenience store, your signs must advertise LAIT not MILK, PAIN not BREAD, BIÈRE not BEER. The rules of the game may have been distasteful to some, they may have seemed oppressive to others, but they were clear. And when you stopped to think about it, you realized that Quebec had simply made *de jure* what was *de facto* elsewhere in the country: if a Spanish-speaker arrived in Toronto, he would necessarily have to live much of his life—to engage with the society—in English. Quebec was simply saying that, *chez nous*, the same thing must be done in French.

Le Devoir publisher Lise Bissonnette once wrote, "In the eyes of English Canadians, who like to believe that they practice the canons of multiculturalism, Québécois culture is just one stem in the great and colourful cultural bouquet which blossoms from coast to coast."[6] If multiculturalism was meant, in part, to cast Quebecers as just another ethnic group, to reduce the distinctiveness of the province's history and place in Confederation to parity with the other provinces, then it has worked to a large extent—outside Quebec at least. Evidence of this is found in the resistance to affording the province special constitutional status; the insistence that it is simply one of ten equal provinces, with the same powers, same rights, same obligations. But this is a simple-minded view of equality. It is obvious to anyone with a nodding acquaintance of Quebec that it is different. It has obligations—to its language, to its culture, to its view of life—that the other provinces do not. And if you have special obligations, then you need special powers to fulfill those obligations. But if Quebecers are just another ethnic group, their needs can be, politically speaking, safely ignored.

The problem, of course, is that Quebecers themselves have never bought into the Canadian idea of multiculturalism. Its dangers were self-evident. "Carried over into Quebec," Ms. Bissonnette has written, "this multiculturalism would be suicidal, since it tends to make francophones a minority like the others."

In addition, reservations have been expressed by Claude Corbo, rector of l'Université du Québec à Montréal and himself the grandson of Italian immigrants. Declaring multiculturalism to be a dead-end for immigrants, Mr. Corbo pointed out that the policy has kept many "from integrating naturally into the fabric of Canadian and Quebec society."[7] He called for its abolition, adding that "We tell people to preserve their original patrimony, to conserve their values, even if these values are incompatible with those of our society."

Quebec is no haven for immigrants. It too has its share of racists, and an undeniable strain of xenophobia runs through its nationalism. Parti Québécois leader Jacques Parizeau has mused in the past about an independent Quebec reducing the number of English-language radio and television stations in the province to reflect the percentage of Anglophones—which is, philosophically at least, a gesture of tyranny. And it is M.Parizeau too who indulges in intimidation of financial institutions that question the benefits of separatism to the Quebec economy. These are not ideas that reassure.

Certain linguistic expressions, too, prove unsettling. *"Québécois pure laine,"* an identification that hints of notions of racial purity, causes me to reflect that my *"laine"* will never be *"pure"* enough to allow me, in the eyes of some, to fully belong to the family: "I will always be the Other. *"Le Québec aux Québécois,"* the vociferous chant of the crowds marching in celebration of St.Jean-Baptiste, evokes the question of who is a Quebecer — and the politically expedient answer first offered by René Lévesque and parroted by national spokesmen ever since, that a Quebecer is anyone who lives in Quebec, is at best disingenuous, for it implies an absurd corollary: If a Quebecer is anyone who lives in Quebec, then a Quebecer who leaves the province ceases to be a Quebecer, unless, one imagines, the Quebecer happens to be *"pure laine"* or *"de vieille souche."* The answer, meant to disarm, is meaningless.

[...] Migration — the act of leaving, the act of reestablishment — creates its own experience, effects its own change. One is no longer simply who one was in the first part of one's life. To pretend that one has not evolved, as official multiculturalism so often seems to demand of us, is to stultify the personality, creating stereotype, stripping the individual of uniqueness: you are not yourself, you are your group. It is not really a mosaic that one joins — the parts of a mosaic fit neatly together, creating a harmonious whole — but rather a zoo of exoticism that one enters. Some are scandalized to speechlessness when I mention that the Trinidad Carnival leaves me unmoved, that I never pine for sandy beaches. Stereotype comforts; its demise disorients. But how wearying it can become.

An unusual view of the discomfort of exoticism was presented in *The Globe and Mail* in November 1993 by a woman named Sherrill Johnson.[8] At the time a graduate student working in developing countries, she wrote of the special treatment she received in India and Guyana by virtue of her exoticism: being a white foreigner in a non-white land opened doors, afforded ease of access denied to others. At the time, engrossed in her work, she unhesitantly accepted the special treatment, and it was only after her return to anonymity in Canada that unease set in. "It's disturbing being singled out on the basis of one's appearance," she wrote, "receiving special favors based on nothing more than the colour of my skin ... " In

Guyana, she was called "white meat" in the streets. "[T]he label that I was tagged with started to chafe and it became harder and harder to forget, or perhaps more accurately ignore, the effects of my skin colour—both positive and negative. I longed to walk down a street and not be seen as a blond white woman, or a piece of 'white meat,' but simply as an ordinary person. Nothing more and nothing less."

The struggle against stereotype, the basis of all racism, is, in the end, a profoundly personal one. Government programs are essential, but no bureaucratic regime can ever be as effective a stop to stereotype and racist typecasting as an immediate challenge by those who object.

At the same time, to accept the assigned role of multiculturalism—to play the ethnic deracinated and costumed—is to play to stereotype. It is to abdicate one's full humanity in favor of one of its exotic features, ethnicity.

Multiculturalism is ethnicity as public policy: it is society's view of the individual's assigned place within its construct. And yet I would suggest that ethnicity's true value lies in the opposite point of view: as one of the many elements that inform the way the individual views the world.

It may be that one of the unstated desires behind the institution of multiculturalism was a wish to mark ourselves as different from the United States: If they have a melting pot, then we'll have a mosaic. If they ask immigrants to shrug off their past and assume a new identity, we'll ask immigrants to conserve their past and make it their only identity.

Both approaches are essentially illusory, it seems to me, each an exercise in the falsifying of the self. Pretending to continue being simply what one has been in the past, or what one's parents have been, inevitably entails a betrayal of the self—just as pretending, under the assimilative American model, that one is no longer what one has been, that one has completely remade oneself, is also a betrayal of the self. The human personality is not static; it is altered fundamentally, but not wholly, by circumstance and experience. And while the U.S. approach is untrue to both the individual and the state. For if many who immigrate to the United States eventually come to think of themselves as simply "American," strengthening the social fabric, too few who come to Canada end up accepting themselves—and one another—as simply "Canadian," thereby weakening the social fabric.

Certainly, at this point in our social development (or lack of it), ethnic communities have little to gain from multiculturalism, a policy that now serves to make them, more than anything else, simply privy to political manipulation from both inside and outside their communities.

Furthermore, indulging in the game of heightened ethnicity entails the risk of excessive fantasy. It is human to edit the past, to gloss even a harsh reality into a coveted memory: "We were starving, but we were happy." But such memory of a retreating past ever more golden frequently leads to acute personal dissatisfaction. It is easy, in the comforting grip of edited memory, to forget that everything has changed; easy, too, to embrace the miscalculation that arises from an acute yearning for the perfection that, in memory, used to be. Multiculturalism, with its stress on the theatrical, helps concretize such fantasy, and once more both the individual and the state lose — the one by clinging to and at times acting on a fantasy, the other by paling before golden fantasy taken for reality.

In his article, Dr. Sugunasiri suggests several ways in which minority communities can help in "building a just society." He warns against "crying racism at every turn" and urges that they "look inward at the racism and discrimination within [their] own ranks." He encourages them to seek greater co-operation with legal authorities and calls for an effort to "get rid of the dehumanizing aspects" of their cultures. He also insists that historical injustices be left in the past, that they not be allowed to poison the present, and thus, the future — an elegant way of pleading with people to get rid of the chips on their shoulders. Finally, Dr. Sugunasiri offers what seems a radical policy: "Intermarriage must be promoted; it's perhaps our best hope for security and stability. More than 32 per cent of Canadians are the products of mixed marriages; the Japanese-Canadian figure is 50 per cent. Rejuvenate the gene pool."

NOTES

1. Jack Kapica, "Canadians Want Mosaic to Melt, Survey Finds: Respondents Believe Immigrants Should Adopt Canadian Values," *The Globe and Mail*, December 14, 1993.
2. Allyson Jeffs (Southam News), "Canadians Harbour 'Latently Racist' Attitudes: Poll," December 14, 1993.

3. Murray Campbell, "Too Many Immigrants, Many Say," *The Globe and Mail*, March 10, 1994.

4. For Vancouver, the figure was 51 per cent (up 2 points in two years); and for Montreal 39 per cent (up 10 points in two years) — a figure that strikes a serious blow against the widespread belief in Québécois intolerance.

5. Terrance Wills, "Visible-Minority Liberals Criticize PQ, Reform over 'Ghetto' Remark," *Montreal Gazette*, January 1994.

6. Lise Bissonnette, "Culture, Politics and Society in Quebec," in *Boundaries of Identity*, edited by William Dodge (Toronto, 1992).

7. *La Presse* and the *Montreal Gazette*, June 13, 1994.

8. Lysiane Gagnon, "If You Question Quebec Sovereignty, You're a Skunk at a Garden Party," *The Globe and Mail*, April 30, 1994.

ROSEMARY J. COOMBE

THE PROPERTIES OF CULTURE AND THE POSSESSION OF IDENTITY: POSTCOLONIAL STRUGGLE AND THE LEGAL IMAGINATION

In 1992, a longstanding debate in Canadian arts communities erupted in the national public sphere. For three weeks that April, Canadians witnessed a remarkable exchange on the pages of the *Globe and Mail* as controversy raged about the propriety of writers depicting "cultures other than their own," when or if it was appropriate to "tell someone else's story," and whether it was possible to "steal the culture of another."[1] Although the issues addressed there continue to engage critical attention, the *Globe and Mail* debate was significant for it brought into sharp relief the limitations of addressing complex issues of culture and identity politics as a matter of "reading our rights." The positions emergent in this controversy serve to demonstrate how a liberal legal discourse of rights may fundamentally distort issues of cultural politics.

I was initially drawn to the debate because of its ironic implications for my own scholarly work. For too many years I have been working on a book, provisionally called *Cultural Appropriations*; my advance publishing contract specified that nomination.[2] I have been exploring the ways in which subaltern groups use mass media texts, celebrity images, trademarks, and other commodified cultural forms to forge identities and communities. I consider various subcultures that engage movie and TV stars to construct alternative gender identities, and the ways in which trademarks are invoked to challenge concepts of citizenship and reinscribe the space of the nation-state in minority struggles for political recognition.[3] By virtue of the fact that these texts are legally defined as private properties, to which intellectual property holders have rights of exclusivity, the proliferation of meaning in the public sphere is (once again) constrained by forces of capital. Laws that govern the relationship between those who claim a propriety interest in a sign and those who seek to recode it grant enormous power to corporations to control the connotations of those signifiers that increasingly dominate the public sphere.[4]

In short, I have engaged in a consideration of cultural agency and subaltern struggle in consumer society, developing a concept of "cultural appropriation" as progressive cultural politics. Imagine my consternation, then, to find the term "officially defined" by the Advisory Committee for Racial Equality in the Arts (for no less august a body than the Canada Council). The term was deemed to mean "the depiction of minorities or cultures other than one's own, either in fiction or nonfiction" — and designated a serious issue to which the Council must attend.[5] The ironies of my response to this appropriation and definition of the phrase provoked me to reconsider the politics of certain knowledges, in this case, academic theory in law and anthropology. At first I was annoyed; a term I had used to connote progressive, subversive forms of cultural politics on behalf of subordinated social groups had been seized — exclusively to denote the individuous practice of white elites stealing the cultural forms of others for their own prestige and profit. I was uncomfortably aware that I had formed a rather propriety attachment to the term; my own feelings of violation rather closely mirrored those voiced by corporations who were outraged when *their* trademarks were given sanctioned meanings by others.

Exploring my responses to this debate about the "cultural appropriation" of others, I will suggest that my professional identities, both as lawyer and as anthropologist, situate me conflictually with respect to two dominant discourses and their deployment in postcolonial politics. The rhetorical positions of Romanticism and Orientalism, I suggest, function as dangerous supplements in contemporary struggles for political recognition. If my legal knowledge has made me suspicious of the former, my anthropological knowledge makes me uncomfortable with the latter. Struggling to establish positions on issues of cultural representation that avoid these seductive stances is virtually impossible within a discourse of rights and its juridical legacies.

The controversy over cultural appropriation is founded upon particular premises about authorship, culture, property, and identity that are products of a history of colonial appropriation and define the persistent parameters of a European legal imaginary. The limitations of these legal categories for post-colonial struggles, I will suggest, are apparent in responses to First Nations peoples' struggles for self-determination. In addressing First Nations claims here, I seek to avoid speaking "on behalf of" Native peoples, but to speak alongside First Nations activists who have put this issue on the political agenda and to address the dangers of receiving these claims in traditional legal categories. Rather than solve the "problem" of cultural appropriation (which, in any case, is never singular, but specific to particular peoples with particular historical trajectories), I will suggest that we rethink the terms in which we address the question and the ethical responsibilities entailed in its consideration.

The *Globe and Mail* debate centered around a suggestion that government grants should not be made to writers who wrote about cultures other than their own, unless the writer "collaborated" with people of that culture before writing. Although the need to find a "collaborator" is a peculiar and perhaps telling choice of language, this is hardly a suggestion that most scholars, at any rate, were likely to reject. The public controversy evoked by this suggestion, however, was swift and furious, and it quickly polarized around two poles — Romanticism and Orientalism — that structure both our law of property and increasingly configure many political claims for recognition, legitimacy, and self-determination.

In a series of letters to the editor, the tyranny of the state over the individual was invoked, and the transcendent genius of the Romantic author and his unfettered imagination was affirmed. Writers wasted no time evoking the totalitarian state, the memory of the Holocaust and the Gulag. As Timothy Findley forcefully interjected:

> Put it this way: I imagine — therefore I am. The rest — believe me — is silence. What has happened here? Does no one understand? In 1933 they burned 10,000 books at the gate of a German university because these books were written in unacceptable voices. German Jews, amongst others, had dared to speak for Germany in other than Aryan voices. Stop Now. Before we do this again.[6]

Joy Anne Jacoby evoked Russian anti-Semitism to urge the Council "to rethink the implications of imposing any policy of 'voice appropriation' lest they find themselves imitating the Russian approach to cultural censorship"[7]; one letter was addressed "A Letter to the Thought Police."[8]

Other critics proclaimed the absolute freedom of the author's imagination. Neil Bissoondath affirmed the autonomy of his ego in a quotation resplendent with the "I" of Romantic authorship:

> *I reject the idea of cultural appropriation completely .... I reject anything that limits the imagination. No one has the right to tell me who I should or should not write about, and telling me what or how I do that amounts to censorship .... I am a man of East-Indian descent and I have written from the viewpoint of women and black men, and I will continue to do so no matter who gets upset.*[9]

One writer declared that for the past thirty-five years he had been appropriating the "voices of men, women, dogs, cats, rats, bats, angels, mermaids, elephants … [and] salamanders"[10] and that he had no intention of consulting with them or seeking their permission:

> *In common with every writer worthy of his or her vocation, I refuse absolutely to entertain any argument demanding that I do so, or that I am to be in any way restricted in my choice of subject matter. I will not, in short, submit to such censorship.*[11]

Another writer asserted that "appropriation of voice is what fiction is";[12] others lamented that "if cultural appropriation had never been permitted, Puccini could never have written *La Bohème*, Verdi's *Aida* would never have been performed, we would never have thrilled to Lawrence Olivier in *Hamlet* and we would have been denied the music of *Anna and the King of Siam*."[13]

In these constructions of authorship, the writer is represented in Romantic terms as an autonomous individual who creates fictions with an imagination free of all constraint. For such an author, everything in the world must be made available and accessible as an "idea" that can be transformed into his "expression," which thus becomes his "work." Through his labour, he makes these ideas his own; his possession of the work is justified by his expressive activity. As long as the author does not copy another's expression, he is free to find his themes, plots, ideas, and characters anywhere he pleases, and to make these his own. Any attempts to restrict his ability to do so are viewed as an unjustifiable restriction on freedom of expression. The dialectic of possessive individualism and liberal democracy is thereby affirmed. These are also the premises about authorship that govern contemporary intellectual property laws, particularly the law of copyright.

Critical legal scholars have written extensively about the inadequacies of Romantic individualism and its understanding of subjectivity, cultural agency, freedom of speech, and creativity. Often they have done no more than use fairly standard anthropological and poststructuralist insights into the cultural construction of self and discursive formations of subjectivity to counter the universalizing rational individualism that dominates legal thought; it is not necessary to repeat those arguments here. The social experiences of authors inevitably shape their voices, and there is no doubt that the voices of people with remarkably similar social experiences continue to dominate the Canadian culture industries.[14] In a democratic society committed to multiculturalism and social equality, it is surely the work of a federal agency allocating public funds to support the work of marginalized minority writers and artists so that Canadian culture more fully represents national social diversity (and that's putting it in simple liberal terms).

The Romantic individualism expounded by writers in this debate determinedly ignores the balance of power in Canadian publishing. In the worldview presented, everyone is implicitly equal in their capacity to write or be written about—to speak or be spoken for. Such a position purports to be apolitical, but manages only to be ahistorical and blind to relations of power. It ignores the very real social lines along which representation has been structured and the very real difficulties faced by certain social groups to represent themselves and speak on their own behalf. Cultural representation and political representation are closely linked. It is, for example, inconceivable that a vehicle could be marketed as "a wandering Jew," but North Americans rarely bat an eyelash when a Jeep Cherokee® passes them on the road or an advertisement for a Pontiac® flashes across their television screens. More people may know Oneida® as a brand of silverware than as the name of a people and a nation.

For peoples in Canada experiencing discrimination and stereotyping, it must be insulting to have your identity analogized to that of mermaids and elephants, and cold comfort to know that an author has no intention of speaking to salamanders or angels before he writes about *them*, either. One can only assume that minority groups in Canada occupy the same mystical and inarticulate status in the writer's imagination. In such analogies, many Canadians are denied their humanity and deprived of any human knowledge from which others may learn. They are not seen as fellow members of a community whose historical experiences have shaped their current political struggles, but as archetypes and characters; not recognized as human beings to be engaged in dialogue, they are reduced to cultural fodder for the Romantic imagination.

Moreover, the very context in which the debate arose is conveniently elided. Puccini was not, after all, seeking funding from a government committed to multiculturalism when he wrote *La Bohème*, Warner Brothers would have "thrilled" us with Lawrence Olivier in *Hamlet* with or without the Canada Council, and if the Council were asked to fund a musical as blatantly imperialist and paternalistic as *Anna and the King of Siam*, we should indeed question the propriety of public funding.

But if the imperialist claims of the Romantic author coloured one side of this debate, the essentializing voice of Orientalism crept into the other. The article that began the debate was titled "Whose Voice Is It Anyway?" The question presupposed that a "voice" was both unified and singular and could be possessed by an individual or by a collective imagined as having similar abilities to possess its own expressions. Proponents of the Canada Council suggestion defended their position on the grounds of the integrity of cultural identities, authentic traditions, and the need for authenticity in cultural life. In making these arguments, the tropes of possessive individualism become paramount; authors "have identities" which may or may not ensure "their own work's authenticity." The Canada Council director claimed that cultural appropriation was a serious issue, because "we have a need for authenticity. In our society today, there is a recognition that quality has to do with that authenticity of voice."[15] The chair of the Writers' Union of Canada declared that it was no different from a copyright claim in which any unlicensed use of an author's work is theft[16] (in fact there are major difficulties with the copyright analogy, which I will later address).

The *Globe and Mail* debate was soon related back to earlier discussions in which Native writers have appealed to white writers to refrain from telling stories involving Indians so as to enable Native peoples to tell their own stories and claim their own history. Questions of "Who's stealing whose stories and who's speaking with whose voice?"[17] have been posed by some Native cultural activists as "cases of cultural theft, the theft of voice."[18] Canadians were told that "stories show how a people, a culture, thinks"[19] and such stories could not be told by others without endangering the authenticity of cultural works. The Canadian culture industries were accused of stealing the stories of Native peoples. Native artists asked if

"Canadians had run out of stories of their own"[20] and claimed that the telling of Native stories was theft, "as surely as the missionaries stole our religion, the politicians stole our land, and the residential schools stole our language."[21]

In many of the arguments used to support Native claims of cultural appropriation, Canada is either a country with its own culture or one in which there are multiple discrete cultures; one always has a singular culture of one's own, that has a history of its own, and one possesses an authentic identity that speaks in a univocal voice fully constituted by one's own cultural tradition.

Most anthropologists and cultural studies theorists, I suspect, find themselves uneasy in the face of such arguments. It is possible to be simultaneously supportive of First Nations' struggles for self-representation and uncomfortable with the rhetorical strategies employed by many of these who are sympathetic to this end. For anthropologists today, such propositions about culture, authenticity, and identity are extremely contentious ones. Intellectually, we have been called upon to resist the siren call of authenticity, the reification of cultures, and the continuity of traditions.[22] It has become far more intellectually respectable and certainly more fashionable to focus upon improvisation, productive hybridity, the creative poetics of identity creation—cultural conjunctures rather than timeless essences, creolized intercultural processes rather than stable cultural traditions.

The cultural creative processes we celebrate, however, *are* fabrications, and the cultural resources with which emergent identities are fashioned may be tightly embraced by others in alternative systems of value. This is vividly illustrated in George Lipsitz's otherwise politically sensitive book *Time Passages*, discussing American popular culture and memory.[23] He waxes ecstatic about the emancipatory cultural creativity of the "Mardi Gras Indians"—black youths who dress and dance in Plains Indian costume during elaborately rehearsed street pageantry in New Orleans. Their "Indianness" is drawn from the Buffalo Bill imagery ingrained in American mass culture. They know that they are not "real Indians," but one gets little sense that they know there are any or if they believe, as a young child recently told me (as a mark of her worldly sophistication), that "there are no *real* Indians any more than there are real trolls, witches, or fairies." In our constant utopian hope for reinventions of difference, I sometimes fear that we may simply reinscribe the authority of the Romantic author and his unfettered right to creativity. As Annie Coombes suggests, "hybridity" is no guarantee of postcolonial self-determination; it is as equally available to the colonizing practices of capital as it is to local strategies of resistance.[24]

Maintaining respect for cultural tradition, however, also risks reinscribing the authority of our own cultural categories, albeit in the guise of the liberty property holder. The concepts of culture, authenticity, and identity in the *Globe and Mail* debate were posed in *propriety* terms, as debates about *propriety* so often are in contemporary politics. The argument was constructed upon the same philosophy of possessive individualism that grounds our legal categories and historically supported practices of colonial expropriation. The challenges that postcolonial struggles pose for Canadian society may not, however, best be met by reliance upon categories of thought inherited from a colonial era.

Although the term "postcolonial" has engendered controversy and criticism,[25] it is appropriate to the Canadian social and legal context I explore here. Unlike the liberal discourse of multiculturalism or cultural diversity, the term postcolonial and the language of struggle emphasize, rather than obscure, the very real histories of colonialism which we must confront and the relations of power inherited from our multiple colonial pasts that continue to shape social relations of difference. Debates about postcolonialism have particular relevance in a nation that still displays multiple manifestations of British Empire and embraces immigrants from the postcolonial Commonwealth. Furthermore, I think it is important to take up the implicit challenge posed by Linda Hutcheon when she suggests that

> *when Canadian culture is called postcolonial today, the reference is very rarely to the Native culture, which might be the more accurate historical use of the term .... Native and Métis writers are today demanding a voice ... and perhaps, given their articulations of the damage to Indian culture and people done by the colonizers (French and British) and the process of colonization, theirs should be considered the process of colonization, theirs should be considered the resisting, postcolonial voice of Canada.*[26]

To demonstrate how legal rights discourse relies upon the colonial categories that shape its parameters, it is necessary to outline the conceptual logic that developed in the nineteenth century to categorize art, culture, and authorial identity — a logic that continues to mark the limits of the legal imagination. In *The Predicament of Culture*, Clifford describes the "art-culture system" that emerged from European imperialism as a means to categorize arts and cultural goods—categories that continue to inform our laws of propriety in a postcolonial age. We know that the concepts of art and culture are products of the European upheavals and expansions of the early nineteenth century, the ascendancy of bourgeois values, the specter of mass society, imperialist expansion, and colonial rule. Only in the early nineteenth century was art as an imaginative expression abstracted from industry as a utilitarian one. The emergence of an abstract, capitalized "Art," equated with individual creativity and expressive genius, was developed in the same period as the concept of capitalized culture, as a noun or the end product of an abstract process of civilization. It was possible by the end of the nineteenth century to speak of "Culture" with a capital C—representing the height of human development, the most elevated of human expression as epitomized in European art and literature—as well as plural "cultures" with a small c—imagined as coherent, authentic ways of life characterized by wholeness, continuity, and essence.

Clifford argues that two similar categories dominate our evaluation of expressive works. First, he defines the zone of "authentic masterpieces" created by individual geniuses, the category of "Art" properly speaking. Secondly, he designates the category of "authentic artifacts" created by cultures imagined as collectivities. Objects may, therefore, be exhibited in galleries as examples of a human creative ability that transcends the limitations of time and place to speak to us about the "human" condition; they are testaments to the greatness of their individual creators. The artistic imagination is universalized in the European image under the rubric of a universal "human" Culture. Alternatively, objects may be exhibited in museums as the authentic works of a distinct collectivity, integral to the harmonious life of a timeless community and incomprehensible outside of "cultural context"—the defining features of authentic artifacts. Objects may move between categories—occupying liminal zones. But when non-Western objects fully pass from the status of authentic artifact to the status of art, they also escape the ahistorical location of the "tribal," albeit to enter into a "universal" history, defined by the progression of works of great authors (the canon of civilization). They become part of a "human" cultural heritage—Culture capitalized—rather than objects properly belonging to "cultures" anthropologically defined.

These European cultural understandings are mirrored in our legal categories for the valuation and protection of expressive objects. Laws of intellectual property (copyright in particular) and laws of cultural property reflect and secure the logic of the European art/culture system that Clifford outlines. Laws of copyright, for example, developed to protect the expressive works of authors and artists—increasingly perceived in Romantic terms of individual genius and transcendent creativity—in the service of promoting universal progress in the arts and sciences. Copyright laws protect works, understood to embody the unique personality of their individual authors—the expressive component of the "original" is so venerated that even a reproduction or imitation of it is deemed a form of theft.

The idea of an author's rights to control his (the category of the author is a gendered one) expressive creations developed in a context that privileged a Lockean theory of the origin of property in labour in which expressive creation is deemed the author's "work." Intellectual work creates an "Original" arising spontaneously from the vital root of "Genius." Originality in mental labour (as opposed to manual labour) enables the author to claim not merely the physical object produced, but the literary or artistic expression itself—the "work" properly defined.

The literary work, for example, is neither the physical book, nor the ideas contained in it, but the form of the expression which the author gives to those ideas. Literary or artistic works were incorporeal entities that sprang from the "fruitful mind" of an author. The work carries the imprint of the author's personality and always embodies his persona, wherever it surfaces, however it is transmitted, and whatever the sources of its content or the ideas it expresses. He is entitled to exclusive possession of it, wherever it circulates.

If the original, expressive, and possessive individual dominates intellectual property laws, legitimizing personal control over the circulation of text, laws of cultural property protect the material objects of culture. Culture may be defined here in either of the two ways established in the nineteenth century—as the universal heritage of humankind—Culture with a capital C—or in the plural anthropological sense, in which different cultures lay claim to different properties. These two positions on the nature of the "culture" that can rightfully possess the property at issue define the poles of an outgoing controversy in legal scholarship.

On the one hand, we have scholars of cultural property who expound a position of "cultural internationalism," which is nicely deemed a commitment to the cultural heritage of all mankind. On the other hand, we have scholars (and states) that espouse a position of "cultural nationalism" in which particular peoples have particular interest in particular properties, regardless of their current location and ownership. This is currently the position of over sixty nations who are party to a 1976 UNESCO agreement that prohibits importation of objects whose export is prohibited in the country of origin.

Cultural internationalists see the repatriation of cultural objects as "irrational" because in many of the signatory nations, the "supply" of cultural artifacts far exceeds the internal "demand" — "they are rich in cultural artifacts beyond any conceivable use."[27] As relatively poor nations, they would be better off exporting such objects to locations where they are valued. The popularity of cultural nationalism is deemed the result of symbolic values and "lack of ability to deal with cultural property as a resource like other resources to be exploited."[28] The possibility that other peoples may entertain other values is considered no more nor less likely than their sheer ignorance and ineptitude in recognizing cultural property as an exportable resource.

Cultural internationalists suggest that dealers, collectors, and museums should be entitled to participate in the decisions of nations to prohibit exports (after all it is "their" human heritage, too!). Other peoples may have other values, but the "universal human values" embodied in cultural objectives are best evaluated by the one "universal" medium of exchange — money. It is suggested that a "cosmopolitan attitude" would situate objects where they could best be preserved, studied, and enjoyed. The market, of course, will move objects to their locus of highest probable protection — those who are prepared to pay most are most likely to preserve their investment. Nations that "hoard" "unused" objects are denigrated by cultural internationalists because they "fail to spread their culture, and thereby culturally impoverish other peoples in the world."[29] Cultural internationalists are easy to criticize from a cultural studies perspective. Their notions of value and rationality are decidedly Eurocentric; it seems to be beyond their comprehension that there are alternative modes of attachment to objects which do not involve their commodification, objectification, and reification for purposes of collection, observation, and display.

One suspects also that this purported universalism would not support the movement of Rembrandts from the Netherlands to Lagos, despite the fact that Rembrandt's paintings might be "over-represented" in their country of origin, that the Dutch "fail to spread their culture" to the Third World, and that they thereby contribute to the "cultural impoverishment" of Africa's peoples. The existence of vast "underused" holdings in European museums does not appear to have led to movements to establish better museums in Niamey, Lima, or Nanjing despite the vastly larger numbers of people whose "cultural impoverishment" might thereby be alleviated. The "cosmopolitan" attitude espoused appears more Eurocentric than worldly, more monocultural than respectful of cultural difference, and less concerned with the purported "interests of all mankind" than with the interests of maintaining Western hegemony. Culture with a capital C serves very particular cultural interests.

The case for "cultural nationalism," on the other hand, is made on behalf of a people's or nation's patrimony in the name of maintaining and preserving cultural identity. These arguments are bound to find more sympathy with those sympathetic to progressive cultural politics, because they presuppose that values are salient only within local cultural contexts that cannot be reduced to a purported "common" denominator by market principles. Indeed, some cultural objects are seen as so integrally related to cultural identity that they should be deemed inalienable — as essential to the preservation of group identity and self-esteem. The realm of culture with a small c — in the anthropological sense of particular bounded forms of life — is enshrined here.

"Cultural nationalism," however pluralistic in intent, employs a European logic of possessive individualism when it claims objects as essential to identities and elements of authentic traditions. Possessive individualism — the relationship that links the individual to property as formulated in Locke's labour theory of value — increasingly dominates the language and logic of political claims to cultural autonomy. Focusing upon developments in Quebec's cultural heritage laws, anthropologist Richard Handler shows how national culture is envisioned as a kind of property and the nation is imagined as a property-owning "collective individual."[30] The modern individual is the self-contained human monad, one that is completely oneself. "We conceive of this individual as having, as we say, 'an identity.' Identity means 'oneness,' though it is oneness of a special sort ... sameness in all that constitutes the objective reality of a thing."[31] This modern individual is also defined by the property she possesses. Modernity has extended these qualities to nation-states and ethnic groups, who are imagined on the world stage and in political arenas as "collective individuals." Like other individuals, these collective individuals are imagined to be territorially and historically bounded, distinctive, internally homogeneous, and complete unto themselves. In this worldview, each nation or group possesses a unique identity and culture that are constituted by its undisputed possession of property. Within cultural nationalism, a group's survival, its identity or objective oneness over time, depends upon the secure possession of a culture embodied in objects of property.

The UNESCO principle that "cultural property is a basic element of a people's identity" thus begins to look less like respect for cultural diversity and more like another form of Western cultural imperialism. Being is equated with having (and excluding and controlling). What identifies a nation or culture are the traits that distinguish it from other cultures—what it has and they don't. Moreover, those properties that define a nation's culture in a cultural nationalist worldview are characterized by their "originality" or "authenticity." Cultural traits that come from elsewhere are, at best, borrowed and at worst, polluting; by contrast, those aspects of national culture that come from within the nation, that are original to it, are "authentic." Again, contemporary anthropology challenges such claims. The notion that only pristine objects untouched by the forces of modernization bespeak cultural identities has long been discounted as a form of imperialist nostalgia. The capacity of peoples to live in history, and to creatively interpret and expressively engage historical circumstances using their cultural traditions to do so, is now recognized as the very life and being of culture, rather than evidence of its death or decline.

The rhetoric of cultural nationalism that informs cultural propriety rights bears traces of the same logic that defines copyright. Each nation is perceived as an author who originates a culture from resources that come from within and can thus lay claim to exclusive possession of the expressive works that embody its personality. There is, however, a significant difference in the scope of the claims that can be made on behalf of a culture and those that can be made on behalf of an individual author. Copyright laws enable individual authors not only to claim possession of their original works as discrete objects, but to claim possession and control over any reproduction of those works (or any substantial part thereof) in any medium. Cultural property rights, however, enable proprietary claims to be made *only* to original objects or authentic artifacts. The Western extension of "Culture" to cultural Others was limited to objects of property, not to forms of expression. The full authority of authorship was thereby confined to the Western world.

To make this concrete, consider the Picasso paintings that figure so prominently in Clifford's discussion of Primitivism. When an African "statue," produced in a collectivity for social reasons, makes its way into a Picasso painting, the statue itself may still embody the identity of the culture from which it sprang, but any later reproduction of it that alludes back to the Picasso work may be legally recognized as the embodiment of Picasso's authorial personality. The possession of a culture is profoundly limited, whereas the possession of an author extends through time and space as his work is reproduced through mass communication systems. Royalties flow, not to the object's society of origin, but to the estate of the Western author, where the fruits of his originality are realized for fifty years after his death. (We see the same process at work in the expropriation of textile patterns, recipes, and design motifs from Asia and Africa.)

Native people's claims of cultural appropriation cannot be legally resolved as a matter of property rights without doing immense violence to the character of these claims themselves. Native peoples face a legal system that divides the world up in a fashion foreign to their sense of felt need. The law offers two possibilities of property that reflect two visions of culture. Intellectual property laws enable individual artists imagined as acultural Romantic authors to collect royalties for the reproduction of their personal expressions as reward for their contribution to a "human" cultural heritage. Cultural property laws enable collectivities to physically control objects that can be shown to embody the essential identity of a "culture" statistically conceived.

These categories, I would argue, serve only to culturally impoverish the self while they Orientalize the Other. By deeming expressive creations the private property of individuals, who can then control circulations of signification, we deprive ourselves of immense opportunities for creative worldmaking and invest the author with censorial powers. By representing cultures in the image of possessive individuals, we obscure people's histories, their interpretive differences, their ongoing transformations, and the cultural dimensions of their political struggles. The Romantic author and authentic artifacts are both, perhaps, fictions of a world best forgone.

Harvard law professor Martha Minow has suggested that most legal treatments of identity questions fail to acknowledge that the cultural, gender, racial, and ethnic identities of a person are not simply intrinsic to that person, but emerge from relationships between people in negotiations and interactions with others. "The relative power enjoyed by some people compared with others is partly manifested through the ability to name oneself and others and to influence the process of negotiation over questions of identity."[32]

Lawyers and judges who address legal questions of identity should keep in mind its kaleidoscopic nature. They should examine the multiple

contributions given to any definition of identity. They ought to examine the
pattern of power relationships within which an identity is forged. And they
need to explore the pattern of power relationships within which a question of
identity is framed … who picks an identity and who is consigned to it?[33]

It is precisely the inability to name themselves and a continuous history
of having their identities defined by others that First Nations peoples
foreground when they oppose practices of cultural appropriation.

In an effort to create a critical consciousness of racism and its
eradication, cultural critic bell hooks also adopts a pragmatic approach
to questions of identity.[34] She asserts that cultural critics must confront
the power and control over representations in the public sphere, because
social identity is a process of identifying and constructing oneself as a social
being through the mediation of images.[35] Hence subaltern peoples need
to critically engage questions of their representation and its influence on
questions of identity formation. Native peoples are legitimately concerned
with the ahistorical representations of "Indianness" that circulate in
the public sphere and the manner in which such imagery mediates the
capacities of others to recognize their contemporary identities as peoples
with specific needs in the late twentieth century.

Hooks asserts that an identity politics, however necessary as a stage
in the liberation of subordinated peoples, must "eschew essentialist
notions of identity and fashion selves that emerge from the meeting of
diverse epistemologies, habits of being, concrete class locations, and
radical political commitments."[36] A return to "identity" and "culture" is
necessary more as a means of locating oneself in a political practice than
in the embrace of the positivism projected by cultural nationalism. Hooks
links this political project to a feminist anti-essentialism which also links
identity to a history and a politics rather than an essence:

> *Identity politics provide a decisive rejoinder to the generic human thesis, and*
> *the mainstream methodology of Western political theory …. If we combine the*
> *concept of identity politics with a conception of the subject as positionality,*
> *we can conceive of the subject as non-essentialized and emergent from*
> *historical experience.*[37]

In the face of continuing racisms and ethnocentrism, assertions of
identity and culture should not be dismissed and critiques of essentialism
must recognize the very different positions occupied by subaltern groups.

Abstract and universalizing criticisms of essentialism may appear to oppressed peoples as threatening—once again preventing

> those who have suffered the crippling effects of colonization or domination to gain or regain a hearing .... It never surprises me when black folks respond to the critique of essentialism, especially when I denied the validity of identity politics by saying, "Yeah, it is easy to give up identity, when you've got one."[38]

Critiques of essentialism are useful, however, suggests hooks, when they enable African Americans to examine differences within black culture—for example, the impact that class and gender have on the experience of racism. They are also necessary to condemn notions of "natural" and "authentic" expressions of black culture which perpetuate static, ahistorical, and stereotyped images of black people's lives and possibilities.[39] As long as the specific history and experience of African Americans and the cultural sensibilities that emerge from the experience are kept in view, essentialism may be fruitfully criticized. "There is a radical difference between repudiation of the idea that there is a black 'essence' and recognition of the way that black identity has been specifically constituted in the experience of exile and struggle."[40]

First Nations peoples have very different histories and very different contemporary needs, but face similar dilemmas in their representations of identity in contemporary Canadian society. When they specify their unique histories, they are often accused of essentialism, but when they write or paint, their work is often criticized for not being "authentic" or sufficiently "Indian."[41] When First Nations peoples make claims to their own images, stories, and cultural themes, however, they do not do so as Romantic authors nor as timeless homogeneous cultures insisting upon the maintenance of a vanishing authenticity. They do not lay claim to expressive works as possessive individuals, insisting upon permissions and royalties for the circulation of authorial personas in the public realm.[42] The appeals made here cannot be reduced to a purely monetary claim for the royalties due to individuals, because they encompass an insistence upon the respect due to peoples, their histories, and their collective self-determination. Nor is the assertion of cultural presence made in the name of an ahistorical collective essence, but in the name of living, changing, creative peoples engaged in very concrete contemporary political struggles.[43] Our liberal discourses of rights, however, afford them little space to make these kinds of claims.

Native peoples discuss the issue of cultural appropriation in a manner that links issues of cultural representation with a history of political powerlessness; a history of having Indian identity continually defined and determined by forces committed to its eradication. Alienated from their own historical traditions, first by government and now by commerce, they find their "culture" valued while their peoples and their political struggles continue to be ignored. The experience of everywhere being seen, but never being heard, of constantly being represented, but never listened to, of being treated like artifacts rather than peoples, is central to the issue of cultural appropriation. The Canadian public seems intensely interested in things Indian but seem to have less interest in hearing Native peoples speak on their own behalf. When Native writers assert that they are better situated to tell the stories of their experiences, they are accused of curtailing artistic imagination. Such critics reinscribe Native peoples as objects of human culture, rather than authorial subjects in their own right — once again they are "ideas" and themes for the expressive works and propriety claims of others. Like angels and mermaids, they are imagined, rather than engaged, in dialogue.

Despite the immense limitations of the metaphors of possessive individualism, they have become dominant in world political culture. Subaltern groups and less powerful nations must, unfortunately, articulate their political claims in "a language that power understands,"[44] and the language that power understands is increasingly that of possessive and expressive individualism. There are many reasons to be pessimistic about its possibilities. Certainly the perils of making claims in the language of possessive individualism are real ones, as Native peoples in Canada have discovered. For instance, in a presentation on Native cultural autonomy and the appropriation of aboriginal imagery at a meeting of independent filmmakers, Métis videomaker Loretta Todd quoted Walter Benjamin; she was promptly accused of appropriating Western culture![45] She responded that she *was* part of Western culture — as a product of colonization, how could she be otherwise? — and Benjamin was part of that culture. Her interlocutors informed her that white use of Native imagery was equivalent to her use of Benjamin, because Native imagery was now simply a part of contemporary culture.[46]

Other white Toronto artists — self-proclaimed "environmentalist tribesmen" who call themselves Fastwurms — responded to questions about the propriety of their employment of Native ritual themes by slandering their aboriginal critic as "a self-appointed spokesperson for Native artists."[47] In speaking for a culture to which one makes a propriety claim, one always risks allegations that the identity one must possess to make such claims is not the undivided one demanded of the property-holding possessive individual. Once sees continuous attempts to silence Native people's interventions in the debate by questioning their authenticity and representativeness.

This tactic of deeming some people of aboriginal ancestry to be "real Indians" while denying the ability of others to speak on behalf of Native concerns is reminiscent of the historical policies of colonial authorities who arbitrarily conferred and withheld Indian status on spurious grounds that failed to recognize indigenous practices defining community membership. There is also embedded in this argument the notion that all Native peoples must agree for them to have a position that can be recognized as "Native," but as Paul Smith reminds us, "We have differences in political opinion. After all, we come from hundreds of nations and histories."[48]

Curiously, however, there is a constant insistence that aboriginal peoples must represent a fully coherent position that expresses an authentic identity forged from an uncomplicated past that bespeaks a pristine cultural tradition before their voice will be recognized as Native. No one, of course, asks white authors what gives them the authority to speak on behalf of artistic license or what criteria of representativeness they fulfill in order to make claims in the name of the authorial imagination. Nor do we expect uniform positions on the parameters of freedom of speech. The ability to speak on behalf of "universal" values is assumed, even as we argue what their contents might be, whereas people of aboriginal ancestry are often challenged when they name themselves and their experiences. In many ways, this logic mirrors that of the law and its categorizations. In dividing intellectual property and cultural property, authors with intellect are distinguished from cultures with property. Those who have intellect are entitled to speak on behalf of universal principles of reason, whereas those who have culture speak only on behalf of a cultural tradition that must be unified and homogeneous before we will accord it any respect. Such arguments are generally used, moreover, to silence and delegitimate particularly unwelcome Native voices, rather than to invite more indigenous participants to contribute their viewpoints and join the debate.

The Fastwurms, for example, denounced their aboriginal critic by claiming that they consider themselves "intrinsically to be a non-western culture."[49] Situating themselves outside of any cultural history, they attempted to escape inclusion within the history of the Western art world.

Richard Hill, however, suggests that it is impossible to entertain any such "escapist fantasy":

> *Unless whites can acknowledge and respond to their histories of power and racism as it affects all areas of culture, as it inscribes itself in their own minds, an equal and meaningful dialogue is impossible.*[50]

Artists have recently demonstrated more concern with issues of cultural appropriation, and the colonial histories that inform their work, but they have done so in a manner that focuses more attention on the cultural influences upon individual imaginations than upon the lives and contemporary circumstances of Native peoples. When Toronto artist Andy Fabo was chastised for his use of the symbolism of the sweat-lodge ceremony, he defended his work against Cardinal-Shubert's accusation of "cultural plagiarism" on personal grounds:

> *The first art museum that I ever visited was The Museum of The Plains Indians in Browning, Montana. I was eight years old at the time and for better or worse, the experience had an incredible impact on me.*[51]

The museum figures here less as an edifice of imperialism than as the mysterious origin of a personal fetish — as indeed an artist might personally experience it. For a gay artist concerned with questions of AIDS, healing, and otherness, the sweat-lodge might indeed constitute a powerful symbolic image, but Fabo's use of it illustrated no reflexive consideration of the legacy of power that enabled him to exploit its symbolic excess.

Liz Magore, another artist whose work has figured prominently in debates about appropriation, foregrounded the issue in her photography. As Richard Hill describes her show:

> *I notice the photographs on the nearby wall in black and white that depicted a man paddling a canoe, a blond hippy-looking woman in a headband, people camping on the beach, etc. ... The title of the photo of the blonde woman was called "Cheyenne type." ... This must be done ironically but how can I say for sure whether Magore's work was ironic? Maybe she was trying to point out the overlap of cultures, or the richness of First Nations culture as a resource for white artists. I left the work not knowing quite what was going on .... Perhaps it was merely another case of white people talking about themselves using First Nations culture as their medium? Sometime later I*

*read a statement by Magore about the photographs mentioned above. She said
that she wanted to deal with her personal history of appropriating slowly and
gently, in fact, that the work loses any serious claim to criticality. In effect,
it seems to do more to prop up old stereotypes than to aggressively call them
into question. This is especially true when the work is shot in the context of
a national gallery which inevitably lends its authority to the piece .... She
defends her project on the grounds that although the photos are embarrassing,
"a disavowal of my own history is equally uncomfortable."*[52]

Artists who address such issues seem more concerned with delineating
the influence of Native images in their own personal histories and in the
dominant culture from which they draw their artistic inspiration than in
acknowledging the actual histories of colonization in which those images
came to figure as part of a consciousness. When non-Native artists claim
that Native images are a part of their cultural heritage, they are not wrong,
but they are incredibly selective. To claim Native spiritual practices and
traditions of motif and design as part of one's contemporary culture or in
the name of one's personal cultural mediation — while bypassing the history
of racism, institutional abuse, poverty, and alienation that so incorporated
it — is simply to contribute to the process by which the painful realities of
contemporary Native life are continually ignored by those who feel more
comfortable claiming the artifacts they have left behind. Once again the
Romantic author claims the expressive power to represent cultural others
in the name of a universalized cultural heritage.

First Nations peoples may well be compelled to articulate their claims
"in a language that power understands," but in the *substance* of their
claims they contest the logic of possessive individualism, even as they
give voice to its metaphors. Engaging in "double-voiced rhetoric," they
appropriate and subvert these metaphors through the character of the
claims they make. First Nations peoples make it clear that issues of culture
and the proper place of texts cannot be separated from spirituality, political
determination, and title to traditional lands. This nexus of ecological,
spiritual, social, and territorial concerns is central to any understanding
of cultural appropriation.

*Self-determination and sovereignty include human, political, land, religious,
artistic and moral rights. Taking ownership of these stories involves a claim
to Aboriginal title over images, culture and stories.*[53]

In discussions of cultural appropriation, First Nations peoples strive to assert that the relationships that stories, images, motifs, and designs have to their communities cannot be subsumed under traditional European categories of art and culture and the possessive individualism that informs them. It is difficult for Native peoples to even speak about "rights"[54] to cultural expressions or creative skills that may be passed generationally through matrilineal inheritance.[55] Some stories are considered so powerful that one storyteller seeks permission before repeating a tale told by another.[56] To equate the need for such permissions to a copyright license is to reduce the social relationship between Native storytellers to one of contract and the alienation of market exchange relationships. These relationships, however, are ongoing ones which bind generations in a spiritual relationship with land, customs, and ancestors based upon traditions of respect, not the values of commodity exchange.

When Loretta Todd discusses First Nations ideas about ownership in the context of cultural appropriation, she discusses property in terms of relationships that are far wider than the exclusivity of possession and rights to alienate that dominate European concepts:

> *Without the sense of private property that ascended with European culture, we evolved concepts of property that recognized the interdependence of communities, families and nations and favored the guardianship of the earth as opposed to its conquest. There was a sense of ownership, but not one that preempted the rights and privileges of others or the rights of the earth and the life it sustained .... Ownership was bound up with history .... Communities, families, individuals, and nations created songs, dances, rituals, objects, and stories that were considered to be property, but not property as understood by the Europeans. Material wealth was re-distributed, but history and stories belonged to the originator and could be given or shared with others as a way of preserving, extending and witnessing history and expressing one's worldview.*[57]

First Nations peoples are engaged in an ongoing struggle to articulate, define, exercise, and assert aboriginal title, not only in terms of a relationship to territory, but in a relationship to the cultural forms that express the historical meaning of that relationship in specific communities.

For Native peoples in Canada, culture is not a fixed and frozen entity that can be objectified in reified forms that express its identity, but an ongoing living process that cannot be severed from the ecological relationships in which it lives and grows. By dividing ideas and expressions, oral traditions and written forms, intangible works and cultural objects, the law rips asunder what many First Nations people view as integrally related—freezing into categories what Native peoples find flowing in relationships. For those sympathetic to their ends to attempt to reduce these claims to assertions of intellectual property rights is simultaneously to neglect significant dimensions of Native aspiration and impose colonial juridical categories on postcolonial struggles in a fashion that reenacts the cultural violence of colonization. Colonial categories of art, culture, and authorial identity are deeply embedded in our legal categories of property, but the claims of others to objects and representations may well force these Western categories under new forms of scrutiny. As new subjects engaged in postcolonial struggles occupy the categories bestowed upon us by a colonial past, they may well transform the weakening colonial edifice upon which these categories are founded. New agents with new agendas may articulate old categories in new ways; the concept of aboriginal title promises to transform prevailing relations between politics, property, and propriety.

Ultimately the questions of "whose voice it is," who speaks on behalf of whom, and whether one can "steal the culture of another" are not *legal* questions to be addressed in terms of asserting rights, but *ethical* ones to be addressed in terms of moral and political commitments. To come back to the politics of knowledge and its deployment, I would suggest that in contexts of postcolonial struggle, the postmodern claim that cultures are constructed, emergent, mobile, and contested may seem somewhat empty. Such universalizing anti-essentialisms only begs questions of perspective—for whom is culture emergent and contested and in what circumstances? How does this claim sound in the struggles of those for whom "culture" may be the last legitimate ground for political autonomy and self-determination? From what position can one confidently make such a claim? Ultimately, questions of culture and its appropriation are political, rather than ontological, ones that demand empathetic identification rather than formal resolutions—a situational ethics to which we must always attend.

NOTES

1. Although the controversy died down in the national press, references and allusions back to it can be found throughout 1992, as, for example, in a books column by Philip Marchand titled "When Appropriation Becomes Inappropriate," *Toronto Star*, November 23, 1992, B5. I have not pursued the debates in the Canadian press since then.

2. See Rosemary J. Coombe, *Cultural Appropriations: Authorship, Alterity, and the Law* (New York, forthcoming).

3. See Rosemary J. Coombe, "The Celebrity Image and Cultural Identity: Publicity Rights and the Subaltern Politics of Gender," *Discourse* 14, no. 3 (1991), 59–88, and "Tactics of Appropriation and the Politics of Recognition in Late Modern Democracies," *Political Theory* 21 (1993), 411–33.

4. For a discussion of the importance of media in the constitution of contemporary public spheres, see Michael Warner, "The Mass Public and the Mass Subject," in *The Phantom Public Sphere*, edited by Bruce Robbins (Minneapolis, 1993); and Nicholas Garnham, "The Mass Media, Cultural Identity, and the Public Sphere in the Modern World," *Public Culture* 5 (1993), 251–66. I discuss the importance of intellectual properties in "Authorship and Alterity: Democracy in Postmodern Spheres," in *Authorial Imperium: The Politics and Poetics of Intellectual Properties in a Postcolonial Era*, edited by Peter Jaszi and Martha Woodmansee (Durham, forthcoming).

5. S. Godfrey, "Canada Council Asks Whose Voice Is It Anyway?" *Globe and Mail*, March 21, 1992, C1, 15.

6. "Letter to the Editor," *Globe and Mail*, March 28, 1992, D7.

7. "Letter to the Editor," *Globe and Mail*, March 28, 1992, D7.

8. *Globe and Mail*, March 31, 1992, A16.

9. Godfrey, "Canada Council Asks Whose Voice Is It Anyway?" C15.

10. Richard Outram, "Letter to the Editor," *Globe and Mail*, March 28, 1992, D7.

11. Ibid.

12. Russell Smith, "Letter to the Editor," *Globe and Mail*, April 3, 1992, A3.

13. Bill Driedger, "Letter to the Editor," *Globe and Mail*, March 28, 1992, D7.

14. This point was made by Alan Hutchinson, "Giving Smaller Voices a Chance to Be Heard," *Globe and Mail*, April 14, 1992, A16.

15. Godfrey, "Canada Council Asks Whose Voice Is It Anyway?" C1.

16. Godfrey, "Canada Council Asks Whose Voice Is It Anyway?" C15.

17. Lenore Keeshig-Tobias, "Stop Stealing Native Stories," *Globe and Mail*, January 26, 1990, A7.

18. Ibid.

19. Ibid.

20. Ibid.

21. Ibid.

22. See, for example, James Clifford, *The Predicament of Culture: Twentieth-Century Ethnography, Literature, and Art* (Cambridge, 1988); and Renato Rosaldo, *Culture and Truth: Remaking Social Analysis* (Boston, 1989).

23. (Minneapolis, 1991).

24. Annie Coombes, "Inventing the 'Postcolonial': Hybridity and Constituency in Contemporary Curating," *New Formations* 18 (1992), 39–52.

25. See Arun O. Mukherjee, "Whose Postcolonialism and Whose Postmodernism?" *World Literature Written in English* 30, no. 2 (1990), 1; Ella Shohat, "Notes on the Postcolonial," *Social Text* 32 (1992), 99; and Ruth Frankenburg and Lata Mani, "Crosscurrents, Crosstalk: Race, Postcoloniality, and the Politics of Location," in *Displacement, Diaspora, and Geographies of Identity*, edited by Smadar Lavie and Ted Swedenburg (Durham, 1996).

26. "Circling the Downspout of Empire: Post-Colonialism and Postmodernism," *Ariel* 20, no. 4 (1989), 149, 156.

27. John Henry Merryman, "Two ways of Thinking about Cultural Property," *American Journal of International Law* 80 (1986), 831, 832.

28. Ibid., 832 n 5.

29. Ibid., 847.

30. "Who Owns the Past?" in *The Politics of Culture*, edited by Brett Williams (Washington, 1991), 63–74; and "On Having a Culture," in *Objects and Others*, edited by George Stocking (Madison, 1985), 192–217.

31. Handler, "Who Owns the Past?" 64.

32. "Identities," *Yale Journal of Law and the Humanities* 3 (1991), 97, 98–9, citing Angela Harris, "Race and Essentialism in Feminist Legal Theory," *Stanford Law Review* 42 (1990), 584.

33. Ibid., 112.

34. bell hooks, *Yearning: Race, Gender, and Cultural Politics* (Toronto, 1990).

35. Ibid., 5.

36. Ibid., 19.

37. Ibid., 20, citing Linda Alcoff, "Cultural Feminism vs. Poststructuralism: The Identity Crisis in Feminist Theory," *Signs* 13 (1988), 405–33.

38. Ibid., 28.

39. Ibid.

40. Ibid., 29.

41. On accusations of essentialism, see Loretta Todd, "What More Do They Want?" in *Indigena: Contemporary Native Perspectives*, edited by Gerald McMaster and Lee-Ann Martin (Vancouver/Toronto, 1992), 71–9. Lee Maracle notes that

publishers are absolved of charges of censorship when they choose not to publish Native works (often returning works to writers with "Too Indian" or "Not Indian enough" written on them by non-Native editors who presume the authority to judge the works' authenticity), while she is accused of "being a fascist censor" for objecting to non-Native use of Native themes and stories. See Lee Maracle, "Native Myths: Trickster Alive and Crowing," *Fuse Magazine* (Fall 1989), 29.

42. I do not wish to suggest here that artists and authors of First Nations ancestry never wish to have their works valued on the market, or that they would eschew royalties for works produced as commodities for an exchange value on the market. That would be essentialist indeed! Instead, I am suggesting that in the debates surrounding cultural appropriation, Native peoples often assert that there are other value systems than those of the market in which their images, themes, practices, and stories figure and that these modes of appreciation and valuation are embedded in specific histories and relationships that should be accorded respect. Copyright laws, of course, only protect individual authors against the copying of their individual expressions, and do not protect ideas, or cultural themes, practices, and historical experiences from expropriation by cultural others.

43. The best demonstrations of this are found in Native art and literature where issues of identity are engaged in innovative fashions that often appropriate and transform European cultural forms to examine the specificity of First Nations history as it figures in contemporary political struggles and the need to forge alliances with other subordinated groups. The Romantic notion of art for art's sake is often challenged, as is the art/culture system that relegates Native expressive forms to an ethnographic realm, or, alternatively, claims them as Art, only to deny their claims to cultural specificity or political statement. For examples, see the various artists whose work is featured in McMaster and Martin, especially the essay by Cree art instructor Alfred Young Man, "The Metaphysics of North American Art," in *Indigena*, edited by McMaster and Martin, 81–9.

44. Handler, "Who Owns the Past?" 71.

45. Loretta Todd, "Notes on Appropriation," *Parallelogramme* 16 (1990), 24.

46. Ibid.

47. Dai Skuse, Kim Kozzi, and Napoleon Brousseau, "Letter to the Editor," *Parallelogramme* 13 (1989–90), 2.

48. Paul Smith, "Lost in American," *Borderlines* 23 (1991–2), 17–18, 18.

49. Skuse, Kozzi, and Brousseau, "Letter to the Editor," 4.

50. Richard Hill, "One Part per Million," *Fuse Magazine* (Winter 1992), 12–22, 14.

51. Andy Fabo, "Letter to the Editor," *Parallelogramme* 13 (1989–90), 4.

52. Hill, "One Part per Million," 20.

53. McMaster and Martin, "Introduction," in *Indigena*, edited by McMaster and Martin, 17.

54. David Alexis writes that rights are a further imposition upon Native peoples. "Indian people do not think in terms of rights but in terms of responsibility. Whatever flows from the fulfillment of those responsibilities are the gifts in life. The demanding of status from one's mere existence is ludicrous. The so-called fishing rights won by Indian people are not a gift bestowed by white people because of recognition by white people of those rights. Those so called 'rights' are the result of traditional people fulfilling responsibilities to fisheries through traditional ceremony and lifestyle … a gift from the creation [that results from] a fulfillment of responsibility through Indian belief." From "Obscurity as a Lifestyle," *Borderlines* 23 (1991–2), 15.

55. Joane Cardinal-Schubert, "In the Red," *Fuse Magazine* (Fall 1989), 20–8, 20.

56. Keeshig-Tobias, "Stop Stealing Native Stories," 7.

57. Todd, "Notes on Appropriation," 26.

RICK HELMES-HAYES
AND JAMES CURTIS

ETHNICITY AND SOCIAL CLASS THIRTY
YEARS AFTER THE VERTICAL MOSAIC

FROM THE VERTICAL MOSAIC REVISITED

It is probably difficult for recent cohorts of students of sociology to understand the profound ground-breaking impact that *The Vertical Mosaic* had when it first appeared. The discipline of sociology is now well established, and each year the Canadian sociological community produces hundreds of articles and books about matters Canadian. Further, since the 1960s, the discipline has produced a staggering amount of scholarship dealing with a wide range of social issues — class, power, gender, race, ethnicity, education, work, the state, and so forth. As a consequence, we have considerable information on the structure of contemporary Canadian society, enlivened and enriched by a wide range of theoretical interpretations and constructions of these data.

None of this was true in 1965. Indeed, at this time, the Canadian sociological community was just embarking on its rapid-growth phase (the mid-1960s to the mid-1970s), so there were still only 115 university-based sociologists in Canada; and sociology departments were just being set up at a number of universities [....][1] There was not even a Canadian sociology textbook. The nearest thing was a collection of Canadian readings put together by Porter and three colleagues, Bernard Blishen, Frank Jones, and Kaspar Naegele (see Blishen et al., 1961, 1963, 1968, 1971).[2] Also, the first Canadian sociology journal, the *Canadian Review of Sociology and Anthropology*, was not founded until 1964. Certainly there was nothing even approximating the volume of published research on Canadian society that we now take for granted. Thus, Porter and his co-editors had to scour the literature in sociology and political science (including graduate theses) to find enough material to put together an edited book with reasonably broad coverage. In such an environment, the appearance of *The Vertical Mosaic* was of epoch-making significance. Not only did it help to establish the credibility of the discipline in the social science community at a key time in its development, but it provided a macrosociological baseline description and interpretation of Canadian society from which the entire Canadian sociological community could work. As Bruce McFarlane, then Porter's colleague at Carleton, put it, the publication of *The Vertical Mosaic* was the event that marked "the coming of age" of Canadian sociology.[3]

The impact of *The Vertical Mosaic* was immediate and profound. It received almost universal acclaim when it appeared in 1965 [...][4] and the year after won the MacIver Award of the American Sociological Association, the only Canadian sociology book ever to receive that honor. It went on to become the most cited book in the history of Canadian sociology and has sold more copies than any other sociology work ever published by University of Toronto Press.[5] It remains in print to this day, three decades after it was originally released.

In a society which is made up of many cultural groups there is usually some relationship between a person's memberships in these groups and his class position and, consequently, his chances of reaching positions of power. Because the Canadian people are often referred to as a mosaic composed of different ethnic groups, the title, The Vertical Mosaic, was originally given to the chapter which examines the relationship between ethnicity and social class. As the study proceeded, however, the hierarchal relationship between Canada's many cultural groups became a recurring theme in class and power. For example, it became clear that the Canadians of British origin have retained, within the elite structure of the society, the charter group status with which they started out, and that in some institutional settings the French have been admitted as a co-charter group whereas in others they have not. The title, "the Vertical Mosaic," therefore seemed ... appropriate.[6]

Many Canadians are reluctant to admit that their country has a class structure. So far as social classes cannot be demarcated by a hard and fast line ... this reluctance is understandable. But this does not dismiss the other evidence of the class division of the population which exists in terms of inequalities of wealth, opportunity, and social recognition. The barriers are not the horizontal ones of geographic regions or distinctive ethnic cultures but the vertical ones of a large socio-economic hierarchy ... Communities and classes intersect; perhaps in few places more than in Canada, which has regional and ethnic variety ... of formidable magnitude. But these complications merely obscure, they do not eliminate the fundamental problems which class inequalities engender.[7]

THE LASTING RELEVANCE OF *THE VERTICAL MOSAIC*

[There are many] important ways in which Canadian society has changed in the three decades since *The Vertical Mosaic* appeared. Relevant aspects of this change include: the sources of immigration (by country of origin) and the work qualifications required of immigrants have changed; multiculturalism has made the mosaic potentially even more unstable; Aboriginals have found a new voice and power; women have entered the workforce in much larger numbers; foreign ownership of the Canadian economy has increased; Canadian investment abroad has grown; industrial production has been internationalized; the computer and information revolutions have begun; regionalism has intensified; relations between Quebec and the rest of Canada (the latter particularly as represented in the federal government) have become more conflictual — witness the passage of Bill 101 and the results of the 1996 separation referendum; there has been some shift of powers from the federal government to the provinces and a decrease in federal and, more recently, provincial expenditures on social services and the like [....]

Have the many changes in Canadian society meant that the basic images put forward in *The Vertical Mosaic* are no longer accurate characterizations of this society? Judging from the contents of the present volume, the images remain quite appropriate, but how appropriate depends on the image under consideration.

First, Porter's image of a society which locks certain ethnic and racial minorities into entrance statuses at the bottom of the occupational world applies to Canadian society today but less well than it did a generation or two ago [....] This is in part because changed immigration policies have altered the racial and ethnic composition of Canadian society. For example, in 1961, the population of European origin in Canada comprised 23 per cent of the total, and it is now just 15 per cent. Over the same period, the Asian proportion of Canada's population increased from less than 1 per cent to almost 6 per cent. Other ethnics of non-European origin increased from about 1 per cent to almost 5 per cent of the total. And, visible minorities (including Aboriginals) now make up 9 per cent rather than 3 per cent of the population [....] So, Canada is now less British and less European in ethnic background, and it has a larger proportion of visible minorities, than was the case thirty years ago. Moreover, data on the occupational distribution of ethnic groups suggest that some non-charter ethnic groups have more successfully integrated into the occupational structure than was the case three decades ago. Also, they have done so while gaining sociopolitical acceptance. This has occurred because of changing requirements for better work credentials on the part of immigrants, policies of multiculturalism and affirmative action, and efforts by ethnic organizations. Income inequality across some ethnic groups has lessened, too, but income is still distributed unequally with northern and western Europeans and people of British origin remaining more advantaged, and blacks, Aboriginals, and those from Latin, South, and Central America towards the bottom in income. The "visible" racial minorities generally remain lower in income. Native peoples in particular remain at or near the bottom of ethnic hierarchies of every kind — income, occupational status, labour force participation, and so forth [....] In addition, there is still a problem of depressed entrance status for many immigrants, compounded by the structural barriers of labour markets and systematic discrimination. And, as elite studies over the past three decades show, access to the elites remains related to ethnic background. For example, people of British origin continue to do disproportionately well [....] In sum, the vertical mosaic imagery very successfully captured what was occurring in Canada during the first half of the century and before, but there have been some changes in a more egalitarian direction since [....]

Second, the analyses in [*The Vertical Mosaic Revisited*] show that "the class society" image of Canada applies as well today as it did in Porter's time. Indeed, Pat Armstrong's and Julia S. O'Connor's[8] analyses of public policy changes suggest reduced in Canada, we may be entering a period of growing inequalities of each type (compare also Wallace Clement's and Michael Ornstein's analyses).[9] For example, data on the distribution of income suggest that Canada is just as unequal now as it was in 1965 — perhaps worse. Since 1961 the bottom quintile of earners (families) has received about 6 per cent of income, while the top quintile has received approximately 40 per cent. The bulk of the investment income still goes to those at the very top of the class structure only, and RRSPs, which are a development since the period covered by *The Vertical Mosaic*, are for the most part a safe haven from taxes for those earners near the top of the income structure [....][10] Further, something more than 20 per cent of Canadian children currently live below the poverty line [....][11] In 1961 Canada had no food banks. In 1991 there were about 300 [....][12] While more people have access to state-funded medical care, and more people have better education than thirty years ago, efforts at "debt management" by federal and provincial governments have made even these gains precarious for the future.

Porter did not document gender differences in access to jobs and income. When these issues are explored, we find declining but persistent gender inequality, and the trends add moment to the "class society" and "vertical mosaic" images. There have been some gains for women over time in the world of paid work, but women still bear the burden of "the double day" of paid and domestic labour. Thirty years ago less than 30 per cent of women were paid workforce; now 60 per cent are [....][13] (In 1965 women made less than 60 cents for every dollar a man made; that figure is now over 70 cents. Women now make up more than 50 per cent of the undergraduate population at Canada universities, and they account for half those in master's programs and one-third of those in doctoral programs. There are more women in non-traditional occupations than ever before, and at higher levels of authority and pay. Women are still largely missing from the elites Porter described, but some gains have been made in elite access — particularly in the intellectual and labour elites [....] Legislation concerning pay equity, affirmative action, maternity leave, sexual harassment, and so on has been enacted. At the same time these gains have neither shattered nor homogenized the mosaic, for they are spread unevenly across the class and ethnic structure of Canadian society. Further, women suffer higher rates of unemployment and underemployment than men, and lower proportions of women than men are in paid employment full-time year-round (40 per cent today). Women, and particularly women among visible minorities, tend to be the first to suffer from government and private sector cutbacks because they remain overrepresented compared with men among the recently hired, and are concentrated in the clerical, service, teaching, and social service occupations that are currently under fire. Moreover, hard-won legislative gains such as affirmative action and pay equity are currently under attack.

Third, Ornstein's analyses of elite studies suggest that ethnic and racial inequalities in elite recruitment may have lessened somewhat, although a pattern of under representation of minority groups persists. Further, he sees no reason from more recent analyses of who has power in Canadian society to reject or fundamentally alter the conclusions about elite control and elite accommodation presented by Porter. While various elites have received some research attention since Porter's analyses, only the economic elite has received much. For the economic elite, some data suggest that new, regionally based, ethnic capitalist class fragments have emerged (Jewish, Québécois) [....][14] Perhaps the clearest trend is the decline in the percentage of the economic elite that is Anglophone in background. Two recent studies [...][15] suggest that while those of British origin are disproportionately high, they account for only about 55–65 per cent of elites; the French are underrepresented at 7–9 per cent, as are non-charter ethnics at approximately 26–38 per cent. Apparently, class origins of the economic elite also have changed; one major study [...][16] shows that a smaller proportion (62 per cent) than in Porter's results come from middle-class or higher backgrounds. However, despite some shifts in class origin, there is evidence that the Canadian capitalist class is "more robust, centralized, integrated and Canadian than previous studies suggested" and that Canadian, not foreign-controlled, industrial and financial firms are at the centre of this class [....] The limited work on the political elite [...][17] suggests that some diversification of ethnic origins has taken place, with little change in class backgrounds. The situation in the bureaucratic elite at both the federal and provincial levels is different. There has been substantial "downward" shifting of class background change in class backgrounds. The situation in the bureaucratic elite at both the federal and a substantial decline in the percentage from British backgrounds [....][18]

None of the contributors to [*The Vertical Mosaic Revisited*], then, suggests that any of the three basic images from *The Vertical Mosaic* should be set aside in our attempts to analyze contemporary Canadian society. The images are still viable ones, given contemporary social patterns. At the same time, each contributor shows that today we should add some important caveats and qualifiers to Porter's analyses [....] While she does not dispute the continued relevance of the many social inequality-related images in *The Vertical Mosaic*, she takes up the top of gender relations in Canada—one that Porter more or less ignored in *The Vertical Mosaic*—and discusses how the role of gender relations should be understood within the context of Canada as a class- and ethnically stratified society. Armstrong, who coined the phrase "the double ghetto" for the title of one of her books, highlights the issue of gender relations and gender inequality and warns that the gains that have been made in breaking down this aspect of the vertical mosaic are now threatened—especially for women of colour and from visible minority ethnic backgrounds. Moreover, as a feminist political economist she sees a good portion of the push to limit or reverse these gains as coming from those with class-based power. She emphasizes that Canada is not "just" a double ghetto for women; it is a class society. Thus, when we attempt to explain gender relations in Canada we have to explore class relations. Consideration of the most powerful class agents among "accommodating elites" must come into play as well. Further, since classes, dominant or otherwise, are made up of "agents"—real people with ethnic backgrounds, regional ties, and so forth—the facts of Canada as a colony (metropolis—hinterland relations), Canada as "British fragment," and Canada as a "fragile federation" of competing regions and two linguistic "cultures" come into play as well.

We could do a similar analysis of each chapter in [*The Vertical Mosaic Revisited*]. What such analyses would reveal is that the salience of Porter's three central images varies from one chapter to the next but that Porter's basic images constitute the foundation upon which their respective analyses of contemporary Canada are built.

NOTES

1.   Harry H. Hiller, *Society and Change: S.D. Clark and the Development of Canadian Society* (Toronto, 1982), 23, Table 3.

2.   Indeed, as late as 1972–3, only 24 per cent of required texts in 17 sociology departments across Canada were written by Canadians. See Bernard Blishen, Frank Jones, Kaspar Naegle, and John Porter, eds. (Four editions, in 1961,

1963, 1968, 1971). *Canadian Society: Sociological Perspectives* (Toronto). Cited by Redekop 1976, 133 in Robert Brym, with Bonnie Fox, *From Culture to Power: The Sociology of English Canada* (Toronto, 1989).

3.   Interview of Bruce McFarlane by Rick Helmes-Hayes, November 2, 1986.

4.   Rick Helmes-Hayes, "Writings about John Porter and His Work: An Annotated Bibliography, pp. 283–92 in John Porter, *The Measure of Canadian Society*, edited by Wallace Clement (2nd ed.), 283–92 (Ottawa, 1987).

5.   The observation that *The Vertical Mosaic* has sold more copies (over 100,000 copies) than any other sociology book (indeed any other book) published by University of Toronto Press is based on correspondence with Virgil Duff, at the Press, to Rick Helmes-Hayes, May 13, 1997.

6.   John Porter, *The Vertical Mosaic: An Analysis of Social Class and Power in Canada* (Toronto, 1965), xii–xiii.

7.   Ibid., 403–4.

8.   Pat Armstrong, "Missing Women: A Feminist Perspective on *The Vertical Mosaic*," 116, 144; and Julia S. O'Connor, "Social Citizenship, and the Welfare State, 1965–1995: Canada in Comparative Context," 180–233.

9.   Wallace Clement, "Power, Ethnicity, and Class: Reflections Thirty Years after *The Vertical Mosaic*," 34–59; and Michael Orenstein, "Three Decades of Elite Research in Canada: John Porter's Unfulfilled Legacy," 145–79.

10.   Denis P. Forcese, *The Canadian Class Structure* (Toronto, 1997), 148.

11.   Ibid., 47.

12.   Jullian Oderkirk, "Food Banks," in *Social Problems in Canada Reader*, edited by E.D. Nelson and Augie Fleras, 226, Figure 1 (Scarborough, 1995).

13.   Forcese, *The Canadian Class Structure*, 92.

14.   Jorge Niosi, *A Study of Power in the Canadian Business Establishment* (Toronto, 1981).

15.   Alfred A. Hunter, *Class Tells: On Social Inequality in Canada* (Toronto, 1986); Michael Ornstein and H. Michael Stevenson, *In the Bosom of the State: Ideology and Politics in Canada* (Montreal, in press).

16.   Ornstein and Stevenson, *In the Bosom of the State*.

17.   Denis Olsen, *The State Elite* (Toronto, 1980); Rick Ogmundson and J. McLaughlin, "Trends in the Ethnic Origins of Canadian Elites: The Decline of the BRITS," *Canadian Review of Sociology and Anthropology* 29, no. 2 (1992), 227–42.

18.   Colin Campbell and George J. Szablowski, *The Superbureaucrats: Structures and Behaviour in Central Agencies* (Toronto, 1979).

IRSHAD MANJI

BELONGING IN A MULTICULTURAL CONTEXT

FROM RISKING UTOPIA: ON THE EDGE OF A NEW DEMOCRACY

Many refer to me as a Muslim Lesbian Feminist. Labels are simple; the politics behind them are anything but. I cannot deny being an observant Muslim, a committed queer or a practicing feminist, yet with each label comes a set of assumptions that, if explored further, would be punctured.

She must be a socialist. My love of initiative colours me solidly capitalist. At twelve years old, I ran a lucrative lunch business out of the class cloakroom. My few months of operation made me important to my peers. They made me popular. They made me $75.

If she is lesbian and feminist, she hates men. When I came out to my mother, she pleaded with me not to give up on guys. "Give up on guys?" I thought to myself. "Is she kidding? I'm telling her (and everyone else) I'm a lesbian because bisexuality gets no respect." A shame, that. To be pressed against throbbing muscle, enveloped by arms that I can bite but rarely dent, separated merely by a sheet of sweat and a lick of latex, exchanging grunts and grins, all the while knowing he can have me but he cannot keep me: Mum is in luck. That is too good to give up.

She wallows in victimhood. To be a victim is to be immobilized by circumstance, a situation I have always shunned. Even when it meant behaving like a jerk. In a teenage act of pure, lip-smacking spite, I spread a rumor about a friend who had become a born-again Christian. Cautiously passed notes told classmates that I had spotted her hugging a girl. My anonymous phone calls to her home began, "Hey, lezzie, you're being watched." I felt a perverse power surge in singling somebody out. After years of being called a Paki, I was finally showing these missionaries of the supremacist Messiah that I could give as good as I got. To hell with volunteering victimhood for the sake of sisterhood.

She is vegetarian. I adore my burgers, fries, and cheese doodles. "Have your eggplant," I exhort my girlfriend. "Be one with the soil, babe. I choose to be one with the oil." After deconstructing my diet — problematizing my patties and contextualizing my cole-slaw — the post-modernists at my table can only deem me White Trash. Fine, I nod. White Trash captures me better than Muslim Lesbian Feminist.

Identity starts with labels such as Muslim Lesbian Feminist. But when you make the effort to life my label and ask questions — "You don't eat meat, do you?" — you give me the right to be acknowledged and the responsibility to refine or replace your perceptions: "Not only do I eat meat; this dyke devours Whoppers." Rotted in caring sufficiently to be sufficiently curious, that interaction is the mark of belonging. Identity thus emerges from our dialogue, your perceptions meeting mine.

On their own, labels serve as security blankets. They can insulate us when everything else seems to be eroding in the sweep of economic, cultural, and technological change. But also like blankets, labels often restrict movement and conceal the real goings-on underneath. I hope for a world where we turn over the labels and investigate; that is the genesis of belonging.

I understand the advantage of using labels. They are things to which people can react. We all attach ourselves to groups, or are attached to them, as a point of departure for further expression. It is when labels clamp communication that belonging is in jeopardy. By belonging, then, I do mean unconditional acceptance, better known as mindlessness. Belonging is a state in which we accept each other just enough to explore.

The question of belonging is complex not only because of the extent to which I am willing to accept them — their fears no less than their foods. Each of the anecdotes above reflects my lifelong struggle to ensure mutual belonging. Even as a child, I knew that the burden of belonging began with me. To improve my chances of finding a niche, however fleeting, I could not allow myself to feel powerless. I had to grab the opportunity to play lunchtime Santa, bully someone vulnerable or disclose my not-so-straight self. Assimilation is passive, belonging active.

[…] Belonging is a contract in which the dominant culture — of a classroom, a workplace, a society — meets the conditions of human dignity so that it may benefit from the continued contributions of those it dignifies.

Put bluntly, the other side of the belonging bargain is the treatment you get once in the game.

An immigration officer introduced me to that contract when, in October 1972, he refused to settle my family in Montreal. After nationalist dictator Idi Amin seized power in our native Uganda, thousands of Asians were given only days to choose between leaving or dying. With no time to brush up on world geography, my family fled, eventually landing in Montreal. The immigration officer asked my parents why we wanted to live in that city. Desperate not to blow our big chance, my French-speaking mother replied that Montreal begins with the same letter as the family name, so it might make for a happy fit. Upon surveying me and my sisters, the officer told my mother that we would not survive the coming Montreal winter—we were dressed for tropical weather. He offered us Vancouver instead. A few stamps later, the family was bound for the other side of the country.

In retrospect, I would have loved to grow up in a bilingual city. But the officers' move showed that he was paying attention. There is no doubt he had power over us. Even so, this symbol of state hegemony, this gatekeeper of cheap labor, cared enough to view refugee children as human beings with a Canadian future rather than labels lost in a ditched past. He cared enough to wonder what we needed. "A society in which strangers would feel common belonging and mutual responsibility to each other depends on trust," explains Canadian philosopher Michael Ignatieff in his trenchant 1984 book-length essay *The Needs of Strangers*. "[A]nd trust in turn reposes on the idea that beneath difference there is identity."[1]

I doubt that trust would be accorded my refugee family in 1997. The last few years have seen this country suffocate newcomers with suspicion. A federal law requires the finger-printing of refugee claimants. A $975 "right-to-land" fee—the equivalent of a decade's work in areas of the Third World—has been introduced to help sustain the social services used by immigrants (a line routinely rehearsed by politicians and bureaucrats on the evening news. Still, studies conclude that, through taxes, most immigrants give the government far more money than they borrow.) Iron handcuffs and leg shackles adorn some refugees who are kept in crowded Canadian detention centres for months, despite being charged with no crime and, occasionally, despite being as young as thirteen. A prime minister pitching the "politics of inclusion" creates the Ministry of Public Security to "handle" immigrants and refugees. The label implied and imposed by all of these measures: THREAT. Public opinion apparently agrees. Belonging is in jeopardy.

I can think of no collectivity better suited to the experiment [of multiculturalism] than Canadians. In the first place, ours is a heritage of experimentation. It is because the Fathers of Confederation resisted prevailing economic wisdom, bucking the north-south pull of the American continent to carve out a country along the east-west axis, that Canada can be found on a map today. During the 1988 free trade showdown, conservatives brilliantly bottled and sold the value of experimentation by snubbing a century of their own political wisdom and telling Canadians that there is no such thing any more as an unthinkable thought. Strictly speaking, they were correct.

But without counter-experimentation, cautions Richard Gwyn, Canada might coast to oblivion. "As an invented nation, either we reinvent our traditions of egalitarianism and liberalism to accommodate the realities of today's global economy or, some year, some decade, we will simply fade away." His either/or fallacy notwithstanding, Gwyn rightly suggests that counter-experimentation will have to be cultural and psychological more than economic. That is to avoid becoming

> *the national equivalent of a condominium apartment building in which owners and tenants greet each other politely and warmly, and periodically deal sensibly with common practical concerns like maintenance and landscaping, but have no sense of belonging to an enterprise with values and purposes larger than their individual self-interests.*

Rather than giving Canada a new bottom line, more experimentation will have to cultivate an overarching ethos of belonging.

Necessary it might be, but are Canadians willing? Evidently so. "Canadians want to renovate the social contract," observes Judith Maxwell, president of the Canadian Policy Research Network (CPRN). The CPRN's 1995 study, *Exploring Canadian Values,* found that fiscal responsibility and self-reliance cohabit in the Canadian soul with democracy, compassion, equality, and collective responsibility. Reducing the friction between these clusters of principles calls for creativity and negotiation. Canadians, the study concludes, "are able to imagine repairs, renovations, restructuring, and prefer those to the dismantling of social programs. Building a new social contract will require a more holistic approach," whereby elite privileges and not just social programs are put "on the table for trade-off." Maybe most important, "we want to be involved in the renovation process."

Michael Adams confirms the Canadian will to participate. "The kind of authority that gains respect today is not based on fear, intimidation or guilt," his surveys reveal, "but is more voluntaristic and consensual. Not chiseled in marble, but flexible." Flexibility is now "more authentic" to Canadians than rigidity.

Besides the necessity and willingness, Canadians have a capacity for communication that will not let us despair—another dimension of our readiness for the Utopia of Complexity. Significantly, "[w]e're the most heavily cabled country in the world, and the most compulsive makers of long-distance calls," chronicles Richard Gwyn. "It's said that on arriving at the Pearly Gates, all Canadians automatically follow the sign pointing to 'Seminar on Heaven and Hell.'" In other words, we listen. And occasionally, we hear. Whatever the latest stains on its human rights record, Canada remains a remarkable example of common purpose amid competing interests, be they regional, religious, linguistic, ethnic, or class. No other collectivity on earth can claim so much cohesion within so much tension.

Where else can a separatist party be legally elected to the supreme legislature of the land, with enough seats to swear the oath as "Her Majesty's Loyal Opposition," fight for the sovereignty of one province with the funds provided by taxpayers of all provinces and act as the most vociferous parliamentary voice to preserve national social programs? It is barely conceivable. It is Canadian.

Where else can First Nations chiefs put the minister of Indian Affairs on the hot seat for showing up at their 1996 annual meeting late—even though he had just come from fulfilling a long-standing federal promise to move one of Canada's poorest aboriginal communities, the Innu of Davis Inlet, to a less isolated location? Where else could the minister be booed after also committing to accelerated land claim talks with the Labrador Innu? Perhaps achieving all of this during the time of the Assembly of First Nations gathering was a government strategy calculated to keep the minister away yet make the biggest splash. Still, the timing coincided with a deadline imposed by the Labrador Innuit Association, whose president threatened that without progress on land claims, mining of aboriginal territory would come to a halt. Where else would such a threat be peaceably accepted? The minister's response is by no means enough, but neither is it callous indifference.

That Canada was the world's first country to enact multiculturalism does not surprise. Yet who else has a multiculturalism policy that, at rock bottom, trusts people to make nice with each other? It is flawed, but it is a faith in our readiness to accommodate that I am not sure could be felt of any other citizenry.

We can take issue with the nuts and bolts of the UN Human Development Index, which for two years running has ranked Canada as the world's top spot for men, close to top for women. More compelling, I think, are the nakedly subjective judgments from abroad. Canada, a Mexican diplomat has said, is "the solution looking for problems."[2] American actress Jane Fonda seems to agree. Her struggle to belong in the U.S., from being excoriated as a communist for her friendship with the North Vietnamese to being branded as a sell-out for her marriage to billionaire Ted Turner, seeps into her statement that "[w]hen I'm in Canada, I feel like this is what the world should be."[3] If anyone can approach the ideal of interactive complexity, it is us.

NOTES

1.   Michael Ignatieff, *The Needs of Strangers: An Essay on Privacy, Solidarity, and the Politics of Being Human* (London, 1984).

2.   Quoted from speech by Augustine Barrios-Gomez, former Mexican ambassador to Canada, verified by spokesperson Jesus Contreras, author interview by phone, October 1996.

3.   Jane Fonda quoted by John Robert Columbo, *Dictionary of Canadian Quotations* (Toronto, 1991).

T.R. BALAKRISHNAN AND FENG HOU

RESIDENTIAL PATTERNS IN CITIES

FROM IMMIGRANT CANADA: DEMOGRAPHIC, ECONOMIC AND SOCIAL CHALLENGES

In Canada at the present time immigration is as important as natural increase, contributing to about half the annual population growth of the country. Not only the number of immigrants but their composition has drastically changed. Removal of discriminatory clauses in the immigration laws in the early 1960s, combined with the changing push factors in the countries of origin, mean that the ethnic composition of Canada is very different from what it was before. While western European origins predominated before 1960, in the '60s and '70s most immigrants were primarily from southern Europe. Since then, however, populations from the Third World countries have formed the majority of immigrants. Thus, more than one-half of the immigrants in the 1980s were the so-called visible minority groups of blacks, South Asians, Chinese, and many Latin and Central Americans.[1] In 1991, 68 per cent of new arrivals to Canada were visible minority immigrants, about two-thirds of whom were blacks, Chinese, and South Asians (Statistics Canada 1996b).

Unlike the earlier immigrants from western Europe, the new immigrants are more selective in their places of destination in Canada. Larger metropolitan areas attract a disproportionately greater share of recent immigrants. For example, during the decade 1981–91, the percentages of black immigrants who went to Montreal, Toronto, and Vancouver were 20.4, 58.1, and 1.8 respectively. The corresponding percentages for South Asians were 6.5, 52.7, and 16.7 and for Chinese immigrants 6.8, 43.3, and

28.8 respectively. Selectivity in the choice of residential space on the part of ethnic groups is noticeable not only at the regional and city levels but within cities as well, in the creation of distinct neighbourhoods. The changing inter- and intracity ethnic composition forms the focus of study in this chapter.

As the ethnic and racial diversity in Canadian cities changes, concerns arise about the socio-economic integration of minority groups in the larger society as well as problems of discrimination they may face in the housing and labour markets. Two types of integration become particularly relevant, namely, in residential choices of minority groups, and in the occupational structure. Lack of spatial integration is manifested in terms of ethnic neighbourhoods and spatial segregation from other groups, especially the major groups. Ethnic neighbourhoods may also promote retention of ethnic identity. This study focuses primarily on the spatial residential patterns of ethnic groups. Is concentration of recent immigrant groups increasing or decreasing? Are there changes in their segregation from the majority Charter groups of British and French? Do ethnic neighbourhoods differ in their overall socio-economic levels? Can we explain some of these patterns?

The hypothesis that rapid growth of ethnic and racial minorities through immigration will increase their concentration and segregation from major groups has been posited by others and has found some support (Harwood, 1986; Massey, 1986; Massey and Denton, 1987). The premise is that rapid and substantial increase of such immigrants will stimulate negative attitudes toward them. They may be seen as a threat to employment opportunities and a strain on local services and welfare systems. Different customs and lifestyles may also be difficult to accept if the immigrant population of a different ethnic origin increases substantially within a short time (Reitz, 1988a).

Discrimination against immigrant groups in housing and labour markets may force them into certain areas of the city and thus increase their spatial concentration and segregation from specific groups, such as the British or other European origin groups (Olson and Kobayashi, 1993). In the United States much of the non-white segregation is typical of this involuntary segregation (Taeuber and Taeuber, 1965; Taeuber, 1970; Massey and Denton, 1993). The patterns and changes in involuntary residential segregation have been explained in terms of "social class" and "social distance" hypotheses. Residential concentration of social classes may reflect the unequal resources of the classes, which may reduce the choice of residential location for the lower classes. Further, the greater social distance will add to the extent of segregation among certain groups, such as the "visible minorities" (Duncan and Lieberson, 1959; Darroach and Marston, 1971; Richmond, 1972; Kantrowitz, 1973; Driedger and Peters, 1977; Pineo, 1977; Balakrishnan, 1982; Kalbach, 1981; Massey, 1979, 1981a).

On the other hand, concentration can also result from what the minorities perceive as its advantages. Proponents of voluntary segregation, sometimes referred to as the "cultural proximity model," argue that persons of the same ethnic ancestry may choose to live in proximity so that social interaction can be maximized and group norms and values can be maintained (Driedger and Church, 1974; Balakrishnan, 1982). Size and concentration may enable an ethnic group to give its members the comfort of ethnic identity, shared cultural values, language, social institutions such as ethnic clubs, churches, and own language newspapers, and access to economic resources not available elsewhere in the city. One may therefore expect that new arrivals will go to ethnic enclaves first before moving to other areas as their socio-economic conditions and ability to adjust to their new country improve. Most of these studies have been done in the United States with such groups as Mexicans, Puerto Ricans, and blacks. Whether these finding would be duplicated in Canada cannot be taken for granted. Canadian immigrants vary substantially from their American counterparts not only by place of origin but also in their socio-economic characteristics. Moreover, Canada differs from the United States in other respects, for example, the size and history of the black minority. Consequently this hypothesis needs to be tested in the Canadian context.

ETHNIC CONCENTRATION WITHIN THE METROPOLITAN AREAS

Not only are the ethnic profiles of the CMAs (Census Metropolitan Areas) different, but the concentrations within them are as well. Urban sociology is replete with studies of ethnic neighbourhoods such as "Chinatown," "Little Italy," "Greektown," etc. While some ethnic neighbourhoods persist over time, many are swept away by ecological forces. Apart from such factors as ethnic identity, language and duration of stay will influence the continuation of an ethnic neighbourhood. While the assimilation of older immigrants and especially second- or third-generation immigrants

Table 17.1: Percentage Distribution of Immigrants by Period of Immigration and Ethnicity, Canada, 1991

	Percentage of immigrants in total population	Percentage distribution of immigrants by period of immigration				
		Total	<1961	<1961–71	1971–80	1981–91
Total Population	16.1	100	28.5	19.1	23.9	28.5
Single origin British	12.6	100	44.5	23.8	20.5	11.3
French	1.2	100	29.2	24.1	26.5	20.2
Dutch	37.9	100	74.4	10.8	8.6	6.2
German	25.5	100	65.1	16.7	9.3	8.9
Polish	53.4	100	32.2	9.4	7.5	51.0
Ukrainian	12.9	100	80.1	6.9	4.5	8.5
Italian	48.0	100	50.9	37.2	9.0	2.8
Portuguese	68.0	100	8.6	30.0	39.8	21.6
Jewish	33.3	100	35.8	16.0	22.2	26.0
Other European	48.5	100	39.3	24.8	17.5	18.5
Arab/West Asian	71.0	100	2.5	11.9	22.6	63.1
South Asian	68.8	100	.9	10.9	42.0	46.2
Chinese	72.7	100	4.8	9.0	31.3	54.9
Other East/ Southeast Asia	68.4	100	1.0	6.1	38.0	54.9
Latin/Central/ South American	72.7	100	.5	3.0	30.5	66.0
Black/Caribbean	60.9	100	1.5	16.1	41.9	40.5
Aboriginal	.6	100	11.5	16.1	25.3	47.1
Other single	7.5	100	14.4	17.1	26.9	41.6
Multiple origin						
British only	5.2	100	39.4	26.8	23.1	10.7
British & French	2.0	100	29.0	26.4	29.9	14.7
British & other	4.9	100	19.4	26.8	30.6	23.2
French & other	5.7	100	24.8	22.0	28.5	24.7
British/French	3.0	100	16.8	24.0	33.9	25.3
Non-British/ French	20.7	100	21.1	15.7	28.3	34.9

Source: 1991 Census Public Use Sample Tape

will reduce the chances of maintenance of an ethnic neighbourhood, new sustained immigration may increase its salience. We will examine the relative concentration of ethnic groups in the Canadian CMAs using the census tracts as units of analysis.

Before constructing summary measures of concentration, it may be useful to get a descriptive picture of the extent of concentration. Census tracts in each of the metropolitan areas were arranged in decreasing order of ethnic population, so that cumulative proportions of the population could be calculated. Table 17.2 shows the extent of concentration, by examining the proportion of tracts in which 50 and 90 per cent of an ethnic group population is found.

There is very little concentration of the British origin population, which is to be expected, given its size. The French also show low concentrations, even though their numbers are small in many CMAs. They are almost as dispersed as the British in the various metropolitan areas. About 70 per cent of the tracts need to be covered before 90 per cent of the French population is included. Concentration is also low for the northwestern European groups of Germans and Dutch.

Jews are by far the most concentrated minority group in Canada. In Montreal, half of the Jewish population is found in 2 per cent of the census tracts and 90 per cent in 9 per cent of the tracts. They are also heavily concentrated in the other CMAs. Fifty per cent of the Jewish population is found in 3.1 per cent of the census tracts in Toronto and Winnipeg. Italians and Poles are somewhat more concentrated than the western European groups, but much less so than the visible minorities. The highest concentration of Italians is in Montreal, where half of them live in 8.4 per cent of the census tracts.

Apart from the Jewish population, visible minorities are the most concentrated groups in Canada. In Montreal, where the concentrations are highest for every group, half the South Asians live in 5.1 per cent of the census tracts, the corresponding figures for the Chinese and blacks being 8 per cent and 9.5 per cent respectively. In Toronto, the preeminent city in Canada for new immigrants, especially the visible minorities, concentrations persist in spite of their larger numbers. Half the Chinese live in 9.6 per cent of the census tracts, and there are about twenty-eight census tracts where more than a third of the tract population is Chinese. Blacks and South Asians also show concentrations that are only slightly lower than the Chinese.

Table 17.2: Percentage of Census Tracts in which 50 And 90 per cent of Ethnic Group Populations are Concentrated, 1991

CMAs	British	French	Aboriginal	Black	Chinese	Dutch	German	Italian	Jewish	Polish	Scandinavian	South Asian	Ukrainain
Halifax	34.6	30.5	9.3	6.5	10.7	26.5	29.2	16.9	7.9	15.5	11.6	10.7	13.1
Montreal	14.6	23.5	14.3	9.5	8.0	7.6	14.5	8.4	2.0	12.5	4.2	5.1	9.6
Ottawa	25.2	15.6	15.7	12.3	14.7	16.7	25.6	11.9	8.1	17.0	14.1	12.2	16.7
Toronto	28.9	25.1	6.2	12.9	9.6	14.9	26.1	10.8	3.1	10.9	15.6	12.0	13.8
Hamilton	31.1	26.2	10.1	12.0	13.4	14.6	27.6	20.1	4.0	18.8	13.9	11.4	23.9
St.Catharines/ Niagara	32.3	19.1	7.8	7.9	11.9	14.2	21.4	19.2	4.6	21.5	13.7	8.6	24.7
Kitchener/ Waterloo	31.9	28.3	11.9	12.8	13.4	22.2	24.3	19.2	6.4	22.8	14.7	16.6	23.9
London	34.0	28.2	16.7	17.6	11.8	21.9	30.4	17.9	5.1	19.8	17.5	12.7	18.6
Windsor	32.8	26.5	13.1	15.1	14.7	19.7	29.7	21.8	8.5	21.7	12.9	11.0	26.7
Winnipeg	30.1	11.2	8.7	14.6	10.0	22.2	25.4	16.3	3.1	20.9	20.3	8.1	23.5
Calgary	38.5	30.7	15.4	14.0	17.3	30.0	36.2	18.1	4.4	25.1	27.9	10.7	34.4
Edmonton	34.3	28.2	12.8	13.9	15.9	24.4	30.1	11.6	3.9	28.0	24.1	11.0	29.6
Vancouver	32.3	26.7	7.5	14.8	13.5	22.2	30.6	11.9	8.1	21.5	26.8	10.4	29.0
Victoria	36.8	27.5	15.1	10.4	16.4	26.0	33.5	21.3	16.1	21.2	27.1	10.2	31.6
			90%										

Halifax	78.6	74.7	39.9	42.6	38.6	66.5	73.2	51.8	25.1	47.9	34.5	34.6	38.4
Montreal	59.6	67.3	45.5	37.3	36.1	25.6	49.7	42.6	9.0	44.2	13.5	21.3	36.2
Ottawa	65.1	55.5	49.9	42.2	44.9	51.7	65.2	46.4	33.0	49.9	40.7	41.3	47.3
Toronto	72.3	68.1	32.3	46.3	44.4	51.7	68.5	49.9	14.5	51.1	46.8	47.0	55.6
Hamilton	75.9	71.3	34.4	41.7	41.8	56.0	72.4	64.2	20.8	64.1	40.5	39.2	67.7
St. Catharines/ Niagara	75.2	68.2	33.5	25.2	33.4	60.0	56.0	61.3	24.0	63.4	39.5	30.5	65.7
Kitchener/ Waterloo	74.0	70.3	36.8	39.2	49.1	67.7	66.4	59.0	24.5	65.2	43.9	50.1	63.5
London	78.2	73.1	52.1	47.3	42.7	71.2	76.0	64.1	18.7	63.1	50.0	38.0	56.3
Windsor	77.3	72.1	39.0	50.3	44.5	58.9	69.1	63.7	33.2	63.8	42.1	33.4	66.9
Winnipeg	73.9	59.7	47.1	45.7	44.9	63.1	70.1	56.4	17.2	65.4	59.7	31.2	70.5
Calgary	83.4	75.0	49.4	45.5	55.2	76.1	81.5	62.4	30.5	67.0	69.0	45.0	78.9
Edmonton	80.0	74.3	49.5	45.9	52.2	70.7	76.2	51.2	19.9	71.6	65.2	41.6	76.0
Vancouver	77.0	70.6	42.9	44.8	46.9	67.4	75.0	58.0	33.8	64.5	68.7	49.0	72.5
Victoria	82.9	70.4	51.9	28.3	56.7	68.4	79.3	62.7	48.1	59.4	71.9	41.1	76.5

Table 17.3: Gini Indices of Concentration by Ethnic Group for Canada's Major Census Metropolitan Areas, 1986 and 1991

	British		French		Aboriginal		Black		Chinese		Dutch		German	
	1986	1991	1986	1991	1986	1991	1986	1991	1986	1991	1986	1991	1986	1991
Halifax	.226	.238	.312	.305	.652	.703	.728	.716	.643	.690	.338	.391	.319	.323
Montreal	.533	.538	.365	.405	.609	.623	.715	.703	.770	.731	.776	.791	.595	.591
Ottawa	.393	.396	.523	.541	.602	.579	.633	.649	.651	.613	.562	.564	.400	.396
Toronto	.287	.323	.341	.387	.691	.736	.632	.624	.672	.668	.502	.577	.343	.373
Hamilton	.252	.283	.331	.356	.715	.720	.682	.658	.625	.643	.530	.555	.319	.337
St.Catharines/ Niag.	.262	.270	.460	.458	.717	.743	.769	.796	.697	.703	.558	.542	.414	.437
Kitchener/ Waterloo	.308	.280	.366	.341	.737	.703	.692	.664	.647	.619	.415	.424	.402	.406
London	.218	.240	.313	.330	.667	.557	.585	.571	.656	.658	.387	.398	.275	.292
Windsor	.258	.256	.356	.360	.669	.670	.692	.581	.703	.630	.510	.498	.342	.325
Winnipeg	.299	.298	.555	.578	.662	.659	.608	.609	.682	.666	.443	.441	.374	.375
Calgary	.161	.165	.241	.293	.541	.588	.585	.625	.493	.532	.293	.301	.209	.207
Edmonton	.228	.226	.309	.328	.597	.609	.596	.616	.565	.562	.372	.381	.311	.296
Vancouver	.255	.262	.357	.356	.685	.698	.637	.618	.654	.608	.412	.422	.316	.292
Victoria	.205	.189	.353	.355	.703	.585	.774	.745	.576	.538	.313	.371	.264	.251

	Italian		Jewish		Polish		Scandinavian		South Asian		Ukrainian	
	1986	1991	1986	1991	1986	1991	1986	1991	1986	1991	1986	1991
Halifax	.655	.555	.769	.782	.625	.611	.592	.695	.677	.707	.560	.671
Montreal	.715	.688	.922	.924	.651	.639	.860	.883	.804	.834	.704	.717
Ottawa	.636	.634	.713	.744	.350	.564	.562	.644	.704	.655	.566	.580
Toronto	.639	.627	.861	.880	.580	.619	.538	.602	.650	.630	.521	.568
Hamilton	.476	.453	.833	.856	.435	.477	.552	.655	.653	.684	.379	.408
St.Catharines/ Niag.	.480	.485	.862	.832	.437	.454	.573	.658	.746	.755	.356	.404
Kitchener/ Waterloo	.423	.502	.750	.808	.452	.423	.587	.628	.614	.567	.474	.419
London	.465	.489	.820	.854	.413	.467	.521	.568	.632	.676	.438	.518
Windsor	.441	.443	.710	.742	.396	.460	.610	.656	.695	.708	.337	.379
Winnipeg	.563	.535	.860	.870	.451	.443	.394	.492	.733	.753	.404	.391
Calgary	.461	.488	.737	.800	.331	.393	.233	.350	.614	.654	.269	.231
Edmonton	.649	.614	.849	.854	.364	.341	.332	.413	.680	.671	.309	.303
Vancouver	.610	.579	.732	.740	.430	.438	.313	.336	.585	.634	.304	.326
Victoria	.422	.448	.564	.589	.390	.481	.271	.358	.623	.677	.258	.286

A summary measure, "Gini index," was constructed to investigate concentration of a minority group in a city. It is derived from concentration curves, also known as Lorenz curves. For lack of space the curves themselves are not shown here. The vertical axis shows the cumulative percentage of population in the particular ethnic group while along the horizontal axis the census tracts are arranged in decreasing order of the ethnic population. A curve that coincides with the diagonal line indicates that the ethnic population is distributed equally among the census tracts, implying no spatial concentration. The Gini index is the ratio of the area between the curve and the diagonal to the area of the triangle above the diagonal line. Thus the range for the index is from 0 to 1, indicating no concentration or complete concentration.[2]

The Gini indices for each ethnic group in the selected CMAs in 1986 and 1991 are presented in Table 17.3. The indices are highest for the Jewish population, reaching values around .900 in the largest cities of Toronto and Montreal, where most of them live. For the recent Third World immigrant groups of blacks, Chinese, and South Asians, the indices are similar, around .600. Variations among the CMAs are small. The indices are smaller in magnitude for European groups of Italians, Ukrainians, and Polish and still lower for the Dutch and Germans. Variations among the CMAs are greater for the European origin groups.

Has concentration increased for recent immigrant ethnic groups such as Chinese, blacks, and South Asians? A comparison of the Gini indices for 1986 and 1991, a period in which there was a substantial influx of these groups, showed no clear pattern. For example, in CMAs such as Toronto and Halifax, where the black population increased more than the total CMA population, the Gini indices do not show a significant change. The proportion of blacks in Toronto increased from 2.66 per cent of the total population to 3.22 per cent, but the Gini index decreased slightly from .632 to .624. In contrast, in other cities such as Ottawa and Calgary, where the relative increase of blacks has also been substantially more than the average city growth, there were noticeable increases in the indices of concentration. Cities such as London and Windsor, where the proportion of blacks remained the same, showed noticeable decreases in concentration.

Similar observations can be made of the Chinese and, to a lesser extent, South Asians. The proportion of Chinese increased in all the major fourteen CMAs. However, the Gini indices of concentration increased in five CMAs and decreased in the other nine. The two CMAs with the largest absolute increase of Chinese were Toronto and Vancouver. In Toronto, the proportion of Chinese increased from 3.69 per cent to 6 per cent of the total population during the period 1986–91, while Gini index during the same period remained the same. In Vancouver, the proportion of Chinese increased from 7.27 per cent to 10.57 per cent of the population in the tracted areas, but the Gini index of concentration actually decreased from .654 to .608. In the case of South Asians, though still weak, there seems to be a noticeable relationship between population increase and increase in concentration [....]

Conclusion

To summarize, Canada's immigration policy has altered the origin composition of immigrants. No longer from Europe, the United Kingdom, and the United States, today's migrants are admitted under many criteria—family reunification, economic contributions, and humanitarian considerations. Increasingly, these immigrants are from areas in which the main language is not English and/or French. Recent immigrants are the most likely to be unable to converse in English or French, or if they can, to still speak other languages in the home. Women have lower levels of English and/or French language proficiency than men.

Language skills have economic consequences. When in the labour force, persons with low levels of proficiency have higher rates of unemployment compared to groups with higher levels of proficiency. Groups with low levels of proficiency are likely to be employed in production and processing occupations, in low-skill occupations, and in the goods-producing sector of Canada's economy. Correlates of lower levels of language proficiency tend to be more severely felt by the foreign-born visible minority population compared to the foreign-born population without visible minority status.

Perhaps the most important economic variable for economic well-being and life chances is income. Groups with low levels of language skill have, on average, lower wages and salaries compared to other groups. Foreign-born women who are members of visible minority groups and who have low levels of language proficiency have the lowest level of average yearly earnings, even after adjusting for group differences in the amounts of educational attainment, age, and other variables.

The correlates of language proficiency for immigrants and their implications for integration have not gone unnoticed by federal and provincial governments. Policy responses have been twofold. The most long-standing policy response is a remedial solution; the other is a preventive stance.

The "preventive" policy response is directed at persons who seek to enter Canada but have not yet been admitted. A policy initiative that adopts a preventive stance by linking language skills to admissions could in principle reduce the needs of new immigrants for learning English and/or French. Since the 1960s, Canada has given points for English or French language knowledge to immigrants who enter as assisted relatives or in the economic entry categories. However, on 17 November 1995, the federal government announced regulatory amendments to the selection criteria used to admit immigrants in the economic class. These new regulations target the skilled worker component of immigration to Canada, which represented about 25,000 principal applicants for a total of 60,000 persons (excluding those destined to Quebec) in 1994. Both education and ability in English or French will be given greater weight in determining the necessary points for admission, each accounting for a maximum of fifteen points (pass marks depend on the categories of skilled worker, but range from forty-five to fifty-four points).

These regulatory changes may have a modest impact on the numbers of higher skilled workers who might otherwise have faced difficulties in economic integration because of education and language skills. However, throughout the world, the volume of international migration is rapidly growing, frequently fuelled by spontaneous political and economic upheaval, as well as the desire for family reunification. In the face of these numbers and the suddenness of migration flows, fine-tuning the admissions criteria for economic immigrants is not likely to diminish substantially the numbers who arrive without extensive knowledge of English and/or French. The "preventive" policy initiative also does not address the settlement needs of migrants already in Canada.

The "remedial" policy response does provide language training to target groups already residing in Canada. The general rationale has been to further immigrant integration through improved knowledge of the English and French languages. At various times, however, a subset of federally funded language training programs have used the links between language proficiency and enhanced economic productivity to design programs targeted at a subset of workers (see Boyd, 1992).

Despite changing emphases, rationales, and programs over the years, the Canadian federal government has been a long-time player in funding immigrant settlement activities. However, in the 1994 budget, the federal government indicated that it was not longer prepared to be in the business of managing immigrant settlement policies and programs, including directed funding for language training. Following a pattern of decentralization found in other policy domains, the intention of the federal government is to transfer funds to other agencies, including the provinces, who will then set agendas and funding priorities. A critical question for the future is whether or not provinces will fill the void, by establishing and funding immigrant settlement policies and language instruction programs.

These recent policy changes indicate that the preventive stance is become more central at the federal level while the remedial approach is being expelled from the federal arena of responsibility. The consequences of such policy shifts for immigrant integration as yet remain unclear. However, one possibility is that migrants will continue in increasing numbers to enter Canada without high levels of English/French language skills, only to find a dismantled federal language training program and fewer substitutes in the public and provincial government sectors. Data presented in this chapter show that language proficiency, along with gender, nativity, and visible minority status, shapes immigrant integration experience. Those with low levels of language proficiency are the most disadvantaged, and the most likely to be affected by diminished policy responses.

NOTES

1. The Employment Equity Act defines the visible minority population as "persons, other than Aboriginal peoples, who are non-Caucasian in race or non-white in colour" (Employment and Immigration Canada, 1987, B-3). Because there is no census question on whether the respondent is a member of a visible minority group, an operational definition by which a visible minority population could be identified was constructed using available census data (Boxhill, 1990). While the "ethnic origin" question of the census served as the major basis for identifying the visible minority groups, other census variables — e.g., place of birth, mother tongue, and religion — were

used in conjunction with the ethnic origin variable to select and define those who were likely to be members of such groups. A cross-classification of ethnic origin variable with visible minority identifier in the 1991 3 per cent Public Use Sample showed that all the blacks, Chinese, South Asians, Arabs, Filipino, and Vietnamese were "visible," without exception. All the European groups had a visible minority component of less than 1 per cent, except the Spanish (with 47.7 per cent) and Portuguese (with 2.7 per cent). The groups from Latin and Central America showed a visible component of 74.8 per cent. Thus "ethnicity" mostly identifies visible minority groups. For our study, we have concentrated on the three major groups among the visible minorities, namely, blacks, the Chinese, and South Asians, who together account for 64.4 percent, or a total visible minority population of 2.714 million in Canada in 1991, and are entirely in the visible minority category.

2. Our Gini index should not be confused with the Gini coefficient (index) often mentioned in segregation literature. The latter is based on the so-called "segregation curve," which is obtained by plotting the cumulative percentage of majority group against the cumulative percentage of minority group (Duncan and Duncan, 1955). Thus it is a measure of segregation between two groups using areal units in its construction (Massey and Denton, 1988). In comparison, the Gini index used here is based only on the distribution of one ethnic group in space. It is a measure of spatial concentration of each group without being directly relative to another group.

REFERENCES

Balakrishnan, T.R. 1982. "Changing Patterns of Ethnic Residential Segregation in the Metropolitan Areas of Canada." *Canadian Review of Sociology and Anthropology* 19, 92–110.

Boyd, Monica, and John de Vries. "Immigrant Integration: Language, Economic Status and Citizenship in Canada." Presented at the Conference on Immigration and Refugee Policy: The Canadian and Australian Experiences. York University, Toronto, 2–5 May, 1992.

Darroch, A.G., and W.G. Marston. 1971. "The Social Class Basis of Ethnic Residential Segregation: The Canadian Case." *American Journal of Sociology* 77, 491–510.

Driedger, Leo, and Glenn Church. 1974. "Residential Segregation and Institutional Completeness: A Comparison of Ethnic Communities." *Canadian Review of Sociology and Anthropology* 11, 30–32.

Driedger, Leo, and Jacob Peters. 1977. "Identity and Social Distance: Towards Understanding Simmel's 'The Stranger.'" *Canadian Review of Sociology and Anthropology* 14, 158–73.

Duncan, O.D., and S. Lieberson. 1959. "Ethnic Segregation and Assimilation." *American Journal of Sociology* 64, 364–74.

Harwood, Edwin. 1986. "American Public Opinion and U.S. Immigration Policy." *Annals of the American Academy of Political and Social Science* 487, 201–12.

Kalbach, Warren E. 1981. "Ethnic Residential Segregation and Its Significance for the Individual in an Urban Setting." Paper No. 4, Centre for Urban and Community Studies, University of Toronto.

Kantrowitz, N. 1973. *Ethnic and Racial Segregation in the New York Metropolis*. New York: Praeger.

Massey, Douglas S. 1979. "Effects of Socio-Economic Factors on the Residential Segregation of Blacks and Spanish Americans in the U.S. Urbanized Areas." *American Sociological Review* 44, 1015–22.

_____. 1981a. "Social Class and Ethnic Segregation: A Consideration of Methods and Conclusions." *American Sociological Review* 46, 641–50.

_____. 1986. "The Settlement Process among Mexican Migrants to the United States." *American Sociological Review* 51, 670–84.

_____. 1986. "The Social Organization of Mexican Migration to the United States." *Annals of the American Academy of Political and Social Science* 487, 102–13.

Massey, Douglas S., and Nancy A. Denton. 1987. "Trends in the Residential Segregation of Blacks, Hispanics and Asians: 1970–1980." *American Sociological Review* 52, 802–25.

Pineo, Peter C. 1977. "The Social Standing of Ethnic and Racial Groupings." *Canadian Review of Sociology and Anthropology* 14, 47–57.

Reitz, Jeffrey. 1988a. "The Institutional Structure of Immigration as a Determinant of Interracial Competition: A Comparison of Britain and Canada." *International Migration Review* 22, 117–46.

Richmond, Anthony, H. 1972. *Ethnic Residential Segregation in Metropolitan Toronto*. Toronto: Institute for Behavioural Research, York University.

PETER LI

THE SOCIAL CONSTRUCTION OF IMMIGRANTS

FROM DESTINATION CANADA: IMMIGRATION DEBATES AND ISSUES

EXPECTATIONS ABOUT IMMIGRANTS

The three interpretations of immigrants—bureaucratic, folk, and analytical—produce different expectations and approaches about immigrants. For example, the bureaucratic classification inevitably results in immigrants being evaluated in a dichotomy: (1) chosen immigrants who bring in human capital to benefit Canada; and (2) unsolicited immigrants who lack the language capacity and marketable skills to do well in Canadian society. It follows that unsolicited immigrants are by implication a burden to the state since their successful integration to Canada is seen as depending on the state's capacity to provide adequate settlement services to them. The implicit expectation is that unsolicited immigrants do not bring as much value as chosen immigrants to Canada, and that they are costly to integrate into Canadian society. This rationale can easily be used to justify targeting their admission to how much resources the state is prepared to allocate to settle them to avoid undue hardships for the unsolicited immigrants themselves and for Canadian society.

The bureaucratic approach to immigrants means that immigrants, whether chosen or not, are expected to perform as well as native-born Canadians in order to prove their social and economic worth. For selected immigrants, they are expected to match the performance of the average Canadian since they are selected on the basis of their potential labour market contribution. For unsolicited immigrants, their social worth is measured by their not having to rely on the state for settling in Canada and by their

Table 18.1: Temporary Resident and Refugee Claimant Population by Primary Status, Stocks on 1 June 1978–99[1]

Year	Foreign Workers	Foreign Students	Humanitarian[3]	Other	All
1978	9,501	6,124	509	15,812	31,946
1979	33,858	30,587	2,906	29,071	96,422
1980	38,322	33,260	3,957	29,630	105,169
1981	45,679	41,015	8,983	31,790	127,467
1982	48,967	49,077	9,610	29,725	137,379
1983	47,129	49,932	10,004	27,048	134,113
1984	46,943	47,144	13,905	25,577	133,569
1985	49,412	43,260	21,184	25,791	139,647
1986	57,559	39,789	29,754	27,269	154,371
1987	64,425	38,657	44,031	29,632	176,745
1988	73,992	41,781	47,877	29,302	176,745
1989	84,741	46,609	113,025	26,008	270,383
1990	100,100	55,167	145,842	33,150	334,259
1991	105,074	63,147	160,301	36,560	365,082
1992	97,936	67,247	84,776	31,244	281,203
1993	81,885	67,493	79,947	27,694	257,019
1994	71,795	65,630	78,540	27,330	243,295
1995	70,415	64,831	79,015	29,979	244,240
1996	70,833	70,962	81,350	33,861	257,006
1997	71,817	78,249	79,293	35,348	264,707
1998	73,810	79,693	72,331	36,292	262,126
1999	76,853	86,718	69,201	38,863	271,635
Total	1,421,046	1,166,372	1,236,341	656,976	4,480,735

1. This table shows the annal stock statistics measured on the first of June from 1978 to 1999. The figures are broken down by primary status. A person is included in these stock counts regardless of the type of permit or authorization he or she is in possession of. A person who has been given permanent resident status on or before the date of observation is excluded from the stock calculation on that date.
2. *Foreign Workers* are shown according to whether they hold an employment authorization or another type of document on the observation date. For example, in 1999, 76,853 Foreign Workers were deemed to be present in Canada on 1 June. Of those people, 71,834 were authorized to work and 5,019 were authorized to reside in Canada by virtue of being possession of some other type of authorization.
3. *Foreign Students* are shown according to whether they hold a student authorization or another type of document on the observation date. For example, in 1999, 86,718 Foreign Students were deemed to be present in Canada on 1 June. Of those people,

83,510 were authorized to study and 3,208 were authorized to reside in Canada by virtue of being in possession of some other type of permit or authorization.

4. A refugee claimant who has not been issued a permit or authorization by CIC is included in these stock counts as a *Humanitarian case* for two years following the date of his or her most recent appearance in the CIC system. (*Source:* Citizenship and Immigration Canada, *Facts and Figures 1999*, Statistical Overview of the Temporary Resident and Refugee Claimant Population, available at http://cicnet.ci.gc.ca/english/pub/facts99-tem-3.html).

---

ability to catch up with the average Canadian. Given that bureaucratically the immigrant status only applies to those before Canadian citizenship is granted, immigrants, chosen or not, are racing against time to demonstrate their economic contribution in the first few years after arrival before they are "de-classified" as non-immigrants for bureaucratic purposes.

The folk version of immigrants also produces social expectations, which often reflect less on immigrants themselves but more on how race is constructed in Canadian society. In this sense, the notion of immigrants has been racialized in that the term has become a codified concept for some Canadians to focus their opposition to having more non-whites immigrating to Canada. Oppositions to increases in the immigration level take on the social significance of defending the social cohesion in Canadian society, as some Canadians see traditional Canada and its occidental values and symbols being destroyed by hordes of non-white immigrants from countries that represent incompatible values and different traditions (Li, 2000). Since the "immigration problem" is popularly seen as a "race problem" in the sense that "non-white" immigrants and their concentration in urban centers are frequently perceived as producing social stress and tensions that undermine the social cohesion of Canada, the immigration problem is therefore depicted as caused by "too many" non-white immigrants flooding to Canada, at a pace faster than Canada can absorb them. The idea of a finite absorptive capacity is exacerbated by the belief that non-white immigrants are more difficult to integrate because of their fundamental differences in language, culture, tradition, and values. In short, the superficial racial differences of non-white immigrants are normatively transformed into fundamental cultural obstacles that hinder the integration of newcomers.

The folk version of "immigrants" and "their cultural problem" also suggests that despite the official policy of multiculturalism, new immigrants from a different culture are expected to comply with the cultural and normative standards of Canadian society. After all, it is the distinctiveness of the recent non-white immigrants that is seen as causing adjustment problems in Canadian society, unlike European immigrants who are deemed to integrate more easily into Canadian society because of their cultural proximity to native-born Canadians. The undue emphasis on cultural differences creating settlement tensions means that the cultures of new immigrants are not given the same value as Canadian culture and values. These differences, whether superficial or substantive, are made into social problems that are considered to hinder the social cohesion of Canada. It follows that in finding their new place in Canadian society, new immigrants must abandon their cultural distinctiveness in order for them and for Canadian society to avert the problem of integration. In short, the folk version of "immigrants" and "immigration problem" calls for cultural conformity and not acceptance of pluralistic cultures and values.

Compared to the bureaucratic classification and the folk version of immigrants, the analytical understanding of immigrants as people who have immigrated appears to be unproblematic. However, the analytical approach has made normative assumptions about how best to evaluate immigrants. The current state of research is preoccupied with empirical comparisons between immigrants and native-born Canadians. Comparisons are also typically made between those who arrive more recently with those who immigrated earlier to see if the length of residence in Canada makes immigrants more similar to native-born Canadians. To the extent that immigrants, over time, are becoming more like native-born Canadians, immigrants are considered to have assimilated or integrated into Canadian society. Conversely, the display of behavioural patterns and psychological profiles among immigrant groups, which are distinct from that of the majority, is interpreted as the persistence of cultural diversity or ethnicity and a resistance to assimilation. Academic research has implicitly followed the theoretical framework of assimilation in studying the speed and manner by which immigrants become similar to native-born Canadians, despite the popular belief that official multiculturalism has enabled immigrants to preserve their cultural distinctiveness in the process of becoming Canadians. Much research has adopted a benchmark that uses the behavioural standards of those born in Canada to gauge the performance of immigrants.

RODERIC P. BEAUJOT

IMMIGRATION AND DEMOGRAPHIC STRUCTURES

FROM IMMIGRANT CANADA: DEMOGRAPHIC, ECONOMIC AND SOCIAL CHALLENGES

ETHNICITY AND VISIBLE MINORITIES

Immigration increases the ethnic diversity of the Canadian population. In effect, there is a tradition in Canada to focus on the ethnic characteristics of the foreign-born population (Ramirez, 1991). Immigrants can be placed in various categories corresponding to socio-economic characteristics, but they tend to be especially classified into ethnic categories, according to places of origin. All societies have minorities and need to balance assimilation and the respect for differences. The originality of Canada does not come from the presence of minorities and the dynamics of their integration, but from the fact that immigration plays a predominant role in such questions (Lacroix, 1991).

These dynamics of ethnicity are somewhat different in Quebec, where the French-English tensions have increased the opportunity for other ethnic groups to retain more separateness, and where the policy agenda of integration into a French-speaking majority is more recent (Lacroix, 1991). Given the weak position of the French language on the continent, there are difficulties both in integrating immigrants into the French majority and in the French society redefining itself as a receiving and pluralist society.

The ease of demographic classifications by place of birth should not discourage research on the extent to which the classification is relevant for given individuals and groups. This problem of the meaning of categories applies especially to the visible minority designation. Since the 1970s, the fastest growing foreign-born population involves persons born outside of Europe and the United States. In view of employment equity programs, the visible minority population is defined as persons who are neither white, Caucasian, nor aboriginal. In effect, it is the population that originates directly or indirectly from Asia, Latin America, and Africa.

At the 1981 census, the visible minority population was estimated at 1,130,000 persons (4.7 per cent of the total population), of which 85 per cent of immigrants were classified in this category (Beaujot and Hou, 1993; Verma and Hou, 1992). In 1991, this population numbered 2,715,000, or 9.7 per cent of the total population. Among persons with visible minority status aged fifteen and over in 1991, close to two-thirds had arrived since 1971, and 35 per cent since 1981 (Kelly, 1995). Based on slightly lower mortality and slightly higher fertility than the national average, and with a continuation of immigration trends, it is projected that the visible minority population will increase to about seven million in 2016, or close to 20 per cent of the Canadian population (Table 19.1).

Among the demographic components, immigration clearly predominates in the relative growth of the visible minority population (Kalbach et al., 1993). For example, a projection based on 80 per cent visible minority among immigrants produces a total that is 4.5 per cent higher than holding the proportion constant at 68 per cent. In comparison, the difference between a total fertility of 2.11 and 1.87 births per woman produces a difference of only 1.9 per cent in 2016 (Table 19.1).

Immigration therefore plays the dominant role in the socio-cultural transformations of Canada associated with the relative growth of the visible minority population. The immigration factor also dominates in the geographic distribution of this population, in favor of metropolitan areas, and the three largest ones in particular. For persons aged fifteen and over, 93 per cent of the visible minority population was in metropolitan areas in 1991, compared to 59 per cent of the rest of the population (Kelly, 1995). More than two-thirds live in the three largest metropolitan areas, compared to one-third of the remainder of the population. For example, the visible minority population comprises 24 per cent of the metropolitan area of Toronto, 23 per cent for Vancouver, and 10 per cent for Montreal.

While immigration is transforming the Canadian population composition in terms of the relative size of the visible minority component, it is important to appreciate that broad definitions are being used in attempts to capture any element of non-caucasian origin. These definitions are not very sensitive to the appropriateness of the designation, or to the prospects of its reduced relevance over time. The projections used in Table 19.1 may be problematic, since they are based on strong assumptions of ethnic retention, while the very meaning of visible minority status may change considerably over a twenty-year period (Beaujot and Hou, 1993).

Table 19.1: Visible Minority Population, Using Various Assumptions, 1981, 1991, 2016, Canada

	Population	Percentage of total population
1981	1,300,000	4.7
1991	2,714,600	9.7
2016		
High Projection	7,459,500	20.6
Low Projection	7,002,300	19.4
Visible minority Percent in immigration		
68%	7,137,000	
80%	7,459,500	
Difference	322,500 (4.5%)	
Fertility		
2.11	7,137,000	
87.87	7,002,300	
Difference	134,700 (1.9%)	

Source: Samuel 1987; Dai and George, 1996, 29

LANGUAGE COMPOSITION

At the time of arrival, 30 per cent of immigrants of the 1969–77 period, and more than 45 per cent of those of the 1978–90 period, did not know either of the official languages (Thomas, 1992). For the period 1986–91, Termote (1995, 171) estimates that 25 per cent of the net international migration to Quebec was of French home language, along with 0.1 per cent for the rest of Canada. In the 1968–91 cohort, only a third of immigrants were using an official language at home in 1991, and more than 10 per cent knew neither of these languages (Table 19.2).

Over time, the majority of immigrants come to associate with one or the other of the official languages. In order to highlight this tendency, the concept of "predominant language" combines the responses on language spoken at home and knowledge of official languages. Persons who speak English or French at home were assigned this language as their predominant language. Persons speaking "other" languages at home were also assigned to English or French predominant language if they could speak "only" that language among the official languages. In effect, this measures which among the official languages is a given person's predominant language.

Outside of Quebec, the results are simple: immigration contributes to the predominance of the English language, and there is less French spoken among immigrants than in the Canadian-born population (Table 19.3). In Quebec, the foreign born are clearly less French (40.1 per cent) than the Canadian-born population (88.8 per cent). In spite of the minority status of English in Quebec, immigrant cohorts before 1971 were more English than French. For more recent cohorts, close to half are French predominant language, and this predominance is stronger for younger immigrants and for those who did not know English at the time of arrival (Veltman, 1988). Over time, for a given cohort, French tends to gain (Beaujot and Rappak, 1990, 116–17).

Quebec also receives a greater proportion of immigrants who know neither of the official languages, and persons of third languages retain these longer. This longer retention is probably related to the larger potential for ethnic separateness provided by French-English tensions in Quebec. In addition, as we have seen, immigration is concentrated in the one metropolitan area of Montreal, and the City of Montreal in particular (Paillé, 1991). This concentration presents a difficulty for linguistic integration. For instance, in given localities, French mother tongue children can be in a minority, even in French schools. On the other hand, immigrants of third languages are more oriented to French than are non-immigrants of either English or third languages (Castonguay, 1992).

The general linguistic trends in Canada therefore involve decreases in the official language minorities, that is, English in Quebec and French in the rest of Canada. For the rest of Canada, immigration contributes to the trend as there is less French among immigrants than in the native-born population. In Quebec, immigration enhances the English minority because there is more English among immigrants than in the native born, and a sizeable proportion of third-language migrants continue to transfer to the English language.

Table 19.2: Knowledge and Use of Official Languages, by Sex, for Canadian Born and Various Immigrant Cohorts, Canada, 1991

| | Know an Official Language | | | | Do Not Know an Official Language | |
| | Not Spoken at Home | | Spoken at home | | | |
	Male	Female	Male	Female	Male	Female
Canadian born	97.3	97.5	2.3	2.1	0.4	0.4
Immigrants	60.4	59.7	35.1	32.5	4.5	7.7
Before 1946	90.7	88.8	8.5	9.5	0.8	1.7
1946–60	73.4	72.6	24.5	23.3	2.1	4.2
1961–70	71.0	67.6	25.6	25.9	3.4	6.5
1971–75	63.8	63.0	32.9	30.5	3.3	6.4
1976–80	56.8	55.5	38.8	36.2	4.5	8.2
1981–85	44.9	45.6	49.3	43.6	5.8	10.7
1986–91	33.2	34.4	57.1	51.2	9.8	14.4

Source: Special tabulations based on 1991 public use sample.

Immigration therefore plays an important role in Canada's changing linguistic distribution. Although the distribution by languages changes only slowly, immigration is the main element producing an increase in the relative dominance of the English language in comparison to the French language (Lachapelle, 1988a). While language policy in Quebec has promoted a greater association of immigrants with the French language, this is partly at the expense of departures of English and other linguistic groups. Therefore, it is at the expense of a lower total weight of Quebec in the Canadian total and increase the proportion of French in Quebec. The rest of Canada does not have such a problem: more of its international arrivals are English to start with; other immigrants retain their languages to a lesser extent; and almost all transfers favor English. As Lachapelle further observes, only a higher French fertility could both increase the proportion of French and increase the weight of Quebec in Canada.

Clearly, immigration has an impact on the changing socio-cultural composition of the Canadian population. However, we would argue that this impact is especially felt at the time of arrival, and that ethnic and linguistic distinctiveness is reduced over time. This is especially the case outside of Quebec, where immigrants associate with the majority

Table 19.3: Predominant Language for Canadian Born and Various Immigration Cohorts, Quebec and Rest of Canada, 1991

	Quebec			Rest of Canada		
	English	French	Other	English	French	Other
Canadian born	9.3	88.8	2.0	95.4	3.8	0.8
Immigrants	34.7	40.1	25.1	91.7	0.6	7.7
Before 1946	68.9	26.8	4.3	98.1	0.3	1.6
1946–60	46.7	30.4	22.9	96.0	0.3	3.7
1961–70	39.2	36.7	24.2	93.4	0.6	6.0
1971–75	32.3	42.6	25.1	93.1	0.6	6.4
1976–80	25.1	48.6	26.3	90.0	1.0	9.0
1981–85	22.2	49.5	28.2	88.0	0.5	11.4
1986–90	25.7	45.4	28.9	85.4	0.8	13.9

Notes: The predominant language is determined on the bases of language spoken at home and knowledge of official languages. Those who speak one national language at home are assigned this predominant language. Those who do not speak English or French at home are assigned that predominant language if they know only English or French among the official languages. The "other" category comprises those who speak both English and French at home, plus those who speak neither language at home and know both or neither of the official languages.

Source: Special tabulations based on 1991 public use sample.

language. A significant part of the greater sensitivity toward immigration in Quebec results from the fact that immigrants maintain a greater linguistic distinctiveness from the French majority language.

IMMIGRATION AND SOCIO-ECONOMIC COMPOSITION

Immigration is largely justified in economic terms (see, e.g., Employment and Immigration, 1989). In view of the geographic size of the country, and the need to control the resources that were present, immigration has often been seen as necessary if not essential (Sullivan, 1992). However, it does not necessarily follow that immigrants will enhance the socio-economic composition of the population. Discrimination and racism could operate to provide economic benefits through a supply of cheap labour or a dual labour market (DasGupta, 1994). It is therefore important to continuously analyze the economic status of immigrants and to pay attention to disadvantaged groups.

On education, immigrants are more concentrated at the two extremes of the distribution (Beaujot, 1997). At higher levels of education, measured in terms of the proportion with some university education, the immigrant advantage applies especially to the last two decades and especially to men. This advantage is also more likely to apply to persons who are of origins other than Europe and the United States, that is, to persons who are largely of visible minority status. For both men and women, immigrants also have higher proportions with less than nine years of education. However, the greater concentration at higher levels of education means that, on average, the foreign born have more education and immigrants of the 1981–91 period have higher average education than the total foreign born (Badets and Chui, 1994, 41–4).

The foreign born tend to increase not only the average level of education but also labour force participation in Canada. That is, immigrants have higher average levels of labour force participation (Beaujot, 1997). In given age groups, a higher proportion of the foreign-born population is working full-time. However, this advantage does not apply to the persons who arrived in the five-year period preceding the census, where labour force participation is significantly lower.

Average income provides a summary measure of socio-economic composition. Table 19.4 shows two age-adjusted measures of average income. Total income relates to all persons who indicated a positive income in 1990. Employment income is based on persons aged fifteen to sixty-four who worked full-time for at least forty weeks in 1990.

Overall, and in both comparisons, immigrants are very close to the national average. However, this result covers considerable differences by arrival cohort and place of origin. Groups that arrived before 1971 for men and before 1976 for women have average incomes higher than that of the Canadian-born population, while the more recent immigrant cohorts have a disadvantage. Another change is seen to take place over these same cohorts: the average income of immigrants from Europe and the United States moves from being less than to being more than that of immigrants from other continents. In the post-1976 cohorts there is a strong disadvantage for immigrants who are not from Europe and the United States, that is, who are largely visible minorities. For persons admitted in the 1980s, the disadvantage is more than 20 per cent.

The comparison of the 1961 and 1971 censuses had shown a very encouraging outcome for post-war immigrants (the 1946–60 cohort). In the majority of age-sex groups, the average income in 1961 was lower than that of the Canadian-born, but by 1971 these groups had largely exceeded the averages of Canadian-born counterparts (Richmond and Kalbach, 1980). Few similar transitions occurred over the 1971, 1981, and 1986 censuses (Beaujot and Rappak, 1990, 139). In the vast majority of comparisons, a given immigrant cohort was either above or below the average of the Canadian-born population at each census. The transitions that occurred were as follows: the 1961–9 cohort had lower average incomes than the Canadian born in 1971 but exceeded this average in 1981, and women of the 1970–4 cohort made a similar transition by the time of the 1986 census.

Table 19.4 shows no further transitions in the 1991 census. It would appear that the immigrants of cohorts since 1976 may not reach the average income of persons born in Canada, in spite of their educational advantage. The situation is more positive for immigrants from Europe and the United States, who exceed the Canadian-born average except in the last cohort for men and the three last cohorts for women. For the majority of recent immigrants, that is, those from "other continents" who would largely be visible minorities, the three most recent cohorts show serious disadvantages. On the other hand, in the cohorts that preceded 1970, these immigrants from the "other continents" have an average income that is typically superior to the average for immigrants from Europe and the United States.

Our objective here is not to pursue an explanation of these differentials. Nonetheless, it is worth noting the importance of region of residence and socio-cultural characteristics. In particular, the disadvantage of recent cohorts, especially those of non-European origin, applies more to residents of metropolitan areas (Beaujot, 1997. Except for the most recent arrivals, the minority of immigrants who were living in non-metropolitan areas had average incomes that compared favorably to the Canadian born in the same areas. Other results show that the advantages of immigrants of European origin apply to the British but not to the Italians. At the same time, the disadvantage suffered by non-European immigrants does not apply to Chinese arrivals of the 1961–80 period. Also, immigrants who speak one of the national languages at home have average levels of income that compare favorably to that of the Canadian born.

The overall results by socio-economic status are that immigration enhances the Canadian averages, but that the overall differences are small. For education, the more recent cohorts have more advantages, but there is also a higher proportion with lower levels of education among immigrants. The cohort differences by labour force participation and average income

Table 19.4: Indexes of Total Income and Employment Income for Persons Working Full-time at Least 40 Weeks, by Sex, Place of Birth, and Arrival Cohorts, Adjusted for Age, Canada, 1991

	Total Income		Employment Income	
	Men	Women	Men	Women
Canadian born	1.00	1.00	1.00	1.01
Immigrants	1.00	1.00	0.99	0.98
Before 1946	0.99	1.05	1.01	1.07
1946–60	1.10	1.06	1.06	1.07
1961–70	1.09	1.11	1.06	1.07
1971–75	0.99	1.04	0.97	0.99
1976–80	0.93	0.93	0.94	0.92
1981–85	0.86	0.83	0.91	0.84
1986–89	0.75	0.78	0.81	0.79
Europe & U.S.	1.06	1.02	1.04	1.01
Before 1946	0.98	1.05	0.98	1.05
1946–60	1.10	1.05	0.98	1.05
1961–70	1.07	1.06	1.04	1.03
1971–75	1.05	1.02	1.03	1.00
1976–80	1.06	0.97	1.06	0.99
1981–85	1.03	0.93	1.03	0.95
1986–89	0.89	0.80	0.95	0.82
Other	0.88	0.96	0.90	0.92
Before 1946	1.16	1.16	-	-
1946–60	1.10	1.19	1.01	1.08
1961–70	1.17	1.25	1.10	1.13
1971–75	0.94	1.06	0.93	0.98
1976–80	0.85	0.91	0.87	0.89
1981–85	0.78	0.79	0.82	0.78
1986–89	0.70	0.78	0.75	0.78

Notes:
- fewer than 50 cases
Adjustments for age using multiple classification analysis, ten-year age groups, ages 15+
    for total income and ages 15–64 for employment income of persons working full-time
    at least 40 weeks in 1990. Index is based on national average.
Source: Special tabulations based on 1991 public use sample.

clearly show that the strong negative differential at the time of arrival is reduced over time. However, especially on average income of immigrants who are not from Europe and the United States, the disadvantage of the more recent cohorts is not being reduced as quickly. It is even possible to doubt whether these cohorts will arrive at the average incomes of the Canadian born, in spite of their educational advantages.

Summary and Discussion

Our first thesis was that the impact of immigration is especially felt at the time of arrival and conversely that it becomes more diffuse over time. We see that the immigrant population differs from the Canadian-born population more in certain regards than in others. Immigration contributes considerably to demographic growth, to the geographic concentration of this growth, and to ethnic diversity. These aspects of growth, concentration, and diversity are especially felt at the time of arrival. Except on geographic concentration, the impact is reduced over the course of the presence of the foreign-born population. In particular, immigrants do not differ significantly from the receiving population in terms of fertility and mortality. Given in part the advantages in education, the socio-economic differences are reduced with time. The vast majority come to speak the national languages, and even the visibility of ethnic differences lessens, certainly in passing to the second and third generations. Thus, our conclusion is similar to that of Pendakur and Pendakur (1995) when following the occupational distribution of given cohorts of immigrants. Just as the occupation at time of arrival has the largest impact, so too does the demographic impact especially apply to the time of arrival.

Since the influence is especially felt at the time of arrival, it is difficult to know whether the impact of immigration has increased. Nonetheless, our second thesis appears to be supported in terms of growth and socio-cultural and socio-economic composition, where a case can be made for an increased impact associated with more recent immigration. With the exception of the period at the turn of the century, immigration of the period since 1971 is having a larger impact on demographic growth. At least if one considers visible minority status to be a significant ethnic category, the mid-1970s are noteworthy as the turning point after which more than half of immigrants were arriving from Asian, Latin America, and Africa. The longer time taken for immigrants from these continents to reach the Canadian-born average in terms of labour force participation and income also represents a larger differential for recent immigration.

While much attention is paid to demographic growth, the visible minority population, and socio-economic differentials, the differential geographic distribution is also a significant factor, in part because internal migration accentuates the strong original differences at time of arrival. Unlike natural increase, which is rather similar across the country, there are very important geographic differentials for both internal and international migration. With a continuation of current trends, one might argue that only some provinces will have a stake in immigration.

With the diversification of immigration and its concentration in certain regions, the ethnic profile also varies considerably over the geography of the country. In particular, the visible minority population is concentrated in large cities, while rural areas and the Atlantic region reveal a concentration of European ethnicity (White and Samuel, 1991).

In Quebec, immigration is concentrated in the one metropolitan area of Montreal, posing specific challenges for integration. In Toronto and Vancouver, the ethnic concentrations in certain areas of the city could also pose problems. There are advantages to concentration in terms of mutual support and the provision of appropriate services. However, large numbers in a given group can introduce institutional separateness and may undermine the identification with a collective destiny as represented by common social programs. The fact that immigrants, particularly the most visible categories of immigrants, are taking longer to arrive at income levels comparable to the national average poses further challenges to integration.

A broad-ranging book entitled *Age of Migration* argues both that migration is an ever-present phenomenon in human history but that it was never as significant as it is today in terms of the diversity that it brings to most countries (Castles and Miller, 1993). We have proposed here that immigration is playing a larger role in the period since the mid-1970s in terms of (1) a greater impact on population growth, (2) a greater impact on socio-cultural composition through the importance of the visible minority component, and (3) a greater impact on socio-economic composition through more persistent income differentials compared to the Canadian-born.

In order to conclude with some policy reflections, these demographic findings need to be supplemented by other significant observations. Ramacharan (1996) argues that Canada has been and continues to be a racist society. Tator and Henry (1996) find that media and other agencies act for the dominant society in undermining the legitimacy of visible minority groups. Taylor (1996) proposes that there are powerful denial mechanisms in the face of individual level of discrimination. Experimental data show that even a few words on the competitive nature of immigrants can encourage students to have a more negative attitude toward immigration (Esses et al., 1996b). As immigration researchers, we may also have denial mechanisms, especially because we profit from immigration. Other politically correct mechanisms make it difficult to discuss immigration levels; an argument for lower levels can itself be seen as a racist argument.

However, if we accept that immigration is having a larger impact on Canadian society, and that racism and discrimination are persistent, two things are possible. We can argue for changing the society to ensure better integration, as many have suggested. But we can also conclude that immigration levels should be lower to permit the society to better accommodate those immigrants allowed in.

The argument for increasing the levels of immigration is generally made on economic or demographic grounds: that Canada needs more immigrants (Beaujot, 1991, 148–51, 178–201). However, the review by the Economic Council of Canada (1991b) concludes that, in terms of macroeconomic questions, immigration is a fairly neutral phenomenon. In terms of demographics, the projections by Statistics Canada (1994) indicate that even with a fertility rate of 1.7 births per woman and an immigration rate of 150,000 persons per year, the population will still be growing in 2016, that is for the realistically foreseeable future.

I am more sympathetic with the socio-cultural argument for immigration. It is on this ground that the Economic Council of Canada suggests maintaining high levels of immigration. Tepper (1987) makes the case that societies that are better able to "manage ethnicity" will be better equipped to face the twenty-first century. We need to be continuously vigilant with regard to the viability of the "Canadian experiment" with relatively high immigration. This means that questions of integration are particularly significant. If integration is not working, we must consider both alternatives: improve the mechanisms for effective integration and/or ensure that immigration levels are not beyond an appropriate or optimal level.

REFERENCES

Badets, Jane, and Tina W.L. Chui. 1994. *Canada's Changing Immigrant Population.* Ottawa: Statistics Canada Catalogue No. 96-311.

Beaujot, Roderic. 1991. *Population Change in Canada: The Challenges of Policy Adaptation.* Toronto: McClelland & Stewart Inc.

Beaujot, Roderic, and Feng Hou. 1993. *Projecting the Visible Minority Population of Canada: The Immigration Component.* Ottawa: Statistics Canada Employment Equity Data Program.

Beaujot, Roderic, and J. Peter Rappak. 1990. "The Evolution of Immigrant Cohorts." In *Ethnic Demography*, edited by Shiva S. Halli, Frank Trovato, and Leo Driedger. Ottawa: Carleton University Press.

Castles, Stephen, and Mark Miller. 1993. *The Age of Migration: International Population Movements in the Modern World.* New York: Guilford Press.

Castonguay, Charles. 1992. "L'orientation linguistique des allophones à Montréal." *Cahiers québécois de demographie* 21, 95–118.

DasGupta, Tania. 1994. "Political Economy of Gender, Race and Class: Looking at South Asian Immigrant Women in Canada." *Canadian Ethnic Studies* 26, 59–73.

Esses, Victoria, Lynne Jackson, and Jeffrey Nolan. 1996b. "Perceived Economic Threat Influences: Attitudes toward Immigrants and Immigration." Paper presented at the National Symposium on Immigration and Integration, Winnipeg, October 1996.

Kalbach, Warren E., et al. 1993. *Population Projections of Visible Minority Groups, Canada, Provinces and Regions, 1991-2016.* Statistics Canada: Employment Equity Data Program.

Kelly, Karen. 1995. "Visible Minorities: Diverse Group." *Canadian Social Trends* 37, 2–8.

Lachapelle, Réjean. 1988a. *L'immigration et le caractère ethnolinguistique du Canada et du Québec.* Statistics Canada: Direction des études analytiques, Documents de Recherche No. 15.

Lacroix, Jean-Michel. 1991. "Le pluriethnisme canadien: au-delà de la fusion et de la confusion." *Revue internationale d'études canadiennes* 3, 153–70.

Paillé, Michel. 1991. "Choix linguistiques des immigrants dans les trois provinces canadiennes les plus populeuses." *Revue Internationale d'études canadiennes* 3, 185–94.

Pendakur, Krishna, and Ravi Pendakur. 1995. *Earnings Differentials among Ethnic Groups in Canada.* Ottawa: Department of Canadian Heritage. Corporate and Intergovernmental Affairs, Strategic Research and Analysis.

Ramacharan, Subhas. 1996. "Immigrant Minorities in the Canadian Mosaic: Coping with Racism." Paper presented at the National Symposium on Immigration and Integration, Winnipeg, October.

Ramirez, Bruno. 1991. "Les rapports entre les études ethniques et le multiculturalisme au Canada: vers de nouvelles perspectives." *Revue internationale d'études canadiennes* 3, 171–84.

Richmond, Anthony H., and Warren E. Kalbach. 1980. *Factors in the Adjustment of Immigrants and Their Descendents*. Ottawa: Statistics Canada.

Sullivan, Teresa A. 1992. "The Changing Demographic Characteristics and Impact of Immigrants in Canada." In *Immigration, Language and Ethnicity: Canada and the United States* edited by B.R. Chiswick. Washington, D.C.: American Enterprise.

Tator, Carol, and Frances Henry. 1996. "Racism and Resistance in Cultural Production: A Case Study of the Controversy over *Show Boat*." Paper presented at the National Symposium on Immigration and Integration, Winnipeg, October.

Taylor, Don. 1996. "Discrimination in the 1990s: An Invisible Evil." Paper presented at the National Symposium on Immigration and Integration, Winnipeg, October.

Tepper, Elliot. 1987. "Demographic Change and Pluralism." *Canadian Studies in Population* 14, 223–35.

Termote, Marc. 1995. "Tendances démolinguistiques au Canada et implications politiques." In *Towards the XXIst Century: Emerging Socio-Demographic Trends and Policy Issues in Canada*, edited by Federation of Canadian Demographers. Ottawa: Federation of Canadian Demographers.

Thomas, Derrick. 1992. "The Social Integration of Immigrants in Canada." In *The Immigration Dilemma*, edited by S. Globerman. Vancouver: The Fraser Institute.

Veltman, Calvin. 1988. *L'impact de l'immigration internationale sur l'équilibre linguistique à Montréal*. Ottawa: Report for Review of Demography, Health and Welfare.

Verma, Ravi, and Feng Hou. 1992. *Database and Population Estimates for Visible Minorities, 1986–1991*. Ottawa: Demography Division, Statistics Canada.

White, Pamela, and T. John Samuel. 1991. "Immigration and Ethnic Diversity in Canada." *International Journal of Canadian Studies* 3, 69–86.

JAMES S. FRIDERES

MANAGING IMMIGRANT SOCIAL TRANSFORMATIONS

FROM IMMIGRANT CANADA: DEMOGRAPHIC, ECONOMIC AND SOCIAL CHALLENGES

The creation of a multicultural policy in Canada over a quarter of a century ago was both visionary and challenging in attempting to establish a mechanism for managing ethnic-based diversity. Over the years the policy has become a directional beacon for Canadians, although its ability to provoke and confuse both its supporters and critics still remains as we head into the twenty-first century. Nevertheless, multiculturalism is not only consistent with Canadian values but is the quintessential Canadian value.

The concept of multiculturalism is double edged; on the one hand it is seen as contributing to the cultural diversity that enhances the quality of life for Canadians while at the same time it is subject to the criticism that it is the thin end of the wedge that will bring about the disunity of the nation (Schlesinger, 1992; Cochran, 1995–6). Many scholars have maintained that sustaining a stable political system in a multi-ethnic society while remaining committed to democratic norms is a problem. As Cochran (1995–6) points out, "incorporating many ethnic groups into a single political system means incorporating the basic problem of ethnic conflict as well and this causes strain on the political structure" (587). It is a problematic policy, emerging out of two opposing philosophies: the politics of equal recognition, which is constructed out of the principle of universalism, according to which social attributes such as religion, ethnicity, and the race of individuals are irrelevant, and the principle of difference, which recognizes and values distinct dissecting social characteristics such as ethnicity and race (Taylor, 1994). The underlying assumption of this policy is that confidence in one's own cultural traditions will foster a healthy self-identity and a positive "outgroup" attitude and will induce mutually enriching experiences and intergroup harmony.

Multiculturalism, as used in this chapter, refers to "An official ... set of policies and practices in which ethnoracial differences are formally promoted and incorporated as an integral component of the political, social and symbolic order" (Fleras and Elliott, 1992, 22). This definition best reflects both the ideology underlying the policy as well as its applied consequences. First of all, this multidimensional concept recognizes, officially, the positive value of ethnic cultures. Thus, a new moral order has been established in which citizens publicly recognize the value of ethnic minority culture in contributing to the development of both the economics and quality of Canadian society. Second, the policy recognizes the right of the state to become involved in ethnic relations, at a variety of levels. Finally, the concept refers to a philosophy and a set of specific programs that allow ethnic/racial groups to legitimately request state support for maintaining their cultural traditions and incorporating into Canadian society.

The policy of multiculturalism does not operate independently but is integrated with and buttressed by other policies and legislative acts. For example, it is entrenched in section 27 of the Canadian Charter of Rights and Freedoms, 1982, which states that the Charter shall be interpreted in a manner consistent with the preservation and enhancement of the multicultural heritage of Canadians. Sallee (1995) argues that the federal government planned to constitutionalize the Charter because it would counter the rising ethnonationalist forces, reinforce the federal presence, create conditions for the emergence of a national identity, and be positively viewed by Canadians. This perspective is further supported by section 36 of the Constitution Act, 1982, which provides that Parliament and the legislatures are committed to promoting equal opportunities for the well-being of Canadians. As such, the multicultural policy has become part of a large and complex legal and policy network.

This essay attempts to track how the aspirations of Quebec ethnonationalists to acquire greater control over their individual and collective identities has been received or dealt with by the remainder of Canada. The essay builds upon the seminal work of Will Kymlicka (1995a) and W. Connor (1973), showing how immigrants and ethnonationalist groups have been affected by the creation and maintenance of our multicultural policy over the past quarter-century. It concludes by suggesting that immigrants in Canadian society are crucial to the unification and development of a national identity.

IMMIGRANTS AND MULTICULTURALISM

As Burgess (1996) has noted, the issue of minority rights has emerged as a significant feature of post-Cold War international policies. In Canada as elsewhere where governments have experienced high levels of immigration, concerns have been raised (Abu-Laban and Stasiulis, 1992). Criticism has come from a variety of sources, including academics, politicians, lobby groups, and ethnics themselves. Multiculturalism is easy to blame for a variety of social problems because there is no single group supporting such a policy. Critics can escape any concerted rebuttal and the repercussions for the accuser are minimal, regardless of the nature of the criticism. Such criticism is based upon perceptions that the policy has conceded too much power to ethnic communities, that immigrants with skills and money are given preference over Canadians, that the national icons and symbols of Canada will soon disappear because immigrants are allowed to challenge the validity of existing symbols, and the fear that multiculturalism will unravel the national fabric, fragment the ethnic mosaic, and bring about the demise of Canadian society. These arguments are not unique to Canada. Other multicultural societies, such as Australia and New Zealand, have also been subject to these concerns (Blainey, 1984; Rimmer, 1991).

One of the most basic and persistent criticisms of multiculturalism is that it will bring about the demise of Canada as a unified, liberal democratic society and allow for the creation of a myriad of ethnic enclaves. The end result will be the destruction of Canada as a nation. Put another way, the argument is that multiculturalism is undermining the ability and/or willingness of immigrants to incorporate into Canadian society (Bibby, 1990; Castles, 1994). To answer these concerns, we need to determine what evidence is required to support or reject such claims.

If we agree that incorporation (a term introduced by Castles, 1994) must have some empirical counterpart, what might we use as an indicator? For example as Kymlicka (1995b) asked, what is the mother tongue retention rate over the past half-century? What is the level of nonofficial language use in the home over the past fifty years? What kind of interest was there in heritage languages before and after the implementation of multiculturalism? Are fewer immigrants learning to speak one of the two official languages? Moving beyond linguistic indicators, we might ask if membership in ethnic voluntary associations has changed over the past thirty years. Finally, we might ask whether or not the number of interethnic marriages has increased or decreased since the introduction of multiculturalism.

Data with regard to language use are widely available and show that English is the preferred language by immigrants. This is true for all provinces, including Quebec. It was only when Bill 101 was introduced in 1977 that immigrants were forced to speak French in institutional spheres of Quebec, e.g., work, health, education, even though the highest allophone retention rate in Canada is in Quebec. In the western province of Alberta, English is the mother tongue for over 83 per cent of the population, up from 70 per cent in 1921. In other provinces this figure is much higher. In Alberta languages such as Norwegian, German, and French have decreased (as mother tongues) by over 50 per cent in the past half-century. If we compare the pre- and post-1971 periods, we find that the overall increase in English as a mother tongue and the decreasing use of other languages (either in the home or at work) has not changed with the introduction of the multicultural policy. This does not mean that an interest in heritage languages does not exist. On the contrary, there has been a substantial increase in student demand. For example, nearly one-fourth of all students in Alberta are currently enrolled in some form of heritage language course. If we restrict our analysis to immigrants, a similar pattern emerges. Driedger (1996) calculated a language continuity index from 1981 to 1991 and showed that most of the language shift comes from allophones (70 per cent), while French speakers contributed only 20 per cent. Using a ratio of language spoken at home to mother tongue, he also found that language mobility favors English for all of Canada (113:1) while for French it was 95:8. Allophones had a ratio of 54:9. What was even more surprising is that in Quebec the language continuity ratio for French was only 101:2. This figure means that French speakers recruited 1.2 individuals for every 100 French mother tongue speakers over a decade. In all other provinces, the ratio was less than 1:00.

While a definitive study on ethnic organizational membership has not been completed, considerable data has been collected on the number of ethnic voluntary associations and their activities. Again the data show a continual decline in the number of these organizations and their membership. Estimates range from decreases of 30–40 per cent over the past thirty years (Herberg, 1989; Jupp, 1989; Isajiw, 1990).

Data with regard to intermarriage show that over the past century, increasing ethnic intermarriage for heads of husband-wife families is evident. While there are variations among ethnic groups, we find that for most groups over half of the family heads have spouses of a different ethnic origin than themselves. For example, in 1871, about one-quarter of the German marriages were intermarriages; by 1991 this had increased to nearly 60 per cent. While nearly half of the Scandinavian marriages in 1921 were intermarriages, by 1991 the proportion had increased to nearly 85 per cent. In the restricted period 1961 to 1991, we find no specific ethnic group that had lower intermarriage rates in 1991 than thirty years previously (M.Kalbach, personal correspondence, 1996). As Kymlicka (1995c) points out, the evidence suggests that multiculturalism is not producing an unwillingness or inability of immigrants to incorporate into mainstream society. While there are differences among ethnic groups with regard to their level of incorporation, the general pattern holds for most of them.

ETHNONATIONALISTS AND MULTICULTURALISM

The concept of "ethnonationalism" was introduced by Connor (1973), although he never provided a formal definition. For purposes of this chapter, ethnonationalism is defined as an ethnic ideology that involves demands for political autonomy or independence. Thus, there is an explicit linking of nationalism and loyalty to an ethnic group and the relationship between ethnic group and nation is highlighted. (See Norton (1993) for an excellent comparative study on the development of ethnonationalist movements.) Douglass (1988) goes on to note that when an ethnic group aspires to be a "nation," the process of ethnonationalism is born. He argues that an increase in the degree of politicization or the emergence of demands for autonomy constitute one of the components of achieving "nationhood." Further politicization leads to a struggle for independence and success of independence movements results in the formation of a sovereign state. On the other hand, he recognizes that some of these groups/movements are more obsessed with a vision of freedom from domination by non-members than with a vision of freedom to conduct foreign relations with other states (Douglass, 1988). Ethnonationalist groups may be small, local organizations, well within the norms of mainstream society or they may be large, radical, extremist groups spread across the region. They may be located outside the existing political structure, in a "core" political party, or be found in between, such as the many "soft" ethnonationalist groups that occupy the middle ground. In the end there is no homogenous form of ethnonationalist group, as such groups may organize and express their vision in many different ways, both within and outside Quebec.

We now move to the concerns expressed by ethnonationalist groups in Canada. Ethnonationalism is just one form of social movement, which is conceptualized as an organized collective manifestation of issues for which people have considerable concern. These movements attempt to promote change in the society of which they are a part and they do so through different means (Zurcher and Snow, 1981). A social movement is characterized by three features: a program for social change, a plan for satisfying members' needs, and an attempt to gain power for the beneficiaries of the movement (Stephan and Stephan, 1985). The ideologies held by ethnonationalist groups help define and explain the grievances held by individuals, define collective goals and strategies for achieving these goals, and provide moral justification for the pursuit of these goals. The ideology serves to translate private troubles into public issues and describes what must, practically and morally, be done. However, not all participants in collective action will accept every aspect of the proffered ideology.

The existence of ethnonationalism reflects the tendency among individuals to link political legitimacy with ethnic identity. Two elements set the stage for the emergence of ethnonationalism; the first is self-awareness with respect to ethnicity and the realization that a particular group is different from others (Cook, 1986). The second is the success of the notion of popular sovereignty (Macklem, 1993).

Quebec and aboriginal ethnonationalists argue that multiculturalism has prevented them from acquiring more provincial or self-government powers. But since the establishment of the multicultural policy, the Province of Quebec has established its own immigration policy and language laws and developed social contracts with immigrants, to name just a few powers that had previously been in the sole domain of the federal government. Aboriginals likewise have achieved unprecedented self-government powers over the past twenty-five years (e.g., Sechels and the Nisga'a of British Columbia, the establishment of Nunavut). Indians in the Province of Manitoba are concluding an agreement that will phase out the federal Department of Northern and Indian Affairs and turn over all powers to provincial and local Indian organizations. In summary, existing evidence demonstrates that multicultural policy has not thwarted the efforts for more self-government or provincial powers by ethnonationalist groups.

While a number of researchers around the world have focused on the role of ethnonationalist groups there is a paucity of work in Canada (Castles, 1994; Halpern et al., 1992; Jamrozik et al., 1995; Levin, 1993). Due to space limitations, the current discussion will be restricted to Quebec ethnonationalists; nevertheless, many of the processes described are similar for other ethnonational groups, e.g., the Avalogonli in western Kenya; the Biafra and Bette in Nigeria; the Maoris in New Zealand; aboriginals in Canada, the United States, and Sri Lanka.

INCORPORATION INTO CANADIAN SOCIETY

The evidence presented does not support the claim that multiculturalism is hampering the incorporation of immigrants or the goals of ethnonationalist groups. The impact of this policy on immigrant groups and their reaction is easily explained. Immigrants have four options when they arrive in Canada: they can incorporate, remain isolated from mainstream society, try a combination of the two for selected social and cultural institutions, or return to their country of origin (Castles, 1995). We will not discuss the fourth option in this essay, although some immigrants have opted for this alternative. Let us look at each of the remaining possibilities. Most immigrants have left their home because they wanted social change and view Canada as a "lifeboat" from the environment they fled (Cochran, 1995–6). Thus they are predisposed to taking on the social and cultural symbols and behaviors of the host society. There is a willingness to take on new values and mores as they settle into Canada. However, immigrants require a "cushion" as they incorporate the new Canadian way of life into their lives. By the second generation, immigrants tend to downplay their ethnicity and actively search for ways in which they can become further incorporated into the host society (Encel, 1993; Smoliez, 1981). In summary, immigrants are generally committed to living in other people's countries and the last thing they want is to remain isolated or secede from them.

Some ethnic groups—for example, Hutterites, Mennonites, and Hasidic Jews—may opt to remain outside mainstream society in specific institutional spheres. However, they have done so voluntarily and have served notice that while they are prepared to remain apart from some of the dominant institutions of the larger society, they are nonetheless willing to remain within the overall social and political spheres of Canadian society.

If an ethnic group wants to remain isolated and outside mainstream society and yet continue to be a viable cultural community, what would be required of it? As Breton (1964) pointed out, only communities that are institutionally complete and exhibit residential homogeneity and geographical concentration can give any thought to developing a truly alternative system. A full set of parallel institutions such as schools, commercial shops, and religious organizations would have to be established and offer opportunities for members of the ethnic community similar to those offered to mainstream Canadians. In nearly all cases ethnic communities find such a goal unrealistic. However, this does not mean that ethnic communities are not concerned about the retention of their culture. Since the 1980s different ethnic groups have competed in order to acquire legitimacy for their interpretation of social reality (Cairns, 1989), and they continue to try and establish small, independent, community-based ethnic institutions.

A review of the structure of today's ethnic communities reveals that most are small enclaves within a larger mosaic and lack the geographical concentration and/or organizations necessary to become institutionally complete. Many ethnic groups have established extensive networks in areas such as the economic sphere; nevertheless, even those who reside in large metropolitan areas such as Toronto find the establishment of major social and economic institutions—e.g., universities, banks—an unrealistic aspiration.

The fact that immigrants are more vocal and demonstrative of their rights is not evidence that they are less incorporated because of a multicultural policy. To the contrary, it represents the acceptance of multiculturalism and the values it espouses. Immigrants want equality now, not, as in the past, for their children or grandchildren. The idea that immigrants should be quiet and grateful for being allowed into Canada is long out of date. Immigrants are not willing to endure prejudice and discrimination and are prepared to utilize the existing policy and legal system to support their claims.

References

Abu-Laban, Y., and D.Stasiulis. 1992. "Ethnic Pluralism under Siege: Popular and Partisan Opposition to Multiculturalism." *Canadian Public Policy* 18, 365–86.

Bibby, Reginald. 1990. *Mosaic Madness: The Poverty and Potential of Life in Canada.* Toronto: Stoddart.

Blainey, G. 1984. *All for Australia.* North Ryde: Methuen Harper.

Breton, Raymond. 1964. "National Minority Rights and the 'Civilizing' of Eastern Europe." *Contention* 5, 12–25.

Cairns, A. 1989. "Ritual, Taboo and Bias in Constitutional Controversies in Canada. The Timilin Lecture," November 13. Saskatoon: University of Saskatchewan.

_____. 1994. *Migrant Incorporation in Highly Developed Countries: An International Comparison.* Centre for Multicultural Studies, University of Wolllongong, Australia.

_____. 1995. *Multicultural Citizenship.* Canberra: Department of the Parliamentary Library, Parliamentary Research Service.

Castles, Stephen, and Mark Miller. 1993. *The Age of Migration: International Population Movements in the Modern World.* New York: Guilford Press.

Cochran, D.C. 1995–6. "Ethnic Diversity and Democratic Stability: The Case of Irish Americans." *Political Science Quarterly* 110, 587–604.

Connor, W. 1973. "The Politics of Ethnonationalism." *Journal of International Affairs* 27, 1–21.

Cook, R. 1986. *Canada, Quebec, and the Uses of Nationalism.* Toronto: McClelland & Stewart.

Douglass, W. 1988. "A Critique of Recent Trends in the Analysis of Ethnonationalism." *Ethnic and Racial Studies* 11, 192–206.

Driedger, Leo. 1996. *Multi-ethnic Canada: Identities and Inequalities.* Toronto: Oxford University Press.

Encel, S., ed. 1993. *The Ethnic Dimension.* Sydney: George Allen and Unwin.

Fleras, A., and J. Elliott. 1992. *Multiculturalism in Canada.* Toronto: Nelson Canada.

Halpern, M., D. Scheffer, and P. Small. 1992. *Self-Determination in the New World Order.* Washington: Carnegie Endowment for International Peace.

Helly, D. 1994. "Politique québécoise face au pluralisme/culturel et pistes de recherche: 1977–1990." In *Ethnicity and Culture in Canada: The Research Landscape,* edited by J. Berry and J. LaPonce. Toronto: University of Toronto Press.

Herberg, E. 1989. *Ethnic Groups in Canada: Adaptation and Transitions.* Scarborough: Nelson Canada.

Isajiw, Wsevolod W. 1990. "Ethnic Identity Retention." In *Ethnic Identity and Equality,* edited by R. Breton et al. Toronto: University of Toronto Press.

Jamrozik, A., C. Baland, and R. Urquhart. 1995. *Social Change and Cultural Transformation in Australia.* Cambridge: Cambridge University Press.

Jup, J., ed. 1989. *The Challenges of Diversity.* Canberra: Australian Government Publishing Services.

Kymlicka, Will. 1995a. *Multicultural Citizenship.* Toronto: Oxford University Press.

_____. 1995b. *The Bases of Social Unity in a "Multination" Canada.* Ottawa: Heritage Canada.

_____. 1995c. *Multiculturalism and the "Politics of Identity" in Canada.*

Levin, M., ed. 1993. *Ethnicity and Aboriginality: Case Studies in Ethnonationalism.* Toronto: University of Toronto Press.

Macklem, P. 1993. "Ethnonationalism, Aboriginal Identities, and the Law." In *Ethnicity and Aboriginality*, edited by M. Levin, 9–28. Toronto: University of Toronto Press.

Norton, R. 1993. "Ethno-nationalism and the Constitutive Power of Cultural Politics: A Comparative Study of Sri Lanka and Fiji." *Journal of Asian and African Studies* 28, 180–97.

Oberschall, A. 1978. "Theories of Social Conflict." In *Annual Review of Sociology* 82, edited by R. Turner, J.Coleman, and R. Fox, 1212–41.

Sallee, D. 1995. "Identities in Conflict: The Aboriginal Question and the Politics of Recognition in Quebec." *Ethnic and Racial Studies* 18, 277–314.

Saywell, J. 1997. *The Rise of the Parti Québécois, 1967–1976.* Toronto: University of Toronto Press.

Schlesinger, A. 1992. *The Disuniting of America.* New York: Norton.

Smoliez, J. 1981. "Core Values and Cultural Identity." *Ethnic and Racial Studies* 4, 75–90.

Stelcner, Morton, and Natalie Kyriazis. 1995. "An Empirical Analysis of Earnings among Ethnic Groups in Canada." *International Journal of Contemporary Sociology* 32, 41–79.

Taylor, D.M., and F.M. Moghaddam. 1994. *Theories of Intergroup Relations: International Social Psychological Perspectives.* Westport: Praeger.

Zurcher, L., and D. Snow. 1981. "Collective Behaviour: Social Movements." In *Social Psychology: Sociological Perspective*, edited by M. Rosenberg and R. Turner. New York: Basic Books.

DANIEL STOFFMAN

THE ILLUSION OF MULTICULTURALISM

FROM WHO GETS IN: WHAT'S WRONG WITH CANADA'S IMMIGRATION PROGRAM—AND HOW TO FIX IT

Gabriel Yiu, a Vancouver flower merchant and a former columnist for *Ming Pao,* a daily newspaper, was speaking not long ago with a visiting Chinese scholar. "Why," the scholar wanted to know, "is there no dog on the menu in any of the Chinese restaurants in Vancouver? I thought Canada was a multicultural country."

Yiu couldn't come up with a good answer. Like most Canadians, he'd been taught to think of Canada as a multicultural country. The reality, and the answer to the visitor's question, is that while Canada has a diverse urban population, it is not multicultural. The absence of dog from the menus of Chinese restaurants is only one example—perhaps too graphic an example for some—of how this is so.

We learn in school that Canada is a mosaic, not an American-style melting pot. A mosaic consists of tiles, each one separate, that together form a pattern. If each of Canada's multiple ethnic groups is a part of a mosaic, what happens within that part should not be any business of someone who lives in one of the other parts. The visiting scholar had a point.

Many Chinese from mainland China (though not those from Hong Kong) are dog eaters. So are Koreans who, in Korea, frequent specialty dog restaurants that offer such delicacies as "tonic soup." Korean men believe dog meat enhances sexual prowess and have been eating it for centuries. Here dogs are doted upon as part of the family. It's deeply offensive (as well as illegal) in Western countries to sell dog meat. But from the Chinese or Korean viewpoint, there seems no logical reason why it would be acceptable to eat cow, pig, chicken, and lamb but not dog.

Canadian dog lovers, if they really believed in multiculturalism, would respect the right of other cultures to be different. They could be faithful to their own culture by steering clear of restaurants with poodles on the menu. So why can't the Chinese and Korean parts of the Canadian mosaic fully express their culinary cultures? Because all hell would break loose. Dog lovers are passionate and uncompromising. Politicians can yak all they want about multiculturalism, they would say, but this is Canada and nobody had better eat any dogs. Korean-style dog restaurants would need armed guards.

Canadian leaders, from Governor General Adrienne Clarkson on down, use the words "diversity" and "multiculturalism" as if they were synonymous. They're not, and this linguistic misuse is responsible for much of the confusion over cultural differences among Canadians. Diversity encompasses a broad range of characteristics that differentiate people: religion, language, dress, leisure pursuits, and so forth. Diversity is not divisive in a secular Western democracy that upholds the freedom of the individual. But because there are irreconcilable differences between cultures, multiculturalism is divisive. That's why Canadians don't care what people eat—until someone decides to barbecue man's best friend. It's why Canadians don't care what people wear—until an RCMP member demands the right to wear a turban, changing a uniform that's a national symbol.

Some immigrants bring attitudes that are unacceptable to the majority of Canadians and, in some cases, illegal. Just as Canadian Muslims have no right to kill Salman Rushdie, Muslims who emigrate from Africa lose the right to have their daughters circumcised. Men in Canada do not have the right to have more than one wife at a time, even if the culture they brought with them says they do. And they have no right to beat their wives and children or to force a daughter to marry someone she does not want to. Filipino immigrants have no right to stage the cockfights that entertained them at home.

Newcomers might be excused for wondering why they don't have these rights. Why, they might ask, do Canada's leaders boast about its multiculturalism if they do not want the country actually to be multicultural? The answer is that Canada's leaders are hypocrites. As with every aspect of the immigration program, there is the official version and the real version. In the official version, Canada is unlike other countries, such as Britain and France, that also have diverse populations but do not have official multiculturalism. Canada, so the story goes, has found a new model for social harmony by encouraging immigrants to maintain their own cultures rather than expecting them to assimilate into ours.

The reality is quite different. Perhaps that's why two of the most insightful books on the subject of Canadian multiculturalism both have the word "illusion" in their titles. Neil Bissoondath, a novelist of Indian background who was born in Trinidad and now lives in Quebec, thought he was going to become a Canadian when he moved to Canada. He had no intention of becoming an Indo-Trinidadian-Canadian and he wrote a book, *Selling Illusions: The Cult of Multiculturalism in Canada,* explaining why.

In *The Illusion of Difference,* the University of Toronto sociologists Raymond Breton and Jeffrey Reitz examined the widely held belief that Canada is a mosaic in which immigrants retain their identities—unlike the United States, a melting pot in which immigrants swiftly become unhyphenated Americans. They found that, in fact, immigrants to Canada assimilate as quickly as do immigrants to the United States and, indeed, that Canadians are even less inclined than Americans to favour retention of ethnic cultural differences.

Canada's immigration program is based, as we've seen, on demonstrably false claims of economic and demographic necessity. Multiculturalism, an offshoot of our immigration program, consists of rhetoric similarly disconnected from the real world. Hypocrisy is a poor foundation for public policy because it can't help but sow confusion and cynicism.

Khat provides a classic example. I first heard about khat (pronounced "cot") while researching a magazine article about Somali refugee claimants who had settled in Toronto. It was obvious that drug dealing was going on around some suburban apartment buildings favoured by Somalis. It wasn't the usual drugs that were being sold but a leaf known as khat, from a shrub that grows in East Africa and on the Arabian peninsula. The leaf, which resembles rhubarb, is chewed for its euphoric effects, similar to those provided by amphetamines. Khat is used by Somalis as a social lubricant, the way Western people use wine or beer. It's also an important part of weddings and other festive gatherings.

At the time, it was illegal to import khat but legal to possess it. Health Canada has since banned it altogether. (Khat is also illegal in the United States and most European countries, but not Britain.) The active ingredients are prohibited under the Canada Health and Safety Act, following a recommendation of the World Health Organization. In the United States, cathinone, one of the plant's components, is classified as a schedule I controlled substance, a category that includes LSD, heroin, and ecstasy. Health Canada says khat can cause high blood pressure, cardiac problems, hallucination, and insanity. The Somalis I've talked to say it makes people happy and helps conversation to flow. Some Somalis think the prohibition is simply an excuse for the police to harass them.

What to do about khat? The answer depends on one's view of drugs, and of multiculturalism. Many recreational drugs are illegal in Canada. If you think we should lighten up about drugs, you probably favour lifting the ban on khat. If you think not, you would probably leave it, along with LSD and ecstasy, as a banned substance.

From the perspective of multiculturalism, it's a more interesting issue. My own view is that Canada isn't a multicultural country and that real attempts to make it one would cause severe social discord. As for the Somalis, nobody forced them to come here. They came as refugee claimants even though most had already obtained safety elsewhere. For that reason, Canada was under no moral or legal obligation to admit them. Why did they come? Many came because Canada is the easiest place to get welfare, a fact known even in remote parts of Africa and Asia. Easy welfare is part of the "pull factor" that draws refugee claimants to Canada.

By admitting the Somalis and supporting them financially, Canada has bestowed huge favours on them. Now they think Canada's drug laws should be adapted to their social customs? I don't see why, but then I'm not a multiculturalist. If multiculturalism were more than an empty word, its adherents would surely support the Somalis' right to use khat. The dominant culture in Canada makes extensive use of alcohol, but practising Muslims, as many Somalis are, may not use alcohol. If Canada were truly a mosaic, the Somalis would be able to use their intoxicant of choice. But it's not a true mosaic, and the majority culture's emphasis on health and safety supersedes the culture of a minority group.

Canada is officially multicultural; France is officially uni-cultural. Both countries have banned khat. The French give the Somalis a clear message: "You're in France, so you have to do things our way. If you want to chew khat, you must leave. We don't allow that here." The Canadians' message is mixed and mystifying: "We are officially multicultural and proud of it. We wouldn't dream of asking you to abandon your Somali culture, which makes up a valuable part of our mosaic. Oh, and by the way, if you chew khat, we'll put you in jail." To the Somalis, the difference between the French and the Canadians is simply that the French are honest about where they stand while the Canadians aren't. Meanwhile, in non-multicultural Britain, you can buy khat in grocery stores.

In another safety-versus-culture case, a Sikh went to the British Columbia Human Rights Commission to argue that he should be exempt from the law requiring motorcyclists to wear helmets because his religion required him to wear a turban instead. And there have been other cases of the Sikh dress code clashing with Canadian norms. The most famous happened when a controversy erupted after the Royal Canadian Mounted Police granted a Sikh officer's request that he be allowed to wear his turban on duty.

This episode was seen as a victory for multiculturalism; in retrospect, it looks more like a defeat. It showed that the official line about Canada being a multicultural paradise was a lie. The case was a reality check for the ideologues of multiculturalism, who had convinced themselves there was no such thing as a Canadian culture (a Liberal multiculturalism minister, Sheila Finestone, actually said this) or national symbols that Canadians cared about.

In Canada, dress is a matter of individual choice, in contrast to theocratic Muslim countries in which dress codes are forced on the population. Few Canadians would suggest that an orthodox Sikh doctor, bus driver, or store clerk should be denied the right to wear a turban. The RCMP case became a cultural issue, and therefore divisive, because the RCMP, especially in western Canada, is a cherished institution. Moreover, it is a quasi-military organization, and military organizations everywhere require their members to wear identical uniforms. The commissioner of the RCMP sided with the Sikh.

The Sikh Mountie was not merely practising diversity but was challenging deeply felt beliefs of a large segment of the majority culture. A group of retired officers took up the challenge. In federal court they argued that the turban infringed their constitutional right to a secular state free of religious symbols. A petition with an impressive total of 210,000 names backed them up. The court, in ruling in favour of the RCMP, rejected the claim of Sikh organizations that not allowing the turban would amount to religious discrimination. Instead, it upheld the right of the RCMP to change its uniform code.

The Sikhs won but they paid a price—one that most minority groups would prefer to avoid. Many Canadians were embittered by the turban episode and still are. Their message to the ethnic communities was clear: there are limits to how much multiculturalism Canadians will swallow, and if you push those limits, there will be trouble. As it turned out, the RCMP case settled nothing. In March 2002, a Montreal school board ruled that a 12-year-old boy could not wear his religious dagger, or kirpan, because it violated the rule against dangerous objects.

Turbans on Mounties, a leaf chewed by Somalis, the dietary habits of Chinese and Koreans—aren't these rather trivial matters? Perhaps they are, but multiculturalism itself isn't trivial. It touches on such fundamental concepts as separation of church and state, equality of women, and the rights of children. To many immigrants, these are radical, alien concepts, difficult to accept. If Canada is multicultural, some of them believe, maybe they shouldn't have to accept them.

A judge once told me that men who appeared before her charged with assaulting their wives or girlfriends had argued that their culture gave them licence to do so. She did not accept the arguments, but other judges have accepted similar defences. In 1994, a Quebec judge gave a man 23 months in jail, instead of the four years the prosecution requested, for repeatedly sodomizing his 11-year-old stepdaughter. She justified the light sentence on the grounds that, given the man's Islamic faith, he should be given some credit for preserving the girl's virginity. Muslims were as outraged as other Canadians by the judge's suggestion that the man's religion in some way mitigated his actions.

In February 2002, an Ontario couple were arrested for having their 11-year-old daughter circumcised. This practice, involving removal of the clitoris, is widespread in Africa and parts of Asia but illegal in the West. With its official multiculturalism, Canada confuses people who come here, who are urged to retain their cultures and then jailed for doing so. Female circumcision is an important part of the culture of many countries; the United Nations estimates 2 million such procedures are performed annually. "Culturally, fathers and mothers think it's a good thing for their girls," Nadia Badr of the Sudanese Women Association of Niagara told the *National Post*. "They have no idea it's wrong."

At about the same time, a murder trial involving a horrific case of child abuse was unfolding in Toronto. The father of the brutalized little boy said that, in Jamaica, parents have the right to "whip" their children—the multiculturalism defence. How many girls have suffered genital mutilation in Canada, losing a lifetime of sexual pleasure, because immigrants believed Canada's official policy gave them the right to practise their culture? How many children have been beaten under the imprimatur of multiculturalism?

Because of multiculturalism, there is more overt hostility in Canada to those of European ancestry (who made up 87 percent of the population, as of the 1996 census) than to the non-white minority. In the name of multiculturalism, the achievements of Canada's founders have been all but eradicated from school books. Multiculturalists believe English-Canadian schoolchildren should not be allowed to have English historical heroes. Yet, as Richard Gwyn, writing of the demise of English-Canadian nationalism, says, "It was English-Canadians who explored the greater part of the country, cleared it, and settled it. It was they who contributed the overwhelming majority of men who died fighting in wars for democracy and freedom. It was they who created almost all of the country's political and legal infrastructure."

They also opened Canada up to immigrants from all over the world and passed laws outlawing racism and discrimination. And what do they get in return? From Jean Chrétien they get multiculturalism ministers who belittle the English-Canadian culture and vilify them as cross-burning racists.

It's doubtful that Pierre Trudeau intended multiculturalism to become such a nasty business when he enshrined the policy in law in 1971 — although, as Neil Bissoondath pointed out, the Act for the Preservation and Enhancement of Multiculturalism in Canada was notable for its "lack of any mention of unity." Instead, it aimed at "ensuring that the various ethnic groups whose interests it espouses discover no compelling reason to blur the distinctions among them."

Trudeau's multiculturalism act marked the first time in history that a country had deliberately set out to heighten, intensify, and make permanent the ethnic differences among its people. Why would Canada do this to itself? In part, the policy was a response to the Royal Commission on Bilingualism and Biculturalism, which had recommended a two-nations policy — one French, one English — for Canada. At the time, this was also the policy of the Progressive Conservatives under Robert Stanfield.

Trudeau hated the two-nations idea. He envisioned a bilingual Canada with no special status for Quebec. Multiculturalism, as Gwyn points out in *The Northern Magus*, his biography of Trudeau, was a way of forestalling biculturalism. Trudeau seemed to think that French-Canadians would become just another hyphenated group among dozens of others. It didn't work as planned, Gwyn writes, because "French-Canadians escaped easily from the thicket of hyphens Trudeau was trying to plant amongst them by renaming themselves Quebecois."

If anything, the Quebecois were strengthened by multiculturalism, if only because English Canada was weakened by it. By dividing Canadians outside Quebec into dozens of hyphenated groups, multiculturalism amounted to a systematic attempt to eliminate the national identity of English-speaking Canada. In contrast, Quebec's national identity has been reinforced, in part through changes to the immigration program that gave it the right to enhance its francophone character by recruiting francophone immigrants. English Canada has no right to use immigration to enhance its character.

In the 1972 election, Trudeau squeaked back into power with only a two-seat advantage over the Conservatives. Demoted to minority status in Parliament, Trudeau decided to switch his approach from doing what was right to doing what worked. He had to be prepared, Gwyn writes, "to use every tool and all the money in the public purse to win re-election." Trudeau had been accused of neglecting the ethnic vote. That wouldn't do. And so, recounts Gwyn, "up sprang a trebled multiculturalism program that functioned as a slush fund to buy votes."

As an answer to Quebec nationalism, multiculturalism was a flop. Its real value, the Liberals saw, was as part of their electoral machinery. In 2002, with the federal opposition in such disarray that Canada is effectively a one-party state, it's easy to forget that the Liberals' hold on power has, more often than not, been tenuous. The Liberals know the time will come when that hold becomes tenuous again. Immigration and multiculturalism are life rafts on the Liberal ship. They exist to carry a core group of ethnic constituencies that are supposed to prevent the party from sinking whenever it finds itself in rough waters.

After the near defeat of 1972, Trudeau's government began funding dozens of organizations that claimed to represent ethnic Canadians. Some were created for the sole purpose of obtaining these grants. Many were unknown to the people they claimed to represent. A 1976 evaluation of ethnic organizations getting government money found the typical one had only 20 to 85 members.

An umbrella group, the Canadian Ethnocultural Council, claimed to speak for millions of Canadians yet was almost entirely dependent on the government for support. So were the groups within it. In a 1994 study, John Bryden, a dissident Liberal MP, found that the National Association of Canadians of Origins in India, which claimed to speak for 750,000 Canadians, had raised only $4,900 through memberships and donations, relying on the government for the $68,000 it needed to exist. The Liberals were using public money to create a caste of professional multiculturalists dependent on the government for their jobs. In return for their wages, these people were expected to help swing their communities behind the Liberals.

How to sell this crude vote-buying program to the public? Trudeau, with characteristic audacity, argued that multiculturalism would enhance national unity. How so? National unity "must be founded on confidence in one's own individual identity; out of this can grow respect for others and a willingness to share ideas, attitudes, and assumptions."

Like many of Trudeau's statements, this sounded reasonable until you thought about it carefully. Of course people should have confidence in their own identity and respect for others. But where was the evidence that they needed help from Ottawa to build that confidence? And by what bizarre logic could organizations created at taxpayers' expense to reinforce ethnic divisions be seen as contributing to national unity?

Laura Sabia, a prominent feminist and author, was not fooled. In a 1978 speech she attacked politicians "whose motto is 'divide and rule.' I, for one, refuse to be hyphenated. I am a Canadian, first and foremost." Judging from opinion polls, Sabia, like Bissoondath, spoke for the majority. Canadians wanted to be Canadians, not Italian-Canadians or Indo-Canadians. But the newly empowered multiculturalists were determined to give them hyphens whether they wanted hyphens or not. In multicultural Canada, you can be British-Canadian or Sikh-Canadian or Finnish-Canadian, but you can't be Canadian. Your ethnicity resides in the word before the hyphen; the "Canadian" signifies only citizenship, not ethnicity.

From an anthropological view, these distinctions make no sense. And a growing number of Canadians don't agree with them. In a 1991 Angus Reid survey, 63 percent of respondents, told they could choose only one answer for their identity, chose Canadian. Only 13 percent of those born in Canada identified themselves by some other ethnic origin, and only 3 percent born elsewhere chose an ethnic identity other than Canadian.

In 1996, for the first time, Statistics Canada included "Canadian" as an ethnicity option on the census form. A total of 30.9 percent indicated Canadian as their sole or partial ethnic origin. As the idea of Canadian ethnicity gains acceptance, that percentage can be expected to grow. This is a triumph of common sense over official policy.

Ideas about race and ethnicity have evolved in recent decades. Only 60 years ago, Hitler unleashed a world war motivated in part by theories of race that seem insane today but were widely accepted then. Hitler thought the "Aryan race" was superior to others. There is no such thing as an Aryan "race." Nor is there an English or a French "race." Even the standard division of mankind into Asian, black, and Caucasian "races" is under scientific challenge because the genetic differences among these groups are so small.

If ethnicity is not biological—and science tells us it is not—then it can only be linguistic, geographical, and cultural. Anyone who was born in English-speaking Canada or has lived in it for a long time, speaks English fluently, and accepts Canadian values has every reason to identify herself or himself as an ethnic Canadian. And the rapid growth in the number of Canadians with mixed ancestries—36 percent of the population as of 1996— can only accelerate this trend. If your grandparents were Italian, Swedish, American, and Japanese, you might as well call yourself Canadian. And since diversity is one of Canada's cultural characteristics, there's no reason why an ethnic Canadian would not have Asian features or black skin or wear a hijab.

Not far from my home in central Toronto is a cluster of Korean restaurants, nightclubs, and shops. It attracts young people who travel in groups and speak Korean among themselves. This is normal because most of them came to Canada relatively recently, and Korean is their first language. But occasionally I encounter young second-generation Koreans in shops or restaurants. Their English, in both accent and vocabulary, is indistinguishable from that of other Canadians. If they grew up in Korean-speaking homes, they probably speak some Korean as well. The chances that *their* children will speak Korean, however, are slim.

Language is much more than a way of communicating; it is a way of thinking, of organizing perception, of looking at the world. It's the basis of cultural identity. If you don't have Korean language, you don't have much Korean culture. Canada's multiculturalists know this, which is why language is their preoccupation. Millions of dollars are spent on heritage language programs aimed at teaching ancestral languages to the descendants of immigrants. Extreme multiculturalists would go further. A professor at York University, Evelyn Kallen, once proposed that Canada should become a truly multilingual society and that, to accomplish this, all children should be educated in their ancestral languages. In her version of Canada, English and French would have no special status.

Of course, the chances of anything like this happening are zero. Even if a government were crazy enough to try to implement such a policy, few immigrants would want anything to do with it. But this professor's proposal goes to the heart of what multiculturalism is all about.

Canada's diversity is nothing new; the country has accepted immigrants for much of its history. The linguistic history of past immigrant families is identical to what is happening to the Koreans in my neighbourhood. A first-generation immigrant speaks whatever language he brought to Canada. His children—second-generation Canadians—may speak some of that language, but not as well as their native tongue, English. The third generation—the grandchildren of the original immigrant—are almost always unilingual English-speakers. They may have a smattering of old-country words to make Grandpa chuckle, but not enough to carry on a conversation.

With its heritage language programs and its lofty rhetoric about cultural preservation, official multiculturalism attempts to modify this process. The descendants of immigrants are urged to speak their ancestral languages as well as English. This is a worthy goal; in an ideal world, everyone would be multilingual. Not only does learning other languages make one more educated and tolerant and more receptive to the world, there is some evidence it may even make one's brain work better.

The problem is that kids will learn a language only if they see a need for it. Without that need, they won't expend the effort. The issue then becomes whether public funds should be spent on a project doomed to failure. The sociologists Reitz and Breton merely confirm the obvious: fewer than 1 percent of third-generation Canadians speak an ancestral language other than English or French. Which shows that, despite official multiculturalism, assimilation is happening as rapidly as ever.

To most Canadians, including most foreign-born Canadians, this assimilation is a good thing; to multiculturalists it is appalling. I once heard a prominent ethnic bureaucrat describe an immigrant who opposed multiculturalism as an "assimilationist." The venom with which he spat out the word was striking, as if an assimilationist belonged to the same category of repulsive humankind as, say, a pedophile.

If Canada's professional multiculturalists had their way, Germany's immigration system would be replicated here. German society has been unwilling to accept people of other nationalities as Germans. Three million Turkish guest workers have remained Turks rather than become Germans. Sadly, the situation is getting worse instead of better. The German-language skills of German-born children of Turkish parents have been declining in recent years; these children enter school not knowing any German. That's what happens when assimilation is a dirty word.

Ronald Leung once invited his radio listeners to voice their opinions on multiculturalism. Once was enough. Leung did not get to be the most popular talk-show host among people in the Vancouver area who listen to Chinese-language radio by choosing topics nobody wants to talk about. "No one who calls my program has any interest in multiculturalism, except those in the business of multiculturalism," he told me. "I opened the line and nobody called in except the usual people." Leung's Cantonese-speaking listeners don't want to talk about multiculturalism because they are not interested in a government program, created for partisan purposes, that has little to do with anything that matters in their lives.

As of 2002, there are about 400,000 ethnic Chinese in British Columbia, out of a total population of 3.9 million. Of those, 260,000 speak a Chinese language as their mother tongue. Some 90 percent of them live in Greater Vancouver, where a quarter of the population lists Chinese as its mother tongue, a figure that does not include many non-Chinese-speaking people of Chinese ancestry whose families have been in B.C. for generations.

Canada's vaunted diversity is hardly unique. Visitors to major cities in the United States, France, Britain, and many other Western countries will hear many languages in the streets, encounter people in non-Western dress, observe places of worship of different faiths, and see exotic foods in grocery stores. But just as Canada makes a fuss about slower population growth, which the rest of the world sees as normal and manageable, so too does it get unduly excited about diversity.

We call it multiculturalism and claim it makes us different from all other countries. But the truth is that we're not different. As we have seen, if a practice of the minority culture clashes with an important value of the majority culture, we usually don't allow it, just as the Americans or the French wouldn't allow it.

Take the issue of trees, about which people on the West Coast have especially strong feelings. Vancouverites love their stately cedars, some of which soar 200 feet. When large numbers of wealthy Hong Kong Chinese settled on the west side of Vancouver in the 1980s and 1990s, a fight erupted over trees and houses. Immigrants knocked down the old houses and put up huge new ones, "monster houses" to the locals, often made of brick. That was bad enough, but knocking down ancient trees was worse. For many people, these trees had an almost spiritual significance and nobody had a right to knock them down. It wasn't that the Hong Kong people disliked trees; they simply had their own culture with its own belief system. One such belief is that having a tree in front of your house is bad luck; it could make you poor. An immigrant-versus-native battle ensued, and a new bylaw was passed restricting the rights of homeowners to cut down trees.

Multiculturalism policy will never make Canada truly multicultural. Only immigration policy could achieve that. If an "ethnic" community becomes larger than the European-descended community, it will grow more assertive. It will see no reason to defer to a culture that has fewer adherents than its own. It might change the local bylaw so that it can cut down as many trees as it wants. It might want offices and schools to close on its holidays and to remain open on holidays it doesn't celebrate. It might decide to make its language official and have it spoken in the legislature, placed on all public signs, and compulsory in schools.

If that happened, Canada would finally have what it claims to want: true multiculturalism. If it happens anywhere in Canada, it will be in B.C., and it will be the Chinese community that makes it happen, not because its members are power-hungry but because Ottawa's immigration policy will have made them the dominant group, and it is in the nature of dominant groups to exert dominance.

In the late 1980s, the government of Brian Mulroney began a social experiment on a grand scale by dumping the immigration policy that had evolved in Canada since World War II. The jettisoned policy had worked rather well. Its high degree of public acceptance was signalled by the fact that immigration was rarely discussed in Parliament or the media. It was one of those boring government functions—like the management of lighthouses or the mint—that people assumed were in good hands. Annual changes in immigration levels were of no more interest than annual changes in the production of $5 bills. The government could be counted on to provide what was needed. When Mulroney's government replaced the old policy with a new one, unique in the world, it transformed urban Canada. It did so without ever announcing it was doing it, without explaining why it was doing it, and without asking the Canadian people whether they wanted it done. Chrétien continues Mulroney's grand social experiment. Nobody in government, the universities, or anywhere else knows what its ultimate impact on Canada will be. With immigration, we're in uncharted waters.

Historically, immigrants have come in waves. A wave would start gradually, pick up force until it crashed on the shore, then recede. In the past, Canada welcomed waves of Ukrainians, Italians, Hungarians, and many others. Often they came over a relatively short period. The Ukrainians who came during the second decade of the 20th century were quickly cut off from their homeland. Communications were poor, travel was slow, and few could have afforded to go back even had they wanted to. When that wave of immigration stopped, and no new Ukrainians came, they were even more cut off. Canada was now their world.

Thanks to Mulroney, immigrants no longer come in waves from a wide variety of places. Most come in a continuous, relentless flow from relatively few countries. The Liberals set the stage for this in 1978 when they allowed immigrants to sponsor working-age parents, thereby facilitating chain immigration.

This had little immediate impact because, under Trudeau, the annual intake of immigrants remained moderate. Then Mulroney increased immigration to 250,000 a year and made this world-beating level permanent, so that there could be no respite ever, even during a recession. Permanent high levels gave momentum to unskilled, family-class immigration, so that one relative could sponsor another, who could sponsor another, who could sponsor another, in an ever-lengthening chain. That's why Vancouver and Toronto have shopping malls and high schools where Chinese is the first language and English is rarely heard.

Canada's intake is not nearly as diverse as is often claimed. There are 192 countries in the world but, in 1999, 55 percent of new immigrants came from only 10 of those countries. Some countries with huge populations, such as Indonesia, Nigeria, and Brazil, send almost no immigrants to Canada. Why? Because it is difficult to get into Canada as an independent immigrant. It is easy to get in if you're sponsored, but few Indonesians or Nigerians have anyone in Canada to sponsor them.

By contrast, huge numbers of potential sponsors from China, India, and Pakistan are already in Canada. As a result, people from these countries (and a few others) have effectively appropriated Canada's immigration program. Barring the advent of a government with the courage to reclaim immigration from the stakeholders, this situation will be permanent, for the ranks of these émigré communities are swelled daily by new arrivals.

Because of modern travel and communications, new arrivals are no longer cut off from their homelands. It is now possible for a recent immigrant from Hong Kong to live in Richmond, a suburb south of Vancouver, almost as if she had never left home. Perhaps she watches the latest Chinese video release while chatting on her cellphone with her husband, who's back in Hong Kong, where he spends most of his time although he is a Canadian citizen. She's also in phone and e-mail contact with friends back home.

Her neighbours speak Cantonese. At the local shopping mall, she buys the same products she bought in Hong Kong. Her lack of English is not a problem. She may never learn much English, but first-generation immigrants, especially homemakers and older people, often don't. That's normal. Her Canadian-born children may not be learning English either, and that's not normal.

New immigrants of the same language group have always tended to gather in neighbourhoods. What's novel is the scale of these immigrant communities—Richmond is 40 percent Chinese—and the fact that the wave of immigrants never recedes. If the flow of immigrants from China never ends (and with 20,000 new arrivals every year in Vancouver, it shows no sign of ending), how big will the new Chinese-speaking communities grow? Will the Canadian-born children in these communities consider themselves Canadians or Chinese people living in Canada? Will these children learn English? Nobody knows the answers, least of all the politicians, long since booted out of office, who began this social experiment.

If anyone can answer the linguistic questions, it would be Lee Gunderson, head of the Department of Language and Literacy Education at University of British Columbia's Faculty of Education. An expert on language acquisition by immigrants, he recently completed a book, *The Achievement of Immigrant Students in English-Only Schools,* based on 12 years of research and interviews with 417 students in Vancouver schools. [...] Gunderson's findings make clear that the Mulroney-Chrétien immigration program—a relentless influx of large numbers of immigrants coming from the same places and going to the same places—has serious implications for language acquisition.

When my own daughter was seven, our family spent a year in the south of France. She did not speak a word of French and was plunked into the equivalent of grade 2 in a local primary school where nobody spoke

English. She was desperate to communicate, and within weeks she was doing so. In a few months she was speaking French fluently, and she still speaks it well more than 20 years later. Gunderson agrees with me that, had she attended an English school during that year in France, she probably would not have learned French. Kids learn a new language because they need to, not because some adult says it's good for them.

Many of the ethnic Chinese and East Indian kids in Vancouver, including ones born in Canada, are not as fortunate as my daughter was. Though they live in an English-speaking country and attend English-language schools, they don't need to learn a new language to communicate with the other kids. In one Lower Mainland school, 99 percent of the students are Punjabi. Why would they bother trying to speak English to one another? Even if they did, what sort of English would they learn?

In other Richmond schools, large groups of both Cantonese-and Mandarin-speakers speak those languages among themselves. If a Mandarin-speaker were to speak with a Cantonese-speaker, it would have to be in English, Gunderson says. But students from different language groups rarely interact. "For language acquisition, it's very serious," Gunderson points out. "I know kindergartens in Vancouver and Richmond where there may be one native English-speaker. The rest are Cantonese-speakers or Mandarin-speakers."

If the English-speaking toddler is outgoing, maybe she'll learn some Cantonese. Otherwise, she'll be isolated. And the only English the Cantonese-speaking kids will hear is from the teacher. That's not nearly as effective as learning English from native English-speaking children. This linguistic mess, created by reckless mismanagement of the immigration program, turns immigrant language acquisition upside down.

"The whole field of English as a second language [ESL] instruction is based on the notion that the language of the community is the target language," Gunderson explains. "It doesn't work any more in many school situations, because the language of the community is not English. We're now in a situation of teaching English as a foreign language rather than English as a second language. That's the way you learn English in China, where the surrounding language is not English."

In interviews with ESL students, Gunderson found they were distressed about not being immersed in English. "The irony," he says, "is that students in an English-only school system found it impossible for various reasons to interact with English-speakers. A majority reported that it was impossible to talk to English-speakers or to hear English spoken." One ESL student told Gunderson, "There are too many Chinese." Nobody could call him racist, since he's a Cantonese-speaking immigrant himself. This boy was worried that he would never learn "proper English" because he never heard it; all he heard in the halls and in the schoolyard was Cantonese. Other immigrants are also affected. A 14-year-old Spanish-speaking boy told Gunderson: "Too much Chinese. ESL classes are fill with Chinese. Teachers no good, not stop Chinese talk."

In Vancouver, some ESL students were born in Canada. This is of increasing concern to teachers, Gunderson says. "Teachers are beginning to say, 'My God, this child was born in Canada and can't speak a word of English. What's going on here?'"

If a German-born child enters school in Germany not speaking German, many Germans view the matter with concern. When Canadian-born children enter school not speaking English, nobody, other than teachers in the privacy of their staff rooms, says anything. Again, it's because the official orthodoxy is that immigration brings only benefits. To point out obvious problems or shortcomings in a ruined immigration program is in bad taste. Those who question the orthodoxy risk being called nasty names by the stakeholders.

What is not said, but should be, is that in parts of Canada we're seeing the introduction of a German-style immigration system: isolation rather than integration. Once again, this creates winners and losers. The winners are British Columbia real estate developers who make fortunes building houses for the new arrivals. The losers are the students, native English-speakers as well as foreign-language-speakers, whose school experience is diminished as a result of the government's social experiment.

The advent of German-style segregation is not happening because the host community does not wish to accept the newcomers; nor is it the result of standoffishness on the part of the immigrants themselves. Rather, it's happening because the volume and concentration of immigration is so great that integration is impeded. If the flow of new immigrants were more limited and diverse, the problem would disappear.

What will happen to a Canadian-born child who grows up in a Chinese-speaking enclave and enters school as an ESL student not speaking English? Because he's immersed in Cantonese or Mandarin rather than English, his progress in what should be his native language is bound to be slow. At the end of 12 years in the school system, will he speak English like the native Canadian he is, with the same command as other Canadian-born people? If not, once he emerges onto the job market, he'll find that poor communications skills are a crippling handicap. "It's a question we can't yet answer," says Gunderson. "We don't know."

So we find ourselves in uncharted waters. The immigration system is so badly broken that it may no longer be capable of integrating newcomers. Multiculturalists in Vancouver may be getting what they want, though not, ironically, because of our policy of multiculturalism. It's our ill-managed immigration program that's causing some Canadian-born people to retain their ancestral language and speak it better than they speak what should be their native language, English. Previously, this has happened only with small religious groups, such as the Yiddish-speaking ultra-Orthodox Jews in Montreal's Outremont area, who deliberately isolate themselves from the surrounding community.

There's only one way deficient English in a second-generation Canadian would not be a handicap. If Vancouver ever got genuine multiculturalism, Chinese would be as common as English in the life of the city. If that happened, a native-born Vancouverite who spoke minimal English with a strong Chinese accent would feel no more out of place than an anglophone in Montreal who speaks poor French.

This may be the eventual outcome of the social experiment Canada has embarked on, but there's a way to go yet. More than half the immigrants to Greater Vancouver speak Cantonese, Mandarin, or Punjabi, but others come from a variety of places. There are still places where immigration works the way it should. At Vancouver's Brock Elementary School, for example, there are 49 first languages among the pupils. Since none is dominant, the language in the halls and on the playground is English. All the kids learn English quickly and pick up some useful multilingual skills as well. "The first thing they learn," chuckles Gunderson, "is how to swear in lots of different languages."

While many schoolchildren are losers in the current program, Vancouver's Chinese community looks like a winner. Chinese people tell me that they once felt they were just another minority group, and now they feel like "part of the mainstream." That's what constituting almost half the population in a large city will do for you.

Forty years ago, most ethnic Chinese ran restaurants, grocery stores, or laundries. Most lived in the old Chinatown, centred on Pender Street, where everyone, Chinese or not, went for Chinese food. Today Chinese people are more likely to be in business or the professions. They live all over the city and Chinese restaurants are all over the city. That's what people mean when they say they are part of the mainstream, and the change has happened in a generally harmonious fashion. Immigration changes Canada, but Canada changes immigrants, too. After a few years here, a Chinese immigrant is less likely to want to knock down a tree. He may have learned to appreciate its beauty, and he may have learned that it enhances the value of his property.

To the chagrin of politicians who think immigrants should vote for the party that let them in, Vancouver's Chinese community is getting too big and diverse to be manipulated by any political party. At one time you could win a heavily Chinese riding by fielding a Chinese candidate. That's no longer the case. Gabriel Yiu, who used to have a radio show as well as a newspaper column, said things started to change about five years ago. He thinks he had something to do with the change in attitude; he describes what he told his audience: "If a Caucasian said white people should only vote for white candidates, that would be racism. I said that if, after you've done some homework, studied the policies, and don't see much difference, you decide to vote for the Chinese, fine. But if you don't vote for any other reason, that's racism. I was criticized and attacked. But several years later, that's become the mainstream view in the Chinese-language media."

In the 2000 federal election, the Alliance candidate, Joe Peschisolido, won enough Chinese votes to defeat a Liberal cabinet minister, Raymond Chan, in Richmond. Some Chinese voters felt Chan had spent too much time travelling in his role as secretary of state for Asia-Pacific affairs and paid too little attention to constituency matters.

In 2002 Peschisolido angered many of the people who voted him in by switching his allegiance to the Liberals. They said they had voted for a party, not the obscure politician who'd carried its banner. That was significant. The Canadian Alliance has never been in power so it can't take credit for admitting any immigrants. The Richmond election showed that, in a group as large and varied as the Chinese, immigration can't always do what the Liberals expect it to: deliver seats to the Liberals.

Why would anyone expect British Columbians of Chinese ancestry to vote as a bloc in any case? No one speaks of a "Caucasian community" in which someone of Greek background is supposed to think like someone of British background. The so-called Chinese community is just as diverse. There are rich Chinese and poor, educated people and illiterates, speaking several languages that are not mutually comprehensible. Some were born in Canada; some came from mainland China, Taiwan, and Hong Kong, each a distinct society with its own political and social structure. Many of these people have nothing in common save, to a Western eye, their

Asiatic features. No one person or organization could possibly speak for all of them.

If you look for a leader in the so-called "Chinese community" of British Columbia, one name keeps coming up. Lillian To is a stalwart of the immigration industry, although she wouldn't put it that way. SUCCESS, of which she is executive director, may be the most successful social service organization in Canada.

The first time I visited the SUCCESS office, some years ago, it was in an original building in old Chinatown. Since then, it has moved to a lavish new four-storey headquarters. From there, To oversees an empire that includes 11 offices, 350 employees, and 8,000 volunteers. It costs $16 million a year to operate SUCCESS, of which about $11 million comes from the government. The rest comes from its supporters. SUCCESS is the second-largest provider of language training in Vancouver. It has seniors' residences. And it offers, among other services, employment counselling, health promotion, and help for troubled families.

Lillian To knows that some people are concerned about the concentration of Chinese immigrants in parts of Greater Vancouver and is sensitive to suggestions that these new Canadians are not integrating as quickly as they should. "Most people in the Chinese community are very Canadian," she says. "What's wrong with a lot of Chinese living in Richmond close to their friends? In Richmond we have a large number of Chinese living there and we have Chinese malls, Chinese New Year celebrations, Chinese papers, and all of that. I have seen some write-ups about that being an isolated and segregated community. This is far from the truth.

"If you look at the 12-hour day of the average person, they spend most of the time working. Most people who live in Richmond don't work in Richmond; they work elsewhere and not necessarily in the Chinese community. Most are professionals. They may be working as a lawyer downtown or in sales at the Bay. Or they own their own business in Vancouver. That's at least eight hours of the day. Their kids go to Canadian public or private schools.

"So how are they segregated from the rest of the community? In their spare time, maybe they have Chinese food or watch a Chinese movie or shop in a Chinese mall? Don't English-speaking people do that? Don't they have their own friends? Don't they watch what they prefer to watch? Maybe their preference is to watch a Russian film. I am just saying that 10 to 20 percent of their time is their private time."

Ronald Leung, the talk-show host, isn't sure To reflects the views of the majority of the community, though the government assumes that she does. When a parliamentary committee came to Vancouver to gauge public opinion on immigration, it heard from a handful of official spokesmen, including To and Victor Wong, head of the Association of Vancouver Chinese-Canadians, who supported the admission of the boat migrants in 1999. "The government gives money to those organizations that work with immigrants and refugees," says Leung. "Then the government has a meeting to find out public opinion, and who goes there? The same organizations. They're all in the same business. They want more refugees. More lower-income people. More funding for more training courses. My listeners don't want those things, but they don't have time to go to meetings."

Leung has a Ph.D. in computational chemistry from Simon Fraser University. Jobs were available in the United States, but he and his wife wanted to stay in Canada. After a stint in business, he wound up in radio. He has a ready grin and a rapid-fire delivery, and he takes obvious delight in poking the pretensions of the self-appointed spokespersons for the Vancouver Chinese community.

"Our audience is educated and middle class. They are interested in education, taxes, and local and provincial politics. They seldom want to talk about federal politics, except the refugee system. They always complain about it because they came through the regular immigration process."

The local English-language media rarely carry stories about what's happening in the Chinese community, he says. Maybe if they listened to his show they'd have a better idea about what people are thinking. One day, for example, there was a hot discussion about a family living in a million-dollar house in Vancouver. The husband was back in Hong Kong working. He was sending almost no money to his wife and kids. So she applied for, and got, welfare.

Another topic guaranteed to jam up the phone lines is politics in China. Ten years ago, people were critical of the Beijing regime. Though it is still officially Communist, it is presiding over the introduction of capitalism, and the expatriate community has become more sympathetic.

A question that often comes up when you have a large, not fully integrated immigrant community is loyalty. What if Canada and China were in conflict? Where would people's loyalties lie? In the aftermath of September 11, this is a raw issue. "I know what the Chinese people would do," Leung says. "It would depend on where their wealth is. If their relatives and wealth were still in China, they would be pro-China. If their wealth was now in Canada and they no longer had many friends and relatives at home, they would be loyal to Canada. They are very practical. A minority of them, because of their cultural background, would be pro-China all the way. They would just go back."

Leung used to host a show jointly with Thomas Leung, who operates a cultural organization in Vancouver. "I asked Thomas, 'If there is a conflict between Canada and China sometime in the future, and you have your Canadian citizenship and you have done the citizenship ceremony and said you are loyal to Canada, what is your loyalty?'

"He said, 'I am a Canadian citizen today but I am also a Chinese. If there is a war, no matter what, I would go back to China and fight for China.' I said, 'Why are you still in Canada? You should be in China.'"

Then there's the matter of the 200,000 or so Canadian citizens from Hong Kong who have returned there because they can make more money than they can in Canada. "We have a big problem when those people retire and want to come to Canada," Leung says. "We have a universal health system. They haven't paid taxes here and they leave all their money in Hong Kong. They don't pay much tax here. What do we do?"

As a loyal Canadian, Leung is worried by such questions. He thinks they need to be aired. Ironically, the English-language media shy away from them, not wanting to ruffle ethnic sensibilities. Leung keeps his show lively by leaving the political correctness to them.

In 1993 Pushpa Seevaratnam, a doctoral student at the Ontario Institute for Studies in Education, wrote an article in the *Globe and Mail* demanding that math problems using hockey examples be removed from Canadian textbooks. She cited the case of a 10-year-old from Sri Lanka who couldn't figure out how long it would take a Bobby Hull slapshot travelling at 52.9 metres per second to travel 25 metres. Such an example was "ethnocentric," she wrote, and unfair to recent immigrants who don't know anything about hockey.

In 2002, an employee of Edmonton's largest landlord, Boardwalk Equities, slipped a note under the doorway of the apartment of Clark Barr, an 18-year-old student at the University of Alberta. The note ordered him to take down the Canadian flag fastened to the glass door of his ground-floor apartment. When he called to ask why, he was told the flag might offend non-Canadians or new immigrants. (After some embarrassing publicity, the company announced it would erect a flagpole to display the Canadian flag on the property.)

Everyone should be treated with respect and courtesy. Immi-grants, struggling to adjust to a new society and a strange language, deserve special consideration. But the indoctrination of Canadians with the bizarre ideology of multiculturalism has created an odd and embarrassing phenomenon: an attitude of excessive deference towards immigrants. The Economic Council of Canada expressed its disquiet about this attitude a decade ago in its report on the economic impacts of immigration: "Some Canadians are beginning to feel they are expected to be tolerant of immigrants' different ways, but that immigrants are not required, requested, or even expected to adjust to Canadian ways. It almost seems as if Canadianism is underval-ued, as if we were not proud of what our society has to offer."

The council, in its recommendations, proposed the creation of a "moral contract" outlining the responsibilities of both hosts and immigrants. This contract would be widely publicized within Canada as well as to prospective immigrants. No moral contract was ever elaborated; the proposal was denounced by the immigration industry as offensive to multiculturalism, and the government did not go near it.

The two examples above demonstrate what the Economic Council was talking about. They are the logical result of multiculturalism, a creed that seeks to devalue and eliminate anything that is distinctively Canadian. Before multiculturalism, a 10-year-old immigrant would be expected to make the Canadian obsession with hockey his own. Many, of course, did and still do; the National Hockey League is full of Canadian players whose ancestors came from all over the globe. But in multiculturalist ideology, hockey should have no special status in Canada, which is why Pushpa Seevaratnam wanted it out of Canadian textbooks.

For Boardwalk Equities, which had absorbed the same ideology, the Canadian flag had no special status. Its concern was that display of Canada's national symbol in Canada might offend an immigrant, so it ordered it removed. Of the 192 countries in the world, there is only one where such a thing could happen.

These are not mere oddities or extreme cases. The attitude permeates government, universities, and the media and extends all the way to the top of the Supreme Court. In March 2002, the court upheld a policy that gives preference to Canadian citizens for jobs in the federal public service. In doing so, it rejected the claim of three women that the policy is unconstitutional discrimination. Similar policies are common practice all over the world, one of the judges wrote, and the Canadian government has the right to "define the rights and privileges of its citizens."

The court minority, however, including Chief Justice Beverley McLachlin, appeared shocked at the idea that Canadian citizenship should have value, that it should afford those who hold it rights in Canada greater than those who do not. The majority decision, the dissenting judges declared, "violates human dignity."

The mythology underpinning immigration policy—that large-scale immigration is essential for economic growth and demographic survival— feeds into the exaggerated deference promoted by multiculturalism. Here's Royson James, a columnist in the *Toronto Star:* "If it weren't for immigration, we'd have to send out a search party around the world looking for people to keep our country afloat."

[…] [T]here is no evidence that this is true. Most other Western industrialized countries have older populations than Canada, lower fertility rates, slower population growth, and much less immigration. Yet they are doing fine without sending out search parties. Why can these countries, which appear to need immigrants more than Canada does, flourish with few of them whereas we would perish without a lot more? The only possible answer is that Canadian-born people are, in some mysterious way, uniquely deficient. Yet this deficiency is not identified.

James is not the only journalist whose arguments demean Canadian- born people for the sake of exalting immigrants. Neil Swan, the economist who headed the Economic Council study, suggested to me that Canadian attitudes to immigration issues reflect the "Calvinist Presbyterian background in this country that leads to a lot of breast-beating. It's very popular to downplay the virtues of the country." This might explain why the immigration myths and the ideology of multiculturalism have found such fertile soil in Canada. All these beliefs and ideas are based on the conviction that Canada is inadequate—culturally, economically, and in almost every other way.

In my own experience, the Canadians least likely to downplay Canada's virtues are immigrants. Unlike people born here, they chose Canada; they thought it was better than the place they were leaving or other places they might have applied to enter. Few immigrants would dream of suggesting that references to hockey be removed from textbooks or that Canadians should not have the right to display their own flag. Few would object to having to obtain citizenship before applying for a job in the public service.

Nadeem Ahmed, a computer programmer who moved to Toronto from Pakistan in 1996, told me he did not come to Canada to recreate the life of Pakistan in a sealed-off tile of the Canadian mosaic. He came because images of North America—Niagara Falls, the Rockies—that he had seen as a child thrilled him, and he wanted to be part of the place. People like Royson James seem to believe that Canada should be grateful that immigrants condescend to come here. It's an odd belief, given that an estimated 100 million people in the Third World would like to get to a Western country, and the admission tickets are hard to come by.

Ahmed does not think Canada owes anything to immigrants; he thinks it's the other way around. "For too many immigrants, the motive is all material," he says. "They come and they take and don't give back enough. They get free education, free medical care, they even get welfare if they don't have a job. What does Canada get in return? People should do volunteer work. And they should repay Canada by making the strongest possible effort to learn English.

"We Pakistanis have a separate group, the Chinese have a separate group. How long can we stay together if we can't communicate? As a whole society, we are going towards disintegration. If the country gives you a chance to better your life, it's your responsibility to pay it back. We should not take Canadian citizenship for granted as just a materialistic thing. We should be proud of being Canadian."

ALAN B. SIMMONS

IMMIGRATION POLICY: IMAGINED FUTURES

FROM IMMIGRANT CANADA: DEMOGRAPHIC, ECONOMIC AND SOCIAL CHALLENGES

THE CANADIAN CASE

Canadian immigration policy development over the period since Confederation may be understood as a series of historical phases. Each phase is a relatively distinctive period of development in immigration policy. A phase is also understood as an "historical moment" (covering many years) in which the variables shown in Table 22.1 move toward coherence with one another, and, in that sense, provide an interpretation of the immigration policies in that period. That is, in each phase the nation's immigration policy will tend to be consistent with its place in the international system and its related options and preferences with respect to future trade and national culture.

A movement toward coherence does not mean the absence of strain or incoherence. In historical cases, one is likely to find varying degrees of strain and a constant jockeying for improved fit between the policy options concerned. As noted previously, because immigration is an area where opposing economic and cultural values intersect, it tends to be a field of conflict in nations around the world. This explains why Canadian immigration policy has been for years a hotly contested subject, characterized by diverse options and a potential for radical change in direction (Simmons and Keohane, 1992). The same may be said for immigration policy in the United States and Australia, and in many other countries as well.

Given our focus on the latter decades of the twentieth century, it is possible to collapse the history of Canadian immigration policy into three periods. The entire policy history from Confederation to the early 1960s may be considered a single period. This certainly glosses over many changes in national circumstances and immigration policy, but there is also a strong thread of policy continuity in this lengthy phase. The other two phases are shorter, from the early 1960s to the end of the 1980s, and from 1989 to the present. The specific cut-off dates between one period and the next are somewhat arbitrary, since immigration policy often changes in a series of steps spread over several years. In the present case, I have chosen the following key policy events to define the model.

In 1962 Canada abandoned the country preference system for immigrant selection. The formal adoption of a new immigration policy based on the points system did not take place until 1987.

In 1989 Canadian immigration targets began to be set over periods of several years at a time, rather than annually. Prior to 1989, the direction of unemployment levels in a given year were a good predictor of the direction of immigration targets in the following year — that is, a rise in unemployment predicated a subsequent fall in immigration levels. Since 1989, this has no longer been the case. Two important Acts (Bills C-55 and C-84) concerning the control and processing of asylum seekers were implemented in 1989 (Simmons and Keohane, 1992). Some other features of policy that I have included in the post-1989 period actually began earlier. For example, the special programs to attract business and investor immigrants began in 1984. Other policy changes occurred later. For example, the various measures to reduce the proportion of family class immigrants, increase worker immigrants, and to charge much higher application and landing fees were implemented in 1995.

COHERENCE IN EACH PHASE

Table 22.1 summarizes the broad coherence between variables in the "imagined futures" model at each historical phase. The historical trends underlying the arguments are taken from various histories of Canadian immigration, including Corbett (1957), Green (1976), and Hawkins (1988), in addition to assessments of recent policy developments in DeVoretz (1995) and Simmons (1995).

1850–1962

Phase 1 was based on an image of Canada as a promising "European nation" in the New World. This image was hardly surprising. As a former

colony, Canada had very strong political, economic, and cultural ties
to Great Britain. Canada was a secondary yet important nation in the
North Atlantic Economy, hence subject to the power of leading nations
(Great Britain and the United States) as they established rules for trade,
immigration, and culture. As a country in which the native people had
been or were about to be "pacified" Canada offered vast resources and
investment opportunities, provided that needed labour, transportation
infrastructure, and local governance could be established. The system
was ethnocentric (focusing on Europe and its independent "European"
colonies overseas) and racist. Official slavery in the North Atlantic system
ended by the mid-1800s, but racism continued to dramatically restrict the
opportunities for non-European minorities in the system. It was also a
patriarchal system based on an assumption of male workers and female
home-makers.

Canada's immigration policy was based on an imagined future that
incorporated all the underlying assumptions of the system. European
workers and their families were "invited" (with propaganda and land
grants, etc.) to settle in Canada, particularly in decades when Canada faced
good export markets and strong national demand for workers. It was a
system driven by state policies very sensitive to the interests of capital,
hence immigrants judged to be unfit for work in Canada were not admitted
while those who sought to organize radical unions were deported.

A more detailed examination of the long first phase would necessarily
draw attention to the fact that the overall system did not always work well.
Canadian levels of economic growth fluctuated and were generally lower
than those in the United States. Major recessions, the Great Depression,
and the two world wars all disrupted the system and revealed its areas of
weakness. Yet Canada's position in the international system seems not to
have changed radically or sufficiently to permit any real policy departures,
other than shutting down immigration during the periods of system failure
and reinitiating them later.

1962–1989

The end of the Second World War is generally considered to be a major
marker in Canada's evolving status in the international community. The
independent role of Canada in the war, its rising industrial and economic
capacity, and its investment opportunities increasingly placed the nation
as an emerging force on the world stage. Policy changes that reflected
Canada's new role, however, took place gradually in a series of steps largely
concentrated in the 1960s. These changes included:

Table 22.1: Three Historical Phases of Canadian Immigration Policy

Phase	1850–1962	1962–1989	1989–2000
Imagined Future	Rising "European Nation" in the New World	Leading Middle Power on World Stage	Emerging Global Niche Player
Immigration Policy Goals within Imagined Future	Expanding labour force through immigration of farmers and factory workers from Europe.	Expanding labour force through immigration of skilled workers from any country.	Enhance economic prospects with very selective professional and entrepreneurial immigration from any country.
Factors Shaping Imagined Future			
1. Canada's status in the international system.	Secondary power in the North Atlantic Economy.	Middle power on the world stage.	Wealthy nation struggling to adjust to new global markets.
2. Economic options favoured by system.	Trade based on exports of agricultural and semi-manufactured goods.	As before, with new focus on import substitution industrialization. (ISI).	Export-led growth as a niche player in a competitive global system.
3. Cultural options favoured in Canada and permitted in system.	Bilingual European nation.	Bilingual, multicultural nation.	1. Canada: bilingual, multicultural nation. 2. Quebec: unilingual, multicultural nation.
4. Immigration options.	Ready supply of European immigrants.	European immigrants drying up but skilled workers available elsewhere.	1. Canada: ready supply of professional immigrants from non-European countries. 2. Quebec: as above, but supply of those committed to a francophone Quebec nation is limited, creating a policy dilemma.

1. A radical shift in immigration policy away from a preference system favouring European workers to one emphasizing the selection of skilled immigrant workers from any country.
2. Taking on new roles internationally, particularly in the areas of peacekeeping, international development, and anti-racism.
3. By the early 1970s, the first in a series of still continuing efforts to expand Canadian trade to a wider range of nations.

The new imagined future implicitly underlying these various shifts in international policy was that of leading middle power on the world stage. The image implied independence in foreign policy and a progressive stance on social and economic problems. Immigration policy was officially non-racist but not anti-racist, so that racism in Canadian society and in the international system continued to affect immigration policy and its outcomes to some degree (Richmond, 1994, chapter 9; Simmons, 1997). The policy was also officially nonsexist (or gender neutral). Women could apply to come as independent immigrants in their own right, and increasingly they did. However, cultural norms with respect to women's roles clearly influenced actual immigration patterns. Many origin cultures do not favour such independence of women and job markets in Canada were not always favourable to independent female immigrants, although there were exceptions. Caribbean and Philippine women came from cultures that granted greater independence to women with respect to international migration and jobs; these women were also sought for domestic and other low-wage jobs in Canada, as well as in fields such as nurses' aides, thereby leading to a situation reinforcing ethnic/gender stereotypes (Silvera, 1989).

The shift in immigration policy in 1962 may be interpreted as the result of the following changes in context, among others.

First, the supply of qualified European immigrants was beginning to decline, as European economic recovery took place and northwestern Europe itself began to experience labour shortages and to promote "guest-worker" programs to bring in labour from the south and from North Africa.

Second, unequal development in other parts of the world produced a situation in which skilled workers were unemployed or underemployed (low wages) in their home countries and hence very interested in international migration as a way of solving their problems. Some of these countries had long-standing political and cultural links with Canada. This was the case for the Commonwealth Caribbean, India, Sri Lanka, and Hong Kong, all of which have become major contributors to Canadian immigration. Immigrants from countries without such cultural and political links also increased in this period, usually after a bridge was established via initial refugee flows (see Simmons 1989, 1992).

Third, in the 1960s in particular labour demand was high in Canada, related to a still-functioning import substitution industrialization that encouraged the establishment of manufacturing facilities (often American branch plants) in Canada.

Fourth, the long history of Canadian immigration from diverse European countries had created an assumption that there existed in Canada considerable tolerance for cultural diversity. When immigration policy was changed in 1962 it is not clear how much this assumption influenced the shift in policy direction. In fact, it seems that the matter had not been sought out very clearly by political leaders and senior bureaucrats. Whatever the case, by the 1970s it became apparent that the great cultural and ethnic diversity of the new immigration was testing the limits of national tolerance and also challenging the bilingual, bi-national character of Canada. These circumstances led federal authorities to the establishment of multiculturalism as an official state policy in 1978.

1989 to the Present

Immigration policies in Canada are currently "entrepreneurial" in character, related to assumptions about trade imperatives, multicultural tolerance, and immigration possibilities. They include the following features:

1. Competitive skills. Recent policies stipulate that the proportion of immigrants who have higher level work skills or capital and good knowledge of English and or French is to increase. This is based on the assumption that the more skilled, wealthy immigrants with appropriate language capability will contribute to higher national productivity in the near future, and in the process will require less state support for settlement and integration.

2. Economic immigrants. The proportion of economic migrants — workers including professionals, business, and entrepreneurial immigrants — is to increase, while the proportion of "family class" immigrants (spouses and children, namely those not chosen on

skills or capital) is to decrease. The assumptions underlying this policy are identical to those in the point above.

3. Reduced welfare burden. Families wishing to sponsor another member as an immigrant must show higher levels of income and an ability and commitment to support those they sponsor should help be required during the settlement process.

4. Cost recovery. Since 1994, immigrants have been required to pay much more for application and for "landing" fees, if accepted. The current fee schedule implies a total of $3,150 for a family consisting of a couple and two dependent children. Fees for those applying in the business class are much higher. Review of a business proposal (part of the application from business immigrants) alone costs $6,000. These policies presumably tend to reinforce selection favouring individuals from wealthier families and countries who will not need settlement assistance.

The preceding immigration policies are part of a new vision of the nation's future, that of a sophisticated niche player in a competitive global economy. The image is based on the following logic. First, import substitution industrialization is no longer considered a viable option, such that the nation must shift to a competitive export-led economic strategy. Within the dominant political discourse in the global system and within Canada there is no flexibility on this dimension. Canada needs foreign capital and improved professional capacity to meet the trade challenge. Second, Canada's wealth, established contacts with many immigrant source countries, and economic and political uncertainty in other countries together suggest that a portion of the required skills and capital can be obtained by attracting professional and investor immigrants from other countries. This will have the possible advantage of increasing international trade links as a by-product of immigration policy. Third, the legacy of immigration from culturally and ethnically diverse nations over the past thirty years has created a national tolerance for continuing diversity along these dimensions and hence for an immigration policy oriented to current national economic goals.

INTEGRATION AND SOCIETAL TRANSFORMATION

It is important to stress that current immigration policies are part of an imagined future that is based on hopes and, at best, only partially tested assumptions. The assumptions, are, moreover, interdependent. For example, if Canada's hopes for future exports are not realized, the logic of a policy favouring the immigration of skilled foreign labour and entrepreneurs will be called into question. The skilled workers will be without jobs and the entrepreneurs will seek greener pastures elsewhere. Conversely, if ways can be found to ensure that the new skilled immigrants fit into the economy and contribute to rising national productivity, then the future trade dimension of the current imagined future will be more probable, and public support for immigration will tend to be higher. Finally, the image of a harmonious multicultural future society clearly depends on national economic success as well, since such success will promote social mobility among immigrants and provide resources for a strong immigrant settlement program.

Will the direction of Canadian immigration policy in the 1990s facilitate realization of Canada as an agile niche player in the global economy? Such a question cannot be answered with any certainty. However, some of the key research questions that need to be addressed in an effort to provide an answer can be clarified.

Research on patterns of immigrant integration and their implications for societal transformation can contribute to an understanding of how the assumptions of Canada's official imagined future are working out. Various questions concerning immigrant integration and societal transformation are relevant. A number of these are posed in Table 22.1. As noted in the table, questions on immigrant integration have been the subject of considerable past and ongoing research, with the result that much is known about integration and reviews of the field and new empirical evidence are normally broken down by sub-theme [....] Societal transformations — that is, overall social transformations of the nation in areas such as ethnic, class, and regional structure — arising from immigration constitute a related field of research, but one that has been given less attention [....] My objective here is to comment briefly on a number of particular research questions on societal transformation that arise from the model of the immigration process and policy set forth in this essay.

When the impact of immigration policy on societal transformation is addressed from the perspective of imagined national futures and the international system a number of research questions arise. For example, the recent Canadian policy focus on highly skilled immigrants and those with business experience and capital makes sense today only if other aspects of Canadian economic strategy are also successful. Investor immigrants, for instance, have already threatened to pack their bags and leave if tax laws in Canada shift to give greater attention to offshore earnings. The new globalization encourages offshore production and assembly plants to relocate quickly from one country to another in response to offers of tax shelters and other benefits. We should not be surprised if the same thing occurs with investor immigrants, suggesting that they be viewed as "offshore capital."

Current immigration and settlement policy also makes sense only if one can assume that it will not contribute to a crisis of national identity or to social and regional conflict that will consume the nations' political energy. [...]

REFERENCES

DeVoretz, D., ed. 1995. *Diminishing Returns: The Economics of Canada's Recent Immigration Policy*. Ottawa: Renouf Publications for C.D. Howe.

Green, Alan. 1976. *Immigration and the Postwar Canadian Economy*. Toronto: Macmillan.

Hawkins, Freda. 1988. *Canada and Immigration: Public Policy and Public Concern*, 2nd ed. Montreal and Kingston: McGill-Queen's University Press.

Richmond, Anthony H. 1994. *Global Apartheid: Refugees, Racism, and the New World Order*. Toronto: Oxford University Press.

Silvera, Makeda. 1989. *Silenced: Talks with Working Class Caribbean Women about Their Lives and Struggles as Domestic Workers in Canada*. Toronto: Sister Vision.

Simmons, Alan. 1989. "World System Linkages and International Migration: New Directions in Theory and Method with an Application to Canada." In *Proceedings of the IUSSP General Conference, New Delhi, 20–27 September, 1989*, vol. 2. Liege, Belgium: International Union for the Scientific Study of Population.

_____. 1992. "Canada and Migration in the Western Hemisphere. Canada's Role in the Hemisphere." In *A Dynamic Partnership: Canada's Changing Role in the Hemisphere,*, edited by Jerry Haar and Edgar Disman. Miami: Transaction Publishers, University of Miami North-South Center.

_____. 1995. *Economic Globalization and Immigration Policy: Canada Compared to Europe. Organizing Diversity: Migration Policy and Practice, Canada and Europe*. Toronto: Oxford University Press.

Simmons, Alan, and Kearan Keohane. 1992. "Shifts in Canadian Immigration Policy: State Strategies and the Quest for Legitimacy." *Canadian Review of Anthropology and Sociology* 29, 421–52.

SECTION TWO

EXPERIENCE

EVA TIHANYI

THE CHILD EVENTUALLY GROWS UP

At six months
you tossed me into my grandmother's arms
like a basketball to the nearest teammate, then
ran from the court

The two of you—my mother, my father—
in your hopeful daring twenties
haycarting across the Hungarian border
in the January night

Too much risk with an infant
you thought, and we all survived

Six years later
you collected me at the airport,
a long-lost suitcase, contents
not remembered

What you found was, in your view,
mouthy, clumsy, undignified;
a child in need of lessons

And so you forced me to the top bunk
to cure my fear of heights,
cut my hair short enough
to ensure it could no longer hold
my grandmother's ribbons
(you said I needed style)

I was not like my four-year-old brother,
by birth an instant North American kid
to match the Campbell's soup,
the chrome and plastic furniture

What I was you did not want—
a small self
flying open-souled and curious
to her faraway fairytale parents
who now expect
all they could not give

ADELE WISEMAN

FROM THE SACRIFICE

CHAPTER ONE

The train was beginning to slow down again, and Abraham noticed lights in the distance. He shifted his body only slightly so as not to disturb the boy, and sank back into the familiar pattern of throbbing aches inflicted by the wheels below. A dim glow from the corridor outlined the other figures in the day coach as they slept, sprawled in attitudes of discomfort and fatigue. He tried to close his eyes and lose himself in the thick, dream-crowded stillness, but his eyelids, prickly with weariness, sprang open again.

Urgently the train howled the warning of its approach to the city. Facing him, Abraham's wife seemed to seize the same wailful note and draw it out plaintively as she sighed in her sleep. Her body huddled, strained and unnatural, on the faded green plush seat. He could feel the boy, slack and completely pliant, rolling to the motion of the train. The whistle howled again, the carriage jolted, and his son lurched heavily, almost lifelessly against him.

Enough! With a sudden rush of indignation, as though he had been jerked awake, it came to Abraham that they had fled far enough. The thought took hold in his mind like a command. It came alive in his head and swept through him angrily, in a wave of energy, a rebellious movement of blood. It was as simple as this. Enough. He must act now.

He sat up carefully, shifting Isaac's limp form into another position, fired in his new determination by the boy's weak protesting mumble. Slowly, he stretched, feeling his joints crackle, willing the cramp out of his body. He looked about him impatiently.

As though summoned, the conductor entered the coach. Abraham turned his head and beckoned imperatively.

"Where are we?" he asked in Ukrainian, tentatively, his red-rimmed eyes gleamed with excitement, his loud voice muted to a hoarse whisper.

The man stooped, his face polite, questioning, and to Abraham offensively vacant in his noncomprehension. "I beg your pardon?" he said in English.

"Where are we stopping, please?" Abraham asked urgently in Yiddish, speaking slowly and patiently so that the man must understand.

The conductor shook his head. "No speak, no speak," he said, pointing to Abraham's mouth, then to this own, with a deprecating gesture.

Abraham looked at the man with irritation. Was there anyone on the train who could do anything, but make faces and smile? "Why does the train stop?" he asked suddenly, hopefully, in Polish.

The conductor shook his head helplessly.

Abraham leaned forward and gestured wildly toward the window to where the lights blinked in the distance.

The conductor, as though realizing something, smiled a broad, reassuring smile, shook his head vigorously, patted Abraham lightly on the arm, and made as if to move on.

"The train! Stop! Why? What city?" roared the Jew in exasperation, spitting out the words in broken German.

At the sound his son jerked suddenly awake, frightened, and looked blindly about for a moment. Other passengers groaned, stirred their numb bones, and mumbled in protest. The conductor swayed on down the car, shrugging apologetically at drowsy faces.

"Animals here," muttered Abraham, subsiding and turning helplessly to his son. "They can only gibber and gesticulate."

"What's the matter, Pa?" Isaac yawned. "Can't you sleep?"

"*No!*" With a gesture, he flung aside the overcoat he had used as a cover. "The train is stopping. We're getting off."

"But we have two more days."

"Who awaits us?"

There was no answer to this that the boy knew of. Who awaited them? What awaited them? It did not really matter whether they stopped here blindly, or went blindly on to the other city for which they had bought the tickets. Isaac crouched for another moment and watched his father, who was collecting their bundles. His own limbs were so knotted that it took him a moment to gather the strength to get out from under his warm coat and stretch.

The conductor called out the name of the city.

"No; enough, I say," said Abraham. "Fifteen months and eleven days. If I had to spend more days and nights worrying about a new beginning I would not have the strength to begin. Two more days and nights in this position, and this whole human being that you call your father will make sense only to an upholsterer. I do not know where we will sleep tomorrow, but at least our beds will lie flat and we will rock no more."

"But our tickets —" Isaac rubbed his eyes with numb fingers and shook his head to clear his thoughts.

"Ah, our tickets." Abraham scratched the itching skin under his forked beard reflectively. "Well, it's senseless trying to explain anything to that fellow. Listen to him. He can't answer a simple question, and now he wakes up the whole train with his shouting up and down. Well, I suppose he can't help himself. Would I have understood him even if he had understood me?"

Strength and humor returned with his decision. He moved around and stretched; his blood began to circulate again. Like a young man entering deliberately into an adventure, he felt excited at making a positive gesture in the ordering of his fate.

"In fact, come to think of it, we'll be saving money. If we get off here we save the rest of our fare, so just in case they're not clamoring for a butcher and I don't get a job here right away, we'll save that much more money to live on in the meantime. That's why it's such a good idea to get off here. You see, your father has not lost his common sense. In fact, it's a wise decision I have made with God's help. And we can see about our tickets in the station."

Lights flashed by; at the other end of the car a young couple were gathering their belongings.

"The important thing now," Abraham continued, "is that we must stop running from death and from every other insult. We will seize our lives in these scarred hands again." He paused to consider his words with pleasure.

"Come, boy, we must wake your mother — but gently. How weary she is."

When the train grunted to a halt Abraham and his family, his wife blinking and shivering with sleep, stood among the few waiting with their bundles in their arms. The conductor, noticing the group assembled to leave, rushed up to them.

"No, no, no!" He shook his head and reached for Abraham's suitcase. "This isn't your stop!"

Abraham brushed his arm away firmly.

"Shalom," he said, politely, yet with a certain fierceness that prevented the conductor from persisting. They descended to the platform. The conductor stood shaking his head in exasperation over these immigrants. Abraham cast him a last, forgiving glance. As though it were written, he could see what they must do. First, to find the immigration barracks — to sleep, at last, without the artificial pulse of engines to remind them even in sleep that they were wanderers. Then, with the new day, to settle themselves gingerly on the crust of the city, perhaps someday even to send down a few roots — those roots, pre-numbed and shallow, of the often uprooted. But strong. Abraham felt strength surge up in him, excitement shaking the tiredness out of his body. No matter what is done to the plant, when it falls, again it will send out the tentative roots to the earth and rise upward again to the sky. The boy was young, the boy was blessed, the boy would grow.

Isaac shifted his bundle uncomfortably under curious stares and raised his eyes upward and ahead in imitation of the oblivious purposefulness of his father. He moved stiffly, aware of the difference in dress between these people and himself, and listened, lonely among the strange rhythms about him, for voices of warmth.

That morning they had found a place to live, and now they were bringing their belongings to install in the room. Isaac thought of the new home with trepidation, perhaps not so much in spite of but because of the fact that the landlady had told him happily that she had two daughters just his age. What would two native girls think of him? What if they were like their mother — two garrulous girls with sharp noses, the tips moving like rabbits', incessantly up and down as they talked?

Sarah, Isaac's mother, who had lived for months as in a dream, found herself hypnotized, watching the face of Mrs. Plopler as she talked. When the woman addressed persuasively, woman to woman, reiterating the merits of this furnished room with its bed, its couch, its bureau, its chair, and its big window, she merely nodded up and down, unthinking.

The landlady was a thin, flat-fronted woman with nothing to draw the eye from her hyperactive nose other than a head of tightly grizzled hair that started upward from her head in stiff, small waves. As she talked she examined her prospective roomers and saw that they were no longer young, this straight-backed Jew with his beard thrust forward, as though starched, away from his chest, and his wide-eyed, unresponsive wife. Still talking, she swept her eyes over their pale adolescent son, who stood looking at her in a way which she found vaguely irritating. Her eyes took in their portable belongings. She concluded that they were lucky to get her room, and, reminding them again that they would have the benefit of a furnished room with a bed, a couch, a bureau, a chair, and a big window, as well as kitchen and bathroom facilities, which they would share with her family, she asked for her rent in advance.

Half an hour after they were securely installed and she had their rent pinned away warmly, their landlady was telling a neighbor how she had taken a poor immigrant family into the house, practically right off the train, and how she made them feel immediately at home. "Why, they're taking baths already."

Shortly afterward she met her adolescent daughters at the door with the whispered news that she had rented the room to an immigrant family with a son of about sixteen, who, however, didn't look like much, but that they would nevertheless have to stop running about the house half-naked in the mornings. She added that the tenants had taken baths already, three separate baths, and that she had served them tea in the kitchen and had learned that the father was a butcher. At present, she told the girls, they were asleep after their long trip.

Leaving her daughters at home—two overgrown girls who began to wander up and down outside the room, pausing to listen and giggle at the door of their tenants—she went off to shop for supper. At the grocery she mentioned that she had taken an immigrant family into her house, people she knew nothing about, that they had taken baths already, that she had served them tea, that the husband was a butcher, that they were resting at present, and that it was hard for two families to share one bathtub.

When her husband came home she told him that they had finally rented the furnished room to an immigrant family, that the husband was a butcher who didn't have a job yet, though they'd paid rent in advance, that they were at present asleep in their room, that they had taken baths already, and that she wondered how often they intended to take baths during the week, all three of them.

"You have to show them that we have a bathtub right away," said her husband, who was a joker and jolly good fellow at a party but surly, with secret grievances, at home.

"Well, it's by the toilet," she defended herself. "They would have found out anyway. And besides, it's because of the long train ride that they bathed. They're greenhorns; they won't want to bathe very often. You know how filthy these people are apt to be."

"We have too much hot water for you," he grumbled.

"She served them tea, too," chimed in Gertie and Goldie eagerly, happy for some diversion after having palpitated around the house all afternoon in vain.

The Ploplers waited to get a glimpse of their tenants, but Abraham and his family slept on until the evening. Then the Ploplers noted that the lights went on and heard their voices murmuring, the man's louder than the rest. But they couldn't catch the words. From the moving about they assumed that the new tenants were unpacking and putting the room in order. Possibly, even, they were eating something from one of their outlandish bundles. Then the lights went out.

"Certainly sleep a lot," commented their landlord. "Why you didn't knock on the door and ask them if they want anything is beyond me. I think I have as much right to see them as you have. I go out in the morning and come back to find half my house rented away, and nobody thinks to introduce me to my new tenants. Nobody thinks fit to ask me if maybe in my opinion they're not suitable for tenants in my house. Who rents a room just like that?"

"Why didn't you tell me when the lights were on to knock on the door?" said his wife. "You'd think they'd come out by themselves to be sociable. They know I have a husband."

"Thank you for telling them you have a husband. What are they hiding themselves away for?"

"Maybe they're tired," suggested one of the girls.

"I'm tired too," said her father. "So what?"

"What does the son look like?" asked the other girl, who had heard at least half a dozen times before. They both listened eagerly while their mother described how thin and wretched-looking a boy he was, but not, for all that, entirely ugly. The landlord resigned himself sullenly to waiting till morning.

Maybe they're whispering that we might want some water during the night, Isaac lay, sleepy and thirsty, conjuring up this fanciful hope because he was ashamed to venture out of the room in his bathrobe among all those feminine voices that whispered in the kitchen. It seemed to him that he had not had any water for a long time. The taste of salt herring was in his mouth. He got up and brushed against the chair, making a noise so that the whispering in the kitchen held its breath for a moment. His father's deep, open-mouthed breathing continued to purr and chortle from the bed, and his mother lay silent, curled up under the bedclothes. Isaac found an orange to suck and lay back down on the couch with it.

It was different when they had changed boats and were in England for a short while. There it didn't matter that his clothes were different. He could walk with his hands in his pockets, knowing he'd be leaving soon, and pretend he was a tourist—wealthy, idle, indolent, even perhaps at times a bit supercilious. He saw himself back in London when he had stood for a long time watching people buy bananas, wondering what was done with them. Yet he had not let on, just cocked his head carelessly to one side and whistled a short snatch of melody, as it were absent-mindedly, as though speculating on some subject far off from these petty transactions.

At last a man and a little boy had bought some of the bananas, and the little boy peeled one of them and began to gobble greedily. So Isaac had bought and peeled to take, tentatively, taste …. Pleasant … Floating in to confront his parents. Mother's gasp. "What are you eating?" Father: "Raw!" … Isaac, enormously sophisticated, wearing no clothes at all, prowling a strange house with raw girls, whispering, "It's a fruit to gobble greedily in English." Tasting-sipping-drinking deeply. Suddenly, his brothers' heads crowding among the immigrants. Moses: "Like water." "No, like herring." Jacob, the learner, in the darkened room. "Like watered herring"—definitely. "Like water." Moses, the singer, adamant. "Raw water." "Can't get water from a torn bathrobe"—contemptuously.

The orange didn't help much, ventured Isaac. She still wagged her yellow nose …

As Isaac slept.

After lunch, when Isaac went to the English-language course that had been organized in the district high school, Abraham left the house with him. Isaac pointed at objects, enunciating carefully the English names.

"Tree. Sky. Cloud. House. Mountain."

Abraham would repeat, fingering the syllables clumsily with his tongue, but with immense satisfaction listening to the sound of his son's apparently adroit mastery. When they parted, the young voice continued to repeat itself in his head, raised, clear, ardent, for to Abraham his son's voice must be ardent. Nothing grows but by desire.

Sky. Houz. He stopped in front of a tree, frowning at it demandingly. Now what did he call this?

His beard jutted out in vexation, and his eyes traveled up the trunk in search of a clue.

Boim. Isaac's voice, speaking clearly in Yiddish, came to his mind.

"*Boim,*" said Abraham out loud to the tree with satisfaction and proceeded toward the busy avenue.

The little leaves are falling from the trees. Abraham expanded his scope, carefully enunciating his thought mentally, as though it were an elementary language lesson, thinking in Yiddish, but laboriously, so that he could feel pleasantly as though it were the English equivalent.

He stopped as he reached the avenue and pulled out his little snap purse to look for the address the butcher had given him that morning.

Today I may find work. Then we will go to night school. It may be that there are new thoughts in English. The Russians, too, have very clever sayings.

The chill autumn winds ruffled the hair on his face, outlined his bare cheeks where they met his beard, and crept, clean-smelling, into his nostrils.

Isaac will yet do something fine. He was not spared for nothing.

He looked into the shop windows as he passed and checked the numbers above their doors.

The butcher had said, looking at him in a sly way, "Polsky might be needing a new man now that he's opened up again. His business is booming. The women can't resist nosing around now that he's back. You know how women are."

Abraham had asked for and written down the address of this Polsky's shop.

"Quite a man, Polsky," the butcher had begun again. "And when the women get hold of something like that their tongues run ahead of them. Can't talk of anything else."

"Yes," agreed Abraham, who only half heard. "You think perhaps that he might need someone?"

"Never can tell. He's got a pretty big place there. Used to have someone to help him. And now that he's just back from his little holiday, as they say, and his mind probably isn't altogether on his work yet—well, he probably needs someone." The butcher chuckled wisely and winked. "Only you'd better watch; it may be catching. How does your wife feel about that sort of thing?"

Abraham saw himself already on the way. Immediately after lunch he would go. It was no good to go with a hungry look. He thanked the butcher and left, leaving the man to look after him with some annoyance, the frustrating taste of an untold story on his lips.

That was a strange man, that butcher, full of funny looks and hints. But maybe this man will really need me. Abraham paused before two large windows, aware that he was nervous and anxious. He looked about him at the preparations nature was making for winter.

If I get work we will walk in the park this evening, he promised himself as he opened the door to the store. The large bell tinkled distantly in his ears. He closed the door behind him carefully. If not — we will walk in the park.

He straightened up and walked through the sawdust to the counter, where the butcher was waiting on a customer. Standing a little to one side, his hands behind his back, he waited tensely till the man should be through.

Isaac walked to school, studying signs and faces, learning the contours of the city, wondering what was to come for him. The city rose about him, planted on an undulating countryside that seemed to have spilled over from the ridge of dark hills in the western distance. The life that he remembered wavered uncertainly forward to meet the life that he seemed just about to live. In the morning he had wandered around in the flats of the city, the crowded, downhill area in which he lived. The flats scooped down toward the edge of the brown river with a sort of lilting quality, as though the earth had lifted a shoulder and the houses had slid closer together and the factories had slipped and jostled one another to the river bank.

Westward, above the flats, grand houses spread themselves. Their rocky gardens and many trees prepared, with an autumnal festival of color, for the austerities of winter. Along the edge of the sharp incline which, like a small cliff, separated the heights from the flats, the streets lit up brightly at night and were crowded with people. In the day they were filled with traffic and the commerce of the city.

Beyond the river to the east, and beyond the township and truck gardens that dotted its farther bank, was another gradual rise, which gathered breath for several miles and heaved up finally with a tremendous effort to a double-crested hill that dominated the eastern landscape. To Isaac the land seemed like a great arrested movement, petrified in time, like his memories, and the city crawled about its surface in a counterpoint of life.

He was aware of the hill to the east as he walked. When he didn't look at it, it seemed to crowd up closer, as though it were watching, absorbing every gesture in its static moment. He look sideways and back toward it, and the mountain assumed its proper proportion, the sweeping double hump carelessly mantled in splotches of autumn color.

The mountain reminded him of how he had asked the giggling daughters of his landlady the source of the lights that peered at night from behind its first hump. They had crowded close beside him at the window, Gertie and Goldie, the younger one right up against his side. The older one had held her finger to her ear, described a circle with it several times, then pointed to the lights. The younger whispered, "Crazy-house," giggled, and shuddered fearfully closer to him. This was why it was called Mad Mountain—a strange name to call a mountain that looked so intimately on all the affairs of the city. Strange to think of the people that it had gathered up to live with itself. It was not a thing to laugh and giggle about as these girls did. But with women it is always so, Isaac told himself sagely. What they said meant little. It was merely to draw your attention to the other things that their eyes and lips could tell you.

It was because of a girl that his brothers had discovered one night that he sometimes stayed awake and listened to them talking. How young he had been then! That night back in the old country returned to him now with a vividness that banished the warm immediacy of the sun and the keen-smelling breeze from his senses. He had lain awake as he had intended, hoping to hear another argument about God, so that he could finish explaining to the incredulous Menasha Roitman across the street why some great thinkers thought that maybe there couldn't be a God. He had forgotten, because of Menasha's interruptions and arguments, the lofty line of reasoning that Jacob had followed some nights before. Now he listened, puzzled, while his brothers crawled into their places on the huge stove beside him and whispered about an ordinary girl.

Minutely they debated whether the carpenter's daughter had really spent all afternoon picking flowers in her front yard solely because Moses himself had spent all afternoon walking back and forth past her house.

"You say she was picking flowers for two whole hours?" asked Jacob, the thinker, man of reason. "She must have picked a good many flowers in that time," he continued thoughtfully. "And what would she do with all of them?" It followed, obviously, that the flowers were only an excuse. And what other reason could she have?

"Do you really think so?" Moses had asked in such a pathetic voice that Isaac had wanted to giggle. And Moses tried to remember out loud what kind of flowers and how many flowers she had picked, and whether that was all she had really been doing in the garden. He went carefully over the many times that he had wandered back and forth down the street, pretending to be immersed in thought, until the smell of hops from the brewery two blocks down, combined with his excitement, had nearly overcome him. He recalled that she had kept slightly turned toward the walk, that when he glanced her way he had caught her eyes several times lowering hastily to her work in the garden. Once when he had passed she actually raised herself up and stretched, with one hand on the back of her hip and the other wiping across her lovely brow and fine black eyes. But even though her lips seemed to be smiling she might just have been shading her eyes from the sun and not really looking at him. Thus reasoned Moses the singer, humbly, his voice filled with emotions that Isaac had never heard there before, except, perhaps, when he sang one of those love songs that his mother liked with so much feeling that the neighboring women gathered around to hear. The desire to giggle surged up in Isaac again, and he stiffened against it.

But Jacob was alert and serious in his brother's behalf. "How could she have been shading her eyes from the sun? You said that it happened in the late afternoon. If it did, since her house is on the west side of the street, the sun would be behind her and shining toward you, so she couldn't have been shading them; she was just pretending. She must have been looking at you. The sun would be in your eyes. Do you remember if you had to squint when you looked at her?"

"Squint," said Moses brokenly, "I love her."

Isaac snickered, choking over the piece of bedcover that he was stuffing into his mouth.

There was a moment of utter silence, during which Isaac tried desperately to fall suddenly asleep. Then Moses pounced.

"Pest! You were listening! What did you hear? What did you hear, little devil?"

Isaac, though he was a little frightened, tried to sound innocent and injured and sleepy with Moses breathing heavily over him, but the question itself seemed so silly that his voice broke on a quavering giggle. "You like girls." Now it was afterward, with another sun and a breeze that smelled of laying the old earth to sleep. How old had Moses been then? His own age; and it did not seem so silly now to want a girl to look at him. He thought, as he awoke to the pattern of the stone high-school steps that he was ascending, of what Jacob had said after he had rescued him from the "lesson" that Moses had begun to teach him.

"Wait, wait, little knacker, you'll grow up yet."

Who could have dreamed then that they would not wait with him? Sometimes the very thought that it was he who still lived frightened him. It made him now, as the high-school bell rang, rush into the classroom and, without even seeing the welcoming smile of his friend who sat beside him, sit down quickly and bury his mind in the grammar book.

During the absence of her men Sarah stayed in the house and made a home of their room. Gentle as a nutcracker, Mrs. Plopler took her under her wing. She introduced her, with significant looks, to the neighbors. She accompanied her to the grocer's, and introduced her with more significant looks to the grocer and the customers who were waiting to be served. The significant look was a staple in the social equipment of Mrs. Plopler. She considered herself a past mistress in the art of talking between the lines. So she let Sarah know, or thought she let Sarah know, that this was the grocer about whom she had already spoken and would speak again as soon as they returned home. At the same time she let the grocer know with expressive movements of the nose, eyes, and lips, that this was the immigrant of whom she had spoken, and that there was much to be said further about her. Back home, she laid open the lives of the grocer and his customers and the neighbors before Sarah in a constant flow of Yiddish.

Sometimes Sarah felt as though the nibbling face were pursuing her. Unobtrusive though she tried to make herself, standing in a corner by the sink, preparing a meal for her men, her mind still in its customary reverie, Mrs. Plopler would appear, hair and nose over her shoulder, holding forth on how she herself preferred to prepare that particular dish. Almost invariably, just as Sarah was ready to cook her dinner, the landlady managed to reach the stove and plunk down a kettle on the only empty element. Then Sarah had to wait and listen to the endless flow of words. Sometimes the words seemed to recede and become like little human cries that pierced into the back of her mind. Then Sarah would look up, startled into sympathy, with her dazed brown eyes full on Mrs. Plopler's face. And

Mrs. Plopler would feel the warm reassurance that somehow this silent woman recognized that she too had a soul.

But Mrs. Plopler's soul was a voraciously sociable one. She would follow Sarah into the bedroom hungrily, talking. Sarah had to listen, clasping and unclasping her hands, looking one way and another to avoid the peripatetic face. Why did she have to talk so? Why did she have to beat upon the air with sounds? And those things that she said sometimes that were not from the mouth of a friend.

"You know," said Mrs. Plopler one morning, "you have the room very nicely arranged, but I'm afraid you haven't got enough floor space. In all the interior decoration books nowadays they talk about floor space. Just the other day Gertie and I were reading in a magazine with pictures, how floor space gives a room a new look. Maybe you don't need the chair. It clutters up the place."

Sarah roused to what she sensed was a threat to the comfort of her men. "We need the chair. Isaac studies his lessons on the chair by the bureau."

"Oh, I thought you could do without it. Why should he study here? Will we bite off his head if he sits in the kitchen?" asked the landlady, who did not particularly want Isaac in the kitchen but thought the boy held aloof from her daughters. Not, of course, that she would approve if they got too friendly. As she told one of the neighbors, it was enough of a worry to her just to have a strange boy in the house. A mother has to use her eyes. Mrs. Plopler let the neighbor know that she was equal to the task.

"Thank you," said Sarah. "But he likes to work by himself where it's quiet."

"Oh," said the woman. "I didn't know it was so noisy in my kitchen."

And she told her husband that night that their roomers didn't feel that the house was quiet enough for them, that they were complaining already. Mr. Plopler slept turned away from his wife, and she had to lean forward to catch his mutterings. Sometimes he did turn to her but completed his attentions with a brusque dispatch that left her quickly alone again, like a used utensil.

Mrs. Plopler had married for love. But never from the first day of her marriage, in spite of the fact that she had brought with her such a nice dowry, had she been able to please her husband. She lay back again. "Cuff for kindness," she concluded, "was all you could expect from these people."

Abraham paced home over ground that met his strides firmly, as though he had just learned to walk. Before the man, Polsky, who had finally given him a job, there had been a variety of butchers who looked at him, estimated his age, added five years for his beard and the furrows between his eyes, and five more because he spoke no English, and shook their heads. His employer looked to be a good-natured man, large and ruddy and as rudimentary as the red meat that his arms slung so easily on and off the hooks on the wall.

"So you're a butcher." He looked Abraham up and down. "In the old country they turn out even the butchers like rabbis, ha-ha-ha, eh? Don't take offense. I'm a man who doesn't blow in lace handkerchiefs. I say a girl should know what a pinch is for. Straight and to the point, ha-ha-ha, eh? One thing I know about an old-country man. He knows his craft. You can pickle meat?"

"Of course," said Abraham loudly, for his voice was loud and strong.

"Of course. Well, I need a man who knows the subtleties. I always throw a little bit too much of this, of that. I'm more of a business man myself," the butcher continued with pride. "We'll get along, eh?"

Abraham was grateful to this man—a rather coarse fellow, from the way he talked, but a man who in his own way seemed to have a heart—and some discernment. He had, after all—rather rudely, of course, in keeping with his nature—noticed that he, Abraham, had a certain air about him, that he had the appearance of a holy and a learned man. Well, hadn't that been the dream of his father? And if his father hadn't died so young, leaving him with a mother to take care of and five sisters to worry about, would he have been a butcher? And his own sons—did not a man take on dignity from their achievement, their near-achievement of his dream? But what would another care about this? What did it matter to them that he had had a son who would have been a great cantor and another who was a scholar already when yet a child. Did other men care that he had had a son miraculously returned to him? This was for time to tell the world. Now they looked at the furrows about his eyes as though he were the trunk of some tree and shook their heads. And he himself could rely only on his powerful voice, which resounded so in his own head, and on his upright bearing to show that he had still the strength of a young man.

What did it matter to destiny, the age of a man? A God who could pluck the fruit of a man's desire when it was scarcely ripe and strangle such seed as could have uplifted the human race did not think in terms of days and years.

But I am not—his steps paused with his mind's anxious scruple—angry with You, Lord, any longer. One son at least shall not precede his father to the grave.

"*Tree.*" It came to him suddenly, out loud. Tree. This means *boim* in Canada. Abraham beamed at a stranger who passed him. We will surely walk in the little park by the river this evening. And I will buy bananas. He had become inordinately fond of the new fruit his son discovered. Isaac should be home soon from the English school. He himself would come in, carrying a bag with bananas, and maybe something else, something else that was good. Perhaps he would wait for a little while before he told them. Yes. They would know by the bananas and the other something that it was not bad news. So he would hold it in for a while and wait for the right moment to tell them that he had found work, that they were on their feet again.

Just thinking about it as he walked along, and then while he bought the bananas and the other treat at the grocery—the very thought of it made him feel so enthusiastic about the prospect of coming in and making them wonder a little about what had happened to him that somehow he couldn't help himself. The minute he stepped over the threshold, his face beaming, he announced that he had found a job. Without even waiting to put down the bags that he carried, he told them everything—where he had been, what had been said, and that he had already worked a few hours just to get used to it.

"Polsky! Him! Not *him!*" Into their eager discussion erupted the ecstasies of the landlady. "But he's just the man I was telling you about yesterday." She turned on Sarah vivaciously. "And this morning—no, wait—yes, I think I must have mentioned him to you this morning too. As though it were fated!"

Sarah looked up at her blandly. "Yes." She didn't remember, but it seemed likely that within all that Mrs. Plopler had said this Polsky, who have given her Avrom a job and had enabled him to relax now for the first time in so long, should be included.

Abraham recalled, as he had recalled in those anxious moments of waiting while Polsky dealt with a customer, how the other butcher had sounded as though sending him to this man was something of a practical joke, almost as though Polsky might be dealing in not strictly kosher meat.

Mrs. Plopler, who saw happily that she wasn't going to get any help from Sarah, plunged into her story.

Polsky was a scandal. One day, suddenly, with no warning, he had walked out of his shop, closed up and disappeared. But that wasn't it, that wasn't it at all. Polsky was a married man with a wife and children—a sloppy wife and scruffy children, but that wasn't the shame of it. The shame of it was that Polsky had a customer, a married woman, a woman who was not so young as she made out and certainly not as attractive as some of the men made out, although he, Avrom, would no doubt have the chance to judge for himself. This Laiah had a husband who was a nice quiet young man, who made her a living. And of course, now it began to appear, who knows how many other men she had as well? Such a woman seems to know well enough how to prevent herself from having children and having to remember how many fathers each child has. So she was free to run around turning other men's heads. Although what kind of man her husband could be was hard to understand. A man who could stand around and let his own wife make—they should excuse the expression—a public urinal of herself. *But.* That was the beginning. Without anybody even suspecting, this Laiah had been carrying on a relationship with this Polsky. Only such things can't be kept from the eyes of the world for long. When Polsky locked his shop that day and disappeared, Laiah also walked out of her house and disappeared—with Polsky.

The landlady paused, surveyed them significantly, and went on that they might not interrupt.

People talked, of course. People were horrified. Here was this wife, here were these children. What was to become of them? Who would have imagined that Polsky, laughing and joking with the customers, would someday desert his wife and children? What was going to happen? The whole world knew that this was not the end. Then one day, just about two weeks ago, after a whole month—pouf! They're back. All of a sudden a big wagon of meat pulls up outside of Polsky's shop, right there on the avenue. Polsky jumps out and opens the place for business. But that's not all. Where is Polsky living? With his wife! They say he brought her presents, and the kids presents, and they're living the same as before. One thing is certain, that no man could stuff Sonya Plopler's mouth with presents and sneak in the back way. And that one, his paramour? Pooh pooh! She's back with her husband. With her own eyes Mrs. Plopler had seen them parading around together at the Free Loan Society banquet. They say she has the nerve to show her face in the butcher shop too. God, what's happening in the world? Mrs. Plopler took a long, deep breath and exhaled emphatically.

"He must be doing good business too," she added as an afterthought, "if he can afford to take on help again after being closed for a month."

During her recital Mrs. Plopler had ignored the fact that Isaac was present. Abraham thought of this with disapproval as he noticed that his son was leaning forward with his mouth open, apparently anxious to enter the conversation. He tried with a frown to catch Isaac's eye.

Mrs. Plopler looked at Abraham. It was time for him to break the significant silence which she had allowed for her information to sink in.

"I suppose," ventured Sarah, who was, as always, vaguely distressed to see two human beings perish in the jaws of another, "we don't know exactly what—" she trailed off lamely, made aware by Mrs. Plopler's stare that she had not risen to the occasion.

"But how do people know," said Isaac cleverly, bubbling with his brother Jacob's favorite dialectical approach, "that they were together? Just because they were gone at the same time doesn't mean—" His voice faded away as he caught his father's eye.

Mrs. Plopler's ardor, though dampened, still flickered. To Isaac's bewilderment, after she had progressed from damning Polsky and Laiah through all the people who by their passivity condoned such affairs, she darted suddenly to the conclusion that it would be only decent for her to patronize the place where her tenant worked. Tomorrow she would go herself to make an order. "I'll help you to pay your rent," she concluded in high good humor.

Later on, when they had escaped from the house and were sitting together on a bench in the little park by the river with few words passing between them, each one made their own silent voyage into the past and the future. Sarah remembered with a certainty in her mother's heart her intuition that Moses had had his eye on a girl already. Isaac watched the double-crested mountain, towering in front of them, and was aware of it even as his mind jumped from thought to thought. It was strange that, no matter where his mind went, the hill remained there, solid in his vision, every time he looked up. It was a comfort that it didn't change, like the people he had known and the other things that had once stood rooted, it had seemed, forever. It was like the sight of his father's face when he had opened his eyes for the first time after the fever, towering over him, claiming him.

Now that Abraham thought of it he determined to buy permanent seats at the neighboring synagogue for himself and his family as soon as possible. After all these sorrows, God had chosen to set him and his family down in this strange city to await what further He had in store for them. Very well.

CLARK BLAISE

A CLASS OF NEW CANADIANS

FROM A NORTH AMERICAN EDUCATION

Norman Dyer hurried down Sherbrooke Street, collar turned against the snow. "Superb!" he muttered, passing a basement gallery next to a French bookstore. Bleached and tanned women in furs dashed from hotel lobbies into waiting cabs. Even the neon clutter of the side streets and the honks of slithering taxis seemed remote tonight through the peaceful snow. *Superb,* he thought again, waiting for a light and backing from a slushy curb: a word reserved for wines, cigars, and delicate sauces; he was feeling superb this evening. After eighteen months in Montreal, he still found himself freshly impressed by everything he saw. He was proud of himself for having steered his life north, even for jobs that were menial by standards he could have demanded. Great just being here no matter what they paid, looking at these buildings, these faces, and hearing all the languages. He was learning to be insulted by simple bad taste, wherever he encountered it.

Since leaving graduate school and coming to Montreal, he had sampled every ethnic restaurant downtown and in the old city, plus a few Levantine places out in Outremont. He had worked on conversational French and mastered much of the local dialect, done reviews for local papers, translated French-Canadian poets for Toronto quarterlies, and tweaked his colleagues for not sympathizing enough with Quebec separatism. He attended French performances of plays he had ignored in English, and kept a small but elegant apartment near a colony of *émigré* Russians just off Park Avenue. Since coming to Montreal he'd witnessed a hold-up, watched a murder, and seen several riots. When stopped on the street for directions, he would answer in French or accented English. To live this well and travel each long academic summer, he held two jobs. He had no intention of returning to the States. In fact, he had begun to think of himself as a semi-permanent, semi-political exile.

Now, stopped again a few blocks farther, he studied the window of Holt-Renfrew's exclusive men's shop. Incredible, he thought, the authority of simple good taste. Double-breasted chalk-striped suits he would never dare to buy. Knitted sweaters, and fifty-dollar shoes. One tanned mannequin was decked out in a brash checkered sportscoat with a burgundy vest and dashing ascot. Not a price tag under three hundred dollars. Unlike food, drink, cinema, and literature, clothing had never really involved him. Some day, he now realized, it would. Dyer's clothes, thus far, had all been bought in a chain department store. He was a walking violation of American law, clad shoes to scarf in Egyptian cottons, Polish leathers, and woollens from the People's Republic of China.

He had no time for dinner tonight; this was Wednesday, a day of lectures at one university, and then an evening course in English as a Foreign Language at McGill, beginning at six. He would eat afterwards.

Besides the money, he had kept this second job because it flattered him. There was to Dyer something fiercely elemental, almost existential, about teaching both his language and his literature in a foreign country — like Joyce in Trieste, Isherwood and Nabokov in Berlin, Beckett in Paris. Also it was necessary for his students. It was the first time in his life that he had done something socially useful. What difference did it make that the job was beneath him, a recent Ph.D., while most of his colleagues in the evening school at McGill were idle housewives and bachelor civil servants? It didn't matter, even, that this job was a perversion of all the sentiments he held as a progressive young teacher. He was a god two evenings a week, sometimes suffering and fatigued, but nevertheless an omniscient, benevolent god. His students were silent, ignorant, and dedicated to learning English. No discussions, no demonstrations, no dialogue.

I love them, he thought. They need me.

He entered the room, pocketed his cap and ear muffs, and dropped his briefcase on the podium. Two girls smiled good evening.

They love me, he thought, taking off his boots and hanging up his coat; I'm not like their English-speaking bosses.

I love myself, he thought with amazement even while conducting a drill on word order. I love myself for tramping down Sherbrooke Street in zero weather just to help them with noun clauses. I love myself standing behind this podium and showing Gilles Carrier and Claude Veilleux the difference between the past continuous and the simple past; or the sultry Armenian girl with the bewitching half-glasses that "put on" is not the same as "take on"; or telling that dashing Mr. Miguel Mayor, late of Madrid, that simple futurity can be expressed in four different ways, at least.

This is what mastery is like, he thought. Being superb in one's chosen field, not merely in one's mother tongue. A respected performer in the lecture halls of the major universities, equipped by twenty years' research in the remotest libraries, and slowly giving it back to those who must have it. Dishing it out suavely, even wittily. Being a legend. Being loved and a little feared.

"Yes, Mrs. David?"

A *sabra:* freckled, reddish hair, looking like a British model, speaks with a nifty British accent, and loves me.

"No," he smiled, "I *were* is not correct except in the present subjunctive, which you haven't studied yet."

The first hour's bell rang. The students closed their books for the intermission. Dyer put his away, then noticed a page of his Faulkner lecture from the afternoon class. *Absalom, Absalom!* his favourite.

"Can anyone here tell me what the *impregnable citadel of his passive rectitude* means?"

"What, sir?" asked Mr. Vassilopoulos, ready to copy.

"What about *the presbyterian and lugubrious effluvium of his passive vindictiveness*?" A few girls giggled. "O.K.," said Dyer, "take your break."

In the halls of McGill they broke into the usual groups. French Canadians and South Americans into two large circles, then the Greeks, Germans, Spanish, and French into smaller groups. The patterns interested Dyer. Madrid Spaniards and Parisian French always spoke English with their New World co-linguals. The Middle Europeans spoke German together, not Russian, preferring one occupier to the other. Two Israeli men went off alone. Dyer decided to join them for the break.

Not *sabras,* Dyer concluded, not like Mrs. David. The shorter one, dark and wavy-haired, held his cigarette like a violin bow. The other, Mr. Weinrot, was tall and pot-bellied, with a ruddy face and thick stubby fingers. Something about him suggested truck-driving, perhaps of beer, maybe in Germany. Neither one, he decided, could supply the name of a good Israeli restaurant.

"This is really hard, you know?" said Weinrot.

"Why?"

"I think it's because I'm not speaking much of English at my job."

"French?" asked Dyer.

"French? Pah! All the time Hebrew, sometimes German, sometimes little Polish. Crazy thing, eh? How long you think they let me speak Hebrew if I'm working in America?"

"Depends on where you're working," he said.

"Hell, I'm working for the Canadian government, what you think? Plant I work in—I'm engineer, see—makes boilers for the turbines going up North. Look. When I'm leaving Israel I go first to Italy. Right away— bamm I'm working in Italy I'm speaking Italian like a native. Passing for a native."

"A native Jew," said his dark-haired friend.

"Listen to him. So in Rome they think I'm from Tyrol—that's still native, eh? So I speak Russian and German and Italian like a Jew. My Hebrew is bad, I admit it, but it's a lousy language anyway. Nobody likes it. French I understand but English I'm talking like a bum. Arabic I know five dialects. Danish fluent. So what's the matter I can't learn English?"

"It'll come, don't worry," Dyer smiled. *Don't worry, my son;* he wanted to pat him on the arm. "Anyway, that's what makes Canada so appealing. Here they don't force you."

"What's this *appealing?* Means nice? Look, my friend, keep it, eh? Two years in a country I don't learn the language means it isn't a country."

"Come on," said Dyer. "Neither does forcing you."

"Let me tell you a story why I come to Canada. Then you tell me if I was wrong, O.K.?"

"Certainly," said Dyer, flattered.

In Italy, Weinrot told him, he had lost his job to a Communist union. He left Italy for Denmark and opened up an Israeli restaurant with five other friends. Then the six Israelis decided to rent a bigger apartment downtown near the restaurant. They found a perfect nine-room place for two thousand kroner a month, not bad shared six ways. Next day the landlord told them the deal was off. "You tell me why," Weinrot demanded.

No Jews? Dyer wondered. "He wanted more rent," he finally said.

"More—you kidding? More we expected. *Less we* didn't expect. A couple with eight kids is showing up after we're gone and the law in Denmark says a man has a right to a room for each kid plus a hundred kroner knocked off the rent for each kid. What you think of that? So a guy who comes in *after* us gets a nine-room place for a thousand kroner *less.*

Law says no way a bachelor can get a place ahead of a family, and bachelors pay twice as much."

Dyer waited, then asked, "So?"

"So, I make up my mind the world is full of communismus, just like Israel. So I take out applications next day for Australia, South Africa, U.S.A., and Canada. Canada says come right away, so I go. Should have waited for South Africa."

"How could you?" Dyer cried. "What's wrong with you anyway? South Africa is fascist. Australia is racist."

The bell rang, and the Israelis, with Dyer, began walking to the room.

"What I was wondering, then," said Mr. Weinrot, ignoring Dyer's outburst, "was if my English is good enough to be working in the United States. You're American, aren't you?"

It was a question Dyer had often avoided in Europe, but had rarely been asked in Montreal. "Yes," he admitted, "your English is probably good enough for the States or South Africa, whichever one wants you first."

He hurried ahead to the room, feeling that he had let Montreal down. He wanted to turn and shout to Weinrot and to all the others that Montreal was the greatest city on the continent, if only they knew it as well as he did. If they'd just break out of their little ghettos.

At the door, the Armenian girl with the half-glasses caught his arm. She was standing with Mrs. David and Miss Parizeau, a jolly French-Canadian girl that Dyer had been thinking of asking out.

"Please, sir," she said, looking at him over the tops of her tiny glasses, "what I was asking earlier—*put on*—I heard on the television. A man said *You are putting me on* and everybody laughed. I think it was supposed to be funny but *put* on we learned means get dressed, no?"

"Ah—*don't put me on*," Dyer laughed.

"I yaven't erd it neither," said Miss Parizeau.

"To put *somebody* on means to make a fool of him. To put some*thing* on is to wear it. O.K.?" He gave examples.

"Ah, now I know," said Miss Parizeau. "Like bullshitting somebody. Is it the same?"

"Ah, yes," he said, smiling. French Canadians were like children learning the language. "Your example isn't considered polite. 'Put on' is very common now in the States."

"Then maybe," said Miss Parizeau, "we'll ave it ere in twenty years."

The Armenian giggled.

"No—I've heard it here just as often," Dyer protested, but the girls had already entered the room.

He began the second hour with a smile which slowly soured as he thought of the Israelis. America's anti-communism was bad enough, but it was worse hearing it echoed by immigrants, by Jews, here in Montreal. Wasn't there a psychological type who chose Canada over South Africa? Or was it just a matter of visa and slow adjustment? Did Johannesburg lose its Greeks, and Melbourne its Italians, the way Dyer's students were always leaving Montreal?

And after class when Dyer was again feeling content and thinking of approaching one of the Israelis for a restaurant tip, there came the flood of small requests: should Mrs. Papadopoulos go into a more advanced course; could Mr. Perez miss a week for an interview in Toronto; could Mr. Giguere, who spoke English perfectly, have a harder book; Mr. Coté an easier one?

Then as he packed his briefcase in the empty room, Miguel Mayor, the vain and impeccable Spaniard, came forward from the hallway.

"Sir," he began, walking stiffly, ready to bow or salute. He wore a loud grey checkered sportscoat this evening, blue shirt, and matching ascot-handkerchief, slightly mauve. He must have shaved just before class, Dyer noticed, for two fresh daubs of antiseptic cream stood out on his jaw, just under his earlobe.

"I have been wanting to ask *you* something, as a matter of fact," said Dyer. "Do you know any good Spanish restaurants I might try tonight?"

"There are not any good Spanish restaurants in Montreal," he said. He stepped closer. "Sir?"

"What's on your mind, then?"

"Please—have you the time to look on a letter for me?"

He laid the letter on the podium.

"Look *over* a letter," said Dyer. "What is it for?"

"I have applied," he began, stopping to emphasize the present perfect construction, "for a job in Cleveland, Ohio, and I want to know if my letter will be good. Will an American, I mean—"

"Why are you going there?"

"It is a good job."

"But Cleveland—"

"They have a blackman mayor, I have read. But the job is not in Cleveland."

"Let me see it."

Most honourable Sir: I humbly beg consideration for a position in your grand company ...

"Who are you writing this to?"

"The president," said Miguel Mayor.

I am once a student of Dr. Ramiro Gutierrez of the Hydraulic Institute of Sevilla, Spain ...

"Does the president know this Ramiro Gutierrez?"

"Oh, everybody is knowing him," Miguel Mayor assured, "he is the most famous expert in all Spain."

"Did he recommend this company to you?"

"No—I have said in my letter, if you look—"

An ancient student of Dr. Gutierrez, Salvador del Este, is actually a boiler expert who is being employed like supervisor is formerly a friend of mine ...

"Is he still your friend?"

Whenever you say come to my city Miguel Mayor for talking I will be coming. I am working in Montreal since two years and am now wanting more money than I am getting here now ...

"Well ... " Dyer sighed.

"Sir—what I want from you is knowing in good English how to interview me by this man. The letters in Spanish are not the same to English ones, you know?"

I remain humbly at your orders ...

"Why do you want to leave Montreal?"

"It's time for a change."

"Have you ever been to Cleveland?"

"I am one summer in California. Very beautiful there and hot like my country. Montreal is big port just like Barcelona. Everybody mixed together and having no money. It is just a place to land, no?"

"Montreal? Don't be silly."

"I thought I come here and learn good English but where I work I get by in Spanish and French. It's hard, you know?" he smiled. Then he took a few steps back and gave his cuffs a gentle tug, exposing a set of jade cufflinks.

Dyer looked at the letter again and calculated how long he would be correcting it, then up at his student. How old is he? My age? Thirty? Is he married? Where do the Spanish live in Montreal? He looks so prosperous, so confident, like a male model off a page of *Playboy*. For an instant Dyer felt that his student was mocking him, somehow pitting his astounding confidence and wardrobe, sharp chin and matador's bearing against Dyer's command of English and mastery of the side streets, bistros, and ethnic restaurants. Mayor's letter was painful, yet he remained somehow competent. He would pass his interview, if he got one. What would he care about America, and the odiousness he'd soon be supporting? It was as though a superstructure of exploitation had been revealed, and Dyer felt himself abused by the very people he wanted so much to help. It had to end someplace.

He scratched out the second "humbly" from the letter, then folded the sheet of foolscap. "Get it typed right away," he said. "Good luck."

"Thank you, sir," said his student, with a bow. Dyer watched the letter disappear in the inner pocket of the checkered sportscoat. Then the folding of the cashmere scarf, the draping of the camel's hair coat about the shoulders, the easing of the fur hat down to the rims of his ears. The meticulous filling of the pigskin gloves. Mayor's patent leather galoshes glistened.

"Good evening, sir," he said.

"*Buenas noches*," Dyer replied.

He hurried now, back down Sherbrooke Street to his daytime office where he could deposit his books. Montreal on a winter night was still mysterious, still magical. Snow blurred the arc lights. The wind was dying. Every second car was now a taxi, crowned with an orange crescent. Slushy curbs had hardened. The window of Holt-Renfrew's was still attractive. The legless dummies invited a final stare. He stood longer than he had earlier, in front of the sporty mannequin with a burgundy waistcoat, the mauve and blue ensemble, the jade cufflinks.

Good evening, sir, he could almost hear. The ascot, the shirt, the complete outfit, had leaped off the back of Miguel Mayor. He pictured how he must have entered the store with three hundred dollars and a prepared speech, and walked out again with everything off the torso's back.

I want that.

What, sir?

That.

The coat, sir?

Yes.

Very well, sir.

And *that*.

Which, sir?

All that.

"Absurd man!" Dyer whispered. There had been a moment of fear, as though the naked body would leap from the window, and legless, chase him down Sherbrooke Street. But the moment was passing. Dyer realized now that it was comic, even touching. Miguel Mayor had simply tried too hard, too fast, and it would be good for him to stay in Montreal until he deserved those clothes, that touching vanity and confidence. With one last look at the window, he turned sharply, before the clothes could speak again.

JOY KOGAWA

ROAD BUILDING BY PICK AXE

FROM WOMAN IN THE WOODS

The Highway
Driving down the
highway from Revelstoke—
forced labour—all the
Nisei[1] having no
choice etcetera etcetera
and mentioning this in
passing to this Englishman
who says when he
came to Canada from
England he wanted to
go to Vancouver too but
the quota for professors
was full so he was
forced to go to Toronto.

1.   Pronounced "knee-say," a name for second-generation Japanese-Canadians;
     "Issei" means first-generation. "Sansei" third-generation.

FOUND POEM

Uazusu Shoji
who was twice wounded
while fighting with the Princess Pats

in World War I
had purchased nineteen acres of land
under the Soldiers Settlement Act
and established a chicken farm.

His nineteen acres
a two-storied house
four chicken houses
and electric incubator
and 2,500 fowl
were sold for $1,492.59.

After certain deductions
for taxes and sundries were made
Mr. Shoji received a cheque
for $39.32.

The Day After

The day after Sato-sensei
received the Order of Canada
he told some of us Nisei
the honour he received
was our honour, our glory
our achievement.

And one Nisei remembered
the time Sensei went to Japan
met the emperor
and was given a rice cake
how Sensei brought it back to Vancouver
took the cake to the baker and
had it crushed into powder
so that each pupil might
receive a tiny bit.

And someone suggested
he take the Order of Canada medal
and grind it to bits
to share with us.

MEMENTO

Trapped in
a clear plastic
hockey-puck
paperweight
is a blank ink sketch
of a jaunty outhouse.

Slocan Reunion—
August 31, 1974
Toronto.

MAY 3, 1981

I'm watching the flapping
green ferry flag on the
way to Victoria—
the white dogwood flower
centred by a yellow dot.
A small yellow dot
in a BC ferry boat—

In the Vancouver Daily Province
"Western Canada Hatred
Due to Racism."

Ah my British
British Columbia, my
first brief home.

FOR ISSEI IN NURSING HOMES

Beneath the waiting
in the garden in
late autumn—how
the fruit falls without
a thud, the white
hoary hair falls and
falls and strangers
tread the grey walk ways
of the concrete garden.

How without vegetation how
without touch the old ones
lie in their slow days.

With pick axe then
or dynamite

that in their last breaths, a
green leaf, yes, and
grandchild bringing gifts.

AUSTIN C. CLARKE

GRIFF!

From When Women Rule

Griff was a black man from Barbados who sometimes denied he was black. Among black Americans who visited Toronto, he was black: "Right on!" "Peace and love, Brother!" and "Power to the people!" would suddenly become his vocabulary. He had emigrated to Toronto from Britain, and as a result, thought of himself as a black Englishman. But he was blacker than most immigrants. In colour, that is. It must have been this double indemnity of being British and black that caused him to despise his blackness. To his friends, and his so-called friends, he flaunted his British experience, and the "civilized" bearing that came with it; and he liked being referred to as a West Indian who had lived in London, for he was convinced that he had an edge, in breeding, over those West Indians who had come straight to Canada from the canefields in the islands. He had attended Ascot many times and he had seen the Queen in her box. He hated to be regarded as just black.

"Griff, but you're blasted black, man," Clynn said once, at a party in his own home, "and the sooner you realize that fact, the more rass-hole wiser you would be!" Clynn usually wasn't so honest, but that night he was drunk.

What bothered Griff along with his blackness was that most of his friends were "getting through": cars and houses and "swinging parties" every Friday night, and a yearly trip back home for Christmas and for Carnival. Griff didn't have a cent in the bank. "And you don't even have *one* blasted child, neither!" Clynn told him that same night.

But Griff was the best-dressed man present. They all envied him for that. And nobody but his wife really knew how poor he was in pocket. Griff smiled at them from behind his dark-green dark glasses. His wife smiled too, covering her embarrassment for her husband. She never criticized him in public, by gesture or by attitude, and she said very little to him about his ways, in their incensed apartment. Nevertheless, she carried many burdens of fear and failure for her husband's apparent ambitionless attitudes. England had wiped some British manners on her, too. Deep down inside, Griff was saying to Clynn and the others, *godblindyougodblindyou!*

"Griffy, dear, pour your wife a Scotch, darling. I've decided to enjoy myself." She was breathing as her yoga teacher had taught her to do.

And Griffy said, *godblindyougodblindyou!* again, to Clynn; poured his wife her drink, poured himself a large Scotch on the rocks, and vowed, *I am going to drink all your Scotch tonight, boy!* This was his only consolation. Clynn's words had become wounds. Griff grew so centred around his own problems that he did not, for one moment, consider any emotion coming from his wife. "She's just a nice kid," he told Clynn once, behind her back. He had draped his wife in an aura of sanctity; and he would become angry to the point of violence, and scare anybody, when he thought his friends' conversation had touched the cloud and virginity of sanctity in which he had clothed her: like taking her out on Friday and Saturday nights to the Cancer Calypso Club, in the entrails of the city, where pimps and doctors and lonely immigrants hustled women and brushed reputations in a brotherhood of illegal liquor. And if the Club got too crowded, Griff would feign a headache, and somehow make his wife feel the throbbing pain of his migraine, and would take her home in a taxi, and would recover miraculously on his way back along Sherbourne Street, and with the tact of a good barrister, would make tracks back to the Cancer and dance the rest of the limp-shirt night with a woman picked from among the lonely West Indian stags: his jacket let loose to the sweat and the freedom, his body sweet with the music rejoicing in the happy absence of his wife in the sweet presence of this woman.

But after these hiatuses of dance, free as the perspiration pouring down his face, his wife would be put to bed around midnight, high up in the elevator, high off the invisible hog of credit, high up on the Chargex Card, and Griff would be tense, for days. It was a tenseness which almost gripped his body in a paralysis, as it strangled the blood in his body when the payments of loans for furniture and for debts approached, and they always coincided with the approaching of his paycheque, already earmarked against its exact face value. In times of this kind of stress, like his anxiety at the racetrack, when the performance of a horse contradicted his knowledge of the Racing Form and left him broke, he would grumble, "Money is *naught* all."

Losing his money would cause him to ride on streetcars, and he hated any kind of public transportation. He seemed to realize his blackness more intensely; white people looking at him hard — questioning his presence, it seemed. It might be nothing more than the way his colour changed colour, going through a kaleidoscope of tints and shades under the varying ceiling lights of the streetcar. Griff never saw it this way. To him, it was staring. And his British breeding told him that to look at a person you didn't know (except she was a woman) was *infra dig*. *Infra dig* was the term he chose when he told Clynn about these incidents of people staring at him on the streetcars. The term formed itself on his broad thin lips, and he could never get the courage to spit it at the white people staring at him.

When he lost his money, his wife, after not having had dinner nor the money to buy food (the landlord locked the apartment door with a padlock one night while they were at a party), would smile in that half-censuring smile, a smile that told you she had been forced against the truth of her circumstances, to believe with him, that money was "not all, at-all." But left to herself, left to the ramblings of her mind and her aspirations and her fingers over the new broadloom in her girl-friend's home, where her hand clutched the tight sweating glass of Scotch on the rocks, her Scotch seeming to absorb her arriving unhappiness with the testimony of her friend's broadloom, or in Clynn's recreation room, which she called a "den"; in her new sponge of happiness, fabricated like the house in her dreams, she would put her smile around her husband's losses, and in the embrace they would both feel higher than anybody present, because, "Griffy, dear, you were the only one there with a Master of Arts."

"I have more brains than *any one* there. They only coming-on strong. But I don't have to come on strong, uh mean, I don't *have* to come on strong, but ... "

One day, at Greenwood Race Track, Griff put his hand into his pocket and pulled out five twenty-dollar bills, and put them on one race: he put three twenty-dollar bills on Number Six, on *the fucking nose — to win! Eh?* (he had been drinking earlier at the Pilot Tavern); and he also put two twenty-dollar bills on Number Six, *to show.* He had studied the Racing Form like a man studying his torts: he would put it into his pocket, take it out again, read it in the bathroom as he trimmed his moustache; he studied it on the sweet-smelling toilet bowl, he studied it as he might have studied laws in Britain; and when he spoke of his knowledge in the Racing Form, it was as if he had received his degrees in the Laws of Averages, and not in English Literature and Language.

And he "gave" a horse to a stranger that same day at Greenwood. "Buy Number Three, man. I read the Form for three days, taking notes. It *got* to be Number Three!" The man thanked him because he himself was no expert; and he spent five dollars (more than he had ever betted before) on Number Three, to *win*. "I read the Form like a blasted book, man!" Griff told him. He slipped away to the wicket farthest away; and like a thief, he bought his own tickets: "Number Six! Sixty on the nose! forty to show!" and to himself he said, smiling, "Law o' averages, man, law of averages."

Tearing up Number Six after the race, he said to the man who had looked for him to thank him, and who thanked him and shook his hand and smiled with him, "I don't have to come on strong, man, I *mastered* that Form." He looked across the field to the board at the price paid on Number Three, and then he said to the man, "Lend me two dollars for the next race, man. I need a bet."

The man gave him three two-dollar bills and told him, "*Any* time, pardner, any time! Keep the six dollars. Thank *you!*"

Griff was broke. Money is *naught* all, he was telling the same man who, seeing him waiting by the streetcar stop, had picked him up. Griff settled himself back into the soft leather of the new Riviera, going west, and said again to the man, "Money is naught all! But I don't like to come on strong. Uh mean, you see how I mastered the *Form,* did you?"

"You damn right, boy!" the man said, adjusting the tone of the tape-deck. "How you like my new car?"

The elevator was silent that evening, on the way up to the twenty-fifth floor; and he could not even lose his temper with it: "This country is uncivilized—even the elevators—they make too much noise a man can't even think in them; this place only has money but it doesn't have any culture or breeding or style so everybody is grabbing for money money money." The elevator that evening didn't make a comment. And neither did his wife: she had been waiting for him to come from work, straight, with the money untouched in his monthly paycheque. But Griff had studied the Racing Form thoroughly all week, and had worked out the laws and averages and notations in red felt-pen ink; had circles all the "long shots" in green, and had moved through the "donkeys" (the slow horses) with waves of blue lines; had had three "sure ones" for that day; and had averaged his wins against heavy bets against his monthly salary, it was such a "goddamn cinch"! He had developed a migraine headache immediately after lunch, slipped through the emergency exit at the side, holding his head in his hand, his head full of tips and cinches, and had caught the taxi which miraculously had been waiting there, with the meter ticking; had run through the entrance of the racetrack, up the stairs, straight for the wicket to be on the Daily Double; had invested fifty dollars on a "long shot" (worked out scientifically from his red-marked, green-and-blue wavy-line Form), and had placed "two goddamn dollars" on the favourite—just to be sure!—and went into the clubhouse. The favourite won. Griff lost fifty dollars by the first race. But had won two dollars on his two-dollar bet.

"I didn't want to come on strong," he told the man who was then a stranger to him. The man could not understand what he was talking about: and he asked for no explanation. "I didn't want to come on strong, but I worked out all the winners today, since ten o'clock last night. I *picked* them, man. I can pick them. But I was going for the 'long shot'. Hell, what is a little bread? Fifty dollars! Man, that isn't no bread, at all. If I put my hand in my pocket now, look ... *this is* bread! ... five *hundred* dollars. I can lose, man, I can afford to lose bread. Money don't mean anything to me, man, money is no *big* thing! ... money is *naught* all."

His wife remained sitting on the Scandinavian couch, which had the habit of whispering to them, once a month, "Fifty-nine thirty-five owing on me!" in payments. She looked up at Griff as he gruffed through the door. She smiled. Her face did not change its form, or its feeling, but she smiled. Griff grew stiff at the smile. She got up from the couch. She brushed the anxiety of time from her waiting miniskirt ("My wife must dress well, and look *sharp*, even in the house!"), she tidied the already-tidy hairdo she had just got from Azans, and she went into the kitchen, which was now a wall separating Griff from her. Griff looked at the furniture, and wished he could sell it all in time for the races tomorrow afternoon: the new unpaid-for living-room couch, desk, matching executive chair, the table and matching chairs where they ate, desk pens thrown in, into the bargain the salesman swore he was giving them, ten Friday nights ago down Yonge Street, scatter rugs, Scandinavian-type settee with its matching chairs, like Denmark in the fall season, in style and design; he looked at the motto, CHRIST IS THE HEAD OF THIS HOME, which his wife had insisted upon taking as another "bargain"; and he thought of how relaxed he felt driving in the man's new Riviera. He took the new Racing Form, folded in half and already notated, from his breast pocket, and sat on the edge of the bed, in the wisteria-smelling bedroom. His wife had been working, he said to himself, as he noticed he was sitting on his clean folded pyjamas. But he left them there and perused the handicaps and histories of the horses. The bundle buggy for shopping was rolling over the polished wood of the living-room floor. The hinges of the doors of the clothes cupboard in the hallway were talking. A clothes hanger dropped on the skating rink of the floor. The cupboard door was closed. The bundle buggy rolled down from its prop against the cupboard and jangled onto the hardboard ice. Griff looked up and saw a smooth brown, black-maned horse standing before him. It was his wife.

"Griffy, dear? I am ready." She had cleaned out her pocketbook of old papers, useless personal and business cards accumulated over drinks and at parties; and she had made a budget of her month's allowance, allowing a place in the tidied wallet section for her husband's arrival. The horse in Griff's mind changed into a donkey. "Clynn called. He's having a party tonight. Tennish. After the supermarket, I want to go round to the corner, to the cleaners' and stop off at the liquor store for a bottle of wine. My sisters're coming over for dinner, and they're bringing their boy-friends. I want to have a roast. Should I also buy you a bottle of Black-and-White, Griffy, dear?": *they're at post! they're off!* ... as *they come into the backstretch, moving for the wire ... it's Phil Kingston by two lengths, Crimson Admiral, third, True Willie ... Phil Kingston, Crimson Admiral, True Willie ...* but Griff had already moved downstairs, in the direction of the cashiers' wicket: "Long shot in your arse! Uh got it, this time, old man!" *True Willie is making a move. True Willie! ... Phil Kingston now by one length, True Willie is coming on the outside! True Willie! It's True Williel*

"It's almost time for the supermarket to close, Griff dear, and I won't like to be running about like a race horse, sweating and perspiring. I planned my housework and I tried to finish all my housework on time so I'll be fresh for when you came home. I took my time, too, doing my housework and I took a shower so I won't get excited by the time my sisters come and I didn't bother to go to my yoga class" *it's True Willie by a neck! True Willie! What a run, ladies and gentlemen! what a run! True Willie's the winner, and it's now official!* "and I even made a promise to budget this month so we'll have some money for all these bills we have to pay. We have to pay these bills and we never seem to be paying them off and the rent's due in two days, no, today! oh, I forgot to tell you that the bank manager called about your loan, to say that" *it's True Willie, by a neck!*

Griff smashed all the furniture in the apartment in his mind, and then walked through the door. "Oh Griffy, dear! Stooly called to say he's getting a lift to the races tomorrow and if you're going he wants you to ... "

Griff was standing in the midst of a group of middle-aged West Indians, all of whom pretended through the amount of liquor they drank, and the "gashes they lashed" that they were still young black studs. "Man, when I entered that door, she knew better than to open her fucking mouth to me! To *me? Me?*" The listening red eyes understood the unspoken chastisement in his threatening voice. "Godblindyou! she knew better than, *that*, me? if she'd only opened her fucking mouth, I would have ... " They raised their glasses, all of them, to their mouths, not exactly at the same time, but sufficiently together, to make it a ritualistic harmony among men. "As man!" Griff said, and then wet his lips. They would, each of them, have chastised their women in precisely the same way that Griff was boasting about disciplining his. But he never did. He could never even put his hand to his wife's mouth to stop her from talking. And she was not the kind of woman you would want to beat: she was much too delicate. The history of their marriage had coincided with her history of a woman's illness which had been kept silent among them; and its physical manifestation, in the form of a large scar that crawled halfway around her neck, darker in colour than the natural shade of her skin, had always, from the day of recovery after the operation, been covered by a neckline on each of her dresses. And this became her natural style and fashion in clothes. Sometimes, in more daring moods, she would wear a silk scarf to hide the scar. "If my wife wasn't so blasted sickly, I would've put my hand in her arse, *many times!* I've thought o' putting my hand in her arse, after a bad day at the races!" He had even thought of doing something drastic about her smile and about his losses at the track and at poker. It was not clearly shaped in his mind: and at times, with this violent intent, he could not think of whom he would perform this drastic act on. After a bad day at the track, the thought of the drastic act, like a cloud over his thoughts, would beat him down and take its toll out of his slim body which itself seemed to refuse to bend under the great psychological pressure of losing, all the time. He had just lost one hundred dollars at Woodbine Race Track, when one evening as he entered Clynn's living-room, for the usual Friday night party of Scotch and West Indian peas and rice and chicken, which Clynn's Polish wife cooked and spoiled and learned how to cook as she spoiled the food, he had just had time to adjust his shoulders in the over-sized sports jacket, when he said, braggingly, "I just dropped a hundred. At Woodbine." He wet his lips and smiled.

"Dollars?" It was Clynn's voice, coming from the dark corner where he poured drinks. Clynn was a man who wouldn't lend his sister, nor his mother—if she was still alive—more than five dollars at one time.

"Money don't mean anything, man."

"A *hundred* dollars?" Clynn suddenly thought of the amount of Scotch Griff had been drinking in his house.

"Money is *naught* all."

"You're a blasted ... boy, do you lose *just* for fun or wha'?" Clynn sputtered. "Why the arse you don't become a *groom,* if you like racehorse so much? Or you's a ... a *paffological* loser?"

"Uh mean, I don't like to come on strong, or anything, but, money is *naught* all ... "

"Rass-hole put down my Scotch, then! You drinking my fucking Scotch!"

And it rested there. It rested there because Griff suddenly remembered he was among men who knew him: who knew his losses both in Britain and Canada. It rested there also, because Clynn and the others knew that his manner and attitude towards money, and his wife's expressionless smile, were perhaps lying expressions of a turbulent inner feeling of failure. "He prob'ly got rass-hole ulcers, too!" Clynn said, and then spluttered into a laugh. Griff thought about it, and wondered whether he had indeed caused his wife to be changed into a different woman altogether. But he couldn't know that. Her smile covered a granite of silent and apparent contentment. He wondered whether he hated her, to the bone, and whether she hated him. He felt a spasm through his body as he thought of her hating him, and not knowing about it. For so many years living together, both here and in Britain; and she was always smiling. Her constancy and her cool exterior, her smiles, all made him wonder now, with the Scotch in his hand, about her undying devotion to him, her faithfulness, pure as the sheets in their sweet-smelling bedroom; he wondered whether "I should throw my hand in her arse, *just* to see what she would do." But Clynn had made up his own mind that she was, completely, destroyed inside: her guts, her spirit, her aspirations, her procreative mechanism, "Hysterectomy all shot to pieces!" Clynn said cruelly, destroyed beyond repair, beneath the silent consolation and support which he saw her giving to her husband; at home among friends and relations, and in public among his sometimes silently criticizing friends. "I don't mean to come on strong, but ... "

"You really want to know what's wrong with Griff?" Clynn's sister, Princess, asked one day. "He want a *stiff lash* in his backside! He don't know that he's gambling-'way his wife's life? He doesn't know that? Look, he don't have chick nor child! Wife working in a good job, for *decent* money, and they don't even live in a decent apartment that you could say, well, rent eating out his sal'ry. Don't own no record-player. *Nothing.* And all he doing is walking 'bout Toronto with his blasted head high in the air! He ain' know this is North America? Christ, he don't even speak to poor people. He ain' have no motto-car, like some. Well, you tell me then, what the hell is Griff doing with thirteen-thousand Canadian dollars a year? Supporting race-horse? No, man, you can't tell me that, 'cause not even the *most* wutless o' Wessindians living in Toronto, could gamble-'way thirteen thousand dollars! Jesuschrist! that is twenty-six thousand back in Barbados! Think o' the land he could buy back home wid thirteen-thousand Canadian dollars. And spending it 'pon a race-horse? What the hell is a race-horse? *Thirteen thousand?* But lissen to me! One o' these mornings, that wife o' his going get up and tell him that she with-child, that she *pregnunt* ... " ("She can't get pregnunt, though, Princess, 'cause she already had one o' them operations!") "Anyhow, if his wife was a diff'rent person, she would 'ave walked-out on his arse *long ago!* Or else, break his two blasted hands! and she won't spend a *day* in jail!"

When Griff heard what Princess had said about him, he shrugged his shoulders and said, "I don't have to come on strong, but if I was a different man, I would really show these West Indian women something ... " He ran his thin, long, black fingers over the length of his old-fashioned slim tie, he shrugged the grey sports jacket that was a size too large, at the shoulders, into shape and place, wet his lips twice, and said, "Gimme another Scotch, man." While Clynn fixed the Scotch, he ran his thumb and index finger of his left hand down the razor edge of his dark brown trouser seams. He inhaled and tucked his shirt and tie neatly beneath the middle button of his sports jacket. He took the Scotch, which he liked to drink on the rocks, and he said, "I don't have to come on strong, but I am going to tell you something ... "

The next Friday night was the first day of fête in the long weekend. There hadn't been a long weekend in Canada for a long time. Everybody was tired of just going to work, coming home, watching CBC television, bad movies on the TV, and then going to bed. "There ain' no action in this fucking town," Clynn was saying for days, before the weekend appeared like raindrops on a farmer's dry-season head. And everybody agreed with him. It was so. Friday night was here, and the boys, their wives, their girl-friends, and their "outside women" were noisy and drunk and happy. Some of the men were showing off their new bell-bottom trousers and broad leather belts worn under their bulging bellies, to make them look younger. The women, their heads shining like wet West Indian tar roads, the smell from the cosmetics and grease that went into their kinky hair and on their faces, to make them look sleek and smooth, all these smells and these women mixed with the cheap and domestic perfumes they used, whenever Avon called; and some women, wives whose husbands "were getting through," were wearing good-looking dresses, in style and fashion; others were still back home in their style, poured in against their wishes and the better judgement of their bulging bodies; backsides big, sometimes too big, breasts bigger, waists fading into the turbulence of middle age and their behinds, all poured against the shape of their noisy bodies, into evil-fitting, shiny material, made on sleepy nights after work, on a borrowed sewing machine. But everybody was happy. They had all forgotten now, through the flavour of the calypso and the peas and the rice, the fried chicken, the curry-chicken, that they were still living in a white man's country; and it didn't seem to bother them now, nor touch them now. Tonight, none of them would tell you that they hated Canada; that they wanted to go back home; that they were going "to make a little money, first"; that they were only waiting till then; that they were going to go back before the "blasted Canadian tourisses buy-up the blasted Caribbean"; they wouldn't tell you tonight that they all suffered some form of racial discrimination in Canada, and that that was to be expected, since "there are certain things with this place that are not just right"; not tonight. Tonight, Friday night, was forgetting night. West Indian night. And they were at the Cancer Club to forget and to drink and to get drunk. To make plans for some strange woman's (or man's) body and bed, to spend "some time" with a real West Indian "thing," to eat her boiled mackerel and green bananas, which their wives and women had, in their ambitions to be "decent" and Canadian, forgotten how to cook, and had left out of their diets, especially when Canadian friends were coming to dinner, because that kind of food was "plain West Indian stupidness." Tonight, they would forget and drink, forget and dance, and dance to forget.

"Oh-Jesus-Christ, Griff!" Stooly shouted, as if he was singing a calypso. He greeted Griff this way each time he came to the Club, and each time it was as if Stooly hadn't seen Griff in months, although they might have been together at the track the same afternoon. It was just the way Stooly was. "Oh-Jesus-Christ, Griff!" he would shout, and then he would rush past Griff, ignoring him, and make straight for Griff's wife. He would wrap his arms round her slender body (once his left hand squeezed a nipple, and Griff saw, and said to himself, "Uh mean, I won't like to come on strong about it, but ... "; and did nothing about it), pulling up her new minidress above the length of decency, worn for the first time tonight, exposing the expensive lace which bordered the tip of her slip. The veins of her hidden age, visible only at the back of her legs, would be exposed to Griff, who would stand and stare and feel "funny," and feel, as another man inquired with his hands all over his wife's body, the blood and the passion and the love mix with the rum in his mouth. Sometimes, when in a passion of brandy, he would make love to his wife as if she was a different woman, as if she was no different from one of the lost women found after midnight on the crowded familiar floor of the Cancer.

"Haiii! How?" the wife would say, all the time her body was being crushed. She would say, "Haiii! How?" every time it happened; and it happened every time; and every time it happened, Griff would stand and stare, and do nothing about it, because his memory of British breeding told him so; but he would feel mad and helpless afterwards, all night; and he would always want to kill Stooly, or kill his wife for doing it; but he always felt she was so fragile. He would want to kill Stooly more than he would want to kill his wife. But Stooly came from the same island as his wife. Griff would tell Clynn the next day, on the telephone, that he should have done something about it; but he "didn't want to come on strong." Apparently, he was not strong enough to rescue his wife from the rape of Stooly's arms, as he rubbed his body against hers, like a dog scratching its fleas against a tree.

Once, a complete stranger saw it happen. Griff had just ordered three drinks: one for his wife, one for himself, and one for Stooly, his friend. Griff looked at the man, and in an expansive mood (he had made the "long shot" in the last race at Woodbine that afternoon), he asked the stranger, "What're you drinking?"

"Rum, sah!"

"I am going to buy you a goddamn drink, just because I like you, man."

The stranger did not change the mask on his face, but stood there, looking at Griff's dark-green lenses. Then he said, "You isn' no blasted man at all, man!" He then looked behind: Stooly was still embracing Griff's wife. It looked as if he was feeling her up. The man took the drink from Griff, and said, "You is no man, sah!"

Griff laughed; but no noise came out of his mouth. "Man, that's all right. They went to school together in Trinidad."

"In *my* books, you still ain' no fucking man, boy!" The stranger turned away from Griff: and when he got to the door of the dance floor, he said, "Thanks for the drink, *boy*."

The wife was standing beside Griff now, smiling as if she was a queen parading through admiring lines of subjects. She looked, as she smiled, like she was under the floodlights of some premiere performance she had prepared herself for a long time. She smiled, although no one in particular expected a smile from her. Her smiling went hand in hand with her new outfit. It had to be worn with a smile. It looked good, as usual, on her; and it probably understood that it could only continue to look good and express her personality if she continued smiling. At intervals, during the night, when you looked at her, it seemed as if she had taken the smile from her handbag, and had then powdered it onto her face. She could have taken it off any time, but she chose to wear it the whole night. "Griffy, dear?" she said, although she wasn't asking him anything, or telling him anything, or even looking in his direction. "Haiii! How?" she said to a man who brushed against her hips as he passed. The man looked suddenly frightened, because he wanted his advance to remain stealthy and masculine. When he passed back from the bar, with five glasses of cheap rum-and-Cokes in his hands, he walked far from her.

Griff was now leaning on the bar, facing the part-time barman, and talking about the results of the last race that day; his wife, her back to the bar, was looking at the men and the women, and smiling; when someone passed, who noticed her, and lingered in the recognition, she would say, "Haiii! How?"

A large, black, badly dressed Jamaican (he was talking his way through the crowd) passed. He stared at her. She smiled. He put out his calloused construction hand, and with a little effort, he said, "May I have this dance, gal?" Griff was still talking. But in his mind he wondered whether his wife would dance with the Jamaican. He became ashamed with himself for thinking about it. He went back to talking, and got into an argument with the part-time barman, Masher, over a certain horse that was running in the feature race the next day at Greenwood. Masher, ever watchful over the women, especially other men's, couldn't help notice that the calloused-hand Jamaican was holding on to Griff's wife's hand. With his shark-eyes he tried to get Griff's attention off horses and onto his wife. But Griff was too preoccupied. His wife placed her drink on the counter beside him, her left hand still in the paws of the Jamaican construction worker, whom nobody had seen before, and she said, "Griffy, dear?" The man's hand on her manicured fingers had just come into his consciousness, when he wheeled around to give her her drink. He was upset. But he tried to be cool. It was the blackness of the Jamaican. And his size. Masher knew he was upset. The Jamaican reminded Griff of the "Congo-man" in one of Sparrow's calypsos. Masher started to laugh in his spitting kee-kee laugh. And when Griff saw that everybody was laughing, and had seen the Congojamaican walk off with his wife, he too decided to laugh.

"It's all right, man," he said, more than twice, to no one in particular, although he could have been consoling the Jamaicancongo man, or Masher, or the people nearby, or himself.

"I sorry, suh," The Jamaican said. He smiled to show Griff that he was not a rough fellow. "I am sorry, suh. I didn't know you was with the missis. I thought the missis was by-sheself, tonight, again, suh."

"It's no *big* thing, man," Griff said, turning back to talk to Masher, who by now had lost all interest in horses. Masher had had his eyes on Griff's wife, too. But Griff was worried by something new now: the man had said, *"by-she-self, tonight, again, suh"*; and that could mean only one thing: that his wife went places, like this very Club, when he wasn't with her; and he had never thought of this, and never even imagined her doing a thing like this; and he wasn't sure that it was not merely the bad grammar of the Jamaican, and not the accusation in that bad grammar, *"but language is a funny thing, a man could kill a person with language, and the accusation can't be comprehended outside of the structure of the language ... wonder how you would parse this sentence, Clynn ... a Jamaican fella told me last night, "by-sheself, tonight, again, suh"; now, do you put any emphasis on the position of the adverb, more than the conditional phrase ?"* Griff was already dozing off into the next day's dreams of action, thinking already of what he would tell Clynn about the accident: *"Which is the most important word in that fellow's sentence structure? 'By-sheself,' 'again,' or 'tonight'?"*

"Never mind the fellow looks like a canecutter, he's still a brother," Griff said to Masher, but he could have been talking into the future, the next day, to Clynn; or even to himself. "I don't want to come on strong, but he's a brother." The CBC television news that night dealt with the Black Power nationalism in the States. The Jamaican man and Griff's wife were now on the dance floor. Griff stole a glimpse at them, to make sure the man was not holding his wife in the same friendly way Stooly, who was a friend, would hold her. He thought he would be able to find the meaning of *"by-sheself,"* *"again,"* and *"tonight"* in the way the man held his wife. Had the Jamaican done so, Griff would have had to think even more seriously about the three words. But the Jamaican was about two hundred and fifty pounds of muscle and mackerel and green bananas. "Some other fellow would have come on strong, just because a rough-looking chap like him, held on ... "

"Man, Griff, you's a rass-hole idiot, man!" Masher said. He crept under the bar counter, came out, faced Griff, broke into his sneering laugh, and said, "You's a rass-hole!" Griff laughed too, in his voiceless laugh. "You ain' hear that man say, *'by-sheself,' 'tonight,' 'again'*? If I had a woman like that, I would kiss her arse, by-Christ, just for *looking at* a man like that Jamaikian-man!" Masher laughed some more, and walked away, singing the calypso the amateur band was trying to play: "*Oh Mister Walker, Uh come to see your daughter …*"

Griff wet his lips. His bottom lip disappeared inside his mouth, under his top lip; then he did the same thing with his top lip. He adjusted his dark glasses, and ran his right hand, with a cigarette in it, over his slim tie. His right hand was trembling. He shrugged his sports jacket into place and shape on his shoulders … "*Oh, Mister Walker, uh come to see ya daughterrrrr …* " He stood by himself in the crowd of West Indians at the door, and he seemed to be alone on a sun-setting beach back home. Only the waves of the calypsonian, and the rumbling of the congo drum, and the whispering, the loud whispering in the breakers of the people standing nearby, were with him. He was like the sea. He was like a man in the sea. He was a man at sea … "*tell she is the man from Sangre Grande …* "

The dance floor was suddenly crowded, jam-packed. Hands were going up in the air, and some under dresses, in exuberance after the music; the words in the calypso were tickling some appetites; he thought of his wife's appetite and of the Jamaican's, who could no longer be seen in the gloom of the thick number of black people; and tomorrow was races, and he had again mastered the Form. And Griff suddenly became terrified about his wife's safety and purity, and the three words came back to him: "*by-sheself*," "*tonight*," "*again*." Out of the crowd, he could see Masher's big red eyes and his teeth, skinned in mocking laugh. Masher was singing the words of the calypso: "*Tell she I come for she …* " The music and the waves on the beach, when the sun went behind the happy afternoon, came up like a gigantic sea, swelling and roaring as it came to where he was standing in the wet white sand; and the people beside him, whispering like birds going home to branches and rooftops, some whispering, some humming like the sea, fishing for fish and supper and for happiness, no longer in sight against the blackening dusk … "*she know me well, I had she already! …*" Stooly walked in front of him, like the lightning that jigsawed over the rushing waves; and behind Stooly was a woman, noisy and Trinidadian, "this part-tee can't done till morning come!" like an empty tin can tied to a motor car bumper. All of a sudden, the fishermen and the fishing boats were walking back to shore, climbing out of their boats, laden with catches, their legs wet up to their knees; and they walked with their boats up to the brink of the sand. In their hands were fish. Stooly still held the hand of a woman who laughed and talked loud, "Fête for so!" She was like a barracuda. Masher, raucous and happy, and harmless, and a woman he didn't know, were walking like Siamese twins. One of his hands could not be seen. Out of the sea, now resting from the turbulent congo drumming of the waves in the calypso, came the Jamaicancongoman, and his wife.

"Thank you very much, suh" he said, handing Griff his wife's hand. With the other hand, she was pulling her miniskirt into place. "She is a first class dancer, suh."

"Don't have to come on *strong*, man."

"If I may, some other time, I would like to ... " the man said, smiling and wiping perspiration from his face with a red handkerchief. His voice was pleasant and it had an English accent hidden somewhere in it. But all the words Griff heard were "I know she well, I had she already." ... "*by-sheself*," "*again*," "*tonight*" ... and there were races tomorrow. His wife was smiling, smiling like the everlasting sea at calm.

"Haiii!" she said, and smiled some more. The Jamaicanman moved back into the sea for some more dancing and fish. The beach was still crowded; and in Griff's mind it was crowded, but there was no one but he standing among the broken forgotten pieces of fish: heads and tails, and empty glasses and cigarette butts, and some scales broken off in a bargain, or by chance, and the ripped-up tickets of wrong bets.

Masher appeared and said in his ear, "If she was my wife, be-Christ, I tell you ... " and he left the rest for the imagination.

Griff's wife's voice continued, "Griffy, dear?"

Masher came back from the bar with a Coke for the woman he was with. When he got close to Griff, he said in his ear, "Even if she was only just a screw like that one I have there ... "

"Griffy, dear, let's go home, I am feeling ... "

" ... and if you was *something*," Masher was now screaming down the stairs after them. Griff was thinking of the three little words which had brought such a great lump of weakness within the pit of his stomach.

"Masher seems very happy tonight, eh, Griffy, dear? I never quite saw Masher so happy."

" ... you, *boy! you, boy!* ... "

"Masher, Haiii! How?"

"If it was mine," Masher shouted, trying to hide the meaning of his message, "if it was mine, and I had put only a two-dollar bet 'pon that horse, that horse that we was talking about, and, and that horse *behave so*, well, I would have to *lash* that horse, till ... *unnerstan*?"

"Griffy, dear? Masher really loves horses, doesn't he, eh?"

They were around the first corner, going down the last flight of stairs, holding the rails on the right-hand side. Griff realized that the stairs were smelling of stale urine, although he could not tell why. His wife put her arm round his waist. It was the first for the day. "I had a *great* time, a real ball, a *lovely* time!" Griff said nothing. He was tired, but he was also tense inside; still he didn't have the strength or the courage, whichever it was he needed, to tell her how he felt, how she had humiliated him, in that peculiar West Indian way of looking at small matters, in front of all those people, he could not tell her how he felt each time he watched Stooly put his arms round her slender body; and how he felt when the strange Jamaican man, with his cluttered use of grammar broken beyond meaning and comprehending, had destroyed something, like a dream, which he had had about her for all these fifteen years of marriage. He just couldn't talk to her. He wet his lips and ran his fingers over the slim tie. All she did (for he wanted to know that he was married to a woman who could, through all the years of living together, read his mind, so he won't have to talk) was smile. That goddamn smile, he cursed. The sports jacket shoulders were shrugged into place and shape.

"Griffy, dear? Didn't you enjoy yourself?" Her voice was like a flower, tender and caressing. The calypso band, upstairs, had just started up again. And the quiet waltz-like tune seemed to have been chosen to make him look foolish, behind his back. He could hear the scrambling of men and crabs trying to find dancing partners. He could imagine himself in the rush of fishermen after catches. He was thinking of getting his wife home quickly and coming back, to face Stooly and the Jamaican man; and he wished that if he did come back, that they would both be gone, so he won't have to come on strong; but he was thinking more of getting rid of his wife and coming back to dance and discuss the Racing Form; and tomorrow was races, again. He imagined the large rough Jamaican man searching for women again. He saw Stooly grabbing some woman's hand, some woman whom he had never seen before. But it was *his* Club. He saw Masher, his eyes bulging and his mouth wide open, red and white, in joy. And Griff found himself not knowing what to do with his hands. He took his hands out of his jacket pockets; and his wife, examining her minidress in the reflection of the glass in the street door they were approaching, and where they always waited for the taxicab to stop for them, removed her arm from his waist. Griff placed his hand on her shoulder, near the scar, and she shuddered a little, and then he placed both hands on her shoulders; and she straightened up, with her smile on her face, waiting for the kiss (he always kissed her like that), which would be fun, which was the only logical thing to do with his hands in that position around her neck, which would be fun and a little naughty for their ages like the old times in Britain; and his wife, expecting this reminder of happier nights in unhappy London, relaxed, unexcited, remembering both her doctor and her yoga teacher, and in the excitement of her usually unexcitable nature, relaxed a little, and was about to adjust her body to his, and lean her scarred neck just a little bit backward to make it easy for him, to get the blessing of his silent lips (she remembered then that the Jamaican held her as if he was her husband) when she realized that Griff's hands had walked up from her shoulders, and were now caressing the hidden bracelet of the scar on her neck, hidden tonight by a paisley scarf. She shuddered in anticipation. He thought of Stooly, as she thought of the Jamaican, as he thought of Masher, as he squeezed, and of the races — tomorrow the first race goes at 1:45 P.M. And the more he squeezed the less he thought of other things, and the less those other things bothered him, and the less he thought of the bracelet of flesh under his fingers, the bracelet which had become visible, as his hands rumpled the neckline. He was not quite sure what he was doing, what he wanted to do; for he was a man who always insisted that he didn't like to come on strong, and to be standing up here in a grubby hallway killing his wife, would be coming on strong: he was not sure whether he was wrapping his hands round her neck in a passionate embrace imitating the Jamaican, or whether he was merely kissing her.

But she was still smiling, the usual smile. He even expected her to say, "Haiii! How?" But she didn't. She couldn't. He didn't know where his kiss began and ended; and he didn't know where his hands stopped squeezing her neck. He looked back up the stairs, and he wanted so desperately to go back up into the Club and show them, or talk to them, although he did not, at the moment, know exactly why, and what he would have done had he gone back into the Club. His wife's smile was still on her body. Her paisley scarf was falling down her bosom like a rich spatter of baby food, pumpkin, and tomato sauce; and she was like a child, propped against a corner, in anticipation of its first step, toddling into movement. But there was no movement. The smile was there, and that was all. He was on the beach again, and he was looking down at a fish, into the eye of reflected lead, a fish left by a fisherman on the beach. He thought he saw the scales moving up and down, like small billows, but there was no movement. He had killed her. But he did not kill her smile. He wanted to kill her smile more than he wanted to kill his wife.

Griff wet his lips, and walked back up the stairs. His wife was standing against the wall by the door, and she looked as if she was dead, and at the same time she looked as if she was living. It must have been the smile. Griff thought he heard her whisper, "Griffy, dear?" as he reached the door. Stooly, with his arm round a strange woman's body, took away his arm, and rushed to Griff, and screamed as if he was bellowing out a calypso line, "Oh-Jesus-Christ-Griff!"

Masher heard the name called, and came laughing and shouting, "Jesus-Christ, boy! You get rid o' the wife real quick, man! As man, *as man.*" Griff was wetting his lips again; he shrugged his sports jacket into place, and his mind wandered ... "show me the kiss-me-arse Racing Form, man. We going to the races tomorrow ... "

ROHINTON MISTRY

SWIMMING LESSONS

FROM TALES FROM FIROZSHA BAAG

The old man's wheelchair is audible today as he creaks by in the hallway: on some days it's just a smooth whir. Maybe the way he slumps in it, or the way his weight rests has something to do with it. Down to the lobby he goes, and sits there most of the time, talking to people on their way out or in. That's where he first spoke to me a few days ago. I was waiting for the elevator, back from Eaton's with my new pair of swimming trunks.

"Hullo," he said. I nodded, smiled.

"Beautiful summer day we've got."

"Yes," I said, "it's lovely outside."

He shifted the wheelchair to face me squarely. "How old do you think I am?"

I looked at him blankly, and he said, "Go on, take a guess."

I understood the game; he seemed about seventy-five although the hair was still black, so I said, "Sixty-five?" He made a sound between a chuckle and a wheeze: "I'll be seventy-seven next month." Close enough.

I've heard him ask that question several times since, and everyone plays by the rules. Their faked guesses range from sixty to seventy. They pick a lower number when he's more depressed than usual. He reminds me of Grandpa as he sits on the sofa in the lobby, staring out vacantly at the parking lot. Only difference is, he sits with the stillness of stroke victims, while Grandpa's Parkinson's disease would bounce his thighs and legs and arms all over the place. When he could no longer hold the *Bombay Samachar* steady enough to read, Grandpa took to sitting on the veranda and staring emptily at the traffic passing outside Firozsha Baag. Or waving to anyone who went by in the compound: Rustomji, Nariman Hansotia in his 1932 Mercedes-Benz, the fat ayah Jaakaylee with her shopping bag, the kuchrawalli with her basket and long bamboo broom.

The Portuguese woman across the hall has told me a little about the old man. She is the communicator for the apartment building. To gather and disseminate information, she takes the liberty of unabashedly throwing open the door when newsworthy events transpire. Not for Portuguese Woman the furtive peerings from thin cracks or spyholes. She reminds me of a character in a movie, *Barefoot in the Park*, I think it was, who left empty beer cans by the landing for anyone passing to stumble and give her the signal. But PW does not need beer cans. The gutang-khutang of the elevator opening and closing is enough.

The old man's daughter looks after him. He was living alone till his stroke, which coincided with his youngest daughter's divorce in Vancouver. She returned to him and they moved into this low-rise in Don Mills. PW says the daughter talks to no one in the building but takes good care of her father.

Mummy used to take good care of Grandpa, too, till things became complicated and he was moved to the Parsi General Hospital. Parkinsonism and osteoporosis laid him low. The doctor explained that Grandpa's hip did not break because he fell, but he fell because the hip, gradually growing brittle, snapped on that fatal day. That's what osteoporosis does, hollows out the bones and turns effect into cause. It has an unusually high incidence in the Parsi community, he said, but did not say why. Just one of those mysterious things. We are the chosen people where osteoporosis is concerned. And divorce. The Parsi community has the highest divorce rate in India. It also claims to be the most westernized community in India. Which is the result of the other? Confusion again, of cause and effect.

The hip was put in traction. Single-handed, Mummy struggled valiantly with bedpans and dressings for bedsores which soon appeared like grim specters on his back. *Mamaiji*, bent double with her weak back, could give no assistance. My help would be enlisted to roll him over on his side while Mummy changed the dressing. But after three months, the doctor pronounced a patch upon Grandpa's lungs, and the male ward of Parsi General swallowed him up. There was no money for a private nursing home. I went to see him once, at Mummy's insistence. She used to say that the blessings of an old person were the most valuable and potent of all, they would last my whole life long. The ward had rows and rows of beds; the din was enormous, the smells nauseating, and it was just as well that Grandpa passed most of his time in a less than conscious state.

But I should have gone to see him more often. Whenever Grandpa went out, while he still could in the days before parkinsonism, he would bring back pink and white sugar-coated almonds for Percy and me. Every time I remember Grandpa, I remember that; and then I think: I should have gone to see him more often. That's what I also thought when our telephone-owning neighbour, esteemed by all for that reason, sent his son to tell us the hospital had phoned that Grandpa died an hour ago.

The postman rang the doorbell the way he always did, long and continuous; Mother went to open it, wanting to give him a piece of her mind but thought better of it, she did not want to risk the vengeance of postmen, it was so easy for them to destroy letters; workers nowadays thought no end of themselves, strutting around like peacocks, ever since all this Shiv Sena agitation about Maharashtra for Maharashtrians, threatening strikes and Bombay bundh all the time, with no respect for the public; bus drivers and conductors were the worst, behaving as if they owned the buses and were doing favours to commuters, pulling the bell before you were in the bus, the driver purposely braking and moving with big jerks to make the standees lose their balance, the conductor so rude if you did not have enough change.

But when she saw the airmail envelope with a Canadian stamp her face lit up, she said wait to the postman, and went in for a fifty paisa piece, a little baksheesh for you, she told him, then shut the door and kissed the envelope, went in running, saying my son has written, my son has sent a letter, and Father looked up from the newspaper and said, don't get too excited, first read it, you know what kind of letters he writes, a few lines of empty words, I'm fine, hope you are all right, your loving son — that kind of writing I don't call letter-writing.

Then Mother opened the envelope and took out one small page and began to read silently, and the joy brought to her face by the letter's arrival began to ebb; Father saw it happening and knew he was right, he said read aloud, let me also hear what our son is writing this time, so Mother read: My dear Mummy and Daddy, Last winter was terrible, we had record-breaking low temperatures all through February and March, and the first official day of spring was colder than the first official day of winter had been, but it's getting warmer now. Looks like it will be a nice warm summer. You asked about my new apartment. It's small, but not bad at all. This is just a quick note to let you know I'm fine, so you won't worry about me. Hope everything is okay at home.

After Mother put it back in the envelope, Father said everything about his life is locked in silence and secrecy, I still don't understand why he bothered to visit us last year if he had nothing to say; every letter of his has been a quick note so we won't worry — what does he think we worry about,

his health, in that country everyone eats well whether they work or not, he
should be worrying about us with all the black market and rationing, has he
forgotten already how he used to go to the ration-shop and wait in line every
week; and what kind of apartment description is that, not bad at all; and if
it is a Canadian weather report I need from him, I can go with Nariman
Hansotia from A Block to the Cawasji Framji Memorial Library and read
all about it, there they get newspapers from all over the world.

The sun is hot today. Two women are sunbathing on the stretch of patchy lawn at the periphery of the parking lot. I can see them clearly from my kitchen. They're wearing bikinis and I'd love to take a closer look. But I have no binoculars. Nor do I have a car to saunter out to and pretend to look under the hood. They're both luscious and gleaming. From time to time they smear lotion over their skin, on the bellies, on the inside of the thighs, on the shoulders. Then one of them gets the other to undo the string of her top and spread some there. She lies on her stomach with the straps undone. I wait. I pray that the heat and haze make her forget, when it's time to turn over, that the straps are undone.

But the sun is not hot enough to work this magic for me. When it's time to come in, she flips over, deftly holding up the cups, and reties the top. They arise, pick up towels, lotions, and magazines, and return to the building.

This is my chance to see them closer. I race down the stairs to the lobby. The old man says hullo. "Down again?"

"My mailbox," I mumble.

"It's Saturday," he chortles. For some reason he finds it extremely funny. My eye is on the door leading in from the parking lot.

Through the glass panel I see them approaching. I hurry to the elevator and wait. In the dimly lit lobby I can see their eyes are having trouble adjusting after the bright sun. They don't seem as attractive as they did from the kitchen window. The elevator arrives and I hold it open, inviting them in with what I think is a gallant flourish. Under the fluorescent glare in the elevator I see their wrinkled skin, aging hands, sagging bottoms, varicose veins. The lustrous trick of sun and lotion and distance has ended.

I step out and they continue to the third floor. I have Monday night to look forward to, my first swimming lesson. The high school behind the apartment building is offering, among its usual assortment of macramé and ceramics and pottery classes, a class for non-swimming adults.

The woman at the registration desk is quite friendly. She even gives me the opening to satisfy the compulsion I have about explaining my non-swimming status.

"Are you from India?" she asks. I nod. "I hope you don't mind my asking, but I was curious because an Indian couple, husband and wife, also registered a few minutes ago. Is swimming not encouraged in India?"

"On the contrary," I say. "Most Indians swim like fish. I'm an exception to the rule. My house was five minutes walking distance from Chaupatty beach in Bombay. It's one of the most beautiful beaches in Bombay, or was, before the filth took over. Anyway, even though we lived so close to it, I never learned to swim. It's just one of those things."

"Well," says the woman, "that happens sometimes. Take me, for instance. I never learned to ride a bicycle. It was the mounting that used to scare me. I was afraid of falling." People have lined up behind me. "It's been very nice talking to you," she says, "hope you enjoy the course."

The art of swimming had been trapped between the devil and the deep blue sea. The devil was money, always scarce, and kept the private swimming clubs out of reach; the deep blue sea of Chaupatty beach was gray and murky with garbage, too filthy to swim in. Every so often we would muster our courage and Mummy would take me there to try and teach me. But a few minutes of paddling was all we could endure. Sooner or later something would float up against our legs or thighs or waists, depending on how deep we'd gone in, and we'd be revulsed and stride out to the sand.

Water imagery in my life was recurring. Chaupatty beach, now the high-school swimming pool. The universal symbol of life and regeneration did nothing but frustrate me. Perhaps the swimming pool will overturn that failure.

When images and symbols abound in this manner, sprawling or rolling across the page without guile or artifice, one is prone to say, how obvious, how skilless; symbols, after all, should be still and gentle as dewdrops, tiny, yet shining with a world of meaning. But what happens when, on the page of life itself, one encounters the ever-moving, all-engirdling sprawl of the filthy sea? Dewdrops and oceans both have their rightful places; Nariman Hansotia certainly knew that when he told his stories to the boys of Firozsha Baag.

The sea of Chaupatty was fated to endure the finales of life's everyday functions. It seemed that the dirtier it became, the more crowds it attracted: street urchins and beggars and beachcombers, looking through the junk that washed up. (Or was it the crowds that made it dirtier? — another instance of cause and effect blurring and evading identification.)

Too many religious festivals also used the sea as repository for their finales. Its use should have been rationed, like rice and kerosene. On Ganesh Chaturthi, clay idols of the god Ganesh, adorned with garlands and all manner of finery, were carried in processions to the accompaniment of drums and a variety of wind instruments. The music got more frenzied the closer the procession got to Chaupatty and to the moment of immersion.

Then there was Coconut Day, which was never as popular as Ganesh Chaturthi. From a bystander's viewpoint, coconuts chucked into the sea do not provide as much of a spectacle. We used the sea, too, to deposit the leftovers from Parsi religious ceremonies, things such as flowers, or the ashes of the sacred sandalwood fire, which just could not be dumped with the regular garbage but had to be entrusted to the care of Avan Yazad, the guardian of the sea. And things which were of no use but which no one had the heart to destroy were also given to Avan Yazad. Such as old photographs.

After Grandpa died, some of his things were flung out to sea. It was high tide; we always checked the newspaper when going to perform these disposals; an ebb would mean a long walk in squelchy sand before finding water. Most of the things were probably washed up on shore. But we tried to throw them as far out as possible, then waited a few minutes; if they did not float back right away we would pretend they were in the permanent safekeeping of Avan Yazad, which was a comforting thought. I can't remember everything we sent out to sea, but his brush and comb were in the parcel, his *kusti*, and some Kemadrin pills, which he used to take to keep the parkinsonism under control.

Our paddling sessions stopped for lack of enthusiasm on my part. Mummy wasn't too keen either, because of the filth. But my main concern was the little gutter-snipes, like naked fish with little buoyant penises, taunting me with their skills, swimming underwater and emerging unexpectedly all around me, or pretending to masturbate—I think they were too young to achieve ejaculation. It was embarrassing. When I look back, I'm surprised that Mummy and I kept going as long as we did.

I examine the swimming-trunks I bought last week. Surf King, says the label, Made in Canada-Fabriqué Au Canada. I've been learning bits and pieces of French from bilingual labels at the supermarkets too. These trunks are extremely sleek and streamlined hipsters, the distance from waistband to pouch tip the barest minimum. I wonder how everything will stay in place, not that I'm boastful about my endowments. I try them on, and feel the tip of my member lingers perilously close to the exit. Too close, in fact, to conceal the exigencies of my swimming lesson fantasy: a gorgeous woman in the class for non-swimmers, at whose sight I will be instantly aroused, and she, spying the shape of my desire, will look me straight in the eye with her intentions; she will come home with me, to taste the pleasures of my delectable Asian brown body whose strangeness has intrigued her and unleashed uncontrollable surges of passion inside her throughout the duration of the swimming lesson.

I drop the Eaton's bag wrapper in the garbage can. The swimming-trunks cost fifteen dollars, same as the fee for the ten weekly lessons. The garbage bag is almost full. I tie it up and take it outside. There is a medicinal smell in the hallway; the old man must have just returned to his apartment.

PW opens her door and says, "Two ladies from the third floor were lying in the sun this morning. In bikinis."

"That's nice," I say, and walk to the incinerator chute. She reminds me of Najamai in Firozsha Baag, except that Najamai employed a bit more subtlety while going about her life's chosen work.

PW withdraws and shuts her door.

Mother had to reply because Father said he did not want to write to his son till his son had something sensible to write to him, his questions had been ignored long enough, and if he wanted to keep his life a secret, fine, he would get no letters from his father.

But after Mother started the letter he went and looked over her shoulder, telling her what to ask him, because if they kept on writing the same questions, maybe he would understand how interested they were in knowing about things over there; Father said go on, ask him what his work is at the insurance company, tell him to take some courses at night school, that's how everyone moves ahead over there, tell him not to be discouraged if his job is just clerical right now, hard work will get him ahead, remind him he is a Zoroastrian: manashni, gavashni, kunashni, better write the translation also: good thoughts, good words, good deeds — he must have forgotten what it means, and tell him to say prayers and do kusti at least twice a day.

Writing it all down sadly, Mother did not believe he wore his sudra and kusti anymore, she would be very surprised if he remembered any of the prayers; when she had asked him if he needed new sudras he said not to take any trouble because the Zoroastrian Society of Ontario imported them from

Bombay for their members, and this sounded like a story he was making up,
but she was leaving it in the hands of God, ten thousand miles away there
was nothing she could do but write a letter and hope for the best.

Then she sealed it, and Father wrote the address on it as usual because
his writing was much neater than hers, handwriting was important in the
address and she did not want the postman in Canada to make any mistake;
she took it off to the post office herself, it was impossible to trust anyone to
mail it ever since the postage rates went up because people just tore off stamps
for their own use and threw away the letter, the only safe way was to hand it
over the counter and make the clerk cancel the stamp before your own eyes.

Berthe, the building superintendent, is yelling at her son in the parking lot.
He tinkers away with his van. This happens every fine-weathered Sunday.
It must be the van that Berthe dislikes because I've seen mother and son
together in other quite amicable situations.

Berthe is a big Yugoslavian with high cheekbones. Her nationality
was disclosed to me by PW. Berthe speaks a very rough-hewn English.
I've overheard her in the lobby scolding tenants for late rents and leaving
dirty lint screens in the dryers. It's exciting to listen to her, her words fall
like rocks and boulders, and one can never tell where or how the next few
will drop. But her Slavic yells at her son are a different matter, the words
fly swift and true, well-aimed missiles that never miss. Finally, the son
slams down the hood in disgust, wipes his hands on a rag, accompanies
mother Berthe inside.

Berthe's husband has a job in a factory. But he loses several days of
work every month when he succumbs to the booze, a word Berthe uses
often in her Slavic tirades on those days, the only one I can understand,
as it clunks down heavily out of the tight-flying formation of Yugoslavian
sentences. He lolls around in the lobby, submitting passively to his wife's
tongue-lashings. The bags under his bloodshot eyes, his stringy moustache,
stubbled chin, dirty hair are so vulnerable to the poison-laden barbs (poison
works the same way in any language) emanating from deep within the
powerful watermelon bosom. No one's presence can embarrass or dignify
her into silence.

No one except the old man who arrives now. "Good morning," he says,
and Berthe turns, stops yelling, and smiles. Her husband rises, positions
the wheelchair at the favourite angle. The lobby will be peaceful as long
as the old man is there.

It was hopeless. My first swimming lesson. The water terrified me. When did that happen, I wonder, I used to love splashing at Chaupatty, carried about by the waves. And this was only a swimming pool. Where did all that terror come from? I'm trying to remember.

Armed with my Surf King I enter the high school and go to the pool area. A sheet with instructions for the new class is pinned to the bulletin board. All students must shower and then assemble at eight by the shallow end. As I enter the showers three young boys, probably from a previous class, emerge. One of them holds his nose. The second begins to hum, under his breath: Paki Paki, smell like curry. The third says to the first two: pretty soon all the water's going to taste of curry. They leave.

It's a mixed class, but the gorgeous woman of my fantasy is missing. I have to settle for another, in a pink one-piece suit, with brown hair and a bit of a stomach. She must be about thirty-five. Plain-looking.

The instructor is called Ron. He gives us a pep talk, sensing some nervousness in the group. We're finally all in the water, in the shallow end. He demonstrates floating on the back, then asks for a volunteer. The pink one-piece suits wades forward. He supports her, tells her to lean back and let her head drop in the water.

She does very well. And as we all regard her floating body, I see what was not visible outside the pool: her bush, curly bits of it, straying out at the pink Spandex V. Tongues of water lapping against her delta, as if caressing it teasingly, make the brown hair come alive in a most tantalizing manner. The crests and troughs of little waves, set off by the movement of our bodies in a circle around her, dutifully irrigate her; the curls alternatively wave free inside the crest, then adhere to her wet thighs, beached by the inevitable trough. I could watch this forever, and I wish the floating demonstration would never end.

Next we are shown how to grasp the rail and paddle, face down in the water. Between practicing floating and paddling, the hour is almost gone. I have been trying to observe the pink one-piece suit, getting glimpses of her straying pubic hair from various angles. Finally, Ron wants a volunteer for the last demonstration, and I go forward. To my horror he leads the class to the deep end. Fifteen feet of water. It is so blue, and I can see the bottom. He picks up a metal hoop attached to a long wooden stick. He wants me to grasp the hoop, jump in the water, and paddle, while he guides me by the stick. Perfectly safe, he tells me. A demonstration of how paddling propels the body.

It's too late to back out; besides, I'm so terrified I couldn't find the words to do so even if I wanted to. Everything he says I do as if in a trance. I don't remember the moment of jumping. The next thing I know is, I'm swallowing water and floundering, hanging on to the hoop for dear life. Ron draws me to the rails and helps me out. The class applauds.

We disperse and one thought is on my mind: what if I'd lost my grip? Fifteen feet of water under me. I shudder and take deep breaths. That is it. I'm not coming next week. This instructor is an irresponsible person. Or he does not value the lives of non-white immigrants. I remember the three teenagers. Maybe the swimming pool is the hangout of some racist group, bent on eliminating all non-white swimmers, to keep their waters pure and their white sisters unogled.

The elevator takes me upstairs. Then gutang-khtang. PW opens her door as I turn the corridor of medicinal smells. "Berthe was screaming loudly at her husband tonight," she tells me.

"Good for her," I say, and she frowns indignantly to me.

The old man is in the lobby. He's wearing thick wool gloves. He wants to know how the swimming was, must have seen me leaving with my towel yesterday. Not bad, I say.

"I used to swim a lot. Very good for the circulation." He wheezes. "My feet are cold all the time. Cold as ice. Hands too."

Summer is winding down, so I say stupidly, "Yes, it's not so warm any more."

The thought of the next swimming lesson sickens me. But as I comb through the memories of that terrifying Monday, I come upon the straying curls of brown pubic hair. Inexorably drawn by them, I decide to go.

It's a mistake, of course. This time I'm scared even to venture in the shallow end. When everyone has entered the water and I'm the only one outside, I feel a little foolish and slide in.

Instructor Ron says we should start by reviewing the floating technique. I'm in no hurry. I watch the pink one-piece pull the swim-suit down around her cheeks and flip back to achieve perfect flotation. And then reap disappointment. The pink Spandex triangle is perfectly streamlined today, nothing strays, not a trace of fuzz, not one filament, not even a sign of post-depilation irritation. Like the airbrushed part of glamour magazine models. The barrenness of her impeccably packaged apex is a betrayal. Now she is shorn like the other women in the class. Why did she have to do it?

The weight of this disappointment makes the water less manageable, more lung-penetrating. With trepidation, I float and paddle my way through the remainder of the hour, jerking my head out every two seconds and breathing deeply, to continually shore up a supply of precious, precious air without, at the same time, seeming too anxious and losing my dignity.

I don't attend the remaining classes. After I've missed three, Ron the instructor telephones. I tell him I've had the flu and am still feeling poorly, but I'll try to be there the following week.

He does not call again. My Surf King is relegated to an unused drawer. Total losses: one fantasy plus thirty dollars. And no watery rebirth. The swimming pool, like Chaupatty beach, has produced a stillbirth. But there is a difference. Water means regeneration only if it is pure and cleansing. Chaupatty was filthy, the pool was not. Failure to swim through filth must mean something other than failure of rebirth—failure of symbolic death? Does that equal success of symbolic life? Death of a symbolic failure? Death of a symbol? What is the equation?

The postman did not bring a letter but a parcel, he was smiling because he knew that every time something came from Canada his baksheesh was guaranteed, and this time because it was a parcel Mother gave him a whole rupee, she was quite excited, there were so many stickers on it besides the stamps, one for Small Parcel, another Printed Papers, a red sticker saying Insured; she showed it to Father, and opened it, then put both hands on her cheeks, not able to speak because the surprise and happiness was so great, tears came to her eyes and she could not stop smiling, till Father became impatient to know and finally got up and came to the table.

When he saw it he was surprised and happy too, he began to grin, then hugged Mother saying our son is a writer, and we didn't even know it, he never told us a thing, here we are thinking he is still clerking away at the insurance company, and he has written a book of stories, all these years in school and college he kept his talent hidden, making us think he was just like one of the boys in the Baag, shouting and playing the fool in the compound, and now what a surprise; then Father opened the book and began reading it, heading back to the easy chair, and Mother so excited, stilling holding his arm, walked with him, saying it was not fair him reading it first, she wanted to read it too, and they agreed that he would read the first story, then give it to her so she could also read it, and they would take turns in that manner.

> *Mother removed the staples from the padded envelope in which he had*
> *mailed the book, and threw them away, then straightened the folded edges of*
> *the envelope and put it away safely with the other envelopes and letters she*
> *had collected since he left.*

The leaves are beginning to fall. The only ones I can identify are maple.
The days are dwindling like the leaves. I've started a habit of taking long
walks every evening. The old man is in the lobby when I leave, he waves
as I go by. By the time I'm back, the lobby is usually empty.

Today I was woken up by a grating sound outside that made my flesh
crawl. I went to the window and saw Berthe raking the leaves in the parking
lot. Not in the expanse of patchy lawn on the periphery, but in the parking
lot proper. She was raking the black-tarred surface. I went back to bed and
dragged a pillow over my head, not releasing it till noon.

When I returned from my walk in the evening, PW, summoned by
the elevator's gutang-khutang, says, "Berthe filled six big black garbage
bags with leaves today."

"Six bags!" I say. "Wow!"

Since the weather turned cold, Berthe's son does not tinker with his van
on Sundays under my window. I'm able to sleep late.

Around eleven, there's a commotion outside. I reach out and switch
on the clock radio. It's a sunny day, the window curtains are bright. I get
up, curious, and see a black Olds Ninety-Eight in the parking lot, by the
entrance to the building. The old man is in his wheelchair, bundled up,
with a scarf wound several times round his neck as though to immobilize
it, like a surgical collar. His daughter and another man, the car-owner,
are helping him from the wheelchair into the front seat, encouraging him
with words like: that's it, easy does it, attaboy. From the open door of the
lobby, Berthe is shouting encouragement too, but hers is confined to one
word: ya, repeated at different levels of pitch and volume, with variations
on vowel-length. The stranger could be the old man's son, he has the same
jet-black hair and piercing eyes.

Maybe the old man is not well, it's an emergency. But I quickly scrap
that thought—this isn't Bombay, an ambulance would have arrived.
They're probably taking him out for a ride. If he is his son, where has he
been all this time, I wonder.

The old man finally settles in the front seat, the wheelchair goes in the trunk, and they're off. The one I think is the son looks up and catches me at the window before I can move away, so I wave, and he waves back.

In the afternoon I take down a load of clothes to the laundry room. Both machines have completed their cycles, the clothes inside are waiting to be transferred to dryers. Should I remove them and place them on top of a dryer, or wait? I decide to wait. After a few minutes, two women arrive, they are in bathrobes, and smoking. It takes me a while to realize that these are the two disappointments who were sunbathing in bikinis last summer.

"You didn't have to wait, you could have removed the clothes and carried on, dear," says one. She has a Scottish accent. It's one of the few I've learned to identify. Like maple leaves.

"Well," I say, "some people might not like strangers touching their clothes."

"You're not a stranger, dear," she says, "you live in this building, we've seen you before."

"Besides, your hands are clean," the other one pipes in. "You can touch my things any time you like."

Horny old cow. I wonder what they've got on under their bathrobes. Not much, I find, as they bend over to place their clothes in the dryers.

"See you soon," they say, and exit, leaving me behind in an erotic wake of smoke and perfume and deep images of cleavages. I start the washers and depart, and when I come back later, the dryers are empty.

PW tells me, "The old man's son took him out for a drive today. He has a big beautiful black car."

I see my chance, and shoot back: "Olds Ninety-Eight."

"What?"

"The car," I explain, "it's an Oldsmobile Ninety-Eight."

She does not like this at all, my giving her information. She is visibly nettled, and retreats with a sour face.

Mother and Father read the first five stories, and she was very sad after reading some of them, she said he must be so unhappy there, all his stories are about Bombay, he remembers, every little thing about his childhood, he is thinking about it all the time even though he is ten thousand miles away, my poor son, I think he misses his home and us and everything he left behind, because if he likes it over there why would he not write stories about that, there must be so many new ideas that his new life could give him.

But Father did not agree with this, he said it did not mean that he was unhappy, all writers worked in the same way, they used their memories and experiences and made stories out of them, changing some things, adding some, imagining some, all writers were very good at remembering details of their lives.

Mother said, how can you be sure that he is remembering because he's a writer, or whether he started to write because he is unhappy and thinks of his past, and wants to save it all by making stories of it; and Father said that is not a sensible question, anyway, it is now my turn to read the next story.

The first snow has fallen, and the air is crisp. It's not very deep, about two inches, just right to go for a walk in. I've been told that immigrants from hot countries always enjoy the snow the first year, maybe for a couple of years more, then inevitably the dread sets in, and the approach of winter gets them fretting and moping. On the other hand, if it hadn't been for my conversation with the woman at the swimming registration desk, they might now be saying that India is a nation of non-swimmers.

The old radiators in the apartment alarm me incessantly. They continue to broadcast a series of variations on death throes, and go from hot to cold and cold to hot at will, there's no controlling their temperature. I speak to Berthe about it in the lobby. The old man is there too, his chin seems to have sunk deeper into his chest, and his face is a yellowish gray.

"Nothing, not to worry about anything," says Berthe, dropping rough-hewn chunks of language around me. "Radiator no work, you tell me. You feel cold, you come to me, I keep you warm," and she opens her arms wide, laughing. I step back, and she advances, her breasts preceding her like the gallant prows of two ice-breakers. She looks at the old man to see if he is appreciating the act: "You no feel scared, I keep you safe and warm."

But the old man is staring outside, at the flakes of falling snow. What thoughts is he thinking as he watches them? Of childhood days, perhaps, and snowmen with hats and pipes, and snowball fights, and white Christmases, and Christmas trees? What will I think of, old in this country, when I sit and watch the snow come down? For me, it is already too late for snowmen and snowball fights, and all I will have is thoughts about childhood thoughts and dreams, built around snowscapes and winter-wonderlands on the Christmas cards so popular in Bombay; my snowmen and snowball fights and Christmas trees are in the pages of Enid Blyton's books, dispersed amidst the adventures of the Famous Five, and the Five

Find-Outers, and the Secret Seven. My snowflakes are even less forgettable than the old man's, for they never melt.

It finally happened. The heat went. Not the usual intermittent coming and going, but out completely. Stone cold. The radiators are like ice. And so is everything else. There's no hot water. Naturally. It's the hot water that goes through the rads and heats them. Or is it the other way around? Is there no hot water because the rads have stopped circulating it? I don't care, I'm too cold to sort out the cause and effect relationship. Maybe there is no connection at all.

I dress quickly, put on my winter jacket, and go down to the lobby. The elevator is not working because the power is out, so I take the stairs. Several people are gathered, and Berthe has announced that she has telephoned the office, they are sending a man. I go back up the stairs. It's only one floor, the elevator is just a bad habit. Back in Firozsha Baag they were broken most of the time. The stairway enters the corridor outside the old man's apartment, and I think of his cold feet and hands. Poor man, it must be horrible for him without heat.

As I walk down the long hallway, I feel there's something different but I can't pin it down. I look at the carpet, the ceiling, the wallpaper: it all seems the same. Maybe it's the freezing cold that imparts a feeling of difference.

PW opens her door: "The old man had another stroke yesterday. They took him to the hospital."

The medicinal smell. That's it. It's not in the hallway any more.

In the stories that he'd read so far Father said that all the Parsi families were poor or middle-class, but that was okay: nor did he mind that the seeds for the stories were picked from the sufferings of their own lives; but there should also have been something positive about Parsis, there was so much to be proud of: the great Tatas and their contribution to the steel industry, or Sir Dinshaw Petit in the textile industry who made Bombay the Manchester of the East, or Dadabhai Naoroji in the freedom movement, where he was the first to use the word swaraj, and the first to be elected to the British Parliament where he carried on his campaign; he should have found some way to bring some of these wonderful facts into his stories, what would people reading these stories think, those who did not know about Parsis — that the whole community was full of cranky, bigoted people; and in reality it was the richest, most advanced and philanthropic community in India, and he did not need to tell his own son that Parsis had a reputation for being generous and family-oriented. And he could have written something also about the historic background, how Parsis came to India from Persia because of Islamic persecution in the seventh century, and were the descendants of Cyrus the Great and the magnificent Persian Empire. He could have made a story of all this, couldn't he?

Mother said what she liked best was his remembering everything so well, how beautifully he wrote about it all, even the sad things, and though he changed some of it, and used his imagination, there was truth in it.

My hope is, Father said, that there will be some story based on his Canadian experience, that way we will know something about our son's life there, if not through his letters then in his stories; so far they are all about Parsis and Bombay, and the one with a little bit about Toronto, where a man perches on top of the toilet, is shameful and disgusting although it is funny at times and did make me laugh, I have to admit, but where does he get such an imagination from, what is the point of such a fantasy; and Mother said that she would also enjoy some stories about Toronto and the people there; it puzzles me, she said, why he writes nothing about it, especially since you say that writers use their own experience to make stories out of.

Then Father said this is true, but he is probably not using his Toronto experience because it is too early; what do you mean, too early, asked Mother and Father explained it takes a writer about ten years time after an experience before he is able to use it in his writing, it takes that long to be absorbed internally and understood, thought out and thought about, over and over again, he haunts it and it haunts him if it is valuable enough, till the writer is comfortable with it to be able to use it as he wants; but this is only one theory I read somewhere, it may or may not be true.

That means, said Mother, that his childhood in Bombay and our home here is the most valuable thing in his life just now, because he is able to remember it all to write about it, and you were so bitterly saying he is forgetting where he came from; and that may be true, said Father, but that is not what the theory means, according to the theory he is writing of these things because they are far enough in the past for him to deal with objectively, he is able to achieve what critics call artistic distance, without emotions interfering; and what do you mean emotions, said Mother, you are saying he does not feel anything for his characters, how can he write so beautifully about so many sad things without any feelings in his heart?

But before Father could explain more, about beauty and emotion and inspiration and imagination, Mother took the book and said it was her turn

now and too much theory she did not want to listen to, it was confusing and
did not make as much sense as reading the stories, she would read them her
way and Father could read them his.

My books on the windowsill have been damaged. Ice has been forming on
the inside ledge, which I did not notice, and melting when the sun shines
in. I spread them in a corner of the living room to dry out.

The winter drags on. Berthe wields her snow pusher as expertly as ever,
but there are signs of weariness in her performance. Neither husband nor
son is ever seen outside with a shovel. Or anywhere else, for that matter.
It occurs to me that the son's van is missing, too.

The medicinal smell is in the hall again, I sniff happily and look
forward to seeing the old man in the lobby. I go downstairs and peer into
the mailbox, see the blue and magenta of an Indian aerogramme with Don
Mills, Ontario, Canada in Father's flawless hand through the slot.

I pocket the letter and enter the main lobby. The old man is there, but
not in his usual place. He is not looking out through the glass door. His
wheelchair is facing a bare wall where the wallpaper is torn in places. As
though he is not interested in the outside world any more, having finished
with all that, and now it's time to see inside. What does he see inside, I
wonder? I go up to him and say hullo. He says hullo without raising his
sunken chin. After a few seconds his gray countenance faces me. "How
old do you think I am?" His eyes are dull and glazed; he is looking even
further inside than I first presumed.

"Well, let's see, you're probably close to sixty-four."

"I'll be seventy-eight next August." But he does not chuckle or wheeze.
Instead, he continues softly, "I wish my feet did not feel so cold all the time.
And my hands." He lets his chin fall again.

In the elevator I start opening the aerogramme, a tricky business
because a crooked tear means lost words. Absorbed in this while emerging,
I don't notice PW occupying the centre of the hallway, arms folded across
her chest: "They had a big fight. Both of them have left."

I don't immediately understand her agitation. "What ... who?"

"Berthe. Husband and son both left her. Now she is all alone."

Her tone and stance suggest that we should not be standing here
talking but do something to bring Berthe's family back. "That's very sad,"
I say, and go in. I picture father and son in the van, driving away, driving
across the snow-covered country, in the dead of winter, away from wife and
mother; away to where? How far will they go? Not son's van nor father's

booze can take them far enough. And the further they go, the more they'll remember, they can take it from me.

> *All the stories were read by Father and Mother, and they were sorry when the book was finished, they felt they had come to know their son better now, yet there was much more to know, they wished there were many more stories; and this is what they mean, said Father, when they say that the whole story can never be told, the whole truth can never be known; what do you mean, they say, asked Mother, who they, and Father said writers, poets, philosophers. I don't care what they say, said Mother, my son will write as much or as little as he wants to, and if I can read it I will be happy.*
>
>   *The last story they liked the best of all because it had the most in it about Canada, and now they felt they knew at least a little bit, even if it was a very little bit, about his day-to-day life in his apartment; and Father said if he continues to write about such things he will become popular because I am sure they are interested there in reading about life through the eyes of an immigrant, it provides a different viewpoint; the only danger is if he changes and becomes so much like them that he will write like one of them and lose the important difference.*

The bathroom needs cleaning. I open a new can of Ajax and scour the tub. Sloshing with mug from bucket was standard bathing procedure in the bathrooms of Firozsha Baag, so my preference now is always for a shower. I've never used the tub as yet; besides, it would be too much like Chaupatty or the swimming pool, wallowing in my own dirt. Still, it must be cleaned.

When I've finished, I prepare for a shower. But the clean gleaming tub and the nearness of the vernal equinox give me the urge to do something different today. I find the drain plug in the bathroom cabinet, and run the bath.

I've spoken so often to the old man, but I don't know his name. I should have asked him the last time I saw him, when his wheelchair was facing the bare wall because he had seen all there was to see outside and it was time to see what was inside. Well, tomorrow. Or better yet, I can look it up in the directory in the lobby. Why didn't I think of that before? It will only have an initial and a last name, but then I can surprise him with: hullo Mr. Wilson, or whatever it is.

The bath is full. Water imagery is recurring in my life: Chaupatty beach, swimming pool, bathtub. I step in and immerse myself up to the neck. It feels good. The hot water loses its opacity when the chlorine, or whatever it is, has cleared. My hair is still dry. I close my eyes, hold my breath, and dunk my head. Fighting the panic, I stay under and count to thirty. I come out, clear my lungs and breathe deeply.

I do it again. This time I open my eyes under water, and stare blindly without seeing, it takes all my will to keep the lids from closing. Then I am slowly able to discern the underwater objects. The drain plug looks different, slightly distorted; there is a hair trapped between the hole and the plug, it waves and dances with the movement of the water. I come up, refresh my lungs, examine quickly the overwater world of the washroom, and go in again. I do it several times, over and over. The world outside the water I have seen a lot of it, it is now time to see what is inside.

The spring session for adult non-swimmers will begin in a few days at the high school. I must not forget the registration date.

The dwindled days of winter are now all but forgotten; they have grown and attained a respectable span. I resume my evening walks, it's spring, and a vigorous thaw is on. The snowbanks are melting, the sound of water on its gushing, gurgling journey to the drains is beautiful. I plan to buy a book of trees, so I can identify more than the maple as they begin to bloom.

When I return to the building, I wipe my feet energetically on the mat because some people are entering behind me, and I want to set a good example. Then I go to the board with its little plastic letters and numbers. The old man's apartment is the one on the corner by the stairway, that makes it number 201. I run down the list, come to 201, but there are no little white plastic letters beside it. Just the empty black rectangle with holes where the letters would be squeezed in. That's strange. Well, I can introduce myself to him, then ask his name.

However, the lobby was empty. I take the elevator, exit at the second floor, wait for the gutang-khutang. It does not come, the door closes noiselessly, smoothly. Berthe has been at work, or has made sure someone else has. PW's cue has been lubricated out of existence.

But she must have the ears of a cockroach. She is waiting for me. I whistle my way down the corridor. She fixes me with an accusing look. She waits till I stop whistling, then says: "You know the old man died last night."

I cease groping for my key. She turns to go and I take a step toward her, my hand still in my trouser pocket. "Did you know his name?" I ask, but she leaves without answering.

Then Mother said, the part I like best in the last story is about Grandpa, where he wonders if Grandpa's spirit is really watching him and blessing him, because you know I really told him that, I told him helping an old suffering person who is near death is the most blessed thing to do, because that person will ever after watch over you from heaven, I told him this when he was disgusted with Grandpa's urine-bottle and would not touch it, would not hand it to him even when I was not at home.

Are you sure, said Father, that you really told him this, or you believe you told him because you like the sound of it, you said yourself the other day that he changes and adds and alters things in the stories but he writes it all so beautifully that it seems true, so how can you be sure; this sounds like another theory, said Mother, but I don't care, he says I told him and I believe now I told him, so even if I did not tell him then it does not matter now.

Don't you see, said Father, that you are confusing fiction with facts, fiction does not create facts, fiction can come from facts, it can grow out of facts by compounding, transposing, augmenting, diminishing, or altering them in any way; but you must not confuse cause and effect, you must not confuse what really happened with what the story says happened, you must not lose your grasp on reality, that way madness lies.

Then Mother stopped listening because, as she told Father so often, she was not very fond of theories, and she took out her writing pad and started a letter to her son; Father looked over her shoulder, telling her to say how proud they were of him and were waiting for his next book, he also said, leave a little space for me at the end, I want to write a few lines when I put the address on the envelope.

NEIL BISSOONDATH

ON THE EVE OF UNCERTAIN TOMORROWS

FROM ON THE EVE OF UNCERTAIN TOMORROWS

It is the violence of beating wings that attracts Joaquin's attention.

Two pigeons, colour only hinted at in the half-light, press in fluttering desperation against the chicken wire enclosing the little wooden balcony. They are too engrossed in battle to notice him at the open door. The air — though soft with the underlying warmth of the spring Jeremy Windhook, the lawyer, says is coming — feels cold, and he folds his arms against its subtle bite.

The wings of the birds flare like pouncing condors, the male — Joaquin now understands — pinning the female beneath him. He sinks his beak into her neck feathers, inflicting submission; steadies himself and, avoiding the ineffectual battering of her wings, awkwardly mounts her.

In the distance, past the complex geometry of withered buildings — garages, storerooms, walls of tin and brick — pressing in on the rear of the rooming house, the colourless towers of a few tall buildings of the city sit one-dimensional against the sky. They suggest an unknown life, a world of blood and flesh and everyday ambition, a life within his sight but not, still, yet, within his grasp.

The wings scratch and scrape at the wire, batter at it. Create, in their terrified clamor, a raucous plea for escape.

His heart races, temples engorge with blood. Lucidity slips, his mind an ungraspable swirl, as he steps out onto the balcony, knowing for the moment nothing but the noise of the birds.

Slaps at the wire with the back of his open hand.

To no sound, no effect.

They cannot — will not — take note of his protest.

He stands back. Horrified. Witness, in the quiet of the morning, to unwilling coupling, an avian rape. It is the way of nature, he tries telling himself. But they are unattractive birds, with panicky, red-rimmed eyes, and this lack of beauty denies them his sympathy: they call to mind infection, physical corruption.

It is all over in seconds. The male has answered the call of nature, the female has been violated. Then, unconcerned, their congress concluded, they wing away in separate directions, are quickly swallowed by the dark gray sky.

Only then does it occur to Joaquin that the wire netting wrapped around the balcony is there not to keep the pigeons in but to keep them out, its function reversed. And he is the one confined, by the chicken wire and by so much more.

"They say that the waiting is the worst thing." Amin, who says he will one day take the name Thomson, carefully pours the boiled coffee into their cups. "But it is not so, I believe." Joaquin silently admires Amin's delicacy, the economy with which he speaks, moves, handles objects, as if he has an abhorrence of excess.

Amin, usually not an early riser, has been up for a while, fussing and puttering in the bathroom. His curly black hair glistens with a shampooed freshness. His every movement tosses off a perfume that conjures for Joaquin a sweet but sweaty armpit. Amin is wearing the outfit that Jeremy Windhook brought him last week: a simple white shirt, pleated trousers, dark socks. It is a specific look that Jeremy Windhook seeks, that of a genteel poverty, an effect he must labor over for people like Amin, who, in their hunger, can so easily look brigand-like. Amin has taken special care this morning. He has showered, he has shaved, he has even clipped his nose hairs — for today, Joaquin knows, is his tomorrow; today is the day that will determine whether tonight he celebrates, or whether tonight he cries.

"The waiting is simple, after what we have been through." The words swish easily from between his barely parted lips, as if he speaks only with his tongue. "The hard part is not knowing what tomorrow will bring for me. Where will I be? What will I do? Will I be happy, or will I be sad?" He lets the condensed milk flow long and thick into his coffee, stirs it without letting the spoon clink against the side of the cup. "These are sad questions, my friend, to ask about tomorrow. No man should have to ask them, I believe."

Joaquin takes his coffee cup in both hands, blinks rapidly at the steam as he raises it to his lips.

"You did not sleep last night," Amin says.

Joaquin smiles minutely at him. The coffee is bitter, the boiled grounds gritty between his teeth.

"I see it in your eyes, my friend. It is not good, I believe."

He sips from his cup, adds, "Eh?" Amin has an ear for language. The exclamation is one of his new acquisitions, Joaquin thinks he is having an affair with one of the secretaries in Jeremy Windhook's office, although Amin says she is only helping him with his English.

Joaquin gives him a thin smile, an acknowledgement of his concern. But he is not sure how he really feels about Amin; he's too self-confident, in the sly way of the street-survivor. Joaquin worries when Amin claims a communality of experience with him. He has never spoken to Amin of his life, has listened with silent skepticism to Amin's eagerly offered autobiography of civil war, starvation, forced conscription. Joaquin wonders whether Jeremy Windhook has told Amin his story; but Jeremy Windhook has never mentioned any of his other clients to Joaquin, so he has no reason to believe this. He thinks instead that Amin is simply assuming the comradeship of those involved in the same enterprise. It is, he thinks, a sign of Amin's struggle with his isolation, the isolation they all share.

Amin reaches into the cupboard for a box of crackers, stuffs two in his mouth with one hand as the other digs into the box for more. He no longer bothers to offer them to Joaquin, knows he does not like their salty dryness.

In the silence disturbed only by Amin's crunching, Joaquin wonders whether he should tell him about the pigeons—it seems somehow important—but Amin's camouflaged nervousness reveals itself in the desperation of his jaw. Joaquin knows that his tale of the pigeons will force Amin's natural melancholia to the surface, will smother his summoned ebullience. So he says nothing.

This day has no dawn.

It is the sun, in any case, and not mechanical precision that marks Joaquin's sense of time. Midday or midnight on his illuminated alarm clock is meaningless. So it is only with the lightening of the sky, its dimming of the lights in the distant buildings, that the day after tomorrow truly becomes tomorrow.

Tomorrow: it is like a forbidden woman, enticing, creeping into his daydreams, invading his fantasies. It robs him of sleep, grates his nerves into a fearful impotence.

It was earlier, when he couldn't stir except with the greatest of effort, when the stillness that gripped his body threatened to harden into a conscious permanence, that he struggled from the clasp of blankets and trudged the cool confines of his room. He was thankful, in those moments of struggle, for the nightlight—the glowing Mickey Mouse face Jeremy Windhook's little daughter no longer needs—that held darkness at bay. Joaquin cannot abide darkness. He has had too much of it, has experienced too intimately the concrete and imagined terrors of it. So he stalked his room in the thin glow, three paces one way, three paces the other, the scuffed boards squeaking like mice underfoot.

Stalked through the figures and effigies of nighttime evocations: the slow tearing of nails from fingers, the cracking of bone, the bite of saw-toothed metal into nipple. Liquid coursed thick and warm across his stomach. The gurgle of strangulated breath caught his throat, a blindfolded darkness pressed in on his eyes. Pain came in vivid memory, flushing hot and cold through his belly and into his chest. His hands throbbed, nipples burned—

Space: he let himself quietly out of the room, padded through the darkened corridor to the kitchen. To the tyranny of shadowed things: the fridge, the stove, the sharp angles of cupboards. The tap dripped rhythmically, maddeningly, into the aluminum sink. He tried the light, but it wouldn't work—the bulb had blown the day before and no one had bothered to change it—and so he opened the door to the little balcony, for space, for air, for escape from the demons of his mind.

Amin, satisfied, belches contentedly into his cupped palm. In the webby light the hairs on the back of his hands and fingers stand out like stiff, black bristles. He offers more coffee and Joaquin accepts with a nod of his head. Amin refills his cup, careful not to pour in too much of the sediment. He empties the grounds into the sink, rinses the pot, places it on the counter; turns on the stove and, hands clenching and unclenching in his pants-pockets, waits for the burner to redden.

From within the house float the distant stirrings of the awakening others: doors and floorboards creaking the splash of water and the tremble of old pipes, throats discreetly cleared. They are seven in all, the Magnificent Seven, as Jeremy Windhook mumbles in moments of exasperation: Joaquin, Amin, a Vietnamese couple, a Haitian, a Sikh, a Sri Lankan. Except for the Vietnamese couple — the man restless, the woman watchful, the two hard-eyed in the way of the ravenous — who spend much time walking the streets of the city, the others keep to themselves, frittering time away in newspapers, television, comic books, or the solitary flipping of cards. Joaquin prefers it this way — life has taught him that the friendliest smile may conceal the sharpest teeth — but he is secretly grateful, too, for Amin's extroversion, the ease of his conversation, the way he will begin talking as if he has been asked a question when he has not been — or as if he is anticipating the questions he may be asked and is eager to provide the answers. Amin fills empty time, provides distraction, but not in the impersonal way of the television; that is what Joaquin appreciates about him, why Joaquin will sit and listen to him, watch the graceful and communicative gestures of his hands, watch his smoke turn the air a soft blue-gray.

Amin takes a cigarette from his shirt pocket, holds the unfiltered end to the glowing element until a thin curl of smoke rises from it. Flicking off the stove, he pulls carefully at the cigarette, encouraging the fire, sucking until the end glows healthily and smoke billows from his nostrils. Sitting on the chair with an uncommon energy, he crosses his legs, looks intently at Joaquin through narrowed eyes, says, "I will tell you why Thomson."

Joaquin already knows why Amin says he will one day change his name to Thomson, but he does not interrupt, for to do so would be to disrupt Amin's optimism, his insistent planning for tomorrow; and thus to disrupt his own. And what else do they have, people like him and Amin and the Vietnamese and the Haitian, but fantasies of tomorrow, how it will be, how they will be? Besides, he likes the deliberation Amin has brought to the enterprise. It shows an initiative he wishes he himself had.

"Because no other name will do, I believe." He sucks at the cigarette held between thumb and index finger. "Canadian people respect certain names, but sometimes they fear them, too. Names of men who are rich and who are bright — maybe too bright, eh? Rich, bright men must not expect popularity in this world."

Joaquin nods in agreement. Amin speaks like a man of the world, a man who understands much beyond his circumscribed experience — and who is he, this Joaquin, electrician by profession, union organizer by necessity, to contradict him? So he listens to Amin, believes he is learning something useful.

"So Thomson it will be. Rich and bright, no doubt. But not a name that makes simple people—what is the word?—thrimble?"

Joaquin nods again. He thinks of the word *temblar*, raises a quivering hand before him.

"Yes, it is thrimble, I believe. This, the name Thomson does not do to simple people. Respect, yes, and admiration. But thrimble, no. So this is who I will be, eh? Amin Thomson, Canadian."

Joaquin smiles thinly at Amin, envies him his certainties.

Amin goes to his room to finish getting dressed. The Vietnamese couple—eyes of a hounded intelligence—come quietly in. With a challenging glare at Joaquin, they slam the balcony door shut and—an eye always on Joaquin—wolf down a couple of peanut-butter sandwiches. They are gone after only a few minutes.

The Sikh, his hair twisted into a knot on top of his head, comes in, makes coffee, and drinks it sitting across the table from Joaquin. They nod at each other, but neither speak.

Outside, the day proceeds through heavy cloud. Pigeons, soaring in the distance, present swift silhouettes.

To Joaquin, the day already feels old.

He looks at his hands, as he does at least once every day. They continue to heal. Slowly, Very slowly. They will never be as they were before, although the doctors tell him greater flexibility will return in time. He will never again hold a screwdriver or a pen—it is how they put it, confirming the expertise of those responsible—but he may, with patience, be able to type.

Jeremy Windhook, a solemn young man intent on evidence, proof, *the full story*, tells him with no hint of irony to look on the bright side. Show them your hands at the hearing, he says, keep them in plain sight, *front and centre*. They have never seen hands like yours. Let them see the fleshy cavities where once there were fingernails, let them see the knotty lumps of crushed knuckles left untended, show them the scars on the back where once flesh was sliced through to the whiteness of bone. Throw the scars at them, he says, bring home to them the enthusiasm with which your hands have been redesigned. Evidence, yes. Dramatic and irrefutable. Jeremy Windhook cannot see his hands without blanching, but it is as if he is in love with them, he speaks of them like a teenager ruminating on imminent coitus: with fascination, with fear.

And what more do you want, Mr. Lawyer? Joaquin thinks. Maybe that I sit there naked so they see the greater mutilation? The hardened welts on back, chest, buttocks?

Tell them about the whip of steel cable, he urges.

The tattoo of cigarette burns on my stomach?

Marlboros, weren't they?

The circle of ragged flesh that has replaced my left nipple?

Make them feel the bit of the sharpened pliers.

All the practiced disfigurement to which I have been subjected, Jeremy Windhook?

But no, Jeremy Windhook has had pictures taken, from every angle. His briefcase is stuffed with medical reports — the language cool and factual, menus of distress that Joaquin has seen — detailing anal violation, organ disruption, bodily dysfunction. It is amazing, Jeremy Windhook says — with fear, with fascination — that he survived.

Joaquin is relieved when, as the Sikh leaves, Amin returns. He is wearing the somber gray jacket that is the final touch to the outfit Jeremy Windhook has provided. He sits and laces up his shoes. They are of brown leather, do not match the rest of the clothes, but they are freshly shined. He has decided not to wear the tie. Ties, like nooses, make him nervous. "Do you know, Hakim — " It is Amin's name for Joaquin, his closest approximation. " — that it take thirty-five gallons of sap to make one gallon of maple syrup?"

"Sap" is not a word Joaquin knows.

"It is juice from a tree," Amin explains. "They take it the way doctors take blood. Then they boil it to make a sweet syrup. It is a Canadian delicacy, I believe."

Joaquin knows where Amin gets all this information, from his friend the secretary and from the newspapers he is always reading. He hopes that one day he, too, will acquire such knowledge.

Amin suddenly stares at him. His eyes, of a glittery and undiluted black, are steady and imploring. "You know, Hakim," he says, his voice breaking, "you know."

Joaquin nods: he knows.

"It is not too much to ask, I believe. A simple life. Khappiness. We forget to enjoy it when we have it, we let it wash over us like water — and then it is gone. If only we knew how to record it, like a film, so that we can recall it and comfort ourselves with the memory. But our brain — it is not strong enough. Khorror will come back with all its power. Khorror will frighten us many months later. But khappiness? Khappiness many months later will make us sad. This is the thing, Hakim. We, you and me, have too many prisons — " He taps at this temple with a finger. " — here." His breathing goes raucous. "We must learn how to make the keys, Hakim, for when our tomorrow comes."

If our tomorrow comes, Joaquin thinks but does not say, for he wants to believe Amin is right yet fears, too, to believe it.

The front door bell buzzes twice. Amin glances at his watch. "Jeremy Windhook," he says.

They hear the door being opened, the Haitian's gravelly voice greeting the lawyer.

Amin stands up tucking his shirt more neatly into his pants. He buttons his jacket, runs his hands through his hair. "Well?" he says.

Joaquin examines him, finds him stiff looking. He reaches out and undoes the jacket button.

Just before Amin leaves, he glances through the window at the sky. The clouds are thinning, beginning to break up.

"Look, Hakim," he says, "the sun! It is a good sign, I believe, eh?"

Joaquin stands up. He cannot speak. Instead, he offers his damaged hand and, for long seconds, they share a firm handshake.

The day advances steadily into the forecaster's prediction of bulky cloud rifting into periods of delicate sunlight. The streets are dry. Cars rumble by spouting music, tires gritty on the asphalt. A sheet of errant paper, whipped along in the wake of the traffic, rasps on the sidewalk. The air teems with sharp, clean sounds unfamiliar from his months of winter waiting.

Joaquin removes his mittens, unzips his parka, the perspiration that is like that of fever drying instantaneously under this clothes. His senses awaken then, nudged through the heaviness of his fatigue into a heightened mindfulness.

There are people all around, people hungry for the sun like prisoners emerging into a prison yard after a too-long, too-dark night. They lounge smoking on benches in snowbound parks, they haul chairs onto their tiny balconies to read or to daydream. Coats are bundled, convertibles converted, sunglasses unfolded. A man and a woman walk by, arms around each other. The woman says, "Spring's around the corner." The man, with a laugh, replies, "Yeah, but it's a big corner."

Joaquin smiles at the little joke. He is enjoying the growing lightness in his legs. He has always been sensitive to weather and is pleased—it is like a sign of a returning normalcy—to find his body reacting with such vigor. For the first time, he feels the city to be a friendly place, an entity apart—so different from the sterile and hermetic offices of officialdom that he cannot imagine the immigration officers he has encountered leading normal lives, relaxing in sidewalk cafés or hugging loved ones. He knows that they must: knows that they watch television, read newspapers, make love. But the implications of their professional functions are, to him, too enormous. Surely they must be immigration officers all the time, as doctors must be doctors all the time, or policemen policemen all the time. So it is, he thinks, so it must be with all people who wield the powers of life and death.

Soon he has left behind the snappier streets, the expensive boutiques and neon-signed cafés and renovated condominiums giving way, as he approaches St-Laurent, to stretches of run-down housing, Korean supermarkets, Portuguese restaurants. The laneways, bordered by crumbling garages, are still dense with snow and dirty ice. Two men in bloodstained lab coats—like morgue attendants, he thinks, clearing the site of a vigorous massacre—unload slabs of fresh-cut meat from a delivery van, while a young boy, attention wandering, sprays a jet of water at the sidewalk.

He turns right at St-Laurent—which Jeremy Windhook calls Saint Lawrence—and walks hurriedly up its length, the crowds here denser, more intent on their business; past the cut-rate stores and dark restaurants, the specialty-food shops and the sex cinema, turning off at last into a quieter street of curtained windows and peeling doors and, quickly, in a movement that feels furtive, into the shadowed cocoon of *La Barricada*.

Miguel, ever watchful, spots him the moment he enters, nods to him, his eyes only slowly losing their suspicion. Satisfied, he puts the beer flute down on the counter and turns away, to prepare, Joaquin knows, two glasses of his spiced coffee.

Miguel keeps his eyes open; is owner, bartender, cook, and watchman all rolled into one. He has installed a bell that warns him when the door is opening; looks for grim men in jackets and ties with badges to flash. They have never come, but all the regulars know that, should Miguel break the beer flute, those who must are to use the door to the second floor in the common washroom while the others, feigning fear, create diversion by heading for the rear exit. It is not a perfect system, but it is a system; it offers a fighting chance—and that, Joaquin appreciates, is all that anyone truly wants.

It is a curious place, small, with whitewashed walls and fake beams overhead, bits and pieces of his country, his continent, scattered around. Baskets hang from the ceiling, shawls cling to the walls, drums and Pan flutes dangle from crooked nails. Travel posters show Andean heights, Machu Picchu, the modernistic sterility of Brasilia. Quietly, as if wafting in from a great distance, the sad music of the mountains lingers just out of reach, a fading memory even before you can seize it.

On one wall, someone has painted lace curtains framing an open window. Through it stretches a field of trimmed grass, trees, flowers, and, in the distance, stark against a perfect and unreal sky, a line of women colourfully unsettling but strangely lifeless. Joaquin finds it a profoundly unsettling work, a vision of a rural paradise in which humans are trespassers. A beautiful and angry work, a work of despair. He sits always with his back to it.

Miguel brings the coffees over, the empty beer flute balanced between them; sits in front of Joaquin with elbows on the table, chin resting on his interlaced fingers. He is a handsome man, his curly black hair, infrequently cut, generously sprinkled with silver. He sleeps little, always looks tired; tends *La Barricada* until late at night, then works into the early hours of morning at the jewellery he fashions as a lucrative hobby. It is these bracelets and earrings and intricate necklaces of silver that keep *La Barricada* afloat; he wholesales them to jewellery shops on St-Denis, enters the profits into the café's books as dinners served and coffees consumed. He sips at the coffee, licks his lips. "You heard about Flavio?" he says in a flat voice.

Joaquin thinks of the sad-eyed young man he's often seen sitting by himself in a corner of the café. Remembers his discomfort at Flavio's hermetic absorption.

The truth is that Joaquin would not come here if he felt he had a choice. The furniture, of worn wood, is too decrepit, lends the place a dismal air, emphasizes somehow its sense of spirit broken into timidity. It is like a closet for the soul, built for containing dusty memories of lives long lost, for perpetuating the resentments of politics long past. Here, he thinks, there is no tomorrow; here, yesterday becomes forever.

"They're sending him back."

Back—a fearful word.

Yet where else is he to go? A chic café on St-Denis? A glitzy bar on Ste-Catherine? He's tried doing both, but in each everyone—or, at least, so it seemed—noticed his hands. Here, too, they are taken note of, but the response is not of questions or queasiness. No, here his hands are accepted as simply part of the universal damage; they evoke no shy curiosity, no willed sympathy, no embarrassed revulsion. Everyone either has endured more or knows of someone who had. And everyone has loved ones who have been, as Miguel says, "thrown through the Devil's Doorway." It is why he is drawn to *La Barricada*, why he feels safer here than anywhere else.

"They say he wasn't involved in enough union activity."

Enough—what is enough?

"Not enough to endanger his life."

Joaquin shivers, twice.

More reason for discomfort: in the corner where Flavio sat, a young woman, Teresa, whom everyone calls Tere, sits biting her nails, or rather not her nails—they are too eaten down for that—but the flesh around them. Joaquin has seen the blood on her fingertips. Miguel has told him Tere's story. They had their Canadian papers, Tere, her husband, and their two children; but on the night before their departure, with their farewell party in full swing, the door burst open. There were scuffles and screams, a brief burst of machinegun fire; and her husband was gone. Embassy officials reacted quickly; saw Tere and the children safely on the plane north, lodged a protest with the government, and demanded that a search be launched for her husband. But they knew—Tere knew—that all the official steps were just a cruel bureaucratic joke.

So Tere arrived, distraught, with the bewildered children; was met by a social worker who took her to a furnished apartment, left her there with mimed instructions—Tere spoke no English, the social worker no Spanish—that she was to prepare dinner for the children. The social worker returned an hour later, to find the apartment thick with smoke and the legs from two of the dining-room chairs smoldering in a cooking fire in the middle of the living room. Someone thought of calling Miguel, and it was up to him to tell Tere, two days later, that her husband had been found shown through the Devil's Doorway. They had identified him by his ring and clothes; it was all they had to go on, considering the condition of his head and fingers.

Miguel made arrangements. A woman he knew in the community looks after the children while Tere attends English classes or, as she has taken more and more to doing, while she comes here to *La Barricada*. It has been six months, and Miguel doesn't have the heart to force her to do what he knows she should be doing. She is torn, Miguel has told him, between returning to her country, where she still has family, and staying here, where her children have a future. She is, Miguel feels, herself seeing the outlines of the Devil's Doorway through the writhing of her demons.

Miguel says, "If Canada will not give Flavio a visa, then God will." Miguel is, in a curious and personal way, a religious man. He can, for hours and with feeling, quote the poetry of the Nicaraguan Cardenal.

Three men huddle in another corner. Two of them are crouched over the hand of the third who sits bolt upright in the chair, eyes shut, lips grimly set. On the table beside them are a box of bandages, a roll of cotton wadding, a bottle of rubbing alcohol, a pair of scissors, and an open package of razor blades.

With a twist of his eyebrows, Joaquin asks Miguel what they are up to.

"Medical care." Francisco, he explains, cut his hand badly at work a couple of weeks before. He was washing dishes, a glass broke. He had no choice but to go to Emergency. When they asked him for his medical insurance card, he said he's forgotten it at home. They sewed up the cut, and warned him to bring the card the next time, when he went to have the stitches removed. Francisco was already paying fifty dollars a week to use someone else's social insurance number, and the man wanted two hundred for use of the medical card. Francisco couldn't afford it, so his friends — one a hospital orderly — were removing the stitches for him. The nightmare, Miguel adds, is if an appendix bursts ....

In the corner, Francisco draws a sharp and lengthy breath.

Joaquin thinks: just another day at *La Barricada*. He knows, and appreciates, that he is among the least damaged, least desperate of Miguel's clients. It is maybe, in the end, why he continues to come here, not just for himself but for Miguel, too.

Miguel prepares lunch for everyone, cheese sandwiches with sticks of carrot. Tere remains at her table, nibbles at the food. Francisco's friends have to leave and Francisco, his right hand roughly bandaged, joins Joaquin and Miguel.

As they eat, Francisco complains about the man whose social insurance number he is using. He is a blackmailer, he says, this man who seemed so sympathetic at the beginning. Even though Francisco has not been able to work for two weeks, the man continues to demand his weekly money, is threatening to tip off Immigration if he is not paid in full.

"Who is this man?" Miguel asks.

"Just a man," Francisco replies.

Joaquin, eating, listening, appreciates Francisco's reticence, understands it. He knows — from the moment his mother's phone call reached him late at work; through the hours? Days? Of darkness to the unexplained release, followed by the harrowing weeks of movement and concealment during the transit north — what it is to be an illegal, understands the fears that lead to continuous vagueness and, eventually, to an invented self. He wonders what Francisco's real name is and for several minutes, as Francisco and Miguel dissect the situation, he tries different names, looking for the one that best matches Francisco's face. It is a haggard face, older than its years, severely scarred by acne; a face that Joaquin could only learn to trust in time. He is neither a Juan nor an Antonio, Joaquin decides, nor a Raul nor an Andres. Luis is too soft, Carlos too round. Alberto, Federico, Mario, Manuel — none quite fits. And then, as he finishes the first half of his sandwich, it comes to him: Francisco has the face of a Jorge.

Jorge. The name echoes in his head, the consonants a harsh whisper. His hands begin to throb and he is forced to drop the carrot stick he has picked up. Francisco and Miguel glance quizzically at him, but return to their conversation after he forces a smile. He tries clenching his hands in his lap — their stiffness prevents the forming of a fist, he can squeeze only so far — but the pain he feels is not a physical one, will not go away so easily.

The pliers, Jorge. No, not those. The smaller ones.

It was his mother who came to him in those moments of searing pain, her teary face alternating with a darkness deeper than that of the blindfold.

You see how he clenches his fist, Jorge. He knows what we want to do, don't you, friend?

A face ageing instantaneously at the news of a daughter's dismemberment. A darkness sparkling with comets and exploding stars.

Any sharp knife will do. You just pull it down, from the wrist towards the fingers. See? Everything opens up. Including the fist.

Dark hairs graying before his eyes. The darkness growing brittle.

You put the pliers just so, getting a tight grip. If he's a nail-biter you have to push it into the flesh, but we're lucky with this one, he's not the nervous type, are you my friend? So you work it as you wish, a quick tug —

Face dissolving. Darkness shattering.

— *or a slow twist, ripping it away* —

Colours, and a roaring in the head.

— either way is effective.

Then only the face, smiling a soothing smile.

Jorge.

A long silence. Then —

Miguel: "Ten minutes?"

Francisco: "At least."

"Maybe a problem with the stomach — "

"Fifteen, even."

"That long?"

"Maybe longer — "

"Joaquin?"

"Yes — "

"Well? Ten, fifteen, longer?"

"Yes, possibly."

Miguel's eyes flicker at him — an annoyed, inquisitive look, a look that in an instant realizes, absorbs, questions Joaquin's distance — then focus on a point past him.

Joaquin turns: a plate with an untouched sandwich, an empty chair pushed back from its table. He realizes how distant he has been, he never noticed Tere leaving.

Miguel considers the chair, the nail of his little finger working at a piece of food stuck between his front teeth.

Francisco drains his beer, draws the back of his hand across his lips. He, too, but with less intensity, considers the empty chair. "So," he says.

"So," Miguel echoes.

Joaquin looks from one to the other. His hands, forgotten, relax in his lap, the pain ebbing.

Miguel dislodges the piece of food, flicks it to the floor. Abruptly pushes himself from the table. The beer flute tips, teeters, crashes onto the tabletop. He frowns at the pieces of broken glass. And then he is running, knocking chairs out of his way.

Blows of his fist on echoing wood.

Joaquin turns, to look.

Miguel is kicking in the bathroom door.

The stickiness that will not wash away from his hands dries quickly in the cold air.

The sidewalks are less crowded now, the streets busy with homebound traffic. The sky, in the glow of the setting sun, is a brittle, icy blue.

Joaquin walks slowly along with his hands secure in his coat pockets, the air washing cool and fresh through his lungs. He feels good, strong; enjoys a physical self-possession too long absent.

On impulse, he stops in at a fruit and vegetable store, buys a couple of oranges. The woman smiles as she hands him his change, and he realizes with a gentle jolt that he feels less distant from these people now, strangers become a little less strange not through any act of their own but—in a twist he cannot understand—through an act of *his* own: in this city, he has helped save a life.

It was his fingers, useless for so much, that Miguel pressed to the cuts on Tere's wrists, his parka snatched from the back of his chair that Francisco threw around her shoulders. Miguel and Francisco, faces glistening with sweat, fingers nimble and efficient, worked quickly with the cotton wadding and bandages.

Tere didn't fight, sat flaccid on the toilet cover, glazed eyes passively watching them. She had rested her hands on the edge of the sink but, growing weaker, hadn't been able to hold them there. The tiled floor was slick with blood.

Francisco's bandage came loose. Joaquin saw the fragile blending of the wound, pinpricks of blood forming on the pulpy skin. Francisco ignored it in the greater urgency, and Joaquin thought with a prickling shame of his judgment of him. This intensity, this urge to heal: he was wrong: Francisco was not a Jorge, he just had a misleading face.

Afterwards, Tere begged them in a voice weakened and fearful not to abandon her to the hospital. Her verb struck them all, prompted among them glances of uncertainty. They had stanched the blood flow and Miguel, soothing, reassuring, murmured his assent. While Francisco disinfected and re-bandaged his own wound, Joaquin and Miguel helped her upstairs, to the bare room in which those who had to could take refuge. She curled up on a mattress on the floor, one hand resting lightly in the other. Miguel gently checked her bandages and, glancing backwards at her, led Joaquin from the room back down the narrow stairs. He would keep her there, he said, would make the necessary arrangements for the children.

Miguel cleared away the broken glass, poured them each a beer. They drank in silence, absorbed. *La Barricada* seemed to have gone inert. The music was off, there was nothing to say.

Eventually, with nothing more than a nod, Francisco left. Joaquin put aside his unfinished glass of beer, offered to help Miguel clean up the bathroom. Miguel refused with a shake of his head; he seemed, in the aftermath, to have no defense against his fatigue; said he would close the place for a few hours, work at his jewellery.

Joaquin walks along, the oranges tucked into the belly of his half-zipped parka. He is not unhappy that Miguel refused his offer. He did not, in truth, relish the thought of returning to the washroom. Much prefers being out here on the sidewalk, in the grip of his sense of having taken a vital step, looking in on the bars and cafés and little restaurants moodily lit behind glass, at the warmth and suggested security of their growing animation.

He lengthens the way back to the house, following streets never before followed, turning left or right or retracing his steps on pure impulse. As the sky darkens into night, windows frame lamplit scenes of comfort and domesticity: a couple preparing a salad; two children tugging at a toy; a man absentmindedly twirling a glass of red wine by candlelight; a woman shuffling through papers in her briefcase. Joaquin drinks them in, these little domestic spectacles; they are so trivial, so inconsequential, so attractive in their banality. And as he watches a cat prancing in pleasure at the opening of a food can, Amin's words come forcefully back to him: *A simple life. Khappiness.*

A faint throb in his hands: Is it too much to ask?

In the sitting room, the radio is on low in the background. The Haitian and the Sri Lankan, both slight, shy men, are hunched over the coffee table playing cards. They glance up without interest as Joaquin comes in, watch without acknowledgement as he removes his parka.

He wonders whether Amin has returned yet, but thinks it best not to ask. It would be like prying, would be frowned upon.

In the kitchen, the Vietnamese couple stands guard over a vigorously bubbling pot. They do not take kindly to his looking in so he goes to his room, puts on the overhead light, and sits on the edge of the bed. His mood, seized in the peculiar tensions of the house, robbed of air by the confines of the room, begins to evaporate. A familiar unease reasserts itself, a vice tightening in his intestines. He takes an orange, nips of chunks of the rind, chews them, the tanginess puckering the fleshy insides of his mouth, invading his nasal passages. It is not a pleasant taste, but is one he has grown to appreciate: for a week during his journey north, fresh oranges were his only sustenance: there was no part he could afford not to consume. The flavor calms him and he closes his eyes, returning in imagination to the scenes witnessed long minutes before. The salad, the toy, the wine glass. The cat circling in hungry anticipation—

The buzz of the doorbell jars him back to his room. He listens: the front door is opened, voices murmur.

Careful footsteps approach his door. He thinks: Amin. Drops the orange onto the bed, stands up, opens the door at the first knock.

No, not Amin. Jeremy Windhook. A jacket is draped over his arm. "For tomorrow," Jeremy Windhook says, holding the jacket out to him. "Eight a.m. sharp. Be ready."

Joaquin takes the jacket, recognizes it. "And Amin?" he says.

Jeremy Windhook hesitates. Then: "Amin was refused."

"Refused?"

"They've classified him an economic refugee."

"*No entiendo.*" Joaquin thinks: Are you less a refugee, Jeremy Windhook, if you are in danger of dying from hunger rather than a bullet?

"He doesn't qualify under the UN definition. He'll be deported tomorrow."

"To his country?"

"To Germany."

"Germany? Why Germany?"

"Because he made his way here from there."

"But if they say he is no danger in his own country, why do they not send him back there?"

"Because—" He shakes his head. "Because it's the rule."

"Why, Jeremy Windhook? Tell me why."

"I don't know why."

"Is it so that another country will do the dirty work for them? The Germans will send him back to his own country, I believe." As he says the last words, Joaquin hears Amin's voice. "And he will die."

Jeremy Windhook says nothing in reply, silently eyes Joaquin.

"You can do nothing?"

"Nothing."

The words hang hollow in the room.

Jeremy Windhook turns, leaves.

Joaquin tosses the jacket onto the bed. He sees Amin in a room he cannot imagine. He is sitting, his face in his hands, in despair: "Amin Thomson," he whispers. "My name is Amin Thomson." Joaquin swallows hard, wipes his eyes on his sleeve. Picks up the orange and makes his way to the kitchen.

The light is off. All that remains of the Vietnamese is the lingering odour of their dinner. He goes to the door, stands, looks out. His hands throb, and he watches for the pigeons, waits for the dawn, here on the eve of his uncertain tomorrows.

SHANI MOOTOO

A GARDEN OF HER OWN

FROM OUT ON MAIN STREET AND OTHER STORIES

A north-facing balcony meant that no sunlight would enter there. A deep-in-the-heart-of-the-forest green pine tree, over-fertilized opulence extending its midriff, filled the view from the balcony.

There was no window, only a glass sliding door which might have let fresh air in and released second- or third-hand air and the kinds of odours that build phantoms in stuffy apartments. But it remained shut. Not locked, but stuck shut from decades of other renters' black, oily grime which had collected in the grooves of the sliding door's frame.

Vijai knew that it would not budge up, down, or sideways. For the amount of rent the husband paid for this bachelor apartment, the landlord could not be bothered. She opened the hallway door to let the cooking lamb fat and garlic smells drift out into the hallway. She did not want them to burrow into the bed sheets, into towels and clothes crammed into the dented cream-coloured metal space-saver cupboards that she had to share with the husband. It was what all the other renters did too; everyone's years of oil—sticky, burnt, over-used, rancid oil—and of garlic, onions, and spices formed themselves into an impenetrable nose singeing, skin-stinging presence that lurked menacingly in the hall. Instead of releasing the lamb from the husband's apartment, opening the door allowed this larger phantom to barge its way in.

Vijai engulfed, slammed the door shut. She tilted her head to face the ceiling and breathed in hard, searching for air that had no smell, no weight. The husband was already an hour late for dinner. She paced the twelve strides, back and forth, from the balcony door to the hall door, glancing occasionally at the two table settings, stopping to straighten his knife, his fork, the napkin, the flowers, his knife, his fork, the napkin, the flowers.

Her arms and legs tingled weakly and her intestines filled up with beads of acid formed out of unease and fear. Seeing a smear of her fingerprint on the husband's knife, she picked it up and polished it on her T-shirt until it gleamed brilliantly, and she saw in it her mother's eyes looking back at her.

Sunlight. I miss the sunlight—yellow light and a sky ceiling miles high. Here the sky sits on my head, heavy gray with snow and freezing rain. I miss being able to have doors and windows opened wide, never shut except sometimes in the rainy season. Rain, rain, pinging on, winging off the galvanized tin roof. But always warm rain. No matter how much it rained, it was always warm.

And what about the birds? Flying in through the windows how often? Two, three times a week? Sometimes even twice in a single day. In the shimmering heat you could see them flying slowly, their mouths wide open as if crying out soundlessly. They would actually be flickering their tongues at the still air, gulping and panting, looking for a window to enter and a curtain rod to land on to cool off. But once they had cooled off and were ready to fly off again, they could never seem to focus on the window to fly through and they would bang themselves against the wall and the light shade until they fell, panicked and stunned. I was the one who would get the broom and push it gently up toward one of these birds after it looked like it had cooled off, and prod, prod, prod until it hopped onto the broom and then I would lower it and reach from behind and cup the trembling in my hand. I can, right now, feel the life, the heat in the palm of my hand from the little body, and the fright in its tremble. I would want to hold on to it, even think of placing it in a cage and looking after it, but something always held me back. I would put my mouth close to its ears and whisper calming shh shh shhhhs, and then take it, pressed to my chest, out the back door and open my hand and wait for it to take its time fluffing out right there in my open hand before flying away.

But here? There are hardly any birds here, only that raucous, aggressive old crow that behaves as if it owns the scraggly pine tree it sits in across the street. This street is so noisy! Every day, all day and all night long, even on Sundays, cars whiz by, ambulances and fire trucks pass screaming, and I think to myself thank goodness it couldn't be going for anyone I know. I don't know anyone nearby.

Too much quiet here, too shut off. Not even the sound of children playing in the street, or the sound of neighbours talking to each other over fences, conversations floating in through open windows, open bricks. Here even when doors are open people walk down hallways with their noses straight ahead, making a point of not glancing to even nod hello.

Oh! This brings all kinds of images to my mind: the coconut tree outside my bedroom brushing, scraping, swishing against the wall. Green-blue iridescent lizards clinging, upside down, to the ceiling above my bed.

And dinnertime. Mama's voice would find wherever I was. "Vijai, go and tell Cheryl to put food on the table, yuh father comin home just now." Standing in one place, at the top of her meagre voice she would call us one by one: "Bindra, is dinner time. Bindra, why you so harden, boy? Dinner gettin cold. Turn off that TV right now! Shanti, come girl, leave what you doin and come and eat. Vashti, go and tell Papa dinner ready, and then you come and sit down." Sitting down, eating together. Talking together. Conversations with no boundaries, no false politeness, no need to impress Mama and Papa.

But that's not how it was always. Sometimes Papa didn't come home till long after suppertime. Mama would make us eat but she would wait for him. Sometimes he wouldn't come for days, and she would wait for him then too.

But there were always flowers from the garden on the table. Pink and yellow gerberas, ferns, ginger lilies. That was your happiness, eh Mama? The garden, eh? And when there were blossoms you and I would go outside together. You showed me how to angle the garden scissors so that the plant wouldn't hurt for too long. We would bring in the bundle of flowers and greenery with their fresh-cut garden smell and little flying bugs and spiders, and you would show me how to arrange them for a centrepiece or a corner table or a floor piece. The place would look so pretty! Thanks for showing that to me, Mama.

Mama, he's never brought me any flowers. Not even a dandelion.

I don't want him to ask how much these cost. Don't ask me who sent them. No one sent them; I bought them myself. With my own money. My own money.

He's never given me anything. Only money for groceries.

Late. Again.

I jabbed this lamb with a trillion little gashes and stuffed a clove of garlic in each one with your tongue, your taste buds in mind. I spent half the day cooking this meal and you will come late and eat it after the juices have hardened to a candle-wax finish, as if it were nothing but a microwave dinner.

I want a microwave oven.

Mama, why did you wait to eat? If I were to eat now would you, Papa, he think I am a bad wife? Why did you show me this, Mama?

I must not nag.

Vijai remained sleeping until the fan in the bathroom woke her. It sputtered raucously, like an airplane engine starting up, escalating in time to fine whizzing, lifting off into the distance.

Five-thirty, Saturday morning.

She had fretted through most of the night, twisting, arching her body, rolling, and nudging him, hoping that he would awaken to pull her body into his and hold her there. She wanted to feel the heat of his body along the length of hers, his arms pressing her to him. Or his palm placed flat on her lower belly, massaging, touching her. He responded to her fidgeting once and she moved closer to him to encourage him, but he turned his naked back to her and continued his guttural exhaling, inhaling, sounding exactly like her father.

Eventually Vijai's eyes, burning from salty tears that had spilled and dampened the pillow under her cheek, fluttered shut and she slept, deep and dreamless, until the fan awakened her.

When the sound of the shower water snapping at the enamel tub was muffled against his body, she pulled herself over to lie in and smell his indentation in the tired foam mattress. She inhaled, instead, the history of the mattress: unwashed hair, dying skin, old and rancid sweat—not the smell she wanted to nestle in. Neither would the indentation cradle her, she could feel the protruding shape of the box-spring beneath the foam.

She debated whether to get up and thanklessly make his toast and tea, or pretend not to have awakened, the potential for blame nagging at her.

She slid back to her side of his bed, the other side of the line that he had drawn down the middle with the cutting edge of his outstretched hand. Vijai pulled her knees to her chest and hugged them. When the shower stopped she hastily straightened herself out and put her face inside the crack between the bed and the rough wall. Cold from the wall transferred itself onto her cheek, and layers upon layers of human smells trapped behind cream-coloured paint pierced her nostrils.

Vijai was aware of the husband's every move as she lay in his bed. Water from the kitchen tap pounded the sink basin, then attacked the metal floor of the kettle, gradually becoming muffled and high-pitched as the kettle filled up. He always filled it much more than was necessary for one cup of tea, which he seldom drank. The blow dryer. First on the highest setting, then dropped two notches to the lowest, and off. The electric razor. Whizzing up and down his cheek, circling his chin, the other cheek, grazing his neck. Snip, snip and little dark half-moon hairs from his nostrils and his sideburns cling to the rim of the white sink basin. Wiping up, scrubbing, making spotless these areas, and others, before he returns, are her evidence that she is diligent, that she is, indeed, her mother's daughter.

At this point in the routine she always expects a handsome aftershave cologne to fill the little bachelor apartment, to bring a moment of frivolity and romance into the room. In one favourite version of her memories, this is what normally happened in her parents' bedroom at precisely this point. But the husband would only pat on his face a stinging watery liquid with the faintest smell of lime, a smell that evaporated into nothingness the instant it touched his skin.

She held herself tensely, still in the crack between the bed and the wall, as he made his way into the dark corner that he called the bedroom. The folding doors of the closet squeaked open. A shirt slid off a hanger, leaving it dangling and tinkling against the metal rod. Vijai heard the shirt that she had ironed (stretched mercilessly tight across the ironing board, the tip of the iron with staccato spurts of steam sniffing out the crevice of every seam, mimicking the importance with which her mother had treated this task) being pulled against his body and his hands sliding down the stiff front as he buttoned it.

Then there was a space empty of his sounds. The silence made the walls of her stomach contract like a closed-up accordion. Her body remained rigid. Her heart sounded as if it had moved right up into her ears, thundering methodically, and that was all that she could hear. She struggled with herself to be calm so that she could know where he was and what he was doing. Not knowing made her scalp want to unpeel itself. Then, the bed sagged as he kneeled on it, leaning across and brushed his mouth on the back of her head. His full voice had no regard for her sleep or the time of morning. He said, "Happy Birthday. I left twenty dollars on the table for you. Buy yourself a present."

The thundering subsided and her heart rolled and slid, rolled and slid, down, low down, and came to rest between her thighs. She turned over with lethargic elegance, as if she were just waking up, stretching out her back like a cat, but the apartment door was already being shut and locked from the outside.

The streets here are so wide! I hold my breath as I walk across them, six lanes wide. What if the light changes before I get to the other side? You have to walk so briskly, not only when you're crossing a wide street but even on the sidewalk. Otherwise people pass you and then turn back and stare at you, shaking their heads. And yet I remember Mama telling us that fast walking, hurrying was very unladylike.

I yearn for friends. My own friends, not his, but I'm afraid to smile at strangers. So often we huddled up in Mama's big bed and read the newspapers about things that happened to women up here — we read about women who suddenly disappeared and months later their corpses would be found, having been raped and dumped. And we also read about serial murders. The victims were almost always women who had been abducted from the street by strangers in some big North American city. Mama and Papa warned me, when I was leaving to come up here, not to make eye contact with strangers because I wouldn't know whose eyes I might be looking into or what I was encouraging, unknowingly. It's not like home, they said, where everybody knows everybody.

No bird sounds — there are not quite so many different kinds of birds here. Yes, Papa, yes, I can just hear you saying to stop this nonsense, all this thinking about home, that I must think of here as my home now, but I haven't yet left you and Mama. I know now that I will never fully leave, nor will I ever truly be here. You felt so close, Papa, when you phoned this morning and asked like you have every past year, how was the birthday girl. You said that in your office you often look at the calendar pictures of autumn fields of bales of hay, lazy rivers meandering near brick-red farmhouses, and country roads with quaint white wooden churches with red steeples, and you think that that's what my eyes have already enjoyed.

"It's all so beautiful, Papa," I said, and knowing you, you probably heard what I wasn't saying. Thanks for not pushing further. I couldn't tell you that he is working night and day to "make it," to "get ahead," to live like the other men he works with. That he is always thinking about this, and everything else is frivolous right now, so we haven't yet been for that drive in the country to see the pictures in the calendars pinned on the wall above your desk. He doesn't have time for dreaming, but I must dream or else I find it difficult to breathe.

At home the fence around our house and the garden was the furthest point that I ever went to on my own. From the house, winding in and out of the dracaenas and the philodendrons that I planted with Mama many Julys ago, feeling the full, firm limbs of the poui, going as far as the hibiscus and jasmine fence, and back into the house again. Any further away from the house than that and the chauffeur would be driving us! And now? Just look at me! I am out in a big city on my own. I wish you all could see me. I wish we could be doing this together.

Papa, you remember, don't you, when you used to bring home magazines from your office and I would flip through them quickly looking for full-page pictures of dense black-green tropical mountains, or snow-covered bluish-white ones? Ever since those first pictures I have dreamt of mountains, of touching them with the palms of my hands, of bicycling in them, and of hiking. Even though I never canoed on a river or a big lake with no shores, I know what it must feel like! I can feel what it is to ride rapids like they do in *National Geographic* magazines. Cold river spray and drenchings, sliding, tossing, crashing! I still dream of bicycling across a huge continent. I used to think, if only I lived in North America! But here I am, in this place where these things are supposed to happen, in the midst of so much possibility, and for some reason my dreams seem even further away, just out of reach. It's just not quite as simple as being here.

This lands stretches on in front of me, behind me and forever. My back feels exposed, naked, so much land behind, and no fence ahead.

Except that I must cook dinner tonight.

What if I just kept walking and never returned! I could walk far away, to another province, change my name, cut my hair. After a while I would see my face on a poster in a grocery store, along with all the other missing persons. The problem is that then I wouldn't even be able to phone home and speak with Mama or Papa or Bindra and Vashti without being tracked and caught, and then who knows what.

Well, this is the first birthday I've ever spent alone. But next time we speak on the phone I will be able to tell you that I went for a very long walk. Alone.

I think I will do this every day—well, maybe every other day, and each time I will go a new route and a little further. I will know this place in order to own it, but still I will never really leave you.

Mama, Papa, Vashti, Bindra, Shanti,

Mama, Papa, Vashti, Bindra, Shanti.

Mama, Papa, Vashti, Bindra, Shanti.

Twenty-four years of Sundays, of eating three delightfully noisy, lengthy meals together, going to the beach or for long drives with big pots of rice, chicken and peas, and chocolate cake, singing "Michael Row Your Boat Ashore," and "You Are My Sunshine," doing everything in tandem with her brother and sisters and Mama and Papa. This particular characteristic of Sundays was etched deeply in her veins. (Not all Sundays were happy ones but recently she seems to have forgotten that.)

It would be her twenty-fourth Sunday here, the twenty-fourth week of marriage.

The only Sunday since the marriage that the husband had taken off and spent in his apartment was six weeks ago, and since he needed to spend that day alone Vijai agreed to go to the library for at least three hours. Before she left the house she thought she would use the opportunity to take down recipes for desserts, but once she began walking down the street she found herself thinking about rivers and mountains. She bypassed the shelves with all the cooking books and home-making magazines and found herself racing toward valleys, glaciers, canoeing, rapids and the like. She picked up a magazine about hiking and mountaineering, looking at the equipment advertisements, read incomprehensible jargon about techniques for climbing.

After about forty minutes, not seeing herself in any of the magazines, she became less enthusiastic, and eventually frustrated and bored. She looked at her watch every fifteen minutes or so and then she started watching the second hand go around and counting each and every second in her head. When three hours had passed she remembered that she had said at least three hours, and she walked home slowly, stopping to window-shop and checking her watch until an extra twenty minutes had passed.

The strength of her determination that they not spend this Sunday apart warded off even a hint of such a suggestion from the husband. What she really wanted to do was to go for the long drive up to a glacier in the nearby mountains. That way she would have him to herself for at least five hours. But he had worked several twelve-hour shifts that week and needed to rest in his apartment.

She went to the grocery store, to the gardening section, and bought half a dozen packages of flower seeds, half a dozen packages of vegetable seeds, bags of soil, fertilizer, a fork and spade, a purple plastic watering can, and a score of nursery trays. She brought it all home in a taxi. Enough to keep her busy and in his apartment for an entire Sunday. She was becoming adept at finding ways to get what she wanted.

He never asked and Vijai did not tell that from her allowance she had paid a man from the hardware store to come over and fix the balcony sliding door. She stooped on the balcony floor scooping earth into nursery trays. He sat reading the newspaper, facing the balcony in his big sagging gold armchair that he had bought next-door at a church basement sale for five dollars. She was aware that he was stealing glances at her as she bent over her garden-in-the-making.

I wore this shirt, no bra, am stooping, bending over here to reveal my breasts to you. *Look at them! Feel something!*

I might as well be sharing this apartment with a brother, or a roommate.

She feels his hands on her waist, leading her from behind to the edge of his bed. Her body is crushed under his as he slams himself against her, from behind, grunting. She holds her breath, taut against his weight and the pain, but she will not disturb his moment. She hopes that the next moment will be hers. She waits with the bed sheet pulled up to her chin. The toilet flushes and, shortly after, she hears newspaper pages being turned in the sagging five-dollar gold armchair.

Later, deep-sleep breathing and low snoring from the bedroom fills the apartment, dictating her movements. She sits on the green-and-yellow shag carpet, leaning against the foot of the husband's armchair, in front of the snowy black-and-white television watching a French station turned down low enough not to awaken him. Something about listening to a language that she does not understand comforts her, gives her companionship in a place where she feels like a foreigner. She is beginning to be able to repeat advertisements in French.

MARIA CAMPBELL

JACOB

FROM STORIES OF THE ROAD ALLOWANCE PEOPLE

Mistupuch he was my granmudder.
He come from Muskeg
dat was before he was a reservation.
My granmudder he was about twenty-eight when he
marry my granfawder.
Dat was real ole for a woman to marry in dem days
but he was an Indian doctor
I guess dats why he wait so long.

Ooh he was a good doctor too
All the peoples dey say dat about him.
He doctor everybody dat come to him
an he birt all dah babies too.
Just about everybody my age
my granmudder he birt dem.

He marry my granfawder around 1890.
Dat old man he come to him for doctoring
and when he get better
he never leave him again.

Dey get married dah Indian way
an after dat my granfawder
he help him with all hees doctoring.
Dats dah way he use to be a long time ago.
If dah woman he work

den dah man he help him an if dah man he work
dah woman he help.
You never heerd peoples fighting over whose job he was
dey all know what dey got to do to stay alive.

My granfawder his name he was Kannap
but dah whitemans dey call him Jim Boy
so hees Indian name he gets los.
Dats why we don know who his people dey are.
We los lots of our relations like dat.
Dey get dah whitemans name
den no body
he knows who his peoples dey are anymore.

Sometimes me
I think dat dah reason why we have such a hard time
us peoples.
Our roots dey gets broken so many times.
Hees hard to be strong you know
when you don got far to look back for help.

Dah whitemans
he can look back thousands of years
cause him
he write everything down.
But us peoples
we use dah membering
an we pass it on by telling stories an singing songs.
Sometimes we even dance dah membering.

But all dis trouble you know
he start after we get dah new names
cause wit dah new names
he come a new language an a new way of living.
Once a long time ago
I could'ave told you dah story of my granfawder Kannap
an all his peoples but no more.
All I can tell you now
is about Jim Boy
an hees story hees not very ole.

Well my granmudder Mistupuch
he never gets a whiteman name an him
he knowed lots of stories.
Dat ole lady
he even knowed dah songs.
He always use to tell me
one about an ole man call Jacob.

Dat old man you know
he don live to far from here.
Well hees gone now
but dis story he was about him when he was alive.
Jacob him
he gets one of dem new names when dey put him in dah
residential school.
He was jus a small boy when he go
an he don come home for twelve years.

Twelve years!
Dats a long time to be gone from your peoples.
He can come home you know
cause dah school he was damn near two hundred miles
away.
His Mommy and Daddy dey can go and see him
cause deres no road in dem days
an dah Indians dey don gots many horses
'specially to travel dat far.

Dats true you know
not many peoples in dem days dey have horses.
Its only in dah comic books an dah picture shows dey
gots lots of horses.
He was never like dat in dah real life.

Well Jacob him
he stay in dat school all dem years an when he come
home he was a man.
While he was gone
his Mommy and Daddy dey die so he gots nobody.
And on top of dat

nobody he knowed him cause he gots a new name.
My granmudder
he say dat ole man he have a hell of time.
No body he can understand dat
unless he happen to him.

Dem peoples dat go away to dem schools
an come back you know dey really suffer.
No matter how many stories we tell
we'll never be able to tell
what dem schools dey done to dah peoples
an all dere relations.

Well anyways
Jacob he was just plain pitiful
He can talk his own language
He don know how to live in dah bush.
It's a good ting da peoples dey was kine
cause dey help him dah very bes dey can.
Well a couple of summers later
he meets dis girl
an dey gets married.

Dat girl he was kine
an real smart too.
He teach Jacob how to make an Indian living.

Dey have a good life togedder an after a few years
dey have a boy.
Not long after dat
dey raise two little girls dat was orphans.

Jacob and his wife dey was good peoples
Boat of dem dey was hard working
an all dah peoples
dey respec dem an dey come to Jacob for advice.

But dah good times dey was too good to las
cause one day
dah Preeses

dey comes to dah village with dah policemans.
Dey come to take dah kids to dah school.

When dey get to Jacob hees house
he tell dem dey can take his kids.

Dah Prees he tell him
he have to lets dem go cause dats the law.
Well dah Prees
he have a big book
an dat book he gots dah names
of all dah kids
an who dey belongs to.

He open dat book an ask Jacob for his name
an den he look it up.
"Jacob" he say
"you know better you went to dah school an you know
dah edjication hees important."

My granmudder Mistupuch
he say Jacob he tell that Prees
"Yes I go to dah school
an dats why I don wan my kids to go.
All dere is in dat place is suffering."

Dah Prees he wasn happy about dat
an he say to Jacob
"But the peoples dey have to suffer Jacob
cause dah Jesus he suffer."

"But dah Jesus he never lose his language an
hees peoples" Jacob tell him.
"He stay home in hees own land and he do hees
suffering."

Well da Prees him
he get mad
an he tell him it's a sin to tink like dat
an hees gonna end up in purgatory for dem kind of
words.

But Jacob he don care
cause far as hees concern
purgatory
he can be worse den the hell he live with trying to
learn hees language and hees Indian ways.

He tell dat Prees
he don even know who his people dey are.
"Dah Jesus he knowed his Mommy and Daddy"
Jacob he tell him
"and he always knowed who his people dey are."

Well
dah Prees he tell him
if he wans to know who hees people dey are
he can tell him dat
an he open in dah book again.

"Your Dad hees Indian name he was Awchak"
dah prees he say
"I tink dat means Star in your language.
He never gets a new name cause he never become a
Christian."

Jacob he tell my granmudder
dat when da Prees he say hees Dad hees name
his wife he start to cry real hard.

"Jacob someday you'll tank the God we done dis."
dah Prees he tell him
an dey start loading up dah kids on dah big wagons.
All dah kids dey was crying an screaming
An dah mudders
dey was chasing dah wagons.

Dah ole womans
dey was all singing dah det song
an none of the mans
dey can do anyting.

Dey can
cause the policemans dey got guns.

When dah wagons dey was all gone
Jacob he look for hees wife but he can find him no
place.
An ole woman he see him an he call to him
"Pay api noosin"
"Come an sit down my granchild I mus talk to you.
Hees hard for me to tell you dis but dat Prees
hees book he bring us bad news today.
He tell you dat Awchak he was your Daddy.
My grandchild
Awchak he was your wife's Daddy too."

Jacob he tell my granmudder
he can cry when he hear dat.
He can even hurt inside.
Dat night he go looking
an he fines hees wife in dah bush
Dat woman he kill hisself.

Jacob he say
dah ole womans
dey stay wit him for a long time
an dey sing healing songs an dey try to help him
But he say he can feel nutting.
Maybe if he did
He would have done dah same ting

For many years Jacob he was like dat
just dead inside.

Dah peoples dey try to talk wit him
but it was no use.
Hees kids dey growed up
an dey come home an live wit him.
"I made dem suffer" he tell my granmudder.
"Dem kids dey try so hard to help me."

Den one day
his daughter he get married an he have a baby.
He bring it to Jacob to see.
Jacob he say
he look at dat lil baby
an he start to cry and he can stop.
He say he cry for himself an his wife
an den he cry for his Mommy and Daddy.
When he was done
he sing dah healing songs dah old womans
dey sing to him a long time ago.

Well you know
Jacob he die when he was an ole ole man.
an all hees life
he write in a big book
dah Indian names of all dah Mommies and Daddies.
An beside dem
he write dah old names and
dah new names of all dere kids.

An for dah res of hees life
he fight dah government to build schools on the
reservation.
"The good God he wouldn of make babies come
from Mommies and Daddies"
he use to say
"if he didn want dem to stay home
an learn dere language
an dere Indian ways."

You know
dat ole man was right.
No body he can do dat.
Take all dah babies away. Hees just not right.
Long time ago
dah old peoples dey use to do dah naming
an dey do dah teaching too.

If dah parents dey have troubles
den dah aunties and dah uncles
or somebody in dah family
he help out till dah parents dey gets dere life work
out.
But no one
no one
he ever take dah babies away from dere peoples.

You know my old granmudder
Mistupuch
he have lots of stories about people like Jacob.
Good ole peoples
dat work hard so tings will be better for us.
We should never forget dem ole peoples.

FRED WAH

From *Diamond Grill*

SITKUM DOLLAH GRAMPA WAH LAUGHS AS HE FLIPS a shiny half-dollar coin into the air. I say tails and he laughs too bad Freddy and shows me the head of King George the sixth. Then he puts a quarter into my hand, closes his brown and bony hand over mine, pinches my cheek while he says you good boy Freddy, buy some candy!

Whenever I hear grampa talk like that, high muckamuck, sitkum dollah, I think he's sliding Chinese words into English words just to have a little fun. He has fun alright, but I now realize he also enjoys mouthing the dissonance of encounter, the resonance of clashing tongues, his own membership in the diasporic and nomadic intersections that have occurred in northwest North America over the past one hundred and fifty years.

I don't know, then, that he's using Chinook jargon, the pidgin vocabulary of colonial interaction, the code-switching talkee-talkee of the contact zone.[1]

I'M JUST A BABY, MAYBE SIX MONTHS (.5%) old. One of my aunts is holding me on her knee. Sitting on the ground are her two daughters, 50% Scottish. Another aunt, the one who grew up in China with my father, sits on the step with her first two children around her. There are 75% Chinese. There is another little 75% girl cousin, the daughter of another 50% aunt who married a 100% full-blooded Chinaman (full-blooded, from China even). At the back of the black-and-white photograph is my oldest boy cousin; he's 25% Chinese. His mother married a Scot from North Battleford and his sisters married Italians from Trail. So there, spread out on the stoop of a house in Swift Current, Saskatchewan, we have our own little western Canadian multicultural stock exchange.

We all grew up together, in Swift Current, Calgary, Trail, Nelson (27% of John A.'s nation) and only get together now every three years (33%) for a family reunion, to which between 70% and 80% of us show up. Out of that, only one (6.6%) married a 100% pure Chinese.

The return on these racialized investments has produced colourful dividends and yielded an annual growth rate that now parallels blue-chip stocks like Kodak and Fuji, though current global market forces indicate that such stocks, by their volatile nature will be highly speculative and risky. Unexpected developments (like Immigration Acts) could throw estimates for a loop. Always take future projections with a grain of salt or better still a dash of soy.

NOTE

1.   Mary Louise Pratt describes this as the practice of *code-switching*, in which speakers switch spontaneously and fluidly between two languages .... In the context of fiercely monolingual dominant cultures like that of the United States, code-switching lays claim to a form of cultural power: the power to own but not be owned by the dominant language. Aesthetically, code-switching can be a source of great verbal subtlety and grace as speech dances fluidly and strategically back and forth between two languages and two cultural systems. Code-switching is a rich source of wit, humour, puns, word play, and games of rhythm and rhyme. "'Yo soy la Malinche,'" in *Twentieth Century Poetry: From Text to Context*, edited by Peter Verdonk, London: Routledge, 1993: 177.

Pratt's description of the "contact zone" is equally useful in considering the dynamics of foreignicity:

> The space of colonial encounters, the space in which peoples geographically and historically separated come into contact with each other and establish ongoing relations, usually involving conditions of coercion, radical inequality, and intractable conflict ....
> "Contact zone" ..., is often synonymous with "colonial frontier." But while the latter term is grounded within a European expansionist perspective (the frontier is a frontier only with respect to Europe), "contact zone" is an attempt to invoke spatial and temporal copresence of subjects previously separated by geographic and

historical disjunctures, and whose trajectories now intersect. By using the term "contact," I aim to foreground the interactive, improvisational dimensions of colonial encounters so easily ignored or supressed by diffusionist accounts of conquest and domination. A "contact" perspective emphasizes how subjects are constituted in and by their relations among colonizers and colonized ... not in terms of separateness on apartheid, but in terms of copresence, interaction, interlocking understandings and practices, often within radically asymmetrical relations of power. (*Imperial Eyes: Travel Writing and Transculturation*. London: Routledge, 1992: 6–7)

See also Monica Kin Gagnon's catalogue essay on Henry Tsang's installation "Utter Jargon":

Chinook Jargon was developed initially as a pidjin language amongst west coast First Nations peoples. Used primarily for trade purposes, Chinook Jargon's (roughly) five-hundred word vocabulary can be more specifically traced to the dialect of the Columbia River Chinook with further influences from English, French and Nuu-chah-nulth (a language group located predominantly on the west coast of Vancouver Island). At the height of its usage, Chinook Jargon had an estimated one hundred thousand speakers throughout a region stretching from northern California to Alaska, and from the Rockies to the Pacific Ocean. As Tsang notes, the jargon was unable to resist the dominance of English, and fell out of use during the first half of the 1900s. (*Dual Cultures*, Kamloops Art Gallery: Kamloops, 1993: 9)

PARIN DOSSA

ON SOCIAL SUFFERING:
FATIMA'S STORY

FROM POLITICS AND POETICS OF MIGRATION:
NARRATIVES OF IRANIAN WOMEN FROM THE DIASPORA

Human suffering has become systemic in our world. Stories of trauma caused by political violence, environmental disasters, civil strife, displacement, and the adverse effects of social policies and practices have become all too common. These occurrences have given rise to a body of literature that has documented the effects of macrosystems on the lived experiences of people (Scheper-Hughes 1992, Das et al. 2001, Das et al. 2000). "Such inquiries, which aim at unveiling the social origins and structural sources of human misery, are particularly crucial for the current historical period, when the dominant voice in the discourse of power persistently and deceitfully insists that responsibility for suffering must be acknowledged by the sufferer himself or herself and thus interprets human suffering in terms of personal stake and individual accountability" (Chuengsatiansup 2001, 31).

The shift from the individual to the social as the cause for human suffering is not easily accomplished as institutional responses mask the workings of the larger system. Institutions isolate and medicalize sufferers to the extent that their lived experiences are appropriated for consumption by global and local audiences. Taking the form of "'infotainment' on the nightly news, images of victims are commercialized; they are taken up into processes of global marketing and business competition" (Kleinman and Kleinman 1997, 1).

Given the above scenario, disciplinary interrogations are at work. Medical anthropologists, in particular, have made a significant contribution towards unmasking the social causes of suffering and pain. Taking a context-specific approach, ethnographers have documented how social suffering and structural violence are mobilized and how these impact on the everyday lives of women and men. Yet, relatively less attention has been given to the political significance of embodied experiences of suffering. This point needs emphasis as human agency is invariably at work, even in the direst situations. The challenge here is to recognize multiple and intricate forms of interventions, keeping in mind that the agency in question is that of people whose social existence has been devalued and silenced by the dominant discourse. Of special importance is the fact that the dominant discourse engages in differential marginalization of people based on such markers as race, class, citizenship, and gender. For example, the media construction of racialized women varies from constructs employed by health policy.

Differential workings of power create spaces and cracks between categories and institutional discourses, making it possible for marginalized people to challenge the dominant system and suggest alternative approaches. This [article] addresses this by reading the narrative of one woman: Fatima. Fatima's narrative is of interest to us as it takes us into heart of marginality, where we can observe not only the workings of the dominant discourse but the ways in which it can be challenged.

PROFILE

Fatima immigrated to Canada with her family (husband, daughter, and son) in 1991. She was a political refugee but was granted landed immigrant status on the strength of her and her husband's U.S. degrees in economics. The family's attempt to settle down in Montreal was thwarted by overt racism. Resettlement in Vancouver helped Fatima to establish her own import-export business — a protected niche. But this was not for long: Fatima was forced to switch roles and become a full-time caregiver following a car accident in which her daughter incurred brain injury. Fatima felt the need to share her story as she found herself battling on two fronts: coping with discrimination against the disabled, compounded in the case of women of colour, and struggling to have her role as a caregiver/a woman/a mother valorized and legitimated by society.

In this [article] I present Fatima's narrative to provide a broader analysis of her and her daughter's lived experiences. Following an account of Fatima's close encounters with racism, I highlight her points of intervention in a layered landscape that includes everyday life, encounters with the medical system, and the public-private divide that disadvantages women.

BREAKING THE SILENCE, CREATING A SPACE FOR DIALOGUE

Each time I met with Khadija (an Iranian therapist/counsellor), she told me stories relating to different subjects. In our third meeting, she related what she referred to as "the veil dilemma" — conflicts encountered by women, regardless of whether they chose to wear or discard the veil.[1] On our fourth meeting (March 2001), Khadija informed me that she was in the midst of hearing Fatima's story concerning her daughter's brain injury. Khadija's response to my question on how she establishes contact with Iranian women in crisis was this: "When I find out that a woman is in a difficult situation, I phone her and ask her if she wants to talk." Khadija explained that most women share their stories with her because there are few other opportunities for them to air their concerns. As noted earlier, storytelling does not constitute a mere account of events. It is in fact an active process of reconfiguration of life.

Iranian women wanted to share their stories with Khadija because she was a good listener and not because she was kith and kin. As a counsellor in Iran, she had learned how to prompt women to give expression to their ideas and feelings. But, as I learnt from Fatima, women also wanted to talk to Khadija because they perceived her to be bicultural and bilingual. In other words, she helped women to ground their stories between the spaces of two worlds: home and host.

Like other Iranian women, Khadija could not find work in her area of expertise in Canada. She therefore established a niche that allowed her to validate herself and remember, in her own words, that "women can think and make a significant contribution to society." As a bilingual counsellor, Khadija was invited by mainstream professionals and civil servants to give talks on "Iranian culture." Khadija did not fall into the trap of merely presenting "how-to-do culture" — a stance that has been problematized as it masks the social causes of suffering. Here, the culture of immigrant communities is held responsible for their inability to settle down, when in fact societal and institutional barriers are to blame. While Khadija did not completely abandon the cultural trope — otherwise she would not be invited — she gently implicated the system by telling the stories of women.

The women presented these stories in the way of testimonial speaking. Fatima's story is related in this genre.

Fatima told her story to Khadija and myself, separately and together, in eight sessions over a period of eight months. Marmar, her daughter, was present in all the sessions. Although Marmar spoke and participated in the discussions as and when she wanted, she was not the principal participant. Fatima had expressed a desire to tell her story ('tell it all") and we respected her wish. Like Zahra, Fatima also wanted her daughter to hear the full story because Marmar did not remember her experiences following the accident. The meetings took place variously at Fatima's house, Khadija's house, and at a restaurant, according to what worked best for everyone. Other than prompting Fatima to elaborate on some aspects, Khadija's role was that of a good listener.

When Khadija first approached Fatima with my inquiry as to whether she was interested in the research project, Fatima jumped at the opportunity. Prior to the storytelling sessions, Fatima submitted the following two paragraphs authored by herself and by her daughter, respectively.

A therapeutic chance/an opportunity was given to me to review and tell out loud or let it out one of the most devastating experience a woman/mom may experience in her life. Which was: lose a daughter in a long battle of life-threatening situation, and suddenly birth was given to a 19-year-old disabled child in replace. Without having the chance or energy to grieve for the loss of the most precious thing in my life, start another harsh struggle, fighting with all obstacles, limitations and difficulties in life to save her life, and then working for her recovery. These are my daughter's words to describe her feelings:

The accident on November 22, 1997, changed my life forever. Since I was released from the hospital, I have been depressed and very lonely. Most people have memories of when they were young. However I have forgotten the first twenty years of my life. I can't remember relatives, the places I've been, and the things I've done. This makes me feel like the first twenty years of my life were just a waste. I have lost touch with many of my friends because it was difficult for me to leave my house and in some cases I cannot even remember them. Furthermore, for the past nine months, I have not been able to live like a normal 20-year-old woman. I can no longer live independently and this has caused a great deal of emotional hardship. It devastates me to think that although I am an adult, I cannot take care of myself.

Since the accident, I have become irritable, impulsive, immature, and impatient. Often I find myself cursing for no reason, yelling at others and becoming frustrated very easily. My daily life has completely changed for the worst. I need help getting in and out of the shower. I also have trouble going up and down the stairs. For example, before my accident, I used to be able to go dancing with my friends whenever I wanted and for as long as I wanted. However, currently I can no longer dance like I used to and I feel that I am a burden to the people I go out with. Additionally, I've been told that I can't go to a normal school of higher learning or hold a job for two years. When I think about these facts, I begin to wonder if I will ever be normal again.

First reading of the above accounts bring home the devastating impact of a major car accident. Woven into the body of this account is a social script. For Fatima, it is "fighting with all obstacles, limitations, and difficulties in life to save her life, and then working for her recovery." Marmar is made to feel that she is a burden on society and she wonders if she will ever be normal again. In a just world, one would expect that one's pain would be lessened by empathy and social support. But this is hardly the case. As Kleinman et al. (1997) and Farmer (2003) have argued, suffering has been rendered into a commodity for consumption by audiences who watch and read about human misery from the comforts of their living rooms. But this is not the end point. There are myriad stories, like those of Fatima and Marmar, that are rendered invisible because they are not considered "worthy" of societal attention. Fatima then takes it upon herself to tell her own story and she does this with vigour and passion. Fatima is also aware that her story will circulate in forums such as the one that Khadija has access to or through print, the medium used by researchers.

Like the Japanese *hibakusha* (bombed) women (Todeschini 2001), Fatima considers it necessary to create a space from which her story will be heard. Such is the silencing of people who are marginalized. Fatima's point of entry is to relate her own experiences of overt racism. In her account, she conveys the injurious effects of racism—an elusive form of suffering. Fatima frames her account in such a way that the reader cannot help but locate what are essentially discrete acts "into a formative relationship with each other, of suggesting a way of thinking them indispensably through each other" (Bannerji 1995, 14). The formative relationship is brought into relief in the reality of everyday life. It is within this realm that trauma and crisis register more deeply. It is also within this space that acts of resistance take place. This context paves the way for Fatima to relate her account of societal response to her daughter's brain injury.

TELLING HER STORY OF BORDER CROSSING

Fatima came to Canada with the expectation that she and her family (husband, 15-year-old daughter, and 11-year-old son) would be well received. Fatima believed that she had the right credentials: she and her husband were political refugees, they both had master's degrees in economics from United States, and they were young. From the point of view of the Canadian state, they were desirable immigrants who would hit the ground running. Fatima and her husband wanted no less. They were keen to settle down quickly and for this reason they decided to live in Montreal: "We were told that it is easier to get jobs here and this is the reason why we went to Montreal." Fatima encountered a world different from the one she had envisioned.

> We moved to Montreal and spent whatever we had saved in Iran in three years. We spend around $125,000. My husband [Mohammed] with his economic background took on a job of a door-to-door salesperson. Even though he was a shy person. There was no other way to live. All these were tortures for him. In our culture there was no such thing as commission job. He could not change his personality but he went through a lot of torture. We received no help from the Iranian community. We never found a reliable job in Montreal.

Note that Fatima first talks about her husband before relating her own experiences. This is because women's subordinate status makes it necessary for them to create their own spaces and establish moral authority before they speak. By highlighting her husband's suffering ("tortures"), Fatima positions herself to tell her tale from the socially valorized role of a wife. Fatima then talks about her distress in not being able to find work in her area of expertise. She intertwines her personal experiences with a collective story of mistreatment of her people in Canada.

> The job that I had found in Montreal was at a very low level. I did not have Canadian experience. I was not accepted/trusted for any jobs. We felt that people had preconceptions about us as being Iranian. People had stereotypes about us, and that is how we would get treated. Fear of financial insecurity affected my relationship with my husband and children. We could not provide a healthy environment for our children.

He would go to twenty places each day looking for a job. When I looked for a job, I would not say that I have a master's degree in economics from the United States. I thought to myself this degree was working against me. When I came here, I registered in a computerized accounting programme, and the school asked me for a resume. I did not write that I have a degree.

In Montreal with the deposit in our bank account, we could not even lease a car. We need someone to come and co-sign for us, someone that has lived there. Even if we wanted to rent a place we needed a co-signer, someone that has a job, and knows us. Silent, she shakes her head, and then continues.

Immigrant women's ties to the marketplace are tenuous and ambiguous. They are largely sought for work in the lower echelons of the labour force and are dispensed with once these positions are eliminated. The ambiguity arises from the fact that the labour of these women is desirable but remains unacknowledged. Acknowledging immigrant women's contributions would mean improving their working conditions, a situation that a profit-based system avoids at all costs. The system in fact deploys the socially constructed categories of race and gender to secure a cheap source of labour. Capitalistic systems are gendered and raced. These observations reveal that Fatima's entry at the lower rungs of the labour force is not coincidental. It is structural, and this aspect prompts Fatima to hide her qualifications, despite the fact that they were acquired in a place (U.S.) where her credentials would not be an issue. A low-end position does not spare Fatima from racism that translates into violence of her self/her body.

They could not accept me between themselves. I would think that I'm boring. I had my own value system. I tried very hard to be accepted. I wasted my time. I even got more humiliated — that made me very angry. I needed to be accepted by them. If I attended a party, no one would even talk to me or even look at me. They gave me the feeling of, "I am really disgusted, why you want to get into our group, get out." I could not be myself.

Das and Kleinman suggest that "the experience of subjugation may itself, when owned and worked upon, become the source of claiming a subject position" (cf. Butler 2001, 6). But in reality, such positions are not claimed with facility and when they do exist, they need to be teased out. This process is revealed in two contexts in the narrative.

First is the crossing of boundaries from the personal to the political. The issue of boundary crossing concerning the moment when an individual gains political consciousness has been subject to debate. One body of work suggests that this form of consciousness requires the availability of the right set of circumstances such as grass-root level movements, a particular crisis, or a critical exposure to the workings of the dominant system (Ross 2001, Todeschini 2001). A second body of work foregrounds the premise that the personal is political regardless of circumstances except that this awareness is latent and may be brought to light through such mediums as stories (Scheper-Hughes 1992).

The moment Fatima stated that she had to hide her qualifications, she entered the political arena. She is suggesting that there must be something amiss in a society that compels people to hide their real qualifications. In making this statement, Fatima reinforced insights from the literature produced by women of colour and transnational feminists, indicating that women of colour are looked upon as a source of cheap labour that can be dispensed with according to the needs of the market (Naples and Desai 2002). In such a situation, as Bannerji (1995) has argued, the bodies of women of colour in white-collar jobs are an anomaly.

Fatima crosses yet another boundary: from speech to the silent language of the body. "Silent, she shakes her head, and then continues." When the body speaks, it conveys a politically charged message (Frank 1995). Fatima conveys the message that she has no words to describe the suffering and the pain caused by social exclusion and racism—the soft knife of politics. Farmer (2003) and Bannerji (1995) have respectively noted that the effects of racism are injurious. The wounds go deep and impact on one's sense of well-being and identity as a person. But there is no closure. People who fight back must also be listened to, because they bring to light the elements of a just world. A first and important step in this direction is to recognize their subjectivity.

The second context is transnational. Being aware of the colonial discourse on the veil/*hejab* which Others Muslim women (Alvi et al. 2003), Fatima takes the reader to her country of birth. She notes that even if she wore the *hejab* in Iran as compelled by the state, she did not lose her identity or dignity. Her work as an economist was recognized and valued. Nevertheless, she does not romanticize her country of birth. She admits that in Iran she was suspected of being a U.S. spy, and that she was pressured to stay at home by the government's ideological stance that "a woman belongs to the house." These were the two reasons why Fatima left Iran.

Yet, for Fatima, these experiences pale in comparison with what she lived through in her adopted country. "I am pushed to lose my identity." "At work," she continued, "they would often talk about immigrant frauds. What should I say ... it is better I go" — that is, she does not want to talk any more. Silence, once again, implicates the system.

Fatima's experiences in the Canadian labour force form part of a structural moment. Long before Fatima stepped into the office, her low-paid work (downward mobility), along with the attitudes and behaviour of her co-workers, were determined by the racialized and gendered Canadian immigration policy (Thobani 1999, Gupta 1996). The policy stipulates that, by and large, women are desirable immigrants only because they are the source of cheap labour that can fill positions that no one else wants to occupy. Of late, immigrant women constitute a pool of volunteers in the downsized social service sector. The fact that Fatima was granted landed immigrant status based on her (also her husband's) U.S. qualifications is of no consequence. Once in the country, the racialized and gendered system channelled her into entry-level work, just as it did Nadia. During a low financial period in their lives, Fatima and her husband applied for welfare.

> They [social service staff] would not let us in. We would often hear, "if you want to leave it [application], but it is going to end up in the garbage." Often in the hallways, on my way from one office to the other, I felt humiliated and cried. I wanted to work for free for three months. My offer was not accepted even on humanitarian basis. It was not their fault because the economic system here does not give them this choice. According to my experience, society does not accept/respect new immigrants. For example, I remember as a new immigrant when I stepped in the coffee room at the office I used to work, they would stop their conversation.

The feminist project in anthropology has been informed by three phases: to make women visible as historical, social, economic, and political actors; to foreground gender as a central analytical category; and to recognize the tightly woven link between gender and social institutions (De Groot 1996). What is of interest in Fatima's account is her point of intervention in this project. Through the sheer act of narration of such events as the incident in the hallway and her encounters in the coffee room, Fatima establishes her position as a political actor. Her implication of the system (society's belittling of immigrant women) does not focus merely on individuals ("it was not their fault"). She concentrates on institutional power and as such her message is a political one that can be placed on a par with critical ethnography. Here the emphasis is on dialogue where "anthropological knowledge may be seen as something produced in human interaction, not merely 'extracted' from native informants who are unaware of the hidden agendas coming from the outsider" (Scheper-Hughes 1992, 25). The issue here is that this approach should not be the exclusive preserve of anthropologists. Research participants may initiate dialogue that evokes the presence of a listening community. Fatima initiates this process through the narrative act where the emphasis is not only on what she says but on how she frames her account. Fatima withdraws and shares information according to her own political project, an important component of which is her gendered identity as a mother and a professional woman.

Unable to stand the humiliation and the pain that Fatima and her husband were subject to in Montreal, the couple moved to Vancouver to make a fresh start. Fatima glossed over this part of her life. She explained that she worked for a firm for three years and then started her own export-import business. This enclave sheltered her from the pain and the humiliation that she experienced in Montreal. She hoped to bury this part of her life, but not for long. Her daughter's accident made it necessary for her to talk about these experiences, if for no other reason than to claim another subject position from which she could speak: that of a caregiver. Fatima found herself carrying the societal burden of care and this social load compelled her to tell her story. Recall her words: "A therapeutic chance/an opportunity was given to me to review and tell out loud or let it out one of the most devastating experience a woman/mom may experience in her life."

BEARING THE SOCIETAL BURDEN OF CARE

As a mom, how I feel about a disabled child. As a mother to protect my child I support her, help her to develop ability and skill to live in the society and protect herself against discrimination that exist against her, not just the right to work or equal opportunity. To protect her from psychological damage. Society here as soon as they see a disabled person, they think of him/her as a lesser person (I mean majority) since there are few who accept and see it any other way of being in this world not just be as someone incapable. However, in public, people don't respect your physical limitation.

These are Fatima's first words on her role as a mother and a caregiver. Unlike people with stories of multiple sclerosis (Monks and Frankenberg 1995), Fatima does not focus exclusively on the adjustment that she and her daughter have to make. For Fatima, the issue concerns societal response to her daughter's brain injury. For Marmar, living in a different body translates into societal rejection of her as a person. She is perceived as a burden, a situation that she internalizes.

Including but also moving beyond the adjustment script takes Fatima into the heart of what disability scholar Oliver (1996) refers to as "disability as social oppression." This form of oppression is multi-dimensional: social, economic, cultural, and psychological. Fatima was compelled to deal with this complex scenario. At one level, she took on the position of a full-time caregiver because Marmar had to start from scratch. Fatima explained that she had to teach her daughter such things as "how to walk" and "how to hold a fork." Rather than receiving any societal support or recognition for her work, Fatima found herself waging a battle against denigration of disabled people, compounded for racialized minorities and women (Asce and Fine 1988, Dossa 2000). This is what Fatima has to say:

> *When I go to Marmar to a concert, mall, or cinema, even in college people don't care about her physical disability. They brush her off. Here people just care about their own business. In a sense selfish, they are self-centred. They don't want to bother to spare any minute of their life for a lesser person (disabled). When she walks with a cane, no one is considerate, to let her go first or slow down so that they don't hit her. Or let her get into the elevator first, or wait a minute for her to get in.*

Societal oppression of the disabled does not exclude family members. Referring to Marmar's visit to her cousins in United States, Fatima observed,

> *They would walk ahead in the restaurant, and for Marmar she could not walk fast. This brought her a bad feeling. Feeling such as being leftover, not wanted, a burden. "I wish I had not gone" is what Marmar said. We are talking about a young adult who is full of life, full of sense of humour, and also very intelligent whenever her mental difficulties do not come out as an obstacle.*

Medical anthropologists have brought to our attention the multifaceted dimensions of what appears to be existential human suffering (Kleinman et al. 1997, Das et al. 2001). First is the corporeal-bodily reality that in disability literature is referred to as impairment (Corker and French 1999). Second is the focus on social conditions such as political conflict, forced migration, and the adverse impact of state policies and practices on communities and individuals. These two levels of suffering are intensified by insensitive institutional and bureaucratic responses that isolate sufferers and subject them to medicalization.

The third dimension of suffering involves the exercise of human agency, which serves a twofold purpose. First, it prevents total appropriation of suffering by the larger and increasingly global systems of power. As Kleinman and Kleinman have noted: "This globalization of suffering is one of the most troubling signs of the cultural transformation of the current era: troubling because experience is being used as a commodity, and through this cultural representation of suffering, experience is being remade, thinned out and distorted" (1997, 2). Second, human agency points to alternative ways that have the potential to effect social change. Note that these ways are not confined to a discrete sphere but exist alongside or in the midst of dominant systems.

A close reading of Fatima's narrative text reveals all the above dimensions. To begin with, Fatima and her daughter highlight the issue of impairment. For Fatima, this means becoming a full-time caregiver. For Marmar, impairment is conveyed in her own words: difficulties in climbing stairs instead of dancing.

Social factors are not easily implicated in a car accident because individuals are held responsible for this occurrence. If we were to engage in what Farmer (2003) refers to as "geographically broad and historically deep analysis," we would be able to establish a correlation between accident-based injuries/death and the social order (read: profit-drive market system). In essence, car accidents are a result of high volume of automobile traffic that has left little room for pedestrians, cyclists, and also public transport. Automobile manufacture, a profit-making industry, epitomizes the capitalistic system. This system's negative impact on the environment and the lives of people is masked by a host of supporting institutions. Given this dense scenario, Fatima does not focus on the cause of the accident. She invests her energy in highlighting societal response to her daughter's brain injury. Through her account of particular incidents in her and her daughter's everyday life (concert, elevator, restaurant), she brings home the social cause of suffering.

Focus on everyday reality is important as it is in this realm that pain and suffering register more poignantly; it is also within this space that social interactions take place and where our bodies' multi-faceted reality is shaped. Equally important is the fact that everyday life is not detached from the larger hegemonic systems that operate in a way so as to make us believe that this reality is a commonsense and taken-for-granted aspect of life. Fatima grounds her experiences in this realm but also expands them to include a transnational dimension. She takes the reader to her home country in Iran "to heal Marmar's wounds." What Fatima and her daughter lived through was day-to-day discrimination experienced on the basis of intersecting inequalities of gender and race and disability. While Fatima bases her narrative on disability, issues of gender and race (Iranian women) are also in the forefront.

> The way they treat her, the way they approach her, the way they care about her, the impact all this kind of support is that she would feel as accepted, respected, and loved as much, if not even more as if she did not have this disability. I took her to Iran to save her heart. To repair her soul because here [in Canada] she was not feeling very much loved, or accepted. She lacked emotional nourishment. The worst of all, she lost all her friends after the accident. She became lonely and all of them disappeared, then she had her major struggle. She was trying so hard to bring back her friends, which did not happen. She was so disappointed she felt as no one loves her, no one wants to be around her because she is disabled.

> But in Iran she was in middle of the crowd, and one of them. One among others, one of them like any others or in another word, to be accepted. A mother understands things that others can't. I could understand her needs. To nurture her spirit and to repair her broken heart, give her a chance to feel good again even with all her disabilities and difficulties. You are as much, if not more, loved and respected, cared as before this incident.

In *Disability and Culture*, Whyte and Ingstad (1995) put forward the method of cultural juxtaposition that enables anthropologists to draw insights from other societies and apply them to problems in their own societies. This anthropological tradition is subject to debate on two grounds. First, there is the danger that the West—the dominant and home territory of anthropologists—would be the reference point for comparison; second, this tradition promotes a divide between the West and the Rest. The latter is considered to have a subordinate status even within the realm of international organizations. Drawing upon her experiential knowledge as a caregiver and as a person who has lived in both the worlds, Fatima engages with this debate.

Fatima's trip to Iran was prompted by a lack in her country of re-settlement. This lack relates to the issue of personhood "seen as being not simply human but human in a way that is valued and meaningful" (Ibid., 10). Why is it the case that in the Western world disability is equated with social oppression? This question does not imply that persons with disabilities are free of oppression in other parts of the world. What is required is a context-specific framework within which to study disability in any society. Taking a sociohistorical perspective, Striker contends that the status of the disabled people in the Western world is best explained in relation to a centralist state. The state has appropriated the lives of disabled persons in a way that renders them dependent and needy. "Thus disability in Europe and North America exists within — and is created by — a framework of state, legal, economic and biomedical institutions. Concepts of personhood, identity, and value, while not reducible to institutions, are nevertheless shaped by them" (cf. Whyte and Ingstad, 10).

Fatima does not comment on the status of the disabled in Iran. To do so would have diluted her context-specific script involving everyday life situations. She focuses on particular but crucial spaces such as that of being in a crowd or among a group of people. Here Marmar is not treated as a lesser person because of her disability. To reiterate Fatima's words, "But in Iran she was in middle of the crowd, and one of them. One among others, one of them like any other or in another word to be accepted." Acceptance in a group/crowd that otherwise did not know Marmar as an individual gave her the assurance that her life is worth living and that she was not a burden on society. In short, Marmar was not marked as negatively different because of her disability. Fatima established a "link" between Iran and Canada by providing a context as to what prompted her to visit Iran.

> *My feeling about taking her to Iran for psychological treatment became a sure idea when my sister [Forouzan] from Iran came to support and help me and Marmar. My sister's three months of therapeutic services that she provided was like a breakthrough point in Marmar's recovery.*

Forouzan's visit to Canada was made possible by the support that she received from her family in Iran. The family (natal and marital) collected funds for her trip and they took care of her children while she was away. Forouzan also made a personal sacrifice as she took an unpaid leave of absence from her teaching job. Through the care and emotional support that she provided to Marmar, Fatima came to know what she lacked in Canada.

Whyte and Ingstad (1995) offer useful comparative insights on attitudinal differences towards disabled persons. They argue that North American society has little to offer to disabled persons as it medicalizes and individualizes their lives — approaches that depoliticize struggles for justice and equality. The opposite situation prevails in the South. There, disabled persons are not subject to essentialized identities ("wheelchair bound" as opposed to "wheelchair user") owing to minimal institutional control. Ironically, the latter translates into minimal state-based services, leaving the family to take care of disabled members. Fatima does not reject the institutional services that Marmar needs for her recovery: physiotherapy, occupational therapy, speech therapy, and psychological counselling. Her activism is based on the conviction that the disabled in the West do not receive emotional support, thus reducing their chances to socially interact and ultimately compromising their sense of who they are as people.

> *In this [Western] culture, there is less emotional support. This society is run by laws [read: institutionalization]. But in Iranian culture, people's support is not generated by law and if they see a disabled person they volunteer to help. They automatically give priority to disabled person. In the eighteen months after Marmar's accident, I realized the need to take her back to Iran for emotional support.*

> *I want to talk about Iran. In Iran everybody first sympathize with a handicap person. There you can have a normal life. Emotionally less under pressure. Here a person is separated from society, and doesn't feel as one with other members of society. One of the biggest pains of a disabled person is that his/her life is separated from everyone else, separated from her old environment. In her new environment she is lonely with no love. This is a major suffering. In Iran, even though people might look at her with pity, nobody behaves around her in a way so that she would feel sorry for herself. She had had the feeling of acceptance, the same amount of love she still would get from people surrounding her the same as before her disabilities.*

In taking issue with institutional services that separate the individual from society, Fatima enters into the heart of one of the main concerns expressed in the literature on social suffering. This body of work is based on the premise that institutions and social conditions must be implicated in all forms of human suffering. Even if human misery cannot directly be linked to societal factors, it is intensified by societal insensitivity and further marginalization of the sufferers.

BATTLING ON TWO FRONTS

Fatima related that she had to wage a battle on two fronts. First there was her daughter, Marmar. Fatima felt her pain very deeply. She could not bear to see the agony that Marmar was going through as she struggled to build her life from scratch. Such activities as walking, eating, taking a bath, and dressing were new to her. Marmar's attempts to relearn what she had learned over nineteen years of her life were frustrated by the obstacles that society placed before her. Fatima related that even going to the doctor was a struggle because she had to help Marmar get dressed and drive her to his office. Yet, every time they went (a couple of times a month), the doctor made them wait for as long as forty-five minutes. It was hard for Marmar to sit this long. Once they were late by fifteen minutes and the doctor shouted at them and said that they were wasting his precious time. It was the same doctor who advised Fatima to "forget" about Marmar as, in his words, "The accident happened and there is nothing more you can do." Fatima gave other examples of insensitivity, such as how Marmar was drugged to numb her pain when all that she needed was a massage from a nurse; how the nurses would shout at her when she did not want to take a shower; how they would take their time to change her position on the bed to prevent sores and so on.

The dehumanized care that Marmar received during her eighteen-month stay at the hospital was not remedied by the outside world.[2] Marmar's experiences are captured in statements cited at the beginning of this [article]. When Fatima realized that society was shunning its responsibility towards the disabled, she took the societal burden onto her own shoulders. This made her fight a second battle: that of ensuring that society recognize her role as a caregiver.

> *I wish that the society or government agencies recognize and appreciate the twenty-four hours of services that I was providing. As the result of me losing my job, a household of two incomes suffered financially and that created lots of problems. Something that I did not need at that time. That job of taking care of a brain-injured young adult is very painful and difficult. If you add to all*

*these difficulties, financial difficulties, you can imagine how bad the situation
can get. I wish that government would compensate at least minimum wage
for eight hours a day. A service that was essential for Marmar's recovery.
If I did not do what I did, she would have never recovered as much, and she
would be left as a disabled who would need twenty-four hours of intensive
care. What I am trying to say is that they should recognize the benefit of
these services provided with love to a fellow citizen and society. At least
compensate a portion of it for the sake of a healthy society.*

Aside from dealing with the issue of recognition, Fatima was belittled
and considered "stupid" for not getting on with her life. "Can you not
understand that brain-injured people's recovery lasts a lifetime? How can
you not get on with your own life?" This is the message that Fatima heard
from medical specialists. Consider the following critical incidents.

First, Fatima related, her psychiatrist, who was helping her cope with
stress and depression, "threw me out of her office. She said that if I was
not willing to put my daughter in a group home, there is nothing more
she can do for me." Second, the psychiatrist's views were reinforced by
family members: her husband and brother-in-law urged her to get on with
her life. They told her that it was not her fault that the accident happened.
Fatima explained that her husband did not "see" how much care she was
putting into Marmar's recovery. She attributes the invisibility of her work
to the fact that "the government does not pay for the full-time work that
I put into my daughter's care." Fatima explained that if she were to put
her daughter into a group home, it would cost the government a lot of
money. Fatima felt that even a minimum wage would enhance her status
as a caregiver.

To make her case, Fatima highlighted the multi-faceted nature of
caregiving. She states that a good caregiver first has to become a student
and learn about the person that she is caring for. In her case, she had to
learn whatever she could about brain injury, but this was not sufficient.
She also had to learn about Marmar as a whole person and not as an
individual splintered by her disability. This meant relating to Marmar
emotionally but also being cognizant of details concerning her body: sore
points, balance, coordination, and so on. Added to this enormous task were
the societal prejudices and discrimination that Fatima had to confront and
whose elimination she had to work towards. As Wendell has expressed it:
"[D]isability is socially constructed through the failure or unwillingness to
create ability among people who do not fit the physical and mental profile

of 'paradigm' citizens. Failure of social support for people with disabilities results in inadequate rehabilitation ... and many other disabling situations that hurt people with disabilities and exclude them from participation in major aspects of life in their societies" (1996, 40).

Disability scholars have argued that disabled people are treated as lesser beings who do not count and whose lives can be dispensed with through such means as abortion of "defected" fetuses, incarceration and gross disregard for their quality of life (Wendell 1996, Oliver 1996). The struggles of disabled persons then begin at the level of basic rights and entitlements that able-bodied people take as given: accessibility, employment, schooling, parenting, sexuality, health, and others. Further, disabled people are labelled as Other and subjected to stigma at multiple levels, compounded in the case of racialized women and other socially disadvantaged minorities. It is these multi-faceted concerns that prompted Fatima to become a full-time caregiver.

Caregiving is not confined to task-oriented work, as common wisdom has it. While this work is crucial (Fatima says that her daughter would have been in a wheelchair if she had not worked towards her recovery), there are other dimensions that are equally daunting and challenging. These dimensions concern overcoming the long-standing Cartesian dichotomy (bed-body work versus social relations) and dealing with societal barriers where disability is nothing less than oppression. For Fatima, caregiving is a mission that she had to undertake; no one around her understood Marmar's needs as a whole person and not a splintered human being. But in the process, Fatima herself was denigrated.

It is a fact that my husband, or even my husband's family, looked at me as an unemployed person. I have lost my self-respect as a professional working woman with a good salary. For three and a half years in the pain of being a nobody, and the feelings that you are only worthy and valued when you bring money home. And I was not able to work anymore because of Marmar; because Marmar's sickness was a mental sickness and I had to always educate myself about her condition and I wanted to be involved in all the therapy sessions so that I would be more informed on what has happened to Marmar and to learn the treatments. And thirdly to be able to follow the practices at home so that I would be more beneficial to her.

And I was the only person that was filling Marmar's loneliness, there was no one else. Her friends were gone as well, and had left her alone. I was her friend, her therapist, massage therapist, her teacher, that was a very hard job, and I had to teach myself on how to work with Marmar. This meant that I was a full-time student so that I could learn so that I could treat Marmar better. A lot of time I had to observe Marmar carefully to find a solution for her problem. I had to create a chart to record all her activities and pain so that I would be able to understand where her pain was coming from.

If the government could provide minimum wage for all these services that I am giving as a mother this would lessen the pressures that have been building up, and maybe I would not be forced to break under all these pressures, and feel the need to see a therapist, and take prescription drugs for my own health.

The question that Fatima raises in her account is this: Why does society not reward a person who takes on multiple roles (teacher, massage therapist, therapist, friend) to take care of another person (in her words, "service from one human being to another")? Aside from the issue of reward, we may state that the person is actually punished. Fatima stated that she lost her social status and her health was jeopardized because society took no notice of her full-time work with Marmar. For a response to the above question, we may turn to the literature.

Caregiving evokes the lesser and more discrete world of home that is run and managed by women. This is a contrived setup put into place by the state, which is interested in securing the unpaid labour of women within a space that remains socially invisible. Furthermore, the state has taken full advantage of the gendered ideology that women by nature are caring, loving, gentle, and sacrificial beings. Feminist intervention into this political economy script has been vigorous. In her work on family caregiving, Anne Opie (1992) suggests that we pay close attention to the way in which what are presented as separate spheres are in fact closely intertwined. This is contrary to the stance taken by the state. Opie argues that the private sphere of home is indeed shaped by social, economic, and political contexts. To effect any kind of change, we need to implicate these contexts. Devaluation of persons providing care translates into devaluation of persons receiving care, and thus it is necessary for us, argues Opie, to deconstruct this conflation. The task of making visible the work of the caregivers is rendered more difficult in the wake of downsizing and privatization of social service programmes, a development that has made the state focus on "community care" that assumes the availability of unpaid female caregivers. The solution proposed by Opie is to question the private and the public divide that the state uses to its benefit—a task that Fatima undertakes based on her experiential knowledge on caregiving. In her own words,

> *From the first day, I did not leave this kid alone as part of being a mother. But it has to be recognized that if it was not for my care this kid would have suffered from another brain injury and not recover as much. The government and society should pay the huge cost of recovery. This did not occur because I was there to take care of her with passion. As a women [sic] and a mother, I suffered in many ways. It all returns to that the government does not recognize and respect biological and natural rights of a free caregiver, who is a mother. It would cost the government more in the end, if I leave this service!*

In this passage, Fatima made a strong case to have her services as a caregiver recognized by the state and by the society. She framed her argument in the language that the state would understand: cost effectiveness. At the same time, she highlighted the enormous cost that she has to bear: "I suffered in many ways." She continues,

> *The whole time I have to struggle with my husband, and myself so that I don't lose my self-esteem because I am always under attack. Because of financial pressures my spouse wanted me to return back to work, and it was me that would not leave this kid alone to return to work even though the whole family was in need of money. If society recognized the value of my services, my family who is also a part of society will also respect my work as well.*

Of interest is the fact that the blurring of the boundaries between the public and the private takes place on the shifting grounds of identity. Fatima refers to herself as a woman, a mother, and a caregiver. The convergence but also disjuncture of these roles—a woman is not invariably a caregiver and, for Fatima, this was especially the case as before the accident she identified herself as a professional woman—makes a powerful script of sacrifice but also highlights the politics of care as revealed in the following passage: "I have a serious claim as a women and as a mother. If I was respected for the care I provide with love, my husband would also understand and appreciate what I am doing." The message conveyed is that she is still a working woman, but on the home front. This intervention—her own take and understanding of the situation—subverts the public/private divide.

It is within this deconstructed space that Fatima tells her story and in the process identifies a niche for remaking a world that is otherwise filled with suffering and pain.

Concluding Note

We began this [essay] with the observation that social suffering is multi-faceted. In particular we noticed that social suffering can either be appropriated or else rendered invisible by the dominant system. Social suffering is also not easy to document in a world where it is taken as a common occurrence that takes place out there in another part of the world. Our role in this respect is to consume images of suffering that the media presents to us in a framework that absolves us from any responsibility both as observers and as participants in a system that isolates sufferers. We have also observed that this political economy script is not complete. People who are subjected to pain and suffering do not maintain silence. They feel the need to tell their stories, often in the form of testimonial speaking.

An intriguing aspect of stories is that they do not exist within a discrete sphere of what the dominant system refers to as "their culture and therefore their stories." In other words, the dominant group would like to hear stories that do not implicate it in any way. As noted in the example of the refugee hearing process, the stories that are validated are those that portray the West as a saviour of people from the Third World. The latter is portrayed as uncivilized where chaos and violence are the order of the day. Given this scenario, stories of marginalized people act as points of intervention into the hegemonic system. While such stories hold the system accountable for their plight, they go beyond this level to include alternative discourses and strategies. Such is the context in which Fatima tells her story.

Through the deployment of narrative strategies — the how, what, and when of storytelling — Fatima first claimed a subject position from which she can speak with authority. Fatima's awareness of the working of the system based on the intersections of inequality of such markers as race, gender, and disability came during the early period of her settlement. Her exclusion and marginalization was total as it not only kept her away from the work that she is qualified to do but affected her sense of identity and well-being. Fatima's implication of the racialized system is intriguing. She uses the colonial narrative of the veil (read: oppression of Muslim women by Islam) to bring into relief an ironic situation: "Even when I wore the veil, I did not lose my identity. I was valued for my work. Here in Canada

I cannot be myself. You are pushed to lose your identity." The message conveyed is to the effect that it is the structural location of immigrant women—lack of opportunities for work and full development of their capacities—that determines their life chances. In her example of the veil and its linkage with women's work, Fatima reverses the hierarchy where the West presents itself as superior and democratic.

Note that Fatima shares her story of re-settlement to lay the groundwork for telling yet another story from the margins of the margins. This second story's marginal status arises from the fact that the issue of disability has not been incorporated into the race/gender/class paradigm. Yet, disability contains intricate layers. The starting point is the existential form of suffering and pain (impairment), intensified by institutional response. It is important to understand how this response is mobilized within particular contexts and in terms of specific discourses. Fatima's narrative provides insights on these aspects. Through her depiction of everyday life situations, we come to know how Marmar's struggle for recovery is made worse by societal indifference and rejection of her racialized, gendered, and disabled body. Everyday life is layered, as it is at this level that pain and suffering are brought into greater relief. Within the space of everyday life, resistance, especially in scattered forms, is exercised.

In the context of everyday life, and between the spaces of the private and the public, Fatima wages her battles: to take care of her brain-injured daughter in a way that goes well beyond what is referred to as bed-and-body work (the physical aspects of recovery). Fatima gives equal and special emphasis to nurturing "Marmar's soul," to use her words. It is for this reason that she takes her daughter to Iran. Reversing the anthropological tradition of cultural juxtaposition, Fatima brings to the fore particular spaces to provide an example of healing of the soul. She uses this example to critique the Western approach that separates the individual from society—a practice that Fatima considers to be injurious to one's well-being. We learn that this form of separation is politically motivated as it absolves society from bearing any responsibility. Canadian society and, more broadly, the West pushes disabled people into the private sphere where they are rendered socially invisible. Fatima ensures that this private space is made public by relating particular incidents that impact on Marmar's recovery and sense of well-being. Fatima also takes on the project of making visible women's work in the private sphere. She presents a powerful script of how her sense of well-being, dignity, and self-worth are negatively affected because society does not validate her full-time work as a teacher, a therapist, a woman, a mother, and a caregiver. Her suggestion that the government should compensate her for this work subverts the public-private divide. She effectively conveys the message that her work in the private sphere should be a societal concern. In light of the fact that neither institutional nor civic society will take responsibility for Marmar, Fatima shouldered the societal burden of care but not without implicating the system and suggesting alternative discourse that kept alive the idea that the private sphere is an integral part of the public sphere.

Note that the speaker is a racialized woman who is effectively given the societal message "You can speak and take action if you like but do not move into our territory. Whatever you do must be confined to your own 'community' and 'culture.'" Referred to as the script of containment of minorities to spaces and places that do not shake the world of the dominant majority, this practice has worked well because the state can continue with its business without having to recognize substantive citizenship rights of this group (Dossa 1999, 2000).

The public-private divide contains other dichotomies such as disability and impairment, emotion and reason, law and sociality, and the West and its Other. Fatima's narrative takes on special meaning because she speaks from between these divided spaces. It is from these spaces that Fatima seeks recognition for herself and her daughter for who they are: whole human beings and not splintered subjects.

NOTES

1. It must be noted that these conflicts arise from external factors. A Muslim woman is "judged" regardless of whether she is veiled or unveiled. A veiled woman is looked down upon as someone who refuses to "integrate" into Canadian society and also as someone who is tradition-bound (read: oppressed). An unveiled woman may also be frowned upon as someone who has become "too Westernized." This dilemma is highlighted in the video documentary *The Green Light*.

2. Fatima stated that the only time Marmar received "good care" was when she was in the Intensive Care Unit. Once she moved to the regular ward, Marmar received the kind of care that is commonly referred to as "bed-and-body" work. Here the emphasis is on personal hygiene. Fatima then felt it necessary to stay

with Marmar every day until late at night. She wants society to recognize her work: "If society as a whole put value on my work, my family who is part of society will also respect my work." In her words, she could then give her daughter the kind of holistic care that a human being is entitled to.

REFERENCES

Alvi, Sajida, Homa Hoodfar, and Sheila McDonough. 2003. *The Muslim Veil in North America: Issues and Debates.* Toronto: Women's Press.

Asce, Michelle, and Adrienne Fine, eds. 1988. *Women with Disabilities: Essays in Psychology, Culture and Politics.* Philadelphia: Temple University Press.

Bannerji, Himani. 1995. *Thinking Through: Essays on Feminism, Marxism, and Anti-Racism.* Toronto: Women's Press.

Chuengsatiansup, Komatra. 2001. "Marginality, Suffering and Community: The Politics of Collective Experience and Empowerment in Thailand." In *Remaking a World: Violence, Social Suffering and Recovery*, edited by Veena Das et al., 31–73. Berkeley: University of California Press.

Corker, Mairian, and Sally French. 1999. "Reclaiming Discourse in Disability Studies." In *Disability Discourse*, edited by Mairian Corker and Sally French, 1–12. Philadelphia: Open University Press.

Das, Veena, and Arthur Kleinman. 2001. "Introduction." In *Remaking a World: Violence, Social Suffering, and Recovery*, edited by V. Das et al., 1–30. Berkeley: University of California Press.

Das, Veena, Arthur Kleinman, M. Ramphele, and P. Reynolds, eds. 2000. *Violence and Subjectivity.* Berkeley: University of California Press.

De Groot, Joanna. 1996. "Gender, Discourse and Ideology in Iranian Studies: Towards a New Scholarship." In *Gendering the Middle East: Emerging Perspectives*, edited by Deniz Kandiyoti, 20–50. Syracuse: Syracuse University Press.

Dossa, Parin. 1999. "(Re)imagining Aging Lives: Ethnographic Narratives of Muslim Women in Diaspora." *Journal of Cross-Cultural Gerontology* 14, no. 3, 245–272.

_____. 2000. "On Law and Hegemonic Moments: Looking Beyond the Law towards Subjectivities of Subaltern Women." In *Law as Gendering Practice: Canadian Perspectives*, edited by Dorothy E. Chunn and Dany Lacome, 138–57. Don Mills: Oxford University Press.

Farmer, Paul. 2003. *Pathologies of Power: Health, Human Rights, and the New War on the Poor.* Berkeley: University of California Press.

Frank, Arthur. 1995. *The Wounded Story Teller*. Chicago: The University of Chicago Press.

Gupta, Tania D. 1996. *Racism and Paid Work*. Toronto: Garamond Press.

Ingstad, Benedicte, and Susan Whyte. 1995. *Disability and Culture*. Berkeley: University of California Press.

Kleinman, Arthur, and Joan Kleinman, eds. 1997. "The Appeal of Experience; The Dismay of Images: Cultural Appropriation of Suffering in Our Times." In *Social Suffering*, edited by A. Kleinman et al., 1–24. Berkeley: University of California Press.

Kleinman, Arthur, Margaret Lock, and Veena Das, eds. 1997. "Introduction." In *Social Suffering*, ix–xxvii. Berkeley: University of California Press.

Monks, Judith, and Ronald Frankenberg. 1995. "Being Ill and Being Me: Self, Body, and Time in Multiple Sclerosis Narratives." In *Disability and Culture*, edited by B. Ingstad and S. Whyte, 107–134. Berkeley: University of California Press.

Naples, Nancy, and Manisha Desai, eds. 2002. *Women's Activism and Globalization: Linking Local Struggles and Transnational Politics*. New York: Routledge.

Oliver, Michael. 1996. *Understanding Disability: From Theory to Practice*. Basingstoke: Macmillan.

Opie, Anne. 1992. *There's Nobody There: Community Care of Confused Older People*. Auckland: Oxford University Press.

Ross, Fiona. 2001. "Speech and Silence: Women's Testimony in the First Five Weeks of Public Hearings of the South African Truth and Reconciliation Commission." In *Remaking a World*, edited by Veena Das et al., 250–80. Berkeley: University of California Press.

Scheper-Hughes, Nancy. 1992. *Death without Weeping: The Violence of Everyday Life in Brazil*. Berkeley: University of California Press.

Thobani, Sunera. 1999. "Sponsoring Immigrant Women's Inequalities." *Canadian Woman Studies* 19 (3):11–17.

Todeschini, Maya. 2001. "The Bomb's Womb? Women and the Atom Bomb." In *Remaking a World*, eds. Veena Das et al., 102–156. Berkeley: University of California Press.

Wendell, Susan. 1996. *The Rejected Body: Feminist Philosophical Reflections on Disability*. New York: Routledge.

Whyte, Susan Reynolds, and Benedicte Ingstadt. 1995. *Disability and Culture*. Berkeley: University of California Press.

SECTION THREE

DOCUMENTS AND TABLES

ETHNIC ORIGIN OF THE CANADIAN POPULATION, 1871-1971[1]

FROM REPORT OF THE ROYAL COMMISSION ON BILINGUALISM AND BICULTURALISM, BOOK IV

Percentages

	1871	1881	1901	1911	1921	1931	1941	1951	1961	1971
Total[2]	100.00	100.00	100.00	100.00	100.00	100.00	100.00	100.00	100.00	100.00
British	60.55	58.93	57.04	55.49	55.41	51.86	49.68	47.89	43.85	44.62
French	31.07	30.03	30.71	28.61	27.91	28.22	30.27	30.83	30.38	28.65
Dutch	0.85	0.70	0.63	0.78	1.34	1.44	1.85	1.89	2.36	1.97
German	5.82	5.88	5.78	5.60	3.35	4.56	4.04	4.43	5.75	6.11
Italian	0.03	0.04	0.20	0.64	0.76	0.95	0.98	1.09	2.47	3.39
Jewish	*	0.02	0.03	1.06	1.44	1.51	1.48	1.30	0.95	1.38
Polish			0.12	0.47	0.61	1.40	1.45	1.57	1.77	1.47
Russian	0.02	0.03	0.37	0.61	1.14	0.85	0.73	0.65	0.65	0.30
Scandinavian	0.05	0.12	0.58	1.56	1.90	2.20	2.12	2.02	2.12	1.78
Ukrainian			0.10	1.05	1.21	2.17	2.66	2.82	2.59	2.69
Other European	0.11	0.13	0.44	1.35	2.44	2.51	2.45	2.47	3.90	3.71
Asiatic	*	0.10	0.44	0.60	0.75	0.81	0.64	0.52	0.67	1.32
Indian and Eskimo	0.66	2.51	2.38	1.46	1.29	1.24	1.09	1.18	1.21	1.45
Others and not stated	0.84	1.51	0.91	0.72	0.45	0.28	0.56	1.34	1.33	0.96

1. Data for 1871 and 1881 are incomplete, particularly in the treatment of small numbers of those from central Europe, 1891 is omitted because of insufficient data.
2. For 1871 includes the population of the four original provinces of Canada only: Nova Scotia, New Brunswick, Quebec, and Ontario. Newfoundland is excluded until 1951.
* Percentage lower than 0.01.

Numbers

	1871	1881	1901	1911	1921	1931	1941	1951	1961	1971
Total[2]	3,485,761	4,324,810	5,371,315	7,206,643	8,787,949	10,376,786	11,506,655	14,009,429	18,238,247	21,568,310
British	2,110,502	2,548,514	3,063,195	3,999,081	4,868,738	5,381,071	5,715,904	6,709,685	7,996,669	9,624,115
French	1,082,940	1,298,929	1,649,371	2,061,719	2,452,743	2,927,990	3,483,038	4,319,167	5,540,346	6,180,120
Dutch	29,662	30,412	33,845	55,961	117,505	148,962	212,863	264,267	429,679	425,945
German	202,991	254,319	310,501	403,417	294,635	473,544	464,682	619,995	1,049,599	1,317,200
Italian	1,035	1,849	10,834	45,963	66,769	98,173	112,625	152,245	450,351	730,820
Jewish	125	667	16,131	76,199	126,196	156,726	170,241	181,670	173,344	296,945
Polish			6,285	33,652	53,403	145,503	167,485	219,845	323,517	316,430
Russian	607	1,227	19,825	44,376	100,064	88,143	83,708	91,279	119,168	64,175
Scandinavian	1,623	5,223	31,042	112,682	167,359	228,049	244,603	283,024	386,534	384,795
Ukrainian			5,682	75,432	106,721	225,113	305,929	395,043	473,337	580,660
Other European	3,830	5,760	23,811	97,101	214,451	261,034	281,790	346,354	711,320	800,300
Asiatic	4	4,383	23,731	43,213	65,914	84,548	74,064	72,827	121,753	285,540
Indian and Eskimo	23,037	108,547	127,941	105,611	113,724	128,890	125,521	165,607	220,121	312,760
Other and not stated	29,405	64,980	49,121	52,236	39,727	29,035	64,202	188,421	242,509	206,090

1. Data for 1871 and 1881 are incomplete, particularly in the treatment of small numbers of those from central Europe, 1891 is omitted because of insufficient data.
2. For 1871 includes the population of the four original provinces of Canada only: Nova Scotia, New Brunswick, Quebec, and Ontario. Newfoundland is excluded until 1951.
* Percentage lower than 0.01.

PIERRE ELLIOTT TRUDEAU

FEDERAL MULTICULTURAL POLICY

HOUSE OF COMMONS DEBATES, OCTOBER 8, 1971

Right Hon. P.E. Trudeau (Prime Minister): Mr. Speaker, I am happy this morning to be able to reveal to the House that the government has accepted all those recommendations of the Royal Commission on Bilingualism and Biculturalism which are contained in Volume IV of its reports directed to federal departments and agencies. Hon. Members will recall that the subject of this volume is "the contribution by other ethnic groups to the cultural enrichment of Canada and the measures that should be taken to safeguard that contribution by other ethnic groups to the cultural enrichment of Canada and the measures that should be taken to safeguard that contribution."

Volume IV examined this whole question of cultural and ethnic pluralism in this country and the status of our various cultures and languages, an area of study given all too little attention in the past by scholars.

It was the view of the Royal Commission, shared by the government and, I am sure, by all Canadians, that there cannot be one cultural policy for Canadians of British and French origin, another for the original peoples, and yet a third for all others. For although there are two official languages, there is no official culture, nor does any ethnic group take precedence over any other. No citizen or group of citizens is other than Canadian, and all should be treated fairly.

The Royal Commission was guided by the belief that adherence to one's ethnic group is influenced not so much by one's origin or mother tongue as by one's sense of belonging to the group, and by what the Commission calls the group's "collective will to exist." The government shares this belief.

The individual's freedom would be hampered if he were locked for life within a particular cultural compartment by the accident of birth or language. It is vital, therefore, that every Canadian, whatever his ethnic origin, be given a chance to learn at least one of the two languages in which his country conducts its official business and its politics.

A policy of multiculturalism within a bilingual framework commends itself to the government as the most suitable means of assuring the cultural freedom of Canadians ....

In implementing [this] policy, the government will provide support in four ways.

First, resources permitting, the government will seek to assist all Canadian cultural groups that have demonstrated a desire and effort to continue to develop a capacity to grow and contribute to Canada, and a clear need for assistance, the small and weak groups no less than the strong and highly organized.

Second, the government will assist members of all cultural groups to overcome cultural barriers to full participation in Canadian society.

Third, the government will promote creative encounters and interchange among all Canadian cultural groups in the interest of national unity.

Fourth, the government will continue to assist immigrants to acquire at least one of Canada's official languages in order to become full participants in Canadian society

[Translation]

Mr. Speaker, I stated at the outset that the government has accepted in principle all recommendations addressed to federal departments and agencies. We are also ready and willing to work cooperatively with the provincial governments towards implementing those recommendations that concern matters under provincial or shared responsibility.

Some of the programmes endorsed or recommended by the Commission have been administered for some time by various federal agencies. I might mention the Citizenship Branch, the CRTC and its predecessor the BBG, the National Film Board, and the National Museum of Man. These programmes will be revised, broadened, and reactivated and they will receive the additional funds that may be required.

Some of the recommendations that concern matters under provincial jurisdiction call for coordinated federal and provincial action. As a first step, I have written to the First Ministers of the provinces informing them of the response of the federal government and seeking their cooperation. Officials will be asked to carry this consultation further.

I wish to table details of the government's response to each of the several recommendations.

It should be noted that some of the programmes require pilot projects or further short-term research before more extensive action can be taken. As soon as these preliminary studies are available, further programmes will be announced and initiated.

Responsibility for implementing these recommendations has been assigned to the Citizenship Branch of the Department of the Secretary of State, the agency now responsible for matters affecting the social integration of immigrants and the cultural activities of all ethnic groups. An Inter-Agency Committee of all those agencies involved will be established to coordinate the federal effort.

[ENGLISH]

In conclusion, I wish to emphasize the view of the government that a policy of multiculturalism within a bilingual framework is basically the conscious support of individual freedom of choice. We are free to be ourselves. But this cannot be left to chance. It must be fostered and pursued actively. If freedom of choice is in danger for some ethnic groups, it is in danger for all ....

Hon. Robert L. Stanfield (Leader of the Opposition): Mr. Speaker, these are excellent words in the Prime Minister's statement. I am sure this declaration by the government of the principle of preserving and enhancing the many cultural traditions which exist within our country will be most welcome ....

[TRANSLATION]

I wish to state immediately, Mr. Speaker, that the emphasis we have given to multiculturalism in no way constitutes an attack on the basic duality of our country. What we want is justice for all Canadians, and recognition of the cultural diversity of this country.

[ENGLISH]

... I am pleased the government has seen the light. But I must also say that, although this is all to the good, I regret that this statement was not made much more promptly.

Apart from what members of our party, among others, have been saying, it is a fact that the fourth volume of the B and B report has been available since early 1970, and I say in all sincerity that the failure of the government to endorse these principles earlier has created some suspicion, some doubts, in the minds of the members of these other cultural groups about the importance the government of Canada has attached to them. I must say that if the effectiveness of the government's action in encouraging the cultural self-fulfillment of the native peoples of Canada can be taken as any kind of an indication of what the practice will be in this broader field, apart from the statement of non-French and non-British ethnic groups within Canada. With regard to the native peoples, there have been many statements about high principles but very little in the way of results and there is some doubt, to mention one example, concerning whether the government is doing enough in northeastern Alberta to help the native people study their own language.

It is fine to announce a principle, but perhaps the most important thing is what the government is going to do to implement this principle. When the Prime Minister uses a phrase such as "within available funds" we must keep in mind the importance of a balance here. There is no indication whatsoever in the Prime Minister's statement this morning that there will be any substantial implementation. I fully agree that a good deal of money must be expended for the encouragement of the development of bilingualism in this country, but I do not think that members of the other cultural groups with other cultural traditions are at all happy with the relatively pitiful amounts that have been allocated to this other aspect of the diversity about which the Prime Minister spoke this morning, multiculturalism.

The Prime Minister has announced the principles. We expect the Prime Minister and his colleagues to give those principles life and meaning, and we will look forward most anxiously to the implementation of these principles.

Mr. David Lewis (York South): I must say, Mr. Speaker, that it is a pleasure to be able to comment on an important aspect of Canadian life that does not have to do with the economy or with unemployment, and it is equally a pleasure to be able to agree with the statement that the Prime Minister made this morning.

As members of this House know, I have not hesitated to criticize government policy, and no doubt a great deal can be said about tardiness and other aspects of the problem which the Prime Minister has put before us. But I propose this morning merely to express my support and our hopes in order to indicate to the people of Canada that this Parliament is united in its belated determination to recognize the value of the many cultures in our country.

[TRANSLATION]

Mr. Speaker, it is with a deep appreciation of both aspects of our Canadian cultural life, official bilingualism and multiculturalism, that my party warmly supports the principles set forth this morning by the Prime Minister.

I have often said that one of the most striking wealths of our country is the fact that it has been founded by two distinctive groups having two distinctive languages well known throughout the world. However, another wealth is also important, since we find in Canada some representatives of almost all the cultures in the world. To all Canadians, whatever their ethnic origin, I say that they must be proud of those two enriching aspects of our country.

[ENGLISH]

Every society has its own cultural treasures which it cherishes with pride. It is a fact of man's history that his preoccupations have been too frequently centered on material development and that his spirit has too often been embittered by conflict and by prejudice. The result has been throughout the world—and this is true of Canadians as well—a failure to appreciate the values of diversity, a tendency to resent rather than to welcome enriching differences. For Canada this attitude is particularly destructive. The diversity of cultures across the land is a source of our greatness as a people .... I suggest that the important point that faces us is that in every society a minority has a problem, the problem of survival, the problem of keeping alive its history, its language, its tradition, its songs, its legends, its identity. When the majority in a society is as cruel as majorities have often been, not only are minorities crushed but the spirit of that society, the soul of that society, is destroyed. It is in that spirit, therefore, that on behalf of my party I welcome the Prime Minister's statement without any reservations.

[Translation]

Mr. Réal Caouette (Témiscamigue): Mr. Speaker, even if I do not always agree with the Prime Minister on various points, I fully agree with the statement he made this morning. Indeed, I have been repeating for thirty years, to those who will hear me, and those who won't, that we have one Canadian nation, and not two, three or ten, that we have two official languages, English and French, and that we have a multiplicity of cultures which are the wealth of our country.

Mr. Speaker, my colleagues and myself are happy the Prime Minister made that statement. However, I find this statement somewhat confusing. The Prime Minister has stated and I quote:

> For although there are two official languages, there is no official culture, nor does any ethnic group take precedence over any other. No citizen or group of citizens is other than Canadian ....

Mr. Speaker, if there is no official culture in Canada, I do not see how we could succeed in really becoming a nation while we would be endowed with only a few cultures unable to get on among themselves or at war with one another. I am positive that we have in Canada a culture peculiar to us. We French Canadians have one that is not at all that of France, just as English-speaking Canadians have a culture which is different from that of Englishmen from England. We have our own Canadian culture. We have our history. Our traditions and customs may differ from one area or ethnic group to another. However, if we cannot change an Englishman into a Frenchman or vice versa, we can nonetheless make good Canadians out of members of all ethnic groups in Canada.

Ukrainians, Italians, and Germans must be able to attain self-fulfillment in Canada ....

[ENGLISH]

What I said in French was that we do not want to have in Canada a little France, a little England, a little Italy, or a little Russia. We want in Canada a great country for all the people of Canada, for all the ethnic groups in our country. Through that channel we will achieve unity and we will reinforce our position in the whole world.

DEPARTMENT OF JUSTICE, CANADA

CANADIAN MULTICULTURALISM ACT, 1985

Whereas the Constitution of Canada provides that every individual is equal before and under the law and has the right to the equal protection and benefit of the law without discrimination and that everyone has the freedom of conscience, religion, thought, belief, opinion, expression, peaceful assembly, and association and guarantees those rights and freedoms equal to male and female persons;

AND WHEREAS the Constitution of Canada recognizes the importance of preserving and enhancing the multicultural heritage of Canadians;

AND WHEREAS the Constitution of Canada recognizes rights of the aboriginal peoples of Canada.

AND WHEREAS the Constitution of Canada and the *Official Languages Act* provide that English and French are the official languages of Canada and neither abrogates nor derogates from any rights or privileges acquired or enjoyed with respect to any other language;

AND WHEREAS the *Citizenship Act* provides that all Canadians, whether by birth or by choice, enjoy equal status, are entitled to the same rights, powers, and privileges and are subject to the same obligations, duties, and liabilities;

AND WHEREAS the *Canadian Human Rights Act* provides that every individual should have an equal opportunity with other individuals to make the life that the individual is able and wishes to have, consistent with the duties and obligations of that individual as a member of society, and, in order to secure that opportunity, establishes the Canadian Human Rights Commission to redress any proscribed discrimination, including discrimination on the basis of race, national or ethnic origin, or colour;

AND WHEREAS Canada is a party to the *International Convention on the Elimination of All Forms of Racial Discrimination*, which Convention recognizes that all human beings are equal before the law and are entitled to equal protection of the law against any discrimination and against any incitement to discrimination, and to the *International Covenant on Civil and Political Rights*, which Covenant provides that persons belonging to ethnic, religious, or linguistic minorities shall not be denied the right to enjoy their own culture, to profess and practice their own religion, or to use their own language;

AND WHEREAS the Government of Canada recognizes the diversity of Canadians as regards races, national or ethnic origin, colour, and religion as a fundamental characteristic of Canadian society and is committed to a policy of multiculturalism designed to preserve and enhance the multicultural heritage of Canadians while working to achieve the equality of all Canadians in the economic, social, cultural, and political life of Canada;

NOW, THEREFORE, Her Majesty, by and with the advice and consent of the Senate and House of Commons of Canada, enacts as follows:

Short Title

1.   This Act may be cited as the *Canadian Multiculturalism Act.*

Interpretation

2.   In this Act, "federal institution" means any of the following institutions of the Government of Canada:

(a) a department, board, commission, or council, or other body or office, established to perform a governmental function by or pursuant to an Act of Parliament or by or under the authority of the Governor in Council, and

(b) a departmental corporation or Crown corporation as defined in section 2 of the *Financial Administration Act,*

but does not include

(c) any institution of the Council or government of the Northwest Territories or the Yukon Territory or of the Legislative Assembly for, or the government of, Nunavut, or

(d) any Indian band, band council, or other body established to perform a governmental function in relation to an Indian band or other group of aboriginal people;

"Minister" means such member of the Queen's Privy Council for Canada as is designated by the Governor in Council as the Minister for the purposes of this Act.

R.S., 1985, c. 24 (4th Supp.), s. 2; 1993, c. 28, s. 78.

MULTICULTURALISM POLICY OF CANADA

3. (1) It is hereby declared to be the policy of the Government of Canada to

   (a) recognize and promote the understanding that multiculturalism reflects the cultural and racial diversity of Canadian society and acknowledges the freedom of all members of Canadian society to preserve, enhance, and share their cultural heritage;

   (b) recognize and promote the understanding that multiculturalism is a fundamental characteristic of the Canadian heritage and identity and that it provides an invaluable resource in the shaping of Canada's future;

   (c) promote the full and equitable participation of individuals and communities of all origins in the continuing evolution and shaping of all aspects of Canadian society and assist them in the elimination of any barrier to that participation;

   (d) recognize the existence of communities whose members share a common origin and their historic contribution to Canadian society, and enhance their development;

   (e) ensure that all individuals receive equal treatment and equal protection under the law, while respecting and valuing their diversity;

   (f) encourage and assist the social, cultural, economic, and political institutions of Canada to be both respectful and inclusive of Canada's multicultural character;

   (g) promote the understanding and creativity that arise from the interaction between individuals and communities of different origins;

   (h) foster the recognition and appreciation of the diverse cultures of Canadian society and promote the reflection and the evolving expressions of those cultures;

   (i) preserve and enhance the use of languages other than English and French, while strengthening the status and use of the official languages of Canada; and

(j)   advance multiculturalism throughout Canada in harmony with the national commitment to the official languages of Canada.

[B]Federal Institutions

(2)   It is further declared to be the policy of the Government of Canada that all federal institutions shall

(a)   ensure that Canadians of all origins have an equal opportunity to obtain employment and advancement in those institutions;

(b)   promote policies, programs, and practices that enhance the ability of individuals and communities of all origins to contribute to the continuing evolution of Canada;

(c)   promote policies, programs, and practices that enhance the understanding of and respect for the diversity of the members of Canadian society;

(d)   collect statistical data in order to enable the development of policies, programs and practices that are sensitive and responsive to the multicultural reality of Canada;

(e)   make use, as appropriate, of the language skills and cultural understanding of individuals of all origins; and

(f)   generally, carry on their activities in a manner that is sensitive and responsive to the multicultural reality of Canada.

Implementation of the Multiculturalism Policy of Canada

[B]General Responsibility for Coordination

4.   The Minister, in consultation with other ministers of the Crown, shall encourage and promote a coordinated approach to the implementation of the multiculturalism policy of Canada and may provide advice and assistance in the development and implementation of programs and practices in support of the policy.

[B]Specific Mandate

5.   (1)   The Minister shall take such measures as the Minister considers appropriate to implement the multiculturalism policy of Canada and, without limiting the generality of the foregoing, may

(a) encourage and assist individuals, organizations, and institutions to project the multicultural reality of Canada in their activities in Canada and abroad;

(b) undertake and assist research relating to Canadian multiculturalism and foster scholarship in the field;

(c) encourage and promote exchanges and cooperation among the diverse communities of Canada;

(d) encourage and assist the business community, labour organizations, voluntary and other private organizations, as well as public institutions, in ensuring full participation in Canadian society, including the social and economic aspects, of individuals of all origins and their communities, and in promoting respect and appreciation for the multicultural reality of Canada;

(e) encourage the preservation, enhancement, sharing, and evolving expression of the multicultural heritage of Canada;

(f) facilitate the acquisition, retention, and use of all languages that contribute to the multicultural heritage of Canada;

(g) assist ethno-cultural minority communities to conduct activities with a view to overcoming any discriminatory barrier and, in particular, discrimination based on race or national or ethnic origin;

(h) provide support to individuals, groups, or organizations for the purpose of preserving, enhancing, and promoting multiculturalism in Canada; and

(i) undertake such other projects or programs in respect of multiculturalism, not by law assigned to any other federal institution, as are designed to promote the multiculturalism policy of Canada.

[B]Provincial Agreements

(2) The Minister may enter into an agreement or arrangement with any province respecting the implementation of the multiculturalism policy of Canada

[B]International Agreements

(3) The Minister may, with the approval of the Governor in Council, enter into an agreement or arrangement with the government of

any foreign state in order to foster the multicultural character of Canada.

[B]RESPONSIBILITIES OF OTHER MINISTERS

6. (1) The ministers of the Crown, other than the Minister, shall, in the execution of their respective mandates, take such measures as they consider appropriate to implement the multiculturalism policy of Canada.

[B]PROVINCIAL AGREEMENTS

(2) A minister of the Crown, other than the Minister, may enter into an agreement or arrangement with any province respecting the implementation of the multiculturalism policy of Canada.

[B]CANADIAN MULTICULTURALISM ADVISORY COMMITTEE

7. (1) The Minister may establish an advisory committee to advise and assist the Minister on the implementation of this Act and any other matter relating to multiculturalism and, in consultation with such organizations representing multicultural interests as the Minister deems appropriate, may appoint the members and designate the chairman and other officers of the committee.

[B]REMUNERATION AND EXPENSES

(2) Each member of the advisory committee shall be paid such remuneration of the member's services as may be fixed by the Minister and is entitled to be paid the reasonable travel and living expenses incurred by the member while absent from the member's ordinary place of residence in connection with the work of the committee.

[B]ANNUAL REPORT

(3) The chairman of the advisory committee shall, within four months after the end of each fiscal year, submit to the Minister a report on the activities of the committee for that year and on any other

matter relating to the implementation of the multiculturalism policy of Canada that the chairman considers appropriate.

GENERAL

[B]ANNUAL REPORT

8.   The Minister shall cause to be laid before each House of Parliament, not later than the fifth sitting day of that House after January 31 next following the end of each fiscal year, a report on the operation of this Act for that fiscal year.

[B]PERMANENT REVIEW BY A PARLIAMENTARY COMMITTEE

9.   The operation of this Act and any report made pursuant to section 8 shall be reviewed on a permanent basis by such committee of the House, of the Senate, or of both Houses of Parliament as may be designated or established for the purpose.

IMMIGRATION
CANADA

SKILLED WORKER SELF-ASSESSMENT

FACTOR 1: EDUCATION (MAXIMUM 25 POINTS)

INDICATE YOUR HIGHEST LEVEL OF EDUCATION

Did not complete secondary school (also called high school)	○
Obtained a secondary school credential	○
Obtained a one-year diploma, trade certificate or apprenticeship, *and* completed at least 12 years of full-time or full-time equivalent studies	○
Obtained a one-year diploma, trade certificate or apprenticeship, *and* completed at least 13 years of full-time or full-time equivalent studies	○
Obtained a one-year university degree at the bachelor's level *and* completed at least 13 years of full-time or full-time equivalent studies	○
Obtained a two-year diploma, trade certificate or apprenticeship, *and* completed at least 14 years of full-time or full-time equivalent studies	○
Obtained a university degree of two years or more at the bachelor's level *and* completed at least 14 years of full-time or full-time equivalent studies	○
Obtained a three-year diploma, trade certificate or apprenticeship (other than university), *and* completed at least 15 years of full-time or full-time equivalent studies	○
Obtained two or more university degrees at the bachelor's level *and* completed at least 15 years of full-time or full-time equivalent studies	○
Obtained a master's or Ph.D. *and* completed at least 17 years of full-time education or full-time equivalent studies	○

Factor 2: English and French Language Ability (maximum 24 points)

To assess your English and French ability, first decide which language you are most comfortable with. This language is your first official language. The language you feel less comfortable communicating in is your second official language.

Determine your language ability, then award points according to your ability to read, write, listen to, and speak English and French.

Check the areas that reflect your ability to read, write, listen to, and speak English and French.

First Canadian Official Language (either English or French)

	Read	Write	Speak	Listen
High Proficiency (Maximum of sixteen (16) points)	O	O	O	O
Moderate Proficiency (Maximum of eight (8) points)	O	O	O	O
Basic Proficiency (Maximum of two (2) points)	O	O	O	O
No Proficiency (No points)	O	O	O	O

Second Canadian Official Language (either English or French)

	Read	Write	Speak	Listen
High Proficiency (Maximum of eight (8) points)	O	O	O	O
Moderate Proficiency (Maximum of eight (8) points)	O	O	O	O
Basic Proficiency (Maximum of two (2) points)	O	O	O	O
No Proficiency (No points)	O	O	O	O

Factor 3: Work Experience (maximum 21 points)

You must have *at least one year* of full-time paid work experience, or the equivalent in part-time work, in an occupation listed in the National Occupational Classification (NOC) list. Your experience must be listed in an occupation listed in Skill Type 0 or Skill Levels A or B of the NOC *and* it must have occurred in the past 10 years. You must have performed most of the duties, including all the essential duties, that are listed for the occupation.

PLEASE NOTE: If your work experience is not listed in Skill Type 0 or Skill Levels A or B of the NOC, or if your experience did not occur in the past 10 years, your application will not be accepted.

To determine your points, first assess your work experience, and then complete the following:

Your Work Experience Is ...

Less than 1 year	O
More than 1 year but less than 2 years	O
More than 2 years but less than 3 years	O
More than 3 years but less than 4 years	O
4 or more years	O

MINIMUM WORK EXPERIENCE REQUIREMENTS

Skilled workers are people who may become permanent residents because they have the ability to become economically established in Canada.

You must meet the following minimum work experience requirements to allow you to apply as a skilled worker:

- You must have at least one year of full-time work experience. You must have been paid for this work.
- Your work experience must be in the category of Skill Type 0, or Skill Level A or B on the Canadian National Occupational Classification (NOC). (See below for instructions.)
- You must have had this experience within the last 10 years.

National Occupation Classification (NOC)

The NOC is a classification system for jobs in the Canadian economy. It describes duties, skills, talents, and work settings for occupations.

Determine Your NOC Category

Follow these steps to see if your work experience meets the requirements to apply as a skilled worker.

1. Find the title of any full-time jobs you had in the past 10 years using National Occupation Classification list. This is a list of all jobs that are in Skill Type 0, Skill Level A or B on the NOC. *Write down the four-digit code located to the left of your job's title.*
2. Go to the NOC Web site and type your four-digit job-code in the "Quick Search" box. Make sure you press the "GO" button. A description of your occupation will appear. Make sure the description and "Main Duties" describe what you did at your last jobs.

   Note: You do *not* have to meet the "Employment Requirements" listed in the description.

   If the initial description and list of main duties *matches* what you did at your last job, you can count this experience when you apply as a skilled worker. You can also earn points in Factor 3 of the Selection Factors.

   If the description *does not match* your work experience then you might not have the experience you need to apply as a skilled worker. Look through the NOC list to see if another occupation matches your experience. Check all of the jobs you had in the past 10 years to see if you have at least one year of work experience in a job that will qualify you as a skilled worker.
3. Check the list of restricted occupations. If your work experience is in a restricted occupation then you *cannot* use it to qualify for the Skilled Worker category.

You do not meet the minimum requirements if:

- none of your work experience is listed in the NOC list;
- your experience did *not* occur in the 10 years before you applied; or
- your only work experience is in a restricted occupation.

If you do not meet the minimum work experience requirements, your application as a Skilled Worker will be refused.

FACTOR 4: AGE (MAXIMUM 10 POINTS)

Points are given for your age at the time your application is received.

Please Enter Your Age in Years

less than 17	O	20	O	52	O
17	O	21 - 49	O	53	O
18	O	50	O	Over 53	O
19	O	51	O		

FACTOR 5: ARRANGED EMPLOYMENT (MAXIMUM 10 POINTS)

To obtain points for this factor, you must have a permanent job offer in Canada and be capable of and likely to accept and carry out the job. One of the following situations must also apply:

1. You have been working in Canada for at least one year on a temporary work permit and:
   a) your temporary work permit was confirmed by HRDC, including sectoral confirmations; b) you are currently working in that employment; c) the work permit is valid for at least another 12 months from the date of your application; and d) your employer has made an offer to employ you on an indeterminate basis if the permanent resident visa is issued.

   OR

2. You have been working in Canada for at least one year on a temporary work permit and:
   a) your temporary work permit is exempt from HRDC confirmation requirements under an international agreement (i.e., NAFTA, GATS) or as a result of the significant benefit to Canada provision (i.e., intra-company transferee); b) you are currently working in that employment; c) the work permit is valid for at least another 12 months from the date of your application; and d) your employer has made an offer to employ you on an indeterminate basis if the permanent resident visa is issued.

OR

3. You do not intend to work in Canada before being issued a permanent resident visa and do not hold a temporary work permit and:
   a) your employer has made an offer to employ you on an indeterminate basis if the permanent resident visa is issued; and b) your job offer has been confirmed by Human Resources Development Canada (HRDC.) You cannot apply to HRDC yourself. Your potential employer must apply for you.

No Arranged Employment	O
Arranged Employment	O

FACTOR 6: ADAPTABILITY (MAXIMUM 10 POINTS)

You can receive a maximum of 10 points based on any combination of the elements listed below:

1. Accompanying spouse/common-law partner's education:

Secondary school diploma or less	O
A one-year diploma, trade certificate or apprenticeship *and* completed at least 12 years of full-time or full-time equivalent studies	O
A one-year diploma, trade certificate or apprenticeship or university degree at the bachelor's level *and* completed at least 13 years of full-time or full-time equivalent studies	O
A two-year diploma, trade certificate or apprenticeship or university degree at the bachelor's level *and* completed at least 14 years of full-time or full-time equivalent studies	O
A three-year diploma, trade certificate or apprenticeship (not university), *and* completed at least 15 years of full-time or full-time equivalent studies	O
Two or more university degrees at the bachelor's level *and* completed at least 15 years of full-time or full-time equivalent studies	O
A master's or Ph.D. *and* completed at least 17 years of full-time or full-time equivalent studies	O
Not Applicable	O

2. Principal applicant or spouse/common-law partner has studied in Canada

No, or has less than two years post-secondary education in Canada	O
Completed at least two years of post-secondary education in Canada since the age of 17	O

3. Principal applicant or spouse/common-law partner has worked in Canada

No, or has worked full-time in Canada for less than one year	O
Worked full-time in Canada for at least one year	O

4. Principal applicant has obtained points under Factor 5, Arranged Employment

You are not eligible to claim points on this question as you do not have arranged employment under Factor 5.

5. Principal applicant *or* spouse/common-law partner has family in Canada

No family in Canada	O
Family in Canada (parent, grandparent, aunt, uncle, sister, brother, niece, nephew, child or grandchild, spouse or common-law partner who is a Canadian citizen or permanent resident living in Canada)	O

SKILLED WORKER SELF-ASSESSMENT
TOTAL POINT SCORE

YOUR FINAL SCORE IS:

HERE IS THE BREAKDOWN OF YOUR TOTAL SCORE:

	Factor	Maximum Points	Your Score
1	Education	25	
2	Language Ability	24	
3	Work Experience	21	
4	Age	10	
5	Arranged Employment	10	
6	Adaptability	10	
	Total Score	**100**	

PASS MARK

The pass mark as of September 18, 2003 is 67.

DID YOU PASS?

If your mark from this test is the same or higher than the pass mark for your application, you may qualify to immigrate as a skilled worker.

If your mark is lower than the pass mark, you might not qualify to immigrate as a skilled worker at this time. The information on the Skilled Worker Class will explain what you need to meet the selection standards.

FINAL DECISION

A CIC officer will make the final decision on the application you submit to a Visa Office. Make sure you fill out the application forms completely. You will need to provide evidence to support your application as well as pass medical and security checks.

The information here is for your advice only. CIC does not keep a record of these results. If you want to keep a record, you can print or save this page from your computer.

See Immigrating to Canada as a Skilled Worker for more information on Skilled Worker immigration.

COPYRIGHT
ACKNOWLEDGEMENTS